Singlehanded Sailing

2nd Edition

THE EXPERIENCES AND TECHNIQUES OF THE LONE VOYAGERS

Written and Illustrated by
Richard Henderson

International Marine Publishing Co.
Camden, Maine

OTHER BOOKS BY RICHARD HENDERSON

First Sail for Skipper
Hand, Reef, and Steer
Dangerous Voyages of Captain William Andrews (ed)
Sail and Power
The Racing Cruiser
Sea Sense
The Cruiser's Compendium
East to the Azores
Choice Yacht Designs
Better Sailing
Philip L. Rhodes and His Yacht Designs
53 Boats You Can Build
John G. Alden and His Yacht Designs (with Robert Carrick)
Encyclopedia of Sailing (with editors of *Yacht Racing and Cruising*)
Heavy Weather Guide (with William J. Kotsch)
Understanding Rigs and Rigging
Sailing At Night
Sailing in Windy Weather

Published by International Marine Publishing Co., a division of Highmark Publishing Ltd., Rt. 1, P.O. Box 220, Camden, Maine 04843.

Typeset by Camden Type 'n Graphics, Camden, ME 04843
Printed and bound by Hamilton Printing Co, East Greenbush, NY 12061
Designed by Deborah Sarafin Davies
Edited by Cynthia Bourgeault, Betsy Holman, and David Oppenheim
Production by Janet Robbins

10 9 8 7 6 5 4 3 2 1

Library of Congress Cataloging-in-Publication Data

Henderson, Richard, 1924-
   Singlehanded sailing / Richard Henderson. — 2nd ed.
      p.   cm.
   Bibliography: p.
   Includes index.
   ISBN 0-87742-972-3 : $24.95
   1. Sailing. 2. Seamanship. I. Title
GV811.6.H46 1988   88-22958
797.1'24—dc19   CIP

Contents

Foreword

SINCE THE FIRST EDITION APPEARED in 1976, Richard Henderson's *Singlehanded Sailing* has been one of the best books for the person who wants to know how to cruise or race without any company except the boat, the wind, the sea, and whatever risks and rewards that they may combine to produce. In this thoroughly revised and updated second edition, Henderson takes into account the many technical advances made after 1976. In those years of intense development in singlehanded sailing, we saw two BOC singlehanded 'round the world races for monohulled boats, the appearance of a new breed of multihulls, a new speed record for a solo circumnavigation set by Dodge Morgan, and an ever enlarging fleet of solo voyagers and cruising sailors.

While singlehanded sailing is not without its opponents—many object to the fact that no lookout can be posted when the crew goes below to eat or sleep—there is a long and honored tradition of lone sailors going long distances. Equally respected is the tradition of returned solo sailors telling as many people as possible how they did it. This marriage of monastic retreat and public confession may seem contrary, but there it is. These loner-publicists have been among the most influential sailors in the history of yachting. From John MacGregor and Joshua Slocum in the nineteenth century through Harry Pidgeon, Ann Davison, Sir Francis Chichester, Bernard Moitessier, Tristan Jones, Dame Naomi James, and Tania Aebi in the twentieth, the world of singlehanding has been peopled by colorful characters who took off on solitary adventures, discovered much on the way, and came back to write or lecture about the lessons learned.

They did not all learn the same lessons. They were, after all, very different people in different boats who had a wide variety of experiences. How big a boat, what kind of self-steerer, how to respond to bad weather, which type of rig, how to stay awake in shipping lanes, what emergency gear to carry—these and other possibilities are even more varied for singlehanders than for any other group of sailors. They are also more hotly debated, since solo sailors have nothing else to fall back on except their boats and themselves. There is no slack in singlehanding.

Therefore, any discussion of singlehanded sailing needs a referee. Richard Henderson fills that role in this book. He has studied the accounts and interviewed living singlehanders, and here he analyzes the lessons that were learned with the same thoughtfulness, objectivity, and broad knowledge of seamanship and yacht design that he demonstrated in his other books (among them *Sea Sense, East to the Azores*, and the definitive study of the designs of John Alden). If you can't take a year or two off to read all the books in his annotated list of sources—which is the most thorough bibliography in any boating book that I am familiar with—then you will do well to read his text. No better survey of singlehanded skills, boats, and hardware exists.

John Rousmaniere
Stamford, Connecticut

In memory of
Dr. Roger P. Batchelor

Acknowledgments

I'LL NOT ATTEMPT to list everyone from whom I've gleaned bits of information used in this book, for I've lost track over the years, and some informants might be inadvertently left out; but a few standouts, who have been most helpful in one way or another, come quickly to mind. My very special thanks go to Roger C. Taylor and Cynthia Bourgeault of International Marine Publishing Company, Betsy Hitz-Holman of *Cruising World* magazine, William W. Robinson and Rosemary Curley of *Yachting* magazine, J. D. Sleightholme of *Yachting Monthly*, Philip L. Budlong of the Mystic Seaport Marine Historical Association, Neal T. Walker of The Slocum Society, Dr. Susie Scholz, D. H. Clarke, Frank Casper, John Letcher, Francis C. Stokes, John Guzzwell, John Rock, Richard C. Newick, Alfred F. Loomis, William Homewood, Mimi Rehor, Donald R. Holm, Helen B. Baldwin, Harald Kolzer, Steven Callahan, Krystyna Chojnowska-Liskiewicz, Marian Hoyt Morgan, Rachel Hayward, Edward Karkow, Irving Groupp, John Moon, James Tazelaar, Pete Hodgins, Sarah S. Henderson, Dennis Guinee, and Patty M. Maddocks.

Preface

M EN SHOULD TELL WHAT THEY KNOW," wrote the British author-sailor Weston Martyr. Singlehanded sailors do not always tell what they know, at least not all of what they know, but when they do speak, we who sail with crew should listen, for we can learn a great deal. Although it has been argued that a singlehander knows only how to handle his own craft, and he has no one to point out his errors, the fact remains that it is far more difficult to manage a boat alone, and a loner learns of necessity how to avoid mistakes. Thus, veteran singlehanders tend to develop a high caliber of seamanship.

The purpose of this book is partly to familiarize the average yachtsman with the history, personalities, and motivations of the great singlehanders, some of whom are not at all well known even to those who follow the literature of the sea. My main purpose, however, is to present and try to analyze the techniques, equipment, and relevant experiences of the singlehanders, so that all sailors can profit. Not all the experiences are examples of what to do, for even the greatest sailors are fallible, and occasionally we may learn what not to do, but the important thing is that we are inspired and taught. The reader may never have any serious intention of embarking on a solo voyage, yet many yachtsmen handle their boats alone when daysailing, sailing overnight, or standing watch. And what veteran sailor has not found himself or herself handling a boat shorthanded at times? Very often there will be children, an inexperienced spouse, or greenhorns aboard, so the skipper will virtually be managing alone.

For the most part, the experiences related between these covers have to do with hard times: gales, capsizings, collisions, hallucinations, groundings, dismastings, and so forth. The difficulties are what concern us, because we should know how they can be handled. As the old adage advises, "Be ready for the worst, and the best will take care of itself."

Nevertheless, solo bluewater sailing need not be hazardous or awkward. A great many voyages have been made without any really unpleasant incidents, and the good times normally far outweigh the bad. There will be plenty of days when the sun is warm on one's back, when fair weather cumuli cast fleeting shadows on rolling blue seas, and the lacelike wake will seem to gurgle and hiss with joy. For a sailor who is well prepared there is probably little risk, but the sea is never completely predictable, and there is always some small element of danger. That is primarily what makes a passage alone or shorthanded a challenge and a true adventure.

Since the first edition of this book in 1976, there have been important developments in the ongoing history of singlehanded sailing. A number of history-making voyages have occurred, and a new generation of colorful, fascinating personalities has appeared on the scene. There is much in the way of new gear, major advances in electronics and electromechanical systems, and ultramodern boats designed specifically for solo sailing and racing. Of course, new doesn't always mean better; sometimes time-proven gear and techniques are more reliable. But it seemed high time for a fresh look at the subject.

As in the first edition, I have attempted to retain a balance between entertainment and useful information. Although this edition puts more emphasis on modern times, with an expanded and updated text and many new illustrations, early history is still featured and little-known pioneers have been further researched. These pages have benefited from correspondence I have had with knowledgeable readers of the original book. This edition continues the work of documenting achievements. Documentation is important not only to give credit to those deserving it, but also to alter the plans of singlehanders attempting to set records which, unbeknownst to them, have already been set.

Through the examples of the great singlehanders included in this book, I hope the reader who habitually sails with full crew will gain the confidence and inspiration to go forth alone or shorthanded. The rewards of doing so are freedom and peace of mind, a feeling of independence, pride of accomplishment, and a sense of belonging to a colorful fraternity of libertarians who happen to be among the world's finest sailors.

Richard Henderson
Gibson Island, Maryland

PART I

A Legacy of Singlehanded Sailing

Blackburn at the helm of his trim little *Great Republic* just before the start of his celebrated Atlantic crossing in 1901. (Courtesy of Sandy Bay Historical Society, from *Lone Voyager* by Joseph E. Garland)

2 A LEGACY OF SINGLEHANDED SAILING

1

Early Voyages and Influential Pioneers

NO ONE WILL EVER know who made the first extended passage singlehanded. It was probably made inadvertently by a castaway or a fisherman who was blown far offshore by a storm. Deliberate singlehanded voyages, though, could have been made in ancient times. It seems quite possible that the early Polynesians, who were such proficient oceanic voyagers, could have produced a few singlehanders. Then there are the tales about Sinbad-type sailors, dating from the Old Kingdom of Egypt (around 2000 B.C.), who, according to records on papyrus scrolls, passed through the gate to the unknown ocean beyond the Red Sea. On the other side of the globe, there is the legend of the Taoist mystic Hsii Shih, who, by himself (he implied), discovered the "Blessed Islands" in about 200 B.C. A number of reports seem to confirm a singlehanded Atlantic crossing in 1786. This voyage was made by an American seaman, Josiah Shackford, who, with only a dog for crew, sailed a 15-ton sloop from Bordeaux, France, to Surinam, South America. It wasn't until the second half of the nineteenth century, however, that authentic solo passages of great distances were recorded with any accuracy.

Several remarkable solo voyages in the early 1800s have been reported, but they have never been authenticated. The first and most improbable of these is the voyage supposedly made by a Captain Cleveland of Salem, Massachusetts, who is said to have sailed a 15-foot boat almost around the world at the turn of the century. It was reported that he crossed the South Atlantic, rounded the Cape of Good Hope, crossed the Indian and then the Pacific Oceans, and eventually reached the west coast of the United States via Alaska. A more probable voyage is one made by J.M. Crenston, who reportedly sailed the 40-foot cutter *Tocca* from New Bedford to San Francisco, a distance of 13,000 miles, which he covered in 226 days. No one seems to know whether or not Crenston passed through the Strait of Magellan. It is conceivable, though not likely, that he was the first singlehander to round Cape Horn. There is also some evidence that Bernard Gilboy made an early passage lasting approximately six weeks from British Columbia to Hawaii.

Much later, in 1882–83, Gilboy made an authenticated Pacific crossing in the tiny double-ender *Pacific*. His log was rediscovered not many years ago and published under the title *A Voyage of Pleasure*. An amazing aspect of this voyage, which lasted for nearly half a year and covered about 7,000 miles, is that Gilboy never stopped and went ashore, although he passed near numerous islands. He had many misadventures, which included a capsizing and consequent loss of mast, compass, rudder, and stores. Eventually, he abandoned his voyage and allowed himself to be picked up by a large schooner a mere 160 miles from Australia, his destination.

Alfred Johnson, a hand-line Banks fisherman, is given credit for the first west-to-east solo Atlantic crossing. His boat was a 20-foot, decked-over dory named *Centennial* in honor of America's 100th anniversary, for the year was 1876, and Johnson hoped to display his boat after her passage in the Philadelphia Centennial Exposition. He sailed from Gloucester on June 15th and landed in Abercastle,

Capt. Johnson was photographed with his dory *Centennial* on a Gloucester dock late in life. Note the low rig, the decking, and the rudder setup. The dory can still be seen at the Cape Ann Historical Society.

Wales, 59 days later. Johnson spoke many vessels during his crossing and kept track of his whereabouts by getting positions from their navigators. One captain of a passing vessel became so concerned about Johnson's welfare that he offered to take the singlehander aboard, boat and all, and then drop him off near Ireland without a word being said, but Johnson firmly declined. Although the singlehander made light of his hardships, he had some rough experiences, including a capsizing during a gale on August 2. Even though *Centennial* carried some ballast, she was caught off guard by a breaking sea and rolled completely upside down.* Fortunately, Johnson was attached to *Centennial* by a long safety line, but it took him 20 minutes to right the boat. Of course, everything on board was soaked, including his bread and other stores, but worse than that, his water was spoiled and his stove lost. Several days later he got some basic supplies from a passing ship and struggled on until reaching the Welsh coast on August 12.

Johnson inspired others to cruise alone, but probably not nearly as much as did two British singlehanders of that era, R.T. McMullen and, particularly, John MacGregor, even though these mariners made no extremely long passages offshore. McMullen was admired for his uncompromising seamanship and his ability to singlehand large, heavy vessels with complicated rigs, such as his 20-ton *Orion*. His exploits were made known through his book, *Down Channel*, first published in 1869. MacGregor started a craze for cruising in canoes. In 1867, he received notoriety by solo-sailing the 21-foot, decked-over but cabinless yawl *Rob Roy* from London to Paris and back, across a wide part of the English Channel, to attend a regatta and "Boat Exhibition." He inspired a great many people to cruise, including sailor-authors E.F. Knight and E.E. Middleton. MacGregor's book, *The Voyage Alone in the Yawl Rob Roy*, which is enhanced by charming engravings showing details of his yawl and her accommodations (see Figure 1-1), especially captured the imaginations of would-be solo sailors.

Seagoing Cockleshells and Early Solo Ocean Racing

In an era noted for cockleshell voyages, the most dedicated singlehander in miniature craft was undoubtedly the Yankee from Beverly, Massachusetts, William Albert Andrews. Although he has often been written off as a stuntsman and a crackpot, Andrews was certainly a true pioneer and a seaman. *Rudder* magazine (June 1891) called him "a man of extraordinary intelligence" and said that he "has more of the practical side to his character than most people would suppose who have followed his career." Of course, it must be admitted that Andrews took some dangerous chances, and he eventually lost his life at sea. He might also be criticized for inspiring emulation. Nevertheless, he is an important figure, historically at least, for he survived six extended voyages in tiny boats, held the record for the smallest boat to cross the Atlantic for about three quarters of a century, and was a participant in the first transatlantic race for singlehanders.

Centennial was gaff rigged and had a short mast that could be lowered in heavy weather. The wisdom of this practice is now considered questionable because recent studies, made after the disastrous Fastnet Race storm in 1979 when about half the fleet of ocean racers were knocked down or rolled over, show that the mast has a favorable effect on a boat's roll inertia, thereby decreasing the likelihood of a capsize.

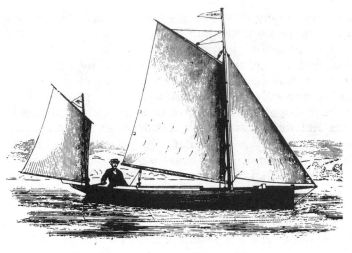

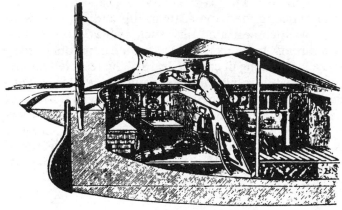

Cooking in rain

Watch on deck

Figure 1-1. The 21-foot canoe yawl *Rob Roy*, sailed by John MacGregor, who did so much to popularize singlehanded cruising in coastal waters.

A former soldier who served for over four years in the Union Army during the Civil War, and a piano maker by trade, Andrews had limited nautical experience before his first voyage in 1878. That year he made a transatlantic crossing with his more experienced brother Asa Walter in *Nautilus*, a 19-foot dory. Brother Walter was ill during much of the 45-day crossing and died not long after returning to the United States. After that, William took to singlehanding.

His first solo voyage, in 1888, was an attempted Atlantic crossing, and one of his purposes was to set a record for the smallest boat to make such a passage. A lot of preparation and unconventional thinking went into the planning of this venture. Some of Andrews' equipment included torpedoes to scare off whales and swordfish, a unique waterproof suit, rubber envelopes for messages, and a contraption for shooting them aboard passing ships. He also had at least one message buoy (see Figure 1-2), which consisted of a cork ring buoy supporting a flag with the words, "Pick This Up" and a Mason jar holding the message. Andrews had a lateen-rigged boat built with such unusual features as watertight bulkheads, a hollow keel that was said to hold 40 gallons of water, and a 200-pound iron shoe that could be dropped off by the untwisting of a single screw. According to a detailed report in the New York *World*, the boat was only 12 feet, 9 inches long, and she was named the *Dark Secret* at the insistence of a sponsor who was promoting a theatrical production of the same name. The voyage itself was a flop, for Andrews had more than his share of headwinds, while his boat leaked badly and was a disappointing performer. He spent 62 miserable days at sea and had not quite reached the mid-Atlantic (longitude 39° 50' W) when he decided to accept being rescued by the westbound Norwegian barque *Nor*.

Undaunted by the failure of the *Dark Secret* venture, Andrews set about preparing for another transatlantic crossing. This time he decided to challenge another singlehander to a race across the ocean, for a prize of $5,000 and a silver cup. The challenge was accepted by Josiah W. Lawlor, son of the famous boat-

Figure 1-2. William Andrews' *Dark Secret*. Andrews undertook six extended voyages on small boats, but was lost at sea with his new wife on the seventh.

builder and designer Dennison J. Lawlor. The younger Lawlor was an experienced sailor, who had recently crossed the Atlantic in an unusual, water-ballasted lifeboat called *Neversink*.

The two competitors built 15-foot boats, both of which were loosely called dories by newspapers of the day. Lawlor's *Sea Serpent* (Figure 1-3) was a double-ender, not unlike a Colin Archer sailing lifeboat. Andrews' *Mermaid* carried a sloop rig with a "bat's wing" mainsail, a sort of cross between a gaff and sliding gunter rig. *Sea Serpent* was sloop-rigged with a bowsprit and a sprit-rigged mainsail, which was divided by a diagonal seam, "lobster boat fashion," running from clew to throat. The two halves of the mainsail were laced together, but they could easily be unlaced to reduce area and convert to a leg-of-mutton rig.

The race began from Crescent Beach, near Boston, on June 21, 1891, the destination Mullion Cove, Land's End, England, where *Nautilus* had landed many years before. Andrews' intended track (as announced before the race) was to be far south of his rival's, but according to their reported positions, Lawlor's track was actually farther south for most of the race (See Figure 1-3). *Sea Serpent* was evidently the better sailer, and she had more favorable winds, for she gradually pulled far ahead of *Mermaid*. With a ballasted keel, she was also the more seaworthy, at least in the important matter of stability and the ability to self-right (*Mermaid* was a centerboarder with no external ballast). Lawlor did capsize on two occasions when *Sea Serpent* broached to, but he had a relatively easy time righting the boat. In contrast, Andrews capsized seven times. The worst of these incidents was reported by Andrews' hometown paper, the *Beverly Citizen*. According to that account, a great sea produced by a summer gale rolled *Mermaid* bottom side up, in which position she remained for some time with Andrews trapped under the vessel's deck. After a considerable struggle, the singlehander escaped through his sliding hatch, swam from under the overturned hull, and grabbed hold of the shallow keel. About 30 minutes later the boat righted, but a great many supplies were lost. The storm raged on, and two days later, on August 20, the cold, wet, and hungry singlehander was rescued by the steamer *Ebrus*, bound for Antwerp. He had raced to within about 600 miles of the English coast.

Si Lawlor reached England at Coverack near the Lizard on August 5, having sailed about 2,800 miles in 44 days. Compared with Andrews he had an easy time of it, but he was not without his share of adventures. Aside from the two capsizings already mentioned, he was also, according to several accounts, attacked by a shark. On the night of July 24, Lawlor was jostled from his sleep by a suspicious motion of his boat and a crunching noise. Leaning over the side, he spotted a large shark gnawing on *Sea Serpent*'s stem. With great resourcefulness, he reached for an exploding yacht salute, wrapped it in paper, lit the fuse, and threw it at the shark's head. The greedy brute snatched the salute and it exploded in his mouth, effectively extricating Lawlor from his predicament.

Andrews must have felt rather humiliated by his defeat, for he made a wager with Lawlor that he would cross the Atlantic the next year in 30 days. Lawlor also decided to make the passage again in an attempt to break his own record. Both men built new boats for the competition. I know little of Lawlor's craft except that she was called *Christopher Columbus*, but the details of Andrews' boat are well known. She was a folding boat built of cedar and canvas, resembling a sneakbox. Her dimensions (as published in Andrews' log) were 14 feet, 6 inches length on

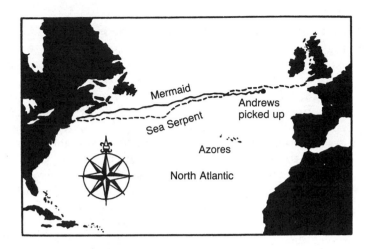

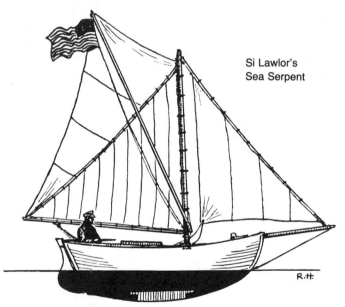

Figure 1-3. The first solo transatlantic race.

deck; 5 feet, 5 inches beam; and 3 feet depth. She had 350 pounds of ballast on her keel, and she could be folded up into a package about 6 inches thick. She was flush-decked and had a sliding hatch that could cover the cockpit in heavy weather. Her rig was similar to *Mermaid*'s with the bat's wing mainsail, except that the new boat had a short bowsprit. Andrews christened her *Sapolio* after the product of the soap manufacturer who sponsored the voyage.

The original plan was to sail the shortest course from Newfoundland to Ireland. But that year, 1892, was the fourth centennial of Columbus' discovery of America, and when Andrews heard of a celebration being held in Palos, Spain, he decided to make that his destination. Lawlor set out much earlier than Andrews and was not heard from again—he was evidently lost at sea. *Sapolio*, however, set sail from Atlantic City on July 20, 1892, and made a successful crossing to Spain by way of the Azores. She was the smallest boat to have crossed the Atlantic, a record that held until Robert Manry's voyage in the 13½-foot *Tinkerbelle* and John Riding's crossing in the 12-foot *Sjo Ag*, both during the summer of 1965.* It took Andrews 31 days to sight the Azores, but he didn't actually land at Angra until six days later, on August 26. Three days after that, he set sail for Spain and reached the village of Burgau, Portugal, on September 20, having had a frightening encounter with finback whales not far from Cape St. Vincent. His crossing took 61 days, counting the three he spent ashore in the Azores. About a week later he reached his eventual destination at Palos and received a hero's welcome.

Although Andrews had fulfilled his dream of a solo crossing in the smallest boat on record, he was not long satisfied, for in 1898 he made another attempt to sail alone from America to Europe in a 13-foot boat called *Phantom Ship.* Departing August 24, he made the mistake of sailing too late in the season and experienced extremely heavy weather. His boat leaked badly, and most of his food spoiled. After enduring 27 days of hardships, the singlehander asked to be taken, boat and all, aboard a passing ship. Yet, on his return home he began making plans for a voyage in an even smaller boat. Since he still had *Phantom Ship,* he decided it would be economical to take her apart and rebuild her into a new boat. The result was another folding craft only 12 feet long with a depth of 22 inches and a beam of 5 feet, which he named *Doree.* He cast off bound for the Azores on June 17, 1899, but again the voyage did not succeed. Three weeks after his departure, he was picked up by the steamer *Holbein,* and headlines in the *World* screamed, "Andrews Was Half Crazy—Privation Had Unhinged the Mind of the Daring Sailor Who Tried to Cross the Ocean in a Dory." The singlehander was reported to be incoherent and semi-delirious when rescued, but he had an explanation for his state. He told a reporter for *The Strand* magazine that he was dazed and nearly asphyxiated from leaking carbonic acid gas, which had escaped from his bottles of Saratoga water. Whether this was true or whether he was suffering from hallucinations I do not know, but he found after speaking a passing ship that he had completely lost track of four days of time.

Andrews' seventh and final voyage was made in what was reported as a 20-foot dory called *Flying Dutchman,* the original name for the older *Sapolio* before she had been sponsored. This was to be a honeymoon cruise, for Andrews had taken a new wife. The two set sail from Atlantic City bound for Spain in the summer of 1901. After about one week at sea, the honeymooners spoke the steamer *Durango,* and that was the last ever heard of William Andrews or his bride. Apparently, they sailed into heavy weather and oblivion.

My correspondent D. H. Clarke, an English authority on small boat voyages, maintains that Andrews' last voyage was actually the third transatlantic race for singlehanders, the second having been between Lawlor and Andrews in 1892, the year of *Sapolio*'s crossing. Andrews' challenger in 1901 was the amazing Howard Blackburn, who singlehanded the 25-foot sloop *Great Republic* from Gloucester to Lisbon that year. Blackburn did challenge "any man" to a solo race, and he made a very fast crossing in 39 days, but the challenge had been dropped a considerable time before he sailed because there had been no takers. Furthermore, he specified that the race be sailed singlehanded (Andrews had his bride, of course) and Black-

---

*According to historian Jean Merrien, however, Harry Young sailed a 13-foot, 9-inch undecked sloop from New York to the Azores in 1939.

The remarkable Howard Blackburn, bluewater singlehander without fingers. (From *Lone Voyager*, by Joseph E. Garland, courtesy of the author)

burn was returning to the United States on a ship at the time of Andrews' departure in *Flying Dutchman*. Thus, not many people would consider it a race. A better case could be made for a race in 1899 between Andrews and Blackburn, for that year the latter crossed in the 30-foot downeast sloop *Great Western*, and he got underway on the same day (though in a different location) as Andrews in his *Doree*. It was said that each singlehander hoped to be the first across.

Howard Blackburn is perhaps the most remarkable of all singlehanders because he had no fingers. He lost them as a young man while a fisherman aboard the Gloucester schooner *Grace L. Fears*, which was working on Burgeo Bank about 65 miles off Newfoundland in mid-winter, 1883. His story is one of incredible courage and endurance.

While tending trawls from a dory, Blackburn and his companion, Tom Welch, became separated from their schooner because of a sudden wind shift and a blinding snow storm. They lay to an improvised drogue for nearly two days, all the while chipping ice from the boat and bailing nearly constantly to keep her from swamping. They never could reach the mother vessel, and Welch died of exposure during the second night. After the storm abated, Blackburn decided to try for the shores of Newfoundland. He had lost his mittens while rigging the drogue and his fingers were frozen stiff, but the tough fisherman had formed his hands into cupped sockets that could receive the oar handles, allowing him to row in a crude fashion. Three days later, with no food or water and with seriously frostbitten hands and feet, he reached Newfoundland, where he was taken in by a destitute family and nursed back to health. Miraculously, he survived, but at the cost of losing many toes, all of his fingers, and half of each thumb.

It is difficult to conceive how Blackburn could have later solo-sailed two boats across the Atlantic when he had no fingers. In *Lone Voyager*, Joseph Garland's biography of Blackburn, he tells us that the singlehander held lines by pinching them between his hands and half-thumbs. To haul on a line, he would take a turn around his waist, lean back, clamp the line with one hand over the cockpit coaming (or elsewhere), take in slack, and then repeat the process. One might say he was "swigging" the line with his body. Of course, there were many other tasks, such as taking sights and lighting his running lights or stove, that were extremely difficult to perform without fingers, but somehow he managed.

After his Atlantic crossings, Blackburn made a remarkable inland voyage in his 25-foot *Great Republic*. He took her from Gloucester down to New York, up the Hudson River, through the Erie Canal, across the Great Lakes to Chicago, and down the Mississippi River to Columbus, Kentucky, where the boat was shipped by rail to Mobile, Alabama. Then he sailed her along the Gulf coast and down around the tip of Florida. The *Great Republic* cruise came to an end when she went hard aground at Coconut Grove. The boat was saved, but Blackburn subsequently sold her. She is still in existence, having recently been bought and preserved by the Gloucester Historical Commission. The really remarkable aspect of her inland cruise was that her draft was almost the same as the depth of some of the waterways on which she traveled. She was towed through the Erie Canal by mule power and through the Chicago Drainage Canal, which was nearly 100 miles long and little more than 3 feet deep, by manpower. Blackburn and a helper took turns walking along the canal's bank with the tow line over their shoulders while, as Blackburn wrote, "Hundreds of snakes would run across the path and sometimes crawl over our feet, many of them six and seven feet long."

The beginning of Blackburn's unsuccessful attempt to cross the Atlantic in the 17-foot dory *America* in June 1903. (Courtesy of Philip Kuuse, from *Lone Voyager*, by Joseph E. Garland)

Another offshore solo voyage was made by Blackburn not long after his return from Florida in 1903. This time he attempted to cross the Atlantic in a 17-foot dory he named *America*. The voyage was extremely rough, with gales and heavy seas. After about two weeks at sea, *America* capsized off Cape Sable, Nova Scotia. Blackburn was trapped below under his sliding hatch, which was jammed shut, but the dory soon righted herself. The compass, lantern, food, and other supplies were lost, so Blackburn headed into Clark's Harbor near Cape Sable when the blow subsided. Some days later he set off again, once more ran into a storm, and again capsized. This time he was on deck and was thrown overboard, but he managed to grab the main boom, haul himself to the side of the dory and right her by putting his weight all on one side. In addition to his problems with the capsizing, Blackburn was sick with an infected knee, so he wisely gave in to the Atlantic and headed back to Nova Scotia.

This voyage might also be considered an attempted transatlantic single-handed race, for Blackburn was competing against a German-American, Ludwig Eisenbraun, who left to cross "the pond" shortly before Blackburn in the 19½-foot "dory" *Columbia*. Eisenbraun was also turned back by the heavy weather, but started off again much later in the season, after Blackburn had abandoned the project, and eventually reached Gibraltar via Halifax and Madeira.

Early Circumnavigations

On May 8, 1898, a heavily built, sea-weary yawl, encrusted with salt and garnished with a fringe of marine growth, tied the knot on a 2½-year voyage around the world. At that moment, when she crossed her outward-bound track, she became the first vessel to make a singlehanded circumnavigation. Large, faded letters across her broad stern proudly proclaimed she was the *Spray* out of Boston. Her lone skipper was Captain Joshua Slocum, who has rightfully been called America's best-known sailor.

He had been given *Spray* when she was the abandoned hulk of a hundred-year-old oyster sloop propped up in a pasture to rot away. With his own hands and the most basic tools he had completely rebuilt the old *Spray* from her keel up, replacing each member piece-by-piece until she was an entirely new boat. Her centerboard well was removed and she was given a shallow keel made from a tough pasture oak felled by Slocum himself. All new structural members were exceptionally heavy, and her planking was 1½-inches thick except at the turn of the bilge where two wales were twice as heavy. She was fastened with copper rivets and a thousand screw bolts. After 13 months of rebuilding, at a cost of $553.62, *Spray* was finally launched, and when she once again met her natural element, Slocum said she sat on the water like a swan.

Born and raised in Nova Scotia, Josh Slocum ran away to sea at an early age to begin an off-and-on professional seagoing career. When only 27 years old, by then an American citizen, he was put in command of a 332-ton bark, the *Washington*. His proudest command, however, was the full-rigged ship *Northern Light*, which he called "the finest American sailing vessel afloat."

Like so many sailors not long before the turn of the century when the glorious age of sail was declining, Captain Josh found himself on the beach, faced with a

Joshua Slocum. (Courtesy of Donald R. Holm)

choice of shore work or going to sea in a "smoke-belcher." No one knows for sure just when he first entertained thoughts of a solo circumnavigation, but the idea of escaping to the open sea alone in a small boat was made conceivable by a 5,500-mile cruise from Brazil to New York he had made with his family in a 35-foot home-built sampan called *Liberdade.* The reborn *Spray* was first envisioned as a floating home and a possible source of income through fishing, but when the fishing did not work out, the captain decided to embark on a loosely scheduled global cruise.

The first leg of his voyage took him from Gloucester, Massachusetts, across the Atlantic by way of the Azores to Gibraltar, but there he was advised by British Naval officers not to cross the Mediterranean alone because of Berber pirates along the North African coast. Heeding this warning, Slocum changed his plans and decided on an east-to-west circumnavigation, so he took the *Spray* back into the Atlantic and headed for South America.

Worries about pirates did not end with the change of course. Before the *Spray* had cleared the African shore, Slocum was chased by a felucca manned by pirates. They almost got him, but in the freshening breeze the felucca, carrying too much sail, broached to and was dismasted. In the same squall *Spray* broke her main boom, but she was able to carry on under reefed main, and her captain soon fished the broken spar. Forty days out of Gibraltar she reached Permambuco, Brazil, where the main boom was permanently shortened by four feet. Later the sloop was converted to a yawl when Slocum added a lug-rigged mizzen mast supported by a semi-circular brace at the stern.

Among Slocum's other adventures during his circumnavigation were a near high-and-dry grounding on the shore of Uruguay, where the captain almost

The famous *Spray*, with Joshua Slocum at the helm, proudly displays her ensign at Hyannis Port, Massachusetts, in 1907. (Courtesy of *Yachting* magazine)

drowned after his half-dory capsized while he was carrying out a large anchor to kedge off. Near the coast of Patagonia his boat was buried by a giant tidal wave just after he had scampered up the mast to avoid being washed overboard. He took the engineless *Spray* through the barren, tortuous Strait of Magellan and along the way had to battle hostile Fuegian Indians and equally savage williwaws that blasted down on him from the mountainous shores. His greatest adventure, though, was sailing through the Milky Way breakers not far from Cape Horn. Blown into this notorious death trap of submerged rocks after being forced to run off before a gale, the *Spray* spent an entire night dodging breakers in the dark during the nastiest kind of weather. Slocum said that God alone knew how his vessel survived.

The next day he escaped through Cockburn Channel, which led back into the Strait of Magellan. A snug anchorage was found, but again he was threatened by Fuegians. Slocum became famous for his clever (but apparently unoriginal) trick of repelling his barefoot Indian invaders by sprinkling the decks with carpet tacks. A test for his "injunuity" was keeping the savages guessing about the number of crew onboard the *Spray*. To this end he made a dummy and changed clothes frequently, creating the impression he was not alone. Outwitting the Fuegians and their murderous halfbreed leader Black Pedro, Slocum got his *Spray* back to the Pacific and finally cleared the shore.

During the rest of her circumnavigation *Spray* crossed waters that were relatively hospitable. She sailed up to the island of Juan Fernandez where Alexander

Selkirk had been marooned (inspiring the story of Robinson Crusoe). Heading more to the west from there, Slocum picked up the tradewinds and made his next landfall at Samoa, where the natives accused him, half seriously, of eating his crew. The next stop was Newcastle, Australia, and then a layover in Sydney, the great yachting center, where Slocum was given a hero's welcome. After a side trip down to Tasmania, *Spray* proceeded north along the Great Barrier reef to Torres Strait, gateway to the lovely Arafura Sea.

Crossing the Indian Ocean, Slocum made several island stops, the first at Keeling Cocos where he took on a load of huge tridacua shells, which he hoped to sell. Not long before he arrived at the island of Rodriguez, the abbé had threatened some misbehaving islanders with a visit from the devil, so when *Spray* arrived with only one man onboard, Captain Josh was at first taken for Satan. After calling at Mauritius, he pushed on through some heavy weather off Madagascar and landed at Durban, South Africa.

Christmas found the old yawl struggling to round the Cape of Good Hope in a wicked seaway. Slocum described his boat as trying to stand on her head, and he was ready for a long rest when he reached Cape Town. Three months later, having been royally entertained, the captain was off again to cross the South Atlantic. Stopping at the midocean island of St. Helena, he took on a passenger in the form of a goat, which devoured everything edible, including his straw hat and a valuable chart of the West Indies. When *Spray* crossed her outbound track off the coast of South America, Slocum said to himself, "Let what will happen, the voyage is now on record." His place in maritime history was secure for all time as the first person to sail around the world alone. On June 27, 1898, three years and two months after setting out, *Spray* reached Newport, Rhode Island, where she ended her 46,000-mile voyage.

Captain Slocum became an overnight celebrity. He was soon in great demand on the lecture circuit, and an audience was requested by another great adventurer, President Teddy Roosevelt. After writing a series of articles about his circumnavigation for *Century* magazine, he produced the book *Sailing Alone Around the World*, which became a best seller and is still popular today. Charmingly written and beautifully illustrated with pen-and-ink drawings (by Fogarty and Varian), the book became a nautical classic. Although intended for the general public and lacking technical details, it has probably inspired more shorthanded voyaging than any other book.

It is interesting to compare Slocum's feat with some of the modern, high-tech circumnavigations. Today great use is made of complicated self-steering vanes and/or autopilots, satellite rescue and navigation systems, roller-furling sails (some of them electrically operated), weather facsimile equipment, ham radios, electricity generators, hydraulic gear, and other gadgetry. Slocum had no engine, no electricity, no self-steering mechanism, no radio, no refrigeration, no hot showers, not even a chronometer. With tongue in cheek he suggested that his longitude was figured from a tin clock which cost him $1.50, but the captain really needed no timepiece at all. He found his longitude through lunar observations, a method that involves measuring the distance of the moon from the sun or a fixed star. For a singlehander on a small boat, lunars require exceptional skill with the sextant.

Unlike many of today's voyagers whose expensive boats are loaded with fancy equipment, Slocum was almost a pauper when he set forth on his circumnavigation. He had but $1.80 in cash, and except for some first-class personal items from

Captain and Mrs. Joshua Slocum on board the *Spray*, in 1902 at Martha's Vineyard. (Photo by Clifton Johnson)

former voyages, like his guns and sextant, he started off with minimal gear. Much of this was scrounged or homemade, such as his turpentine flares, a wooden anchor, and a bucket still. The success of his voyage was largely due to masterful seamanship. He learned to read the weather, maneuver his clumsy craft in tight places, handle her heavy gear, claw to windward when necessary, ride to a sea anchor, lie to or run off in heavy weather, and balance his boat so that she would sail for days with the helm unattended. On the run to Keeling Cocos Island, for instance, *Spray* sailed for 23 days with her skipper's hand on the wheel for a total of three hours. To accomplish this, he extended the bowsprit with a bamboo spar, thus moving the center of effort of his sails far forward. Never one to boast of his seamanship, Slocum said of his circumnavigation that he hoped he had "done nothing that an American sailor should be ashamed of."

Between 1905 and 1908 Captain Josh took three winter cruises to the West Indies in *Spray*. His purpose (or so he said) was "just to save buying a winter coat." The following year he headed south again, but this time he disappeared without a trace. The reason for his loss is a matter of conjecture. Some think the seams of the tired old *Spray* just opened up, but the Captain's son Victor, author of the book *Capt. Joshua Slocum*, thinks it more likely that he was run down by a ship, perhaps in the vicinity of Cape Hatteras where there was a lot of commercial traffic.

Harry Pidgeon, the first man to circumnavigate twice alone, aboard his home-made yawl *Islander*. (Courtesy of *Yachting* magazine)

Another circumnavigation made completely singlehanded did not occur until over a quarter of a century after Slocum's return, when Harry Pidgeon performed the feat in his 34-foot yawl *Islander*. Pidgeon was a landsman until relatively late in life, but he had manual skills and a yearning to visit the South Seas. He built himself a hard-chine yawl, an enlargement of the Sea Bird class (see Chapter 4) and studied navigation in the public library. After making a trial cruise with an unsatisfactory crew, Pidgeon decided to sail alone. He set off from California in 1921, bound for the South Sea islands with little thought of rounding the world, but after reaching his destination and spending some time there, he decided to return home west-about. His track also passed through the Torres Strait and around the southern tip of Africa, but after crossing the Atlantic, *Islander* was able to use the Panama Canal, which did not exist at the time of Slocum's circumnavigation. Pidgeon developed into a first-class seaman and had few untoward experiences except for grounding on a lee shore near Cape Town (see Chapter 11) and having his rig damaged by a steamer that came too close to investigate him.

Pidgeon made a later circumnavigation in the same boat in 1932–37, but on this voyage he had a crew for a small part of the time. In 1947, he attempted a third

A rare photo of Alain Gerbault and Harry Pidgeon as their paths met in Panama. (Courtesy of Donald R. Holm)

rounding of the world in his *Islander*, this time doublehanded with his wife, but the old yawl was wrecked by a tropical storm in the New Hebrides. (Pidgeon and his wife escaped.)

While *Islander* was completing her first voyage around the world, an entirely different kind of boat, an early British racing cutter named *Firecrest*, skippered by the French singlehander Alain Gerbault, was setting out from Gibraltar to cross the Atlantic on the first leg of a circumnavigation. The crossing was very slow, 101 days, and was fraught with gear failure, but nonetheless Gerbault was the first recipient of the Blue Water Medal, an award for meritorious seamanship presented by the Cruising Club of America. Gerbault changed *Firecrest*'s rig from gaff to Marconi and set out from New York in 1924 to continue the circumnavigation. He, too, passed through the Panama Canal, and at Balboa, Gerbault met Pidgeon, who had almost completed his circumnavigation. The two singlehanders, as well as their boats, made an interesting contrast; Gerbault, a former flying ace and tennis champion, was dashing and egotistical, while Pidgeon, a photographer from the American midwest, was plain, modest, and reserved. Their vessels will be compared in Chapter 4.

Gerbault pushed on for the South Seas, where he eventually settled and wrote books extolling the natives' way of life and disapproving of the white man's civilization, but not before he took *Firecrest* entirely around the world. He followed a similar track to Pidgeon's, but after rounding the Cape of Good Hope, he proceeded north for France and suffered a damaging grounding at the Cape Verde Islands. In July 1928 he arrived in his native country and received a hero's welcome with many accolades and awards, including the cross of the Legion of Honor.

The fourth solo circumnavigation was made by American Edward Miles, who set out alone in 1928 on a "goodwill voyage" to spread the message of brotherhood throughout the world. Miles' direction of travel was entirely different from that of the previous circumnavigators, as it was eastabout, and his track passed through the Red Sea rather than around the tip of Africa. Two facts may detract somewhat from the importance of the voyage as a pure sailing feat. The first is that the circumnavigation was made in two different vessels, with a lengthy interval of time between boats. The second is that the boat which traveled the greater distance by far had substantial auxiliary power and used it quite a lot. Both vessels were schooners about 37 feet long named *Sturdy*, built by Miles himself. The first boat burned up as a result of a gasoline fire near the Suez Canal; because of that experience, Miles fit *Sturdy II* with diesel power. He built her in Memphis, Tennessee, and then shipped her to Suez to take up where her predecessor had left off.

Slocum's lone, westabout circumnavigation by way of the Strait of Magellan was duplicated by another retired ship's captain, Louis Bernicot, in 1936–38. This Frenchman had a slight advantage over Slocum in that his 41-foot sloop, *Anahita*, had an engine (of very low power), but Bernicot's fast voyage was nonetheless an exemplary feat of seamanship. Bernicot had his share of heavy weather and actually capsized en route to Cape Horn. Although he did not claim it in his book, *Voyage of the Anahita*, he told one circumnavigator that his boat made a 360-degree roll. Fortunately, she was well ballasted and righted immediately without breaking her Marconi mast. Some years after his voyage around the world, Bernicot was killed in an accident aboard the same sloop.

An entirely different kind of circumnavigation was made by Argentinian Vito Dumas in 1942–43 aboard the double-ended ketch *Lehg II*. His easterly track passed south of the three stormy capes (Good Hope, Leeuwin, and the Horn) and also south of Tasmania. Of course, this was a short route around the world and the winds were almost always astern, which accounts in part for the speed of the voyage (271 sailing days), but it was made in cold, barren waters where the almost unbroken fetch and boisterous winds can produce seas that are often extremely dangerous for small craft. Dumas was the first recipient of the Slocum prize, awarded by the Slocum Society, for a truly outstanding solo voyage.

After World War II, another rugged double-ender, *Stornoway*, sailed alone by American Alfred Peterson, circled the globe in an original way. He made the usual east-to-west rounding, but by the way of the Red Sea, in the opposite direction of Edward Miles. Peterson had few troubles, but most of them occurred in the Red Sea, where he experienced a serious grounding, was held prisoner for a short while, and had his boat plundered by pirates. He reached the east coast of America, from whence he started, in the summer of 1952, completing a voyage of nearly 4 1/2 years.

Before Peterson arrived home, another circumnavigator, Frenchman Marcel Bardiaux, was setting out on one of the most remarkable solo voyages of all time. In a homebuilt, 31-foot racing-cruising sloop, this former kayak champion took about eight years to make a westabout rounding. The astonishing aspect of this voyage was that Bardiaux sailed his little boat, *Les 4 Vents*, around Cape Horn in the beginning of winter against the prevailing winds. The sloop capsized twice when approaching the Horn, an experience that will be described in Chapter 10.*

Jean Gau, a Frenchman who based himself in America, made two circumnavigations alone, the first in 1953–57 and the second from 1962–67. Gau had earned his money between voyages as a chef in a large New York hotel. His vessel and

---

*Bardiaux was not the first singlehander to round Cape Horn the "wrong way," however, for about 20 years earlier, Norwegian Alfon M. Hansen sailed his double-ended cutter *Mary Jane*, east to west around the Horn. Soon afterwards, though, Hansen was wrecked and drowned on the southern coast of Chile. It is also possible but improbable that Crenston (mentioned earlier) sailed around the Stormy Cape in a westerly direction.

Vito Dumas, whose easterly track passed south of the three stormy capes and Tasmania. (Courtesy of Donald R. Holm)

home was the 30-foot Tahiti ketch *Atom*, which not only carried him twice around the world, but also about a dozen times across the Atlantic. As one would expect, Gau and his *Atom* have had many adventures, including surviving the full force of two hurricanes, a lee shore stranding, and a capsizing by a freak wave.

Until fairly recently the smallest boat to be sailed by one man around the earth was *Trekka*, a 21-foot, fin-keel yawl designed by J. Laurent Giles*. She was very capably skippered by a young Briton, John Guzzwell. Like many of his circum-navigating predecessors—Slocum, Pidgeon, Miles, and Bardiaux—Guzzwell built his boat with his own hands (Slocum actually rebuilt his boat). *Trekka*'s voyage, beginning and ending in Victoria, B.C., Canada (1955–59), was in a westerly direction via Torres Strait, the Cape of Good Hope, and the Panama Canal. John wrote me that the same suit of cotton sails, costing "the ridiculous price of £29.10.0" (less than $100 at that time), carried him all the way around the world, which is indicative of his superb seamanship. His most exciting and frightening adventure came when he temporarily left *Trekka* to join Miles Smeeton and his wife Beryl in sailing the ketch *Tzu Hang* from Australia to England via Cape Horn. Many sailors know the story of how, in the Roaring Forties about a thousand miles from South America, *Tzu Hang* pitchpoled and dismasted, her cabin house was seriously damaged, and she nearly sank. Miles Smeeton gives great credit to Guzzwell for his seamanship and skillful carpentry in helping to save *Tzu Hang* by jury-rigging her, making repairs, and helping sail her 1,350 miles to Coronel, Chile.

Another very small boat, the 25-foot, Vertue-class sloop *Cardinal Vertue*, was sailed solo eastabout the world by Australian William E. Nance from 1962–65. The most remarkable aspect of this voyage was that Nance took her across the Pacific through the Roaring Forties and then around Cape Horn. Nance's greatest troubles came earlier, however, on the passage from Cape Town to Melbourne, Australia, when his steering vane was damaged, the mast broke above the spreaders, he was nearly washed overboard, and his boat suffered a series of knockdowns while

*In 1974 Yoh Aoki wrested the record from Guzzwell in the homemade plywood yawl *Ahodori* (Crazy Bird), 20 feet 8 inches LOA. Although it has been argued by Nobby Clarke and others that *Trekka* is smaller, with her deck length of 20 feet 6 inches, Guzzwell wrote that her overall length (from stem to the tip of her reversed transom) is 20 feet 10 inches, making her slightly longer than *Ahodori*. Since 1987, the record has belonged to Australian Sergio Tesra, sailing the 12-foot aluminum cutter *Australis* (see Chapter 2).

Youthful circumnavigator Robin Lee Graham aboard *Dove*. (Courtesy of *Yachting* magazine)

Alec Rose, the popular English grocer who was knighted for his outstanding solo circumnavigation. (Courtesy of John Rock)

rounding Cape Leeuwin. The voyage began in England, but the circumnavigation was completed at Buenos Aires, where he had stopped almost exactly two years earlier.

In the 1960s some of the more highly publicized solo voyages around the world were those made by Robin Lee Graham, Francis Chichester, and Alec Rose. Graham, a teenager from California, was heralded as the youngest circumnavigator. He was only 16 years old when he started his westabout cruise (following a similar track to Pidgeon's) in *Dove*, a stock Lapworth 24, and he was 21 years old when he concluded the voyage in *The Return of Dove*, a stock Luders 33. By contrast, the Englishmen, Chichester and Rose, were comparatively old men (66 and almost 60) when they completed their circumnavigations. They both made fast eastabout roundings, Chichester in about nine months (1966–67) and Rose in slightly less than a year (1967–68), passing south of the three stormy capes as Dumas had done. Unlike the Argentinian, though, the two Englishmen made longer voyages that were considered antipodal since the departure and arrival points were in England. Chichester's boat was the 54-foot ketch *Gipsy Moth IV*; Rose's was the 36-foot yawl *Lively Lady*.

Many other solo circumnavigations were completed in the late 1960s, including those of Frank Casper, Pierre Auboiroux, Alfred Kallies, Wilfried Erdmann, C. H. (Rusty) Webb, John Sowden, Leonid Teliga, Walter Koenig, and Roger Plisson (for a full listing of singlehanded circumnavigators see Appendix A). For some

Francis Chichester, winner of the first OSTAR race (1960) aboard his *Gipsy Moth III*. (Courtesy of *Yachting* magazine)

reason they remain relatively unknown, having received little coverage in the press and popular yachting magazines—although Casper finally received some recognition in the form of the Cruising Club of America Blue Water medal for his circumnavigation made almost entirely alone (1963–66) and for his many solo transatlantic crossings. Certainly these voyagers were not publicity seekers. But the simpler explanation may be that, by the late 1960s, media attention was already shifting toward the dramatic next chapter in the history of singlehanded sailing—the rise of singlehanded racing.

Philippe Jeantot aboard *Credit Agricole*.

2

The Modern Era: Races and Record Breaking

SINCE THE EARLY TRANSATLANTIC SOLO races between Andrews, Lawlor, Blackburn, and Eisenbraun, there were a few informal races across oceans in the decades that followed. However, one event that began in England gave birth to singlehanded ocean racing as we know it today. That event was the Singlehanded Transatlantic Race of 1960, and it started with a wager for half a crown.

The race was the brainchild of Colonel H.G. Hasler, a World War II hero, who had led an attack on German ships in Bordeaux harbor from tiny cockleshell boats. After the war, Hasler took up solo sailing, and he developed a new, almost revolutionary boat and rig for simplified singlehanding. The result of his experiments was the famous, highly modified Folkboat *Jester*, which will be described in Chapter 4. After many discussions and negotiations, Hasler persuaded a prominent London newspaper, the *Observer*, to sponsor the race and the Royal Western Yacht Club to handle the start and other important matters. In America, the Slocum Society, the organization devoted to encouraging long-distance passages in small boats, gave the race publicity and helped in handling the finish. The contestants were Hasler himself, in his 25-foot *Jester*; Francis Chichester, in the 39-foot sloop *Gipsy Moth III*; Valentine Howells, sailing the more conventional Folkboat *Eira*; Jean Lacombe in the smallest boat, the 21-foot *Cap Horn*; and David Lewis, an adventurous doctor who was interested in the medical and survival aspects of the race, sailing the 25-foot *Cardinal Vertue*. (This is the same boat on which William E. Nance later made his eastabout circumnavigation.)

All of the competitors had their share of rough weather. Chichester encountered above-hurricane-force winds on one occasion, and Hasler, pushing far north hunting for easterly winds, weathered a lengthy and what he called "boring" gale. He mentioned "driving the poor little thing [*Jester*] into a filthy breaking sea with

The circular hatch of Hasler's *Jester* which serves as a central control point from which her one sail can be hoisted, trimmed, and reefed without the singlehander's ever leaving the hatchway. (Photo by Bernadette Brennan)

four reefs down." Howells suffered a severe knockdown that resulted in the loss of his chronometer, and he put into Bermuda temporarily. He had already lost electric power for proper time checks (and lights), because he was forced to jettison a huge damaged battery. Lacombe weathered a severe gale lying to a sea anchor, and later he was taken in tow by the Coast Guard for a short while because of a threat from a hurricane and high seas. Dr. Lewis lost the top of his mast soon after the start in Plymouth, but he returned under jury rig and set off again. The race results were: Chichester, first, taking 40 days; Hasler, second, 48 days; Lewis, third, 56 days; Howells, fourth, 63 days; and Lacombe, fifth, 74 days. Times were slow by modern standards, but each competitor felt rightfully proud of his accomplishment, especially Hasler, who had done much to prove his theories.

Thus the stage was set for an event that is raced every four years and has endured to this day as a tough proving ground for solo sailors and high-tech gear. The next OSTAR (*Observer*'s Singlehanded Transatlantic Race) was held in 1964.* This was won in a little over 27 days by a newcomer, the Frenchman Eric Tabarly, sailing an unusual, 44-foot, hard-chined, plywood ketch, *Pen Duick II*. After his victory, Tabarly became a national hero and was made a Chevalier of the Legion of

*The race is now known as the C-Star (Carlsberg Singlehanded Transatlantic Race, reflecting its new sponsorship by Carlsberg Brewing Co.)

Eric Tabarly, who won both the 1964 and 1976 OSTARs and the first singlehanded transpacific race in boats named *Pen Duick*. (Courtesy of Betsy Holman)

Honor. Chichester, again sailing his *Gipsy Moth III*, came in second and bettered his previous time by about 10 days. All the other participants in the 1960 race also competed again. Valentine Howells took third in a new boat, the 35-foot steel sloop *Akka*, and Hasler in his *Jester* took fifth in elapsed time, being beaten by about one day by Alec Rose on *Lively Lady* (Hasler beat Rose on corrected time). Lewis finished seventh in a heavy catamaran *Rehu Moana*, which had previously made a voyage to Iceland (Chapter 11), and which later would carry the doctor and his family to the South Seas. Lacombe finished ninth, beating six other competitors, although he was sailing the smallest boat, the 21-foot *Golif*.

The OSTAR grew so popular that the 1968 race had 35 entries. On this occasion, there were many more multihulls and some large monohulls built especially for the race. Tabarly entered a new 67-foot trimaran, a radical concept for ocean work, *Pen Duick IV*. In this particular competition, she had little chance to show her potential, however, because she collided with a ship soon after the start and had to withdraw. Many of the large, specialized craft, including the winner and second place finisher, were largely paid for by sponsors. This meant that participants sailing unsponsored craft often had to go into considerable debt or spend their life savings in order to get a competitive boat. One man spent so much money simply fitting out a boat he already owned that he had to sell his home to pay expenses.

The winner was Englishman Geoffrey Williams, making his crossing in just under 26 days in the 56-foot, sleek, low-freeboard ketch *Sir Thomas Lipton*. The fast, 49-foot, South African ketch *Voortrekker* sailed by Bruce Dalling was not quite a day behind to take second place on elapsed time and first on corrected time for the monohull award. A most unusual craft took third place. She was the 40-foot, schooner-rigged proa *Cheers*, which will be described in Chapter 4, sailed by an American, Tom Follett. The winning skipper, Williams, had radio communication with a shore-based computer that suggested favorable courses, and evidently this was advantageous, as he was routed north of a storm that a lot of boats did not avoid. Many of the competitors retired from the race mostly because of mast or rudder failure, but two multihulls broke up, and one monohull sank after it was taken in tow following a dismasting. Eight out of 13 multihulls failed to finish. In most cases this was because of various design failures, but one trimaran skipper, Eric Willis, became seriously ill (from contaminated drinking water according to one report), and he had to be taken off his boat, *Coila*, after two medics parachuted down to assist.

This race had a woman participant, a 26-year-old West German secretary named Edith Baumann, but unfortunately her boat, *Koala III*, was one of the two multihulls that came apart in heavy weather.

The Golden Globe—Solo Around the World

In 1968, singlehanded ocean racing took a quantum leap with a bold new race that was far ahead of its time. The previous year, Francis Chichester had completed his highly publicized, one-stop circumnavigation for which he was knighted and became a national hero. Several English sailors and a couple of Frenchmen aspired to outdo him by sailing around the world non-stop. Getting wind of this plan, Chichester's newspaper sponsor, the London *Sunday Times*, decided to create a sensational competition among the aspirants. It would be the ultimate sailboat race, one person per boat with the course running non-stop from a port in the British Isles down to the Southern Ocean, eastward past the great capes and home again to the starting point. Starts could be staggered between June 1 and October 31, 1968. The participant with the fastest elapsed time would receive a prize of £5,000 sterling, and the first home would be awarded a handsome golden globe trophy.

Nine out of 10 entrants started the Golden Globe Race. The first two away were John Ridgeway and Chay Blyth, two former paratroopers who had previously rowed together across the Atlantic. Ridgeway left eight days before Blyth in a stock 30-footer, but after six weeks of hard sailing, a chainplate came loose and he had to put into Recife, Brazil. Blyth, too, had to abandon the race after his 30-foot sloop was struck by a storm and his steering gear was damaged off the coast of southern Africa. (He eventually succeeded sailing around the world alone—non-stop and against the prevailing winds—in another boat, the 58-foot steel ketch *British Steel*.)

Six days later Robin Knox-Johnston, a young shipmaster, sailing the 32½-foot double-ended ketch *Suhaili*, started from Falmouth. He was given little chance of winning the prize as his heavy, modified Colin Archer-type boat was noted for seaworthiness rather than speed.

The two Frenchmen, Bernard Moitessier and Loik Fougeron, started the race on the same day from Plymouth, leaving more than two months after *Suhaili*. Moitessier was already famous and had won the coveted Blue Water Medal for a doublehanded voyage around Cape Horn in his 40-foot steel ketch *Joshua* (named

Robin Knox-Johnston was the only competitor in the 1968 Golden Globe Race to make it back to the starting point. (Courtesy of Betsy Holman)

after Slocum). He was racing the same boat and was given a fair chance of winning the prize money because of *Joshua*'s proven record. Fougeron was sailing an old gaff-rigged cutter named *Captain Browne*. After encountering damaging heavy weather and having second thoughts about the interminable Southern Ocean passage, he decided to withdraw and take a leisurely cruise.

Leaving only a few days after the French boats was *Galway Blazer II*, a junk-rigged schooner skippered by ex-submarine commander Bill King. King was doing well, having passed the Frenchmen, when his boat encountered a blow in the South Atlantic that caused her to capsize and lose a mast and forced King to put in to Cape Town. (His experience will be described in Chapter 11).

Another submarine commander, Nigel Tetley, started about three weeks after King in a 41-foot, Piver-designed trimaran named *Victress*. The spacious, comfortable tri was also fast sailing off the wind. It wasn't very long before she came within striking distance of the competitors that started ahead of her.

On the last day of the starting deadline Alex Corozzo, known as the "Chichester of Italy" and British electronics expert Donald Crowhurst started before they were thoroughly prepared. Corozzo, sailing a 66-foot ketch that was built in a rush to make the deadline, remained in harbor for a week after his official start to ready his boat for sea. Afflicted with a stomach ulcer brought on by the emotional pressures, Corozzo set forth regardless, but was forced to abandon the race and put in at Lisbon.

The most bizarre tale of all is that of Donald Crowhurst, sailing *Teignmouth Electron*, a modified sister tri to Tetley's *Victress*. With certain mental instabilities and growing doubts about the success of his voyage, Crowhurst planned an elaborate hoax whereby he would cruise around the South Atlantic for the time it would take to circumnavigate and then sail back to England ahead of his competitors to collect the prize. A gnawing conscience, solitude, and other pressures seemed to unbalance his mind, and apparently he ended his life with a suicidal jump off the stern.

Despite the many dropouts during the Golden Globe Race, the event resulted in three non-stop circumnavigations. Robin Knox-Johnston proved that a tortoise can really outlast the hares by being the only competitor to make it back to England. He won both awards but generously donated the prize money to Crowhurst's widow. His time for the voyage was approximately 10^1/$_2$ months. The others who made complete circumnavigations were Moitessier and Tetley. *Victress* crossed her outward bound track in what was then a record time of 179 days, but soon after tying the knot, the overstrained tri broke up, and Tetley was forced to abandon her. He was lucky to be rescued by a ship that was directed to him by an American plane.

Moitessier crossed his track, technically completing a global rounding in early March 1969 in the South Atlantic. It has been argued that he was actually the first person to complete a non-stop solo circumnavigation. His rounding, however, was not really antipodal, for after tying the knot, he decided not to finish in England but to keep going and terminate the voyage in the South Seas, where, he said, "You can tie up your boat where you want and the sun is free, and so is the air you breathe and the sea where you swim." So Moitessier was at that time credited with the longest non-stop solo voyage, about 1^1/$_2$ times around the world.

The Golden Globe Race of 1968–69 extracted a high toll from all its participants, both those who finished and those who did not. Fourteen years would pass before another group of solo sailors would gather to meet the ultimate test of racing alone around the world in the 1982–83 BOC Challenge.

Modern Transoceanic Races

By the close of the 1960s, singlehanded racing had come into its own. Each running of the OSTAR saw progressively larger fleets of larger boats and shattered records.

On the West Coast, a transpacific race for singlehanders was held in 1969. Organized by the Slocum Society and the Nippon Ocean Racing Club, the race started in San Francisco and finished in Tokyo. Of five participants, only three finished the race, though René Hauwaert eventually completed the course. The winner was Eric Tabarly, sailing the interesting light-displacement monohull *Pen Duick V*. His time was only 39^1/$_2$ days, about 11 days better than the next boat to finish. Second and third places went to Jean-Yves Terlain and Claus Hehner, sailing 30-foot and 35-foot stock boats respectively. A capable American singlehander, Jerry Cartwright, was forced to retire because of a severe blow to his head received when he was thrown from his bunk during a knockdown (see Chapter 11). Despite being incapacitated by the injury, Cartwright made it to Hawaii without assistance.

Other Singlehanded Transpacific Races starting from San Francisco and crossing almost the entire Pacific took place in 1975 and 1981. They were lightly attended, mostly by Japanese sailors, with only seven finishers in one race and eight in the other. Some of the participants sailed their boats all the way from Japan to the United States to make the starts.

In 1975 Hiroshi Totsuka, sailing the 35-foot *Wing of Yamaha*, was the first-place winner, with Shun Takeich on *Sunbird VI* in second place. The famous Kenichi Horie, who the year before had sailed his 29-foot *Mermaid III* around the world non-stop from west to east in the amazing time of 276 days, took third place on *Mermaid IV*. Notable also was the finish of Noriko Kobayashi, a 90-pound woman sailing a 30-footer appropriately named *Rib*. Two finishers who later completed BOCs were Yoko Tada and David White, the only American in the 1975 event.

Winner of the 1981 race was Fukunari Imada on *Taiyo*, a Sawaji 37. Yoshiji Okamoto on *Ray* and Yoshihide Oda on *Charlie* finished second and third respectively. American Linda Weber-Rettie on *Spirit of Suntory* became the second woman to complete a solo transpacific race. Partly because of a stringent size limitation on the boats, Eric Tabarly's time in the 1969 race remained unbeaten.

Although the transpacific races had few participants, transatlantic solo racing had become so well accepted that the 1972 OSTAR had 55 entries. It was the year for multihulls, huge monohulls, and particular glory for French sailors. First place went to *Pen Duick IV*, formerly Tabarly's trimaran, now sailed by Alain Colas, which logged the remarkable time of 20 days and slightly over 13 hours. The 128-foot monohull *Vendredi 13* (see Chapter 4), skippered by Jean-Yves Terlain, was less than a day behind, while a 53-foot trimaran named *Cap 33*, sailed by another Frenchman, Jean-Marie Vidal, was third with a time of 24 days, 5 hours. Brian Cooke, an Englishman sailing Chay Blyth's former *British Steel*, upheld Britain's reputation by finishing fourth, and American Tom Follett (of *Cheers* fame) sailed the trimaran *Three Cheers* to fifth place. Bill Howell in the catamaran *Tahiti*

The speedy 46-foot trimaran *Three Cheers*, designed by Dick Newick and singlehanded by Tom Follett. (Courtesy of Dick Newick)

Bill probably would have taken fifth had he not collided with a Russian trawler near the finish.

It is almost impossible to cross an ocean at any time without encountering some bad weather, but on the whole the 1972 race had light to moderate winds. After some fresh wind in the first week, the strongest blow was a short-lived gale produced by a fast-moving front, and then there were the usual sudden, isolated squalls. As a result, there were cases of gear failure and a number of dismastings.

Undoubtedly, the greatest tragedy of the 1972 OSTAR was related to the withdrawal of Francis Chichester, who was in poor health. The veteran singlehander, then 70 years of age, radioed that he was not feeling well and decided to retire from the race. He was sailing his *Gipsy Moth V* home to Plymouth when he was intercepted by a French weather ship offering assistance. Chichester declined the offer, but during the communications exchange, the *Gipsy Moth*'s mizzen was damaged by the ship, and then some help really was needed. It came in the form of Chichester's son with others, who were brought to the *Gipsy Moth* by a helicopter and naval vessel. The real tragedy of the affair came when the weather ship collided with the *Lefteria*, an American yacht not in the race, which was coming to Chichester's assistance. The *Lefteria* sank and six crew members lost their lives. Chichester was deeply distressed by the accident. As it turned out, this was his last voyage, for he died not long afterwards. But even before he landed at Plymouth, old, exhausted, and ill, he was reportedly planning another spectacular solo voyage. His spirit simply could not be suppressed.

The largest OSTAR ever in terms of both numbers of competitors and size of boats was the 1976 event. It had 125 starters, and the largest boat was an astonishing 236 feet long. This enormous vessel, derived from the simple premise that the hull with the longest waterline produces the greatest speed, was the *Club Mediterranee*, a four-masted schooner sailed by previous OSTAR winner Alain Colas. That a singlehander could handle such a monster staggers the imagination, and what makes the feat even more incredible is that Colas had not yet fully recovered from an anchoring accident aboard *Manureva* (formerly *Pen Duick IV*), which nearly severed his foot. *Club Mediterranee* did not win the race, but she finished a close second (only 25 miles behind the winner) and probably would have won if Colas hadn't been forced to put into Newfoundland temporarily after most of his halyards parted.

Winner of the 1976 OSTAR was Eric Tabarly (who won the 1964 transatlantic race and the first transpacific race), sailing the 73-foot, ketch-rigged monohull *Pen Duick VI*. Although much smaller than *Club Med* and another competitor, *ITT Oceanic* (formerly *Vendredi 13*), Tabarly's boat was a handful for one man, because she was originally designed to be raced by more than a dozen crewmembers. Tabarly made the crossing in 23 days, 20 hours, 12 minutes despite self-steering gear problems and being forced to lie ahull under bare poles.

Remarkably, the third boat to finish, crossing the line only about 25 hours after *Pen Duick VI*, was one of the smallest boats in the fleet. She was the 31-foot Val Class trimaran *Third Turtle* designed by Dick Newick and skippered by Canadian Mike Birch. Equally remarkable was the fact that the 38-foot monohull *Spaniel*, designed and built by her Polish skipper, Kazimierz Jaworski, finished only a few hours behind *Third Turtle*. Britisher Geoffrey Hales sailing *Wild Rival* won the handicap trophy.

Phil Weld wins the 1980 OSTAR on the Newick-designed trimaran *Moxie*, setting a new course record. (Photo by Paul Mello)

An exceptionally heavy-weather race with a succession of gales gusting as high as Force 11, the 1976 OSTAR resulted in 44 retirements plus two tragic losses of life. Mike Flanagan sailing *Galloping Gael* disappeared, although his boat was found, while Mike McMullen sailing the Newick trimaran *Three Cheers* vanished, boat and all. Four years later, on the eve of the 1980 OSTAR, some wreckage from *Three Cheers* was dredged up off the coast of Iceland, which added weight to the theory that McMullen hit an iceberg. And speaking of ice, Clare Francis was more than a bit shocked after coming on deck to find that her Ohlson 38 had self-steered between two bergs when she was below asleep. Several boats sank in this race including the 70-foot *Kriter III* (formerly *British Oxygen*) sailed by veteran Jean-Yves Terlain.

The next OSTAR in 1980 was a triumph for American singlehanders after years of French domination. Sixty-five-year-old Phil Weld on the 51-foot Newick-designed trimaran *Moxie* was the first boat to finish of 88 starters, and he set a new course record of 17 days, 23 hours, 12 minutes. Second place went to Englishman Nick Keig sailing the trimaran *Three Legs of Mann III*, but another American, Phil Steggall, finished third in the Walter Green-designed trimaran *Jean's Foster*. The latter's finish was remarkable considering that she was only 38 feet long and had to sail the final part of the course without a centerboard, which was lost following a collision with a whale. Canadian Mike Birch finished fourth in the 46-foot trimaran *Olympus Photo II* designed by Dick Newick. Birch had to repair a staved-in aka (connecting arm) with a sheet of plywood. He finished the race with a sign on the patch saying "Phil Weld for president."

Philippe Poupon sails the 56-foot trimaran *Fleury Michon VI* in the 1984 OSTAR. He was the first to finish, but shared the victory with Yvon Fauconnier, who was credited the time he lost assisting in the rescue of Philippe Jeantot. (Photo by Herb McCormick)

Elf Aquitaine II, skippered by Marc Pajot, was tricky to handle but finished second in the 1984 OSTAR. (Photo by Onne Van Der Wal)

Other U.S. boats that did well were the fifth-finishing *Chaussettes Olympia*, a 35-foot trimaran designed and sailed by Walter Green, and the appropriately named *Le First*, a 30-foot Beneteau monohull sailed by Jerry Cartwright, which finished first in the *Jester* class. *Le First* did not actually win, as she was later penalized for receiving engine oil from a Cuban fishing boat for the purpose of charging her dead batteries for radio communication. Apparently, Jerry was exceed-

Warren Luhrs' speedy monohull *Thursday's Child* beat many multihulls in the 1984 OSTAR. (Photo by Karina Paape)

ingly anxious to find out how his daughter had come through an eye operation. Judy Lawson was doing well until her BB10 *Serta Perfect Sleeper* was dismasted as a result of faulty rigging terminals not a great distance from the finish line.

Despite ice warnings that persuaded most racers to take longer, more southerly routes, the 1984 OSTAR was the fastest one so far. In fact, Weld's 1980 record was broken by 13 boats. French multihull ace Philippe Poupon, sailing the 56-foot trimaran *Fleury Michon VI*, was the first to finish, with a time of 16 days, 12 hours, 25 minutes. But another Frenchman, Yvon Fauconnier, actually won the race, because he was given a 16-hour allowance for rescuing Philippe Jeantot (of BOC fame; see ahead) after Jeantot capsized in his over-rigged catamaran *Credit Agricole II*. Fauconnier, sailing the 53-foot trimaran *Umupro Jardin V* stood by while Jeantot waited for the arrival of a French naval vessel to help salvage the capsized catamaran. Phil Weld, who did not race in 1984 but served on the race committee, persuaded the committee to award double victory awards, a first-to-finish prize to Poupon and the winner's prize to Fauconnier. Transatlantic speed record holder *Jet Services*, a 60-foot cat sailed by Patrick Morvan, was leading the fleet until she was abandoned after striking a tree trunk.

The second boat to finish was the radical French catamaran *Elf Aquitaine II* sailed by Marc Pajot. This 60-foot multihull had her mast and sail plan mounted on a turntable between hulls, which made her unusually tricky to handle. In fact, Pajot sometimes found that when his sails accidentally turned the wrong way and went aback, his cat would sail herself backwards at a speed of up to seven knots.

The most remarkable performance for a monohull was that of *Thursday's Child*, sailed by American Warren Luhrs, president of Hunter Marine in Florida. She finished only 10 hours behind the first boat, beating many high-tech multihulls, and broke Phil Weld's 1980 record that was set with a multihull. Designed by Paul Lindenberg with the help of Lars Bergstrom (of Windex wind indicator fame), the 60-foot *Thursday's Child* featured such gadgetry as a pendulum rudder, vortex generators, and a very effective water ballast system (see Chapter 4).

Bill Homewood's speedy Val trimaran *Third Turtle*, temporarily named *British Airways* for the 1984 OSTAR race. (Courtesy of Bill Homewood)

Three other American boats that excelled were the 35-foot Nelson/Marek-designed monohull *City of Slidell* sailed by Luis Tonizzo (winner of class IV despite hitting two whales); the 38-foot trimaran *Destination St. Croix*, skippered by Cruxian Jack Petith; and the OSTAR veteran trimaran *British Airways II* (formerly *Third Turtle*), manned by Chesapeake sailor Bill Homewood, who set a new transatlantic record for a 31-foot boat with a time of 21 days, 5½+ hours.

Perhaps the most heartbreaking incident of the race occurred when the 54-year-old Englishwoman Rachel Hayward, the only one of four women in the 1984 OSTAR to entirely cross the Atlantic, piled up on Point Judith less than seven miles from the finish line. Fatigued and confused after sailing (without electricity) for days in heavy weather and fog, Hayward made a wrong turn and hit the rocks with an impact that dismasted and holed her 35-foot S&S sloop *Loiwing*. Despite her bitterly disappointing finish, Hayward said, "The race was the biggest and most wonderful experience of my life."

In addition to the OSTAR and solo transpacific races, there are other ocean races for singlehanders including those from Newport, Rhode Island, to Bermuda, from England to the Azores and back, and the "pseudo transpacs" from San Francisco to Hawaii. Additional true transoceanics are the Mini Transat races, originally called the PM Star (Poor Man's Singlehanded Transatlantic Race), and the Route du Rhum race from St. Malo, France, to Guadeloupe in the West Indies.

The Mini Transats were two-legged affairs from Penzance, England, to Tenerife, Canary Islands, then to Antigua, West Indies. Conceived by the veteran English singlehander Bob Salmon, the Mini Transats were intended as inexpensive OSTARS for boats with maximum lengths of 6.5 meters (21 feet, 4 inches). The first race in 1977 was won by *Petit Dauphin* sailed by Frenchman Daniel Gilard, who led 19 boats across the finish line, while the Polish singlehander Kazimierz Jaworski finished second. Americans triumphed in 1979 when Norton Smith (winner of the previous year's solo race from California to Hawaii) won overall honors against 24 competitors, and Amy Boyer on *Little Rascal* won the women's prize.

The third Mini Transat race, in 1981, was a disaster, as heavy weather on the first leg caused about half the fleet, all but 13 of the starters, to drop out. A number of boats broke up, but fortunately there was no loss of life. The French dominated this race, with Jacques Peignon on *Les Isles du Ponant* taking the overall honors. Previous race winner *American Express* capsized on her way to the start. The only other American boat to enter was Steve Callahan in his self-designed *Napoleon Solo*, but he was forced to withdraw because of damage. On his way home over a year later his boat sank, possibly due to a collision with a whale, and he was forced to spend 76 days in a life raft. He wrote *Adrift*, a best-selling book, about the experience.

Although most of the Route du Rhum course is sometimes considered easy, a largely downhill slide in the trade winds, these races have had their share of heavy

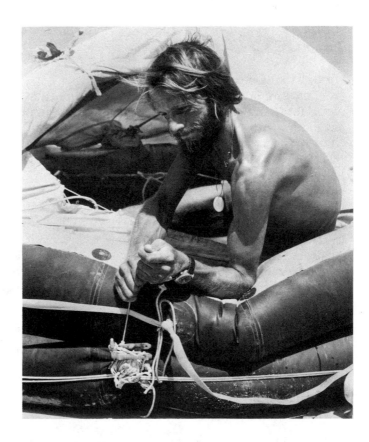

Steve Callahan spent 76 days in a life raft after his boat *Napoleon Solo* collided, possibly with a whale, in the Atlantic. (Photo by Benjamin Mendlowitz)

weather, and they resulted in the loss of two celebrated singlehanders, Alain Colas and Loic Caradec. The former disappeared despite extensive air searches while racing his famous trimaran *Manureva* (formerly *Pen Duick IV*) during the first Route du Rhum in 1978. Winner of that race was Canadian Mike Birch, sailing the Walter Green-designed multihull *Olympus*, with a crossing time of 23 days, 7 hours. She finished only 98 seconds ahead of Michael Malinovsky's *Kriter V*—over a course of about 3,500 miles!

With advances in multihull technology and more favorable weather, the second Route du Rhum, held in 1982, produced much faster elapsed time, with 21 boats beating the time of Birch four years earlier. The winner, Marc Pajot, sailing the 66-foot catamaran *Elf Aquitaine*, took 18 days, 1 hour, 38 minutes to complete the course.

The gale-plagued race of 1986 produced even faster times, with winner Philippe Poupon sailing the course in 14 days, 15 hours, 57 minutes on his hydro-foil-assisted trimaran *Fleury Michon VIII*. This is the race in which Loic Caradec was lost. A top professional multihull racer, Caradec, weighing only 115 pounds, was handling the maxi 85-foot catamaran *Royale*, which carried a sizeable wing mast. The boat was found capsized, but it is not known for certain whether her skipper was lost before or after she flipped. No less a seaman than Eric Tabarly was one of the racers who needed to be rescued. Ironically, he was picked up by his former boat, the monohull *Pen Duick VI*, after his foil-assisted trimaran began to break up.

The BOC Challenge

For every singlehanded sailor who gained experience and tasted competition in the growing number of transoceanic races, there were dozens more who emulated them. It was only a matter of time before some lone sailor, in search of new conquests and the comraderie that surrounds a yacht race, would again issue the challenge to race alone around the world. That person was American David White.

Seventeen men gathered in Newport, Rhode Island, in 1982 for the start of the first BOC Challenge, named for its sponsor, British Oxygen Corporation. Unfortunately, White's boat was forced to withdraw as a result of structural problems and later equipment failure during the first BOC Challenge, but he successfully completed the second race in 1986–87. The two Challenges had identical courses with the first leg from Newport to Cape Town, South Africa; the second leg to Sydney, Australia; the third leg to Rio de Janeiro, Brazil; and the final leg back to Newport.

The contestants had frequent radio contact among themselves as well as with shore-based ham operators, and they were continuously monitored by an Argos satellite receiving signals from transponders on the boats. Considering this communication and the three scheduled layovers, the BOC sailors were not so isolated nor perhaps so independent as were the Golden Globe competitors (Moitessier and Fougeron didn't even carry transmitting radios). Be that as it may, the BOC Challenges produced speed records and outstanding feats of endurance and seamanship as well as technological advances and great publicity for long-distance solo sailing.

These races also created a new singlehanding hero, French oil rig diver-turned-sailor, Philippe Jeantot, who won both BOCs and, in the 1986–87 event, set

Philippe Jeantot won both BOCs with successive *Credit Agricoles*, designed by Guy Dumas. (Photo by Susan Thorpe)

a solo speed record for a monohull circumnavigation of 134 days, 5 hours, 24 minutes. His boat in the first challenge was a 56-foot high-tech cutter named *Credit Agricole.* Designed by Guy R. Dumas, the boat proved exceptionally reliable and, with good handling by her skipper, won every leg. For the second race Jeantot went back to Dumas for a 60-foot *Credit Agricole,* and this boat proved fast but unusually troublesome as a result of some structural problems. Jeantot won the race and set the above-mentioned record only with exceptional perseverance.

During the first BOC there were several mishaps and two spectacular rescues. The first rescue took place during the second leg after Tony Lush pitchpoled while broad reaching before steep seas in his modified Hunter 54 *Lady Pepperell.* The ketch-rigged boat kept her free-standing carbon fiber masts intact but developed a loose keel, which threatened to rupture the boat's bottom. Lush wisely decided to abandon her. Radio contact was made with Francis Stokes sailing the Fast Passage 39 *Mooneshine,* which was about 40 miles to leeward of the strickened vessel. Stokes hove to while Lush, despite having a dangerously swaying keel, managed to sail down to him. The two boats found each other, and after they were lashed together with considerable difficulty in rough seas, Lush was transferred to *Mooneshine.* Stokes finished the leg with his newly acquired "cabin boy," but was not disqualified for sailing with crew, and eventually finished second in his class.

The second rescue was even more dramatic. During the third leg French nuclear submarine officer Jacques de Roux was capsized, dismasted, and holed

Francis Stokes and Tony Lush sail into Sydney, Australia, after a dramatic rescue on the second leg of the BOC. (Photo by Herb McCormick)

while running before gale-produced cross seas in his 41-foot aluminum cutter *Skoiern III*, which was leading her class by a wide margin. The nearest competitor, Englishman Richard Broadhead aboard *Perseverance of Medina*, a Briton Chance-designed 52-foot cutter, had to sail 317 miles to reach de Roux after receiving his distress signal via the Argos satellite tracking system. When Broadhead arrived on the scene, he found *Skoiern III* swamped and her skipper exhausted after bailing for 59 hours. The damaged boat sank within four hours after being abandoned. It was a close call for "the flying Frenchman," but he was not so lucky in the second BOC, as we shall soon see.

There were several groundings in the first BOC, one that took over a month of dislodging effort after New Zealander Richard McBride piled up his 42-foot steel schooner *City of Dunedin* on the Falkland Islands. But the most serious grounding took place when *Gipsy Moth V* (Francis Chichester's last boat) was run onto the rocks of Gabo Island off the southeast coast of Australia as a result of her skipper, Englishman Desmond Hampton, oversleeping and failing to detect a wind shift. Hampton survived by scrambling onto the rocks, but poor *Gipsy Moth V* pounded herself to pieces while Hampton helplessly watched the sickening sight from a rocky ledge.

In addition to Jeantot, Stokes, Broadhead, and McBride, six others completed the course. South African Bertie Reed, sailing the 49-foot, Van de Stadt-designed

John Hughes sails into the Falklands under jury rig after his dismasting in the middle of the Southern Atlantic. (Courtesy of the BOC Group)

Altech Voortrekker, finished second to Jeantot and received an award for best overall performance based on waterline length. Australian Neville Gosson had his hands full with *Leda Pier One*, a 53-footer designed for handling by a full crew. Japanese jazz musician/painter Yukoh Tada, sailing the 44-foot sloop *Koden Okera V*, made good use of information obtained from an Antarctic explorer on the location of pack ice and won Class II, the class for the smaller boats. The Czech author/boat builder who defected to the United States, Richard Konkolski, a veteran of three singlehanded transatlantic races and a previous circumnavigation, made a good showing in his self-designed 44-foot cutter *Nike III*. Skipper of the smallest boat in the fleet of finishers was Frenchman Guy Bernardin sailing *Ratso II*, a light-displacement, 38-foot aluminum cutter. Finally, American Dan Byrne, sailing the first-built Valiant 40, *Fantasy*, a classic stock Robert Perry design, deserves credit for his successful course completion with relatively simple gear and a financial investment that was minuscule compared with the amount spent by others, particularly those who were sponsored.

The second running of the BOC, four years later, drew a larger turnout with 25 starters and 16 finishers. Most of the competitors who retired did so because of rig failures or boat damage, but Jacques de Roux, the Frenchman who was rescued during the first BOC, was lost overboard off the coast of Sydney in the second BOC. Having won his class in the first leg, his new 50-footer, *Skoiern IV* (Chapter 4) was up front in her class during the second leg when she may have hit a submerged object. It is assumed that her skipper hurried on deck without his safety harness and somehow fell overboard. Despite this tragedy, the safety record of the two events is remarkable considering the potential risks involved. The record shows that the participants were not merely individual daredevils, but a unified group of seamen who planned their project meticulously.

Aside from Jeantot, who won the race and set a new circumnavigation record, outstanding performers included American Mike Plant, a former Outward Bound instructor, who won Class II in his homebuilt 50-foot *Airco Distributor*. Frenchman Titouan Lamazou, sailing the 60-foot *Ecureuil d'Aquitaine*, was often nipping at the heels of Jeantot, beat him on one leg, and finished second in Class I. South African John Martin, sailing the 60-foot *Tuna Marine*, did not finish well overall but actually won two legs. Richard Konkolski in *Declaration of Independence*, Bertie Reed in *Stabilo Boss*, and Guy Bernardin (now an American citizen) in *Biscuits Lu* distinguished themselves by completing two BOC Challenges. Perhaps the most remarkable performance of all was that of Canadian John Hughes, sailing the 41-foot sloop *Joseph Young*. After a dismasting in the middle of the Southern Ocean, Hughes erected an A-frame with tiny sails and continued on to the Falkland Islands, rounding Cape Horn under his flimsy jury rig. There he waited for a new mast and completed the circumnavigation in time for the awards ceremony.

Others who completed the second BOC were veteran French singlehander Jean-Yves Terlain in the space age *UAP-Pour Medecins San Frontieres*, Australian Ian Kierman in *Triple M/Spirit of Sydney*, Frenchman Jean-Luc Van Den Heede in *Let's Go* (a class winner of two legs), Harry Harkimo of Finland in *Belmont Finland*, American Blue Water Medalist Hal Roth in *American Flag*, American Mark Schrader (veteran of a 1982–83 Southern Ocean circumnavigation) in *Lone Star*, Pentti Salmi of Finland in *Colt By Rettig*, and race founder David White, who fulfilled his dream of seven years by completing the BOC Challenge.

Modern Feats

While many singlehanders sailed into the limelight in the races that have flourished in the last 30 years, still others found their greatest challenge as individuals breaking new ground, setting new records, and in some cases, challenging their own physical disabilities.

Two Englishmen who were forced to retire from the Golden Globe Race came back more determined than ever to get around the world in an unusual way. William Leslie King, a retired submarine commander, capsized in his specialized, lug-rigged, *Galway Blazer II* (see Chapter 4 and 11), but he set out again on what proved to be another futile attempt the following year. Refusing to give up, King tried again for the third time in 1970, and this time he succeeded in completing a circumnavigation in 1973, although he nearly failed as a result of colliding with a sea creature near Australia. This experience and King's remarkable repair of his vessel will be described in Chapter 11.

Unlike King, who stuck with the same vessel, Chay Blyth, a former paratrooper and transatlantic oarsman, got sponsorship and had a new 58-foot steel ketch built, which he named *British Steel*. The astounding feature of Blyth's 1970–71 circumnavigation was that it was the first singlehanded, non-stop east-to-west circumnavigation via Cape Horn, a route that took Blyth along the Roaring

Chay Blyth made the first
singlehanded non-stop, east-to-west
circumnavigation. (Courtesy of
Donald R. Holm)

Forties against the prevailing winds. Yet, in spite of having to sail to windward, the
voyage was made in the fast time of 292 days.

A remarkable circumnavigation was completed by Webb Chiles in 1976.
Sailing the Ericson 37 *Egregious* around the world from west to east, mostly in the
Roaring Forties, Chiles became the first American soloist with a confirmed Cape
Horn rounding, and he broke Kenichi Horie's aforementioned monohull record
with a total sailing time of 203 days. *Egregious* proved a near perfect handling boat,
but she had at least one serious constructional flaw. Like some of her sisters she
developed a leak abaft the keel, which steadily worsened in the remote southern
seas until the inflow grew to more than 50 gallons per hour. Despite overwhelming

This open, 18-foot Drascombe Lugger yawl *Chidiock Tichborne* has been sailed by Webb Chiles most of the way around the world!

exhaustion from bailing as much as eight hours a day for weeks on end, Chiles kept his "beautiful bitch" afloat and achieved his record-setting goals. Next, Chiles sailed an open 18-foot Drascombe Lugger yawl named *Chidiock Tichborne* from California across the Pacific, then across the Indian Ocean and up into the Red Sea before his boat was damaged and then seized in Saudi Arabia in 1982.

Not much more than a year later, Chiles' record was broken, just barely, by Bulgarian Georgi Georgiev, who sailed the Carter 30 *Cor Caroli* around the world in an east-to-west direction via the Panama Canal and Cape of Good Hope. His total passage time amounted to slightly less than 202 days.

A leading sailing magazine claimed that Englishman David Scott Cowper had the fastest time for a solo circumnavigation in a monohull, when he completed his west-to-east circumnavigation onboard the S&S-designed Huisman 41 *Ocean Bound* in 1980. Though Cowper's time of 224½ days at sea was greater than earlier roundings of Chiles and Georgiev, the Englishman claimed a record for "a true antipodean circumnavigation." Cowper's real distinction came after he completed another, more difficult circumnavigation against the prevailing winds in an east-to-west direction in 1982. On this occasion he became the first singlehander to round the world in both directions via Cape Horn, and being at sea for only 221½ days, he bettered Blyth's time for a westward rounding. In 1985 he completed the first solo powerboat circumnavigation.

The highly publicized American singlehander Dodge Morgan is credited with the fastest non-stop global rounding. The time for his eastward 1985–86 voyage in the 60-foot, Hood-designed *American Promise* amounted to 150 days, 1 hour, 6 minutes. For some reason Morgan's feat is constantly compared with Chay Blyth's non-stop westward circumnavigation. Regarding the comparison, Blyth had this to say: "Nobody goes the other way except me. There's only one person who has done it that way, so what (Morgan) is talking about is a load of rubbish and I find it very boring." Morgan's response was: "I agree with him. The only reason they're compared is they're both non-stop. I salute the bastard. He should get the century's masochist award." Morgan wrested the speed record for a non-stop antipodal

Dodge Morgan, on the high-tech *American Promise*, set a record for the fastest non-stop circumnavigation. (Courtesy of *Cruising World* magazine)

rounding from Dutchman Pleun Van Der Lugt, who circumnavigated via Cape Horn in 1982.

At the time of this writing (1988), the fastest time for a solo global rounding by any kind of sailing yacht is 129 days, 19 hours, 17 minutes. This feat was accomplished by French auto racer Philippe Monnet in 1986–87 when he circled in the 70-foot trimaran *Kriter Brut de Brut*. He chose the southerly route from west to east with several layovers, including an emergency stop at Cape Town, South Africa.

While some singlehanders set out to smash speed records, others are driven to be the first, a distinction that cannot be surpassed by those who follow.

If a sailor can circle the globe without stopping, then surely one can go around twice non-stop. Australian Jonathan Sanders set off in 1981 in the S&S 34 *Perie Banon* and completed two west-to-east roundings below the southernmost capes without stopping. His voyage was continuous but assisted, as he was reprovisioned at sea. One of his circumnavigations was 142 1/3 days, which was less than Dodge Morgan's time, although the Australian sailed considerably less distance in the high latitudes of the Southern Hemisphere.

Still another non-stop rounding along the southern route in the Roaring Forties is the one made by the German soloist Horst Timmreck in 1980. His continuous but assisted voyage in the 31-foot steel sloop *Brigitte* took 163 days according

Tinkerbelle, skippered by Robert Manry, who in 1965 finally wrested from William Andrews the record for the smallest boat to make an eastbound transatlantic crossing. (Courtesy of Keystone Press Agency Ltd.)

to one report. Timmreck may have a record for the closest shaving of Cape Horn, since he bounced off the rocks of that notorious promontory. Englishman Leslie Powles' 239-day circumnavigation in his 34-foot *Solitaire of Hamble* was not only non-stop, but also without replenishment from another vessel. He ran out of food and lost 42 pounds before returning to England in 1981. American Mark Schrader sailed into the records books in 1982–83 when he became the first American to circumnavigate alone via the five capes of the Southern Hemisphere, as well as setting several speed records, in his Valiant 40 *Resourceful.* He was awarded the Slocum Society Medal for this voyage, which was undertaken to raise money for The Resource Foundation for the developmentally disabled, where he served for a decade as executive director.

Like some of the early pioneers, a few modern-day sailors have set out in tiny boats in quest of a record. As mentioned in Chapter 1, during the summer of 1965, Robert Manry in the 13½-foot *Tinkerbelle* and John Riding in the 12-foot *Sjo Ag* finally shattered *Sapolio's* longstanding record for the smallest boat to have crossed the Atlantic. Riding went on to sail halfway around the world in *Sjo Ag* before he was lost at sea.

In 1968 Hugo Vihlen crossed the Atlantic from Casablanca to Miami in *April Fool,* a boat just under 6 feet long, and that set the record for the shortest ocean crosser. But this record was broken or tied (depending on how the measuring was

Gerry Spiess shows *Yankee Girl* to flag officers of the Royal Sydney Yacht Squadron after crossing both the Atlantic and Pacific oceans. (Courtesy of *Cruising World* magazine)

done and whether or not you count fractions of an inch) by Eric Peters in 1982–83 when he sailed across from Spain to Guadeloupe, West Indies, in a barrel-shaped boat named *Toniky Nou*, said to be only 5 feet, 10½ inches long. Another who covered half the globe in a cockleshell was Gerry Spiess when he sailed the 10-foot *Yankee Girl* across the Atlantic from Norfolk, Virginia to Falmouth, England in 1979 and then sailed her across the Pacific from California to Australia in 1981. The following year, Tom Mclean set the west-to-east transatlantic small-boat record when he sailed across in the 9-foot, 9-inch *Giltspur*, but about two weeks later Bill Dunlop made a west-to-east crossing in his *Wind's Will*, which was only 9 feet long.* That record was broken in early 1983 when Wayne Dickinson crossed from Massachusetts to Ireland in the 8-foot, 11-inch *God's Tear*, taking an incredibly long 142 days during the hostile fall and winter seasons and without receiving supplies from ships.**

In the real little league, mention should be made of the sailboard voyages. On a 9-foot windsurfer Frenchman Christian Marty made a 37-day Atlantic crossing from Africa to French Guyana in 1982–83. He lived on board but was supplied with food and drink by an accompanying yacht. In 1987 another Frenchman, Stephane Peyron, made a 46-day passage on a 24-foot sailboard from New York to France without outside assistance. His board boat was sufficiently large for basic supplies and a watertight, coffin-like cabin.

At present, the smallest boat to be sailed alone around the world is *Acrohc Australis*, a 12-foot aluminum cutter sailed by Australian Sergio Testa. Completed in 1987, this westward circumnavigation via Panama had some exciting moments including knockdowns, a serious fire, and a collision with a killer whale. The

*Dunlop was later reported lost in the Pacific in an attempt to sail *Wind's Will* around the world.
**Of course, length is only one aspect of size. Considering other dimensions, the smallest boat to cross the Atlantic must be *Liberia III*, an open, collapsible foldboat that weighed less than 60 pounds. She was sailed from the Canary Islands to the West Indies in 1956 by German doctor Hannes Lindemann.

smallest multihull to solo circumnavigate is the 26-foot catamaran *Amon-Re*, recently sailed around by Canadian Alan Butler in a westward direction via Panama.

Other singlehanding records are set at either end of the age spectrum. The most youthful solo sailors are Americans Robin Lee Graham, already mentioned, and Tania Aebi, whose highly publicized 1985–87 circumnavigation will be discussed just ahead. To this list another name should be added: that of Englishman David Sandeman, who singlehanded across the Atlantic in 1976 when he was 17.

At the opposite end of the age spectrum is Monk Farnham, who is credited with being the oldest sailor to cross the Atlantic alone. In 1981, at the age of 72, he sailed from the Chesapeake to England; then, at 74, he sailed from Ireland to Newport via the Azores and Bermuda on his Shannon 28 *Seven Bells*. Other senior singlehanders include Frank Casper, Marcel Bardiaux, and William Willis, all in their 70s. Tom Blackwell was on his way around the world for the third time when he died of cancer at the age of 72. The oldest of them all, I think, is Josh Taylor, who at 78 completed a circumnavigation on his Cascade 36 *Comitan*, although Josh only singlehanded a small part of the time. He usually had a young female companion, which may help account for his perpetual youth.

Challenging the rigorous high latitudes, a few outstanding singlehanders have made history sailing among the ice. In 1972–74 Dr. David Lewis circled Antarctica on the 32-foot steel sloop *Ice Bird*, during which voyage he capsized three times. In 1977 Belgian Willy de Roos sailed his 43-foot ketch *Williwaw* through the Northwest Passage at the top of Canada and above Alaska. Accomplished in just one season, his voyage was not made entirely alone but mostly so. The famous circumnavigator Kenichi Horie also traversed the Northwest Passage when he circled the North and South American continents, accomplishing what has been called a vertical circumnavigation. This partly solo voyage began when he left Japan in late 1978 and concluded when he limped to Hawaii under a jury rig in 1982 after his 35-foot *Mermaid IV* rolled over twice not far south of the Aleutian Islands.

Then there is that salt-encrusted Welshman, Tristan Jones. I don't quite know how to deal with the page-long list of record claims he sent me, as two Blue Water Medalists of my acquaintance have called him a charlatan. Jones is a colorful writer, and there seems little doubt that he sometimes mixes fiction with fact. But even if he "draws a long bow" on occasions, he has accomplished many astonishing feats. He claims to have sailed "the farthest north ever reached in a sailing vessel," although an Arctic explorer tells me that Jones's geography is mixed up. Nevertheless, he drifted alone for many months, apparently less then 500 miles from the North Pole, after his 36-foot ketch *Cresswell* became trapped in the ice. Other claims include the most singlehanded passages under sail across the Atlantic in craft under 40 feet long—a total of 17 between 1952 and 1975, as well as the most miles of singlehanded sailing in boats under 40 feet—approximately 345,000 miles between 1952 and 1976. Presently Jones is sailing a multihull around the world with one crewmember, after having had his leg amputated. What a man!

Jones is not the only one, however, to have made a shorthanded or singlehanded voyage while battling illness or infirmity. Francis Chichester and Tom Blackwell both singlehanded until the final months of their struggles with cancer,

Adventurer and story-teller Tristan Jones in sheltered waters. (Courtesy of Betsy Holman)

James Hatfield, who overcame a serious heart affliction, gives a thumbs-up gesture as he sails into New York harbor toward the end of his global rounding. (UPI/Bettman Newsphotos)

as did Leonid Teliga and Walter Koenig. The voyages of diabetic George Farley will be described in Chapter 11. Most remarkable of all, perhaps, is cardiac patient James Hatfield, who was born with a hole in his heart. Having been advised by doctors to lead a sedentary life after weathering a ruptured aorta and a number of corrective operations, Hatfield built himself a small boat, crossed the Atlantic in her, and in 1984 set forth from England on an eastabout solo circumnavigation via

Blind sailor Jim Dickson on his Freedom 36, *Eye Opener*, attempted an Atlantic crossing during hurricane season, but was forced to abort at Bermuda. (Photo by Susan Thorpe)

the rugged Southern Ocean. His Cornish crabber *British Heart II* was so badly damaged by storms in the Roaring Forties that he was forced to abandon her and acquire a new boat in New Zealand. Continuing on in *British Heart III*, he crossed the desolate bottom of the Pacific, passed through the Strait of Magellan, and eventually reached his homeport at Penzance, England, from whence he had left 3¹/₂ years earlier.

Among the most amazing solo voyages of them all are those made by blind men. With merely 7-percent vision and only the ability to distinguish light from dark, Hank Dekker sailed his 25-foot *Dark Star* from California to Hawaii in 1983. It took 23 days, an average of 100 miles per day, for Dekker to reach his destination. He lay ahull in heavy weather for two days, and at one point was rolled entirely upside down. In 1986 he successfully completed the Singlehanded Transpac in his Laser 28 *Outta Sight*.

The other blind voyager who made big headlines is Jim Dickson, who attempted an Atlantic crossing in August 1987. His departure from Rhode Island was delayed, and he made the mistake of setting off on his Freedom 36 *Eye Opener* well into the hurricane season. Sure enough, he was caught by tropical storm Arlene, and when a lot of his essential equipment failed, he was forced to terminate the voyage at Bermuda, but planned to try again in 1988. The primary purposes of both Dickson's and Dekker's feats were to disprove the widely held belief that blind people are severely limited in their potential for accomplishment as a result of their handicap.

Transoceanic Women

Crossing oceans, or indeed sailing alone around the world, is not purely a male endeavor. Some of our most celebrated singlehanders have been women.

In 1952–53 Englishwoman Ann Davison sailed alone from Las Palmas to the West Indies in her 23-foot *Felicity Ann*. Much later, in 1969, Ingeborg von Heister crossed the Atlantic alone in the trimaran *Ultima Ratio* and returned in 1970. The following year, Nicolette Milnes-Walker sailed across the Atlantic in her 30-foot sloop *Aziz*, becoming the third woman (not the first, as was often claimed by the press) to cross the Atlantic alone. In 1969, Sharon Sites Adams became the first woman to cross the Pacific alone, from Yokohama to San Diego, taking 75 days in her 31-foot ketch *Sea Sharp II*. She had already sailed from Los Angeles to Hawaii singlehanded in her first *Sea Sharp*, a 25-footer, in 1965. In recent times an increasing number of women are undertaking transoceanic passages, both independently and in the racing arena. Marie-Claude Fauroux (Chapter 3), Teresa Remiszewska, Anne Michailof, Ida Castigliani, and Clare Francis all have completed OSTAR races. Francis already had made an outstanding Atlantic crossing in 1973, when she entered the 1976 OSTAR. During that stormy race, she set a record for the quickest crossing by a lone woman, taking slightly less than 29 days. She placed a remark-

Ann Davison, shown here in the protected cockpit of her 23-foot sloop *Felicity Ann*, made the first authenticated Atlantic crossing by a singlehanded woman. (Courtesy of Patrick Ellam)

Clare Francis set the record for the quickest singlehanded crossing by a woman, finishing 13th in the 1976 OSTAR. (Courtesy of Jonathan Eastland)

Krystyna Chojnowska-Liskiewicz was the first woman to circle the globe singlehanded. (Courtesy of PA Interpress Photos)

Naomi James crosses the finish line in *Express Crusader*, becoming the first woman to sail around the world singlehanded via Cape Horn, and knocking about five days off the record set by Chichester. (Courtesy of Jonathan Eastland)

able 13th out of 121 starters in her Ohlson 38 that measured only 26½ feet on the waterline. Although Judy Lawson and Rachel Hayward failed to finish their OSTARS, both were very close to the finish line when forced to abandon.

Some other accomplished women soloists include Atlantic crossers Florence Arthaud, Amy Boyer, Brigette Aubry, and Margaret Hicks; Tasman Sea Annette Wilde; and Pacific crossers Noriko Kobayashi and Linda Weber-Retti.

The first female singlehander to circle the globe was Krystyna Chojnowska-Liskiewicz from Poland, who sailed the 31-foot *Mazurek* (designed and built by her husband) around east to west via Panama in 1976–78. The first lone woman to circumnavigate by way of the Horn was New Zealand-born Britisher Naomi James, who became Dame Commander Naomi after she completed her voyage in 1978. She made an eastward rounding below the southernmost capes in 267 days (beating Chichester's time), sailing the 53-foot Van de Stadt-designed *Express Crusader* (formerly Chay Blyth's *Spirit of Cutty Sark*).

Still another woman circumnavigated alone later that same year (1978). French model/actress Brigitte Oudry also sailed eastward and rounded Cape Horn in the 34-foot sloop *Gea*. She had a close call in the southern Indian Ocean when she was thrown overboard without a lifeline after *Gea* was knocked down by a huge wave. As the boat righted, Brigitte was able to grab the rail and haul herself onboard.

Also remarkable are the voyages of two Australian women who sailed mostly solo but occasionally had crew. Ann Gash, the "Sailing Granny," took up sailing at

Tania Aebi set out from New York in 1985 at the age of 18 for her successful circumnavigation. (Courtesy of Ernst Aebi/*Cruising World* magazine)

the age of 45. In 1977, when Ann was 55, she made it around the world, although her 26-foot Folkboat *Ilimo* was shipped from Ghana to England after extensive damage from a collision. In addition to her near-circumnavigation, which lasted about 2½ years, Ann has made numerous other long-distance passages, including a two-way Pacific crossing, and she thinks she may have spent more time sailing offshore alone than any other woman.

The other Aussi world cruiser is Julia Hazel, who at this writing has almost completed a westward rounding in the 28-foot steel sloop *Jeshan*. Julia has spent more than 10 years cruising between high latitudes in both hemispheres onboard her beloved boat, which she built with her own hands.

The most celebrated solo circumnavigation by a woman in recent times was that of 21-year-old American Tania Aebi, who set out from New York in 1985 at the age of 18.* Her boat *Varuna* was a J. J. Taylor 26, a stock fiberglass version of the classic Folkboat, bought for her by her father in lieu of a college education. Tania's route was westabout via the Panama and Suez Canals. She took an awful chance crossing the North Atlantic during the peak of the hurricane season, but returned unscathed to a heroine's welcome in New York, where she received congratulatory

*Tania Aebi had hoped to become both the youngest person and the first American woman to sail alone around the world; however on a technicality she just missed claiming those records because she took a passenger on a mere 80-mile passage.

telegrams from Robin Knox-Johnston and President Ronald Reagan, and was awarded the *Cruising World* medal and the Slocum Society Medal for 1987.

History was made in June 1988 when a 34-year old Australian shipbuilder, Kay Cottee, became the first woman to circumnavigate non-stop. She sailed her 36-foot sloop *Blackmore's First Lady* around the world without replenishment via the southern route in 189 days, setting a record for the fastest circumnavigation by a woman.

In this brief history of singlehanding, every solo voyage obviously cannot be described, for there are far too many, and of course, not every one of them is known to the author. Appendix A, however, will at least partially acknowledge some of the most important solo sailors, many of whom have not been mentioned thus far. Some of these will make their appearance later in this book. My apologies to those I have overlooked.

Mark Schrader sailed around the world on his Valiant 40 *Resourceful* to raise money for a charitable organization. (Courtesy of Betsy Holman)

3

Motives, Personalities, and Psychological Aspects

WHAT COMPELS A SAILOR TO undertake a voyage alone? Day sailing or taking a short cruise alone is perfectly understandable. Quite often there are problems in finding a crew; sometimes, in this crowded world, there is a desire to get off by oneself for a short while; or perhaps there is simply the fun of meeting the challenge of sailing unaided. More difficult to understand, perhaps, is the urge to cross oceans or make extended passages alone. In fact, solo voyagers are sometimes thought of as being some combination of reclusive and eccentric. I have even heard it said that such sailors are crazy, or complete "screwballs."

Undoubtedly, a few singlehanders have had some mental problems. Donald Crowhurst, for example, had mental instabilities that certainly contributed to his demise. Yet, in all probability, there is no higher incidence of mental disorder among solo voyagers than any other group of people. As transoceanic singlehander Bill Homewood put it, "A crazy man wouldn't find his way out of the harbor." Dr. John C. Lilly, a psychoanalyst-sailor who made a study of singlehanders, agrees. "A mentally ill person by definition can't successfully cross an ocean singlehanded," says Lilly. Certainly a few solo voyages have been completed by mentally unstable sailors who have had more than their share of luck. But the singlehander with a sickness of the mind is subject to serious errors in judgment and perhaps a complete breakdown under severe stress. Certainly the odds in his case are against the successful completion of a lengthy and difficult passage.

This chapter will touch on the various motives of singlehanders and point out the primary psychological factors with which the lone voyager must contend. Those factors can present serious problems, but the isolated sailor is better able to cope when he or she has an understanding of them and knows how others have dealt with the difficulties.

Motivations and Personalities

When lone sailors are asked about their reasons for singlehanding, they will give a variety of answers: "To prove to myself that I could do it all alone"; "Because I like to sail"; "I longed for new scenes"; "Restlessness was nagging me"; "To put theory to the test"; "I simply had to"; "The best way to find peace"; "Because I bloody-well wanted to." Reasons are difficult to express, and the truth of the matter is that the sailor may not fully understand his or her exact motives. There are ostensible and conscious reasons, but there are also subconscious and sometimes very complex motivations deeply buried in the mind. Of course, it is obvious that solo voyagers are highly individual, and thus motives are highly varied, but nonetheless, there seem to be some basic, commonly shared desires that give impetus to the singlehanding predilection.

If it is possible to simplify and generalize on this involved subject, motivation factors might be put into 10 categories, some of which (or possibly all of which) are shared to some extent by those who go to sea alone. They are as follows: (1) practical purposes, (2) self-significance, (3) curiosity and fullfillment, (4) recognition, (5) independence, (6) escapism, (7) adventurousness, (8) competitiveness, (9) solitude, and (10) the Mother Sea. Granted, such categorization may be oversimplifying the motives, but it offers a framework for more in-depth examination.

(1) The first motive, for practical purposes, is the ostensible, conscious reason (or reasons) for making the singlehanded voyage. In some cases it may be the really significant motive, and in other cases it may only be an excuse for setting forth. This factor is present in many voyages but not in all of them. Practical purposes are often related to testing or proving a theory, gathering research material, or for tangible gains such as winning a prize or monetary rewards. Of course the unavailability of crew is another factor, but this will be examined under category nine.

Notable examples of theory testing are the voyages of Dr. Alain Bombard, Dr. Hannes Lindemann, and to a lesser extent, Jean Lacombe. All of these men set forth in rubber sailing boats for the primary purpose of studying and testing theories and equipment related to survival at sea. Although some aspects of these voyages are controversial, they nevertheless provided some very valuable information for shipwreck victims and offshore castaways. Bombard and Lindemann deliberately endured extremes of privation and suffering for the sake of gaining knowledge and testing theories. More will be said of these theories later. Two others who were dedicated to experimentation and putting theories to test were Dr. David Lewis, who was interested in the medical, psychological, and survival aspects of singlehanding, and H. G. Hasler, who was intrigued with the idea of developing the perfect boat for singlehanding.

There were others with ostensible motives that seemed for the most part to be excuses for extended and difficult solo passages. Francis Chichester, for instance, wanted to break all sorts of speed records, but his powerful competitive spirit seemed secondary to a compulsion for adventure. Ann Davison became the first woman to cross an ocean alone because, as she explained, she wanted something to write about, and sailor-artist Marin-Marie who crossed the Atlantic in his double-ender *Winnibelle* wrote that he needed to "get in touch with his subject" for the

The tenacious Dr. David Lewis after his attempt to circumnavigate Antarctica alone. (Courtesy of Margo Mackay)

painting of seascapes. Tania Aebi wanted to circumnavigate alone for an education and to become an author. Mark Schrader sailed around the world to raise money for a charitable organization, while James Hatfield performed the same feat to raise funds for hospital medical equipment and research. Hank Dekker and Jim Dickson were compelled to prove that blind men could undertake such ventures as solo voyages.

The other factors related to motivation have little to do with pragmatics. They are urges or strong feelings that are sometimes difficult for the singlehander to explain. Some may not even be recognized; they might be buried deeply in the subconscious.

(2) The self-significance factor has to do with finding one's place in the world and acquiring a sense of belonging. Of course, the attempt to discover one's identity is by no means unique for solo voyagers, but singlehanders may have special talents or attributes as seamen, explorers, innovators, handymen, leaders (by inspiring others), theorists, experimenters, artists, transcendentalists, or what have you. There is a need to put these attributes to use. The singlehander discovers in lone voyaging the calling he or she feels uniquely suited for, the most appropriate course of action, the best means of expressing himself or herself. This is particularly evident in those modern professional singlehanders who not only find a satisfying means of self expression, but a remunerative means of earning a living. In France, where singlehanded sailing is a national obsession, superstars like Tabarly and Jeantot may be paid by their commercial sponsors as much or more than their country's other professional athletes.

Though a singlehander may not be understood by the entire world, his rewards are great self-satisfaction and acceptance by his own kind. This motive is strong in singlehanders who have highly developed skills or specialized knowledge, examples being Slocum, Pidgeon, Guzzwell, Chichester, Casper, and so forth. Their particular skills have (or had) to do with boatbuilding and/or navigation. This expertise is not the reason for a voyage, but merely a means of accomplishment that must be exercised.

John Guzzwell wrote in his book *Trekka Round the World*, "I visited friends in Jersey, but my two-year absence had made me a stranger amongst them, and I felt I did not belong there. Out sailing with one of them my old dream of making a long voyage alone returned to me. I was confident I could do so, providing I had a suitable boat. The best idea was to build my own, and with my skill as a joiner, I was sure I could do so." Plainly we are told that the singlehander felt out of place, that he needed a feeling of belonging, and he needed to put his skills to work, not as an end but as a means to his dream. Here are manifestations of factor two, although there were undoubtedly other motives that drove Guzzwell to his remarkable solo circumnavigation.

(3) Curiosity and fulfillment motives are expressed in the desire to see for oneself by actually doing it. This urge may be stimulated by heroes, but it cannot be satisfied vicariously by reading or hearing about the experiences of others; it must be firsthand knowledge learned through physical effort. There is a compulsion to see what it is really like to be alone at sea. Circumnavigator Harold Kolzer wrote, "A person who has not spent one month alone at sea has never really seen it." Not only does the singlehander want to experience the pleasant moments, but often he is curious, perhaps subconsciously, about the more difficult periods. He may wish to test himself, secretly or not, to see how he will stand up to fatigue, loneliness, fear, and hardships, to see if he can manage his vessel by himself in heavy weather at sea. J. R. L. Anderson wrote of Japanese singlehander Kenichi Horie's motives: "He sailed because he had to and he had to sail because he wanted to. That simple passion of wanting to know, to experience, to see for yourself is among the hardest things in the world to put into words."

(4) There is little doubt that offshore singlehanding can produce plenty of recognition. In some countries solo sailors are treated like national heroes, receiving full media coverage, prestigious awards, and even titles. For example, Chichester and Alec Rose were knighted, Tabarly was made Chevalier of the Legion of Honor, Naomi James was made Dame Commander of the Order of the British Empire, and so forth. Then there are such prizes and citations as the Slocum Society Award, Blue Water Medal, Seven Seas Award, Rolex Yachtsman and Yachtswoman of the Year awards, and the *Cruising World* Medal.

The need for recognition seems fairly uncomplicated. It is a desire for fame, for public acclaim, a love of the limelight. The reason for this need, however, is more complex. It may be the manifestation of a genuine sense of superiority, a requirement of the ego, or a stimulant necessary to extract one's best effort; but in a few cases, it might be the mollification of an inferiority complex, the need to build up one's image in the eyes of others. There seems to be little doubt that William Andrews and some other cockleshell voyagers, especially those of the late 1800s, had a large share of this motivation. The voyages of Andrews, for instance, were well advertised, and he delighted in the large crowds seeing him off and the publicity he received after the ventures' completions.

The thirst for fame, however, is by no means limited to the old-time singlehanders. Nicolette Milnes-Walker, a psychologist who crossed the Atlantic alone in 1971, frankly admitted her love of publicity. As she told yachting correspondent Frank Page, "It is marvelous to be famous," and, "It is very attractive to have public recognition." On the other hand, it is only fair to say that a great many singlehanders abhor publicity. In fact, solo voyager Alexander Welsh reportedly knocked a press photographer overboard in an effort to preserve his privacy.

(5) The independence factor is commonly found in the habitual solo voyager, who requires the greatest possible freedom and control over his own destiny. What greater freedom can one have than to be alone at sea, beholden to no one, with no responsibilities other than to oneself, without a time schedule, and free to wander wherever one wishes? Of course a price must be paid for this vagrant pelagic life: the lack of roots, absence of family, lack of companionship, and perhaps a guilty feeling of running away from one's duties. But there are those who abhor dependency in any form and find tremendous satisfaction in self-reliance. This need for independence is typified by Gerbault, who wrote, "I want freedom . . . I am in no hurry . . . I am a-roving, and a rover has no definite plans . . . Now, every minute of the day, I am thinking of departure, and of the great joy called living, when I shall be again alone on the sea."

(6) Escapism is a motive closely related to independence. This is a reaction against the routine life ashore that is so often full of tensions, pressures, boredom, and artificialities. There is often a longing to return to nature. Sometimes the desire to escape from discontent is freely admitted, as in the case of Fred Rebell, who ran away from his problems in Australia. In other cases, there is a reluctance to admit escape for fear people might think it a "cop out" from society. Sometimes rather amusing reasons are given for leaving problems behind, as in the case of Peter Tangvald, a circumnavigator who often sailed alone. Evidently, Tangvald had more than his share of marital problems, and his description of leaving his third wife may or may not have been made with tongue in cheek. He wrote, "I had to choose between her and the boat, she said. Any sailor will know that it is a lot more difficult to get a new boat than a new wife, so I bought a one-way ticket for her to Norway."

It is seldom, if ever, wise to take up voyaging for the sole purpose of escape, for quite often the dissatisfaction which causes the yearning to leave cares behind really comes from oneself. As singlehander Edward Allcard put it, "People who are unhappy here and go somewhere else are usually unhappy there too. It's a thing from within. I don't think anybody can escape from themselves." Tristan Jones put it more strongly, "Anyone who goes to sea to escape problems is a fool."

(7) The quest for adventure is a motive shared to some extent by all singlehanders. It is a characteristic of those with a restless spirit, which some psychologists feel may result, partially at least, from latent wandering instincts inherited from primitive man. For the afflicted sailor there is an urge to travel, to visit new places, a need for a change in routine, a desire for new experiences, excitement, and probably an unconscious wish for some element of danger. As solo sailor Tom Corkill put it, ". . . the bigger the risk, the bigger the adventure." Nearly all adventurers feel they must physically and even emotionally lead the fullest possible life. Of vicarious adventurers, OSTAR veteran Bill Wallace had this to say: "The world is full of guys who mow the lawn and watch TV. They're dead and don't even know it. I think that's terrible." Some sailors readily admit to having this characteristic, while others do not. Chichester wrote, "The same old restlessness was nagging at

me . . . I found myself craving more excitement." One might get the impression that David Lewis is almost bored with the ordinary, for he wrote: "To paraphrase the old saying about kissing a man without a moustache being like eating meat without salt, so is sailing a sea without icebergs—DULL." While both Francis Stokes and Harry Pidgeon said, "I avoid adventure as much as possible," it hardly seems likely that anyone would have chosen the kind of life Pidgeon led without having an adventurous spirit. The very fact that voyages are made alone indicates a possession of this spirit to some degree. As singlehander Bill Howell wrote, "If you love adventure, whatever you do is much more adventurous if you do it alone."

(8) In one form or another, competitiveness is often a driving element among singlehanders. Competitiveness may take its normal form, the desire to win a race or set a record, or it may in some instances be the reverse side of the coin, a desire to avoid competition. In the latter case, there may be an urge to reap the rewards of competition with little risk of being beaten. The solo voyager can often experience a similar kind of satisfaction and glory as that felt by a winning competitor but without entering a race. Then too, if he does enter a formal distance race, the matter of who wins may be of minor importance; the real glory is in successfully completing the course.

One could suspect that Chichester had such motivations, because he invented races in which there were no actual competitors. He tried to break records of his own and others. He raced against the "magic" number of 200 miles a day, and he competed against the runs of square-rigged vessels, the ghosts of clipper ships. But despite this, I am inclined to agree with J. R. L. Anderson who thinks of Chichester as a true competitor, one with an urge for trying to break records and extending man's physical limitations. He really used competition as a spur to get the best from himself, and his competitive ventures were most satisfying when they were done alone. Chichester had little desire for participation in team efforts. As he expressed it, "I don't do a thing nearly as well when with someone. It makes me think I was cut out for solo jobs, and any attempt to diverge from that lot only makes me a half-person."

Within the competitive urge sometimes there is a strong element of nationalism. This is a pride in one's country so powerful that it actually becomes a motivating factor. A case in point is the voyage of Robin Knox-Johnston, who sailed around the world non-stop partly because he ". . . could not accept that anyone but a Briton should be the first to do it." Evidently this was not a mere tongue-in-cheek remark, but a sincere expression of his patriotism. Another remark that gives evidence of intense competitiveness is the one Robin made after an accident during which battery acid was splashed in his eye. He wrote, "I debated turning back for Durban, but Commander King and Bernard Moitessier were in the race. I was in the lead and stood a slight chance of winning, and I felt that this would be worth giving an eye for, so I carried on."

(9) Solitude, of course, is very much a factor in the life of a singlehander, who may or may not enjoy it. Many solo sailors prefer congenial companionship, but they cannot find the right crew. Difficulties with crew are common. Pidgeon, Casper, and many others had such problems in this regard that they preferred to sail alone. Although apprehensive at first, they soon became used to managing by themselves, and life became freer and simpler. Other singlehanders go off alone because it is a necessary condition of a competition they wish to enter. If they have

Francis Stokes, who once declared, "I avoid adventure as much as possible." (Photo by Bernadette Brennan)

a dislike of solitude, however, it is not sufficiently strong to prevent them from embarking. One young singlehander, Dave Englehart, told me that he actually went cruising solo because of his fondness for people. He suggested that his lifestyle gave him a greater opportunity to make new acquaintances, especially with congenial types. In a sense it broadened his social horizon.

Then there are those singlehanders who actually like being alone, at least for certain periods of time. Some lone sailors have admitted a reluctance to end a passage and confessed to a mild dread of going ashore again to mingle with people. Many of these sailors have tendencies toward introversion. There may be a need for inner reflection and contemplation that can only be achieved through isolation. For some there may be a spiritual value in being alone, a feeling of closer contact with God or at least with nature.

One example of a loner who feels at one with God, nature, and the sea is Bernard Moitessier. After the Golden Globe Race when he sailed 1 1/2 times around the world non-stop, he said, "Much of my voyage I sailed under a condition called *Baraka* — a state of grace I could feel, as if I was loved and being looked after by the Olympian Gods above." He spoke of "peace and joy of being in harmony with the universe." After making the difficult decision to withdraw from the Golden Globe Race, he sent a message to his publisher by shooting it aboard a ship with a slingshot (à la William Andrews). It said: "I am continuing non-stop towards the Pacific Islands because I am happy at sea, and perhaps also to save my soul."

Sailing alone may increase one's appreciation of the experience, even sharpen perceptual sensitivities. Circumnavigator Francis Stokes wrote me, "Unless your crew is extraordinarily congenial, the experience shared will be diluted, less vivid, and less well remembered. Solitude sharpens awareness of small pleasures otherwise lost."

In some cases the love of solitude may be a reaction against crowding, the population explosion on shore. Perhaps there is an urge for complete and utter privacy. H. G. Hasler said, "The only pleasure I get at sea really is becoming isolated. I get a tremendous pleasure out of existing in a world that only goes as far as the horizon. I shrink from contact."

Many of the so-called reclusive voyagers simply have an aversion to crowds or groups of people, but they often have a strong need for intimate companionship and closeness to at least one individual. Many have wives, husbands, or sweethearts on which they depend. Naomi James, for instance, said, "I'm antisocial anyway. I can do without the companionship of other people," yet she sorely missed her husband Rob, and became almost dependent on radio communication with him during parts of her solo circumnavigation.

(10) Our last category has a rather strange title, "the Mother Sea." It has to do with the sailor's natural emotions in regard to the sea and his or her vessel. Some of these feelings are deeply buried in the subconscious. They may very well relate to genetic instinct, the sort of thing that tells spiders to build webs or birds to fly south in the winter. Of course, life itself originated in the sea, and perhaps the deep love of the sea possessed by some sailors, the "sea fever" described so well by John Masefield, is in some part the awakening of an instinctive affinity with the mother element. As Robert Manry explained it, "There is an inherited something in the protoplasm of my body cells that feels an agreeable kinship with the sea."

But sometimes the sea's attraction is more a fascination than a love, and there are definitely times when sailors have a downright fear of the sea. In this case, the boat rather than the water may become the mother element, in a sense, the protective womb. This feeling can even extend to the life raft. When David Shaw (not alone, but shorthanded) weathered a lengthy gale in his 37-foot yawl, he became extremely fatigued and developed a strong urge to assume the fetus position in his rubber raft. He described his feeling as being "absolutely straight Freudian because the raft also has a long cord that is attached to the ship. But I envisioned curling up in this thing. It was strictly back to the womb." As H. G. Hasler wrote, "Nothing induces a womb complex more strongly than looking out of a hatch at an angry sea just under your nose."

The affection some sailors have for their boats is well recognized, (Naomi James had an "overwhelming" affection for *Express Crusader*,) and perhaps some parts of this emotion are instinctive. John Guzzwell has written, "A boat seems to have a soul and character of her own. Perhaps it is because of this that boats are usually thought of as being feminine." Singlehander Frank Mulville expands on this thinking when he says, "A boat is a living thing—full of eccentricities, perversities, and endearing quirks. It vibrates with life and gives off sympathy and understanding." Bill Homewood was convinced that his boat was as alive as he was. In fair weather the boat may be like a companion or a girlfriend, but in a hard chance she may seem more like a defending mother. Even in the heaviest weather offshore, the true seaman with confidence in his craft experiences a unique sense of security.

Far from a lee shore with the vessel hove to and all hatches battened down, a snug cabin may seem more protective than a private fortress on land.

There seems to be no motivational common denominator for all singlehanders. Too many contrasting individuals are involved. One sailor may be almost entirely motivated by just one of the 10 factors we've been discussing, while another may, to some degree, be affected by all the factors. Nevertheless, it seems safe to say that all singlehanders possess at least some of these motivations in various combinations. The nearest thing to a common denominator might be what J.R.L. Anderson has called the "Ulysses factor," the exploring instinct in humans. This instinct derives, for the most part, from a primitive need to discover, pioneer, have adventures, investigate, and satisfy one's curiosity through physical effort. Anderson tells us that all of us have the Ulysses factor to some extent, but in modern times, when there are few frontiers left to explore, the instinct is often strong in flyers, mountain climbers, offshore sailors, and especially solo voyagers. This instinctive need is usually best satisfied through individual achievement and not through large-scale team effort.

Furthermore, most solo voyagers probably share what might be called a romantic optimism, the kind of idealistic outlook that allows them to make light of the bad times—the gales, hardships, fatigue, loneliness, worries, and fears. The singlehander thinks mainly of scudding before the trade winds with the warm sun on his back and his dream ship sliding off before foam-flecked seas of the deepest blue. He also dreams of landfalls on tropic isles with palm-fringed lagoons and natives bedecked with flowers. Most, if not all, seagoers have such romantic visions, but those of the solo voyager are so intense and frequent that anxieties are put aside, obstacles are overcome, and dreams are turned into reality.

With the great proliferation of women sailors in recent years it is interesting to speculate on similarities and differences between the sexes with regard to single-handed or shorthanded sailing. Are women as attuned as men to the Mother Sea? Psychologically, there are some intriguing contrasts. At sea both sexes are subject to the same basic stresses and anxieties, but their emotional responses often differ. A woman is more likely to show her emotions, whereas a man more often keeps his emotions bottled up. Some men are afflicted with a high degree of the macho, with an unwillingness to admit to any weaknesses, fears, or mental problems; perhaps this characteristic can be a weakness that will more easily lead to a breakdown. In contrast, the woman may be equipped with a natural safety valve to relieve the build-up of tension and stress.

Even though a woman may lack the muscle power of a man, she can be stronger in other ways. Perhaps nature has endowed her with more patience, endurance, and self-discipline, as well as a higher threshold of pain. Nicolette Milnes-Walker, the sailor/psychologist who was the first female singlehander to sail non-stop across the Atlantic, thinks that a woman is less likely to "crack up" than a man. "It has often been found," she wrote, "that women survive hardship better than men. I think that this is because women are less self-centred than men, for a woman's life is usually centred on her husband and/or children and so she has a motive for fighting on when all is lost. . . . if there is any truth in the argument of evolved innate sex differences, which I think there is, I could expect to have this survival capacity." A confirmation of this theory was given me by Maurice Bailey,

Naomi James, with husband Rob, at the end of her record-setting circumnavigation in *Express Crusader*. (Courtesy of Jonathan Eastland)

who with his wife Marilynn was adrift in a life raft for 117 days after their boat was sunk by a whale. Maurice told me that he might have perished without the psychological strength of his wife.

There is the argument that women are more dependent than men. Singlehander Judy Lawson has written, "Every lady solo sailor needs a good man behind her (witness Jacques for Clare Francis, Rob for Naomi James, etc.). Or maybe several!" But there are some very independent women singlehanders, Ann Gash and Nicholette Milnes-Walker being two examples. Ann Davison set off on an ocean voyage with her husband but lost him in a tragic shipwreck, yet she had the spirit of independence as well as the courage to set off again, this time singlehanded, to become the first woman to cross the Atlantic alone. Many woman singlehanders, such as Naomi James, derive comfort during hard times by depending on thoughts of their loved ones (men do also). But Naomi also revealed a high degree of independence by stating that she derived her inner strength not from the outside, in the form of a strong religious belief, but from faith in herself.

Do women identify with the Mother Sea and relate to their boat in the same way as men? Yes, I believe they do. Tania Aebi gave us a clue when she wrote, "On the ocean, I never feel lonely. There's too much beauty—the sea, the wind, the sky, the animals and fish." I suspect that many women sailors feel a close kinship with the sea. My wife Sally tells me that her outstanding impression of our 27-day transatlantic passage was a previously unrealized sense of the pureness of the environment and an overwhelming feeling of being at one with nature. Every woman sailor with whom I've communicated considers her boat feminine and refers to it as "she" or "her." If the boat is well-mannered, the woman skipper may consider it a comforting female companion. In a gale the boat can assume the role of a protecting mother for either a male or female crew.

A woman can do anything as well or better than a man, as long as it doesn't require a tremendous amount of physical strength. It seems unbelievable that in bygone days women were often considered incapable of sailing a boat. For example, when Thomas Crapo and his wife made a doublehanded Atlantic crossing in a 19-foot ship's boat in 1877, Mrs. Crapo was never allowed to take the helm despite the fact that she was an experienced seagoer, having made several voyages with her husband on larger vessels. This meant that Captain Crapo had to stoically "man" the helm for as long as 72 hours and would heave to in order to sleep rather than allow himself to be spelled by his wife!

As expressed in the Slocum Society's salty journal, *The Spray*, "Since women have such highly refined motor skills, exceptional patience, and a high resistance to both cold and fatigue they are ideal candidates to stand up to the rigors of offshore sailing. In addition most of the old stereotypes and stigmas which have kept women in the galley and not on the foredeck have thankfully been erased and more women will be sharing the unique communion with the sea which only the singlehander experiences."

A few years ago I received a letter from author/journalist/college president Felix Morley, who made some interesting comments on the first edition of this book. Regarding this chapter, Dr. Morley remarked, "Tho' I am not wholly satisfied with the 10 categories, the last of these—'the Mother Sea'—may be so fundamental as to support all the others, as indeed you suggest. Many who are not sailors have no aversion to the idea of having their ashes 'committed to the deep.'" Then Dr. Morley, who was in his eighties at that time, made what I consider a beautiful and provocative comment: "Extrapolating that thought, an octogenarian (like myself) may easily feel associated with those whom you are so carefully preparing for 'singlehanded' sailing. The time is not distant when the last moorings to earth will be withdrawn and the outgoing tide will sweep them to what are at best dubiously charted seas. Of course in this prospect there is cause for apprehension. But surely also an exulting promise of high adventure."

Psychological Factors

Regardless of motivations, the solo voyager will be exposed to certain psychological hazards that could have a great effect on the success of his or her voyage. The most usual problems of this kind arise from loneliness, fears, and hallucinations.

Loneliness is a common hazard to singlehanders, of course, but is seldom extremely serious, and surprisingly, many singlehanders claim that they are never deeply affected. As said earlier, there are some who enjoy or actually need periods of isolation. For them, singlehanding allows an escape from social inhibitions and the claustrophobia of overcrowding. Also, the isolation affords a unique opportunity for contemplation, reflection, obtaining a broader perspective, and perhaps spiritual or at least philosophical meditation. Others, who are not seeking escape from people, are often not adversely affected by the loneliness of singlehanding, for their isolation is completely self-inflicted. They expect solitude, and they don't experience the strong feelings of abandonment and despair so often suffered by castaways. Then, too, there is a definite difference between solitude and loneliness.

It is possible to be lonely when surrounded by people, and this feeling of being alone is probably the most painful kind. As Marin-Marie wrote, "To be alone in the midst of a crowd is much harder to bear than to be a thousand miles from the nearest human being." More recently, solo racer Mike McMullen said, "It is only in big cities where no one is your friend that real loneliness is found."

All of this, however, is not to minimize the problem of loneliness. Slocum was badly afflicted at times, as were Ann Davison, Alain Bombard, Robin Lee Graham, and many others. In a letter to the well-known seaman and author Humphrey Barton, Davison wrote, "I agree with you that singlehanded sailing is not all it might be. The utter aloneness is rather apt to get one down. Didn't know I was quite so gregarious." The youthful Robin Lee Graham reflected, "Loneliness was to ride with me for a thousand days, and throughout the longest nights. At times it was something I could touch." Bill Homewood wrote me, "Every time I have gone long distance offshore the first 24 hours I feel lonely and wonder why I am doing this. My appetite is zero. After five days I'm fine—my spirits are good—all my working systems are in place—I have adapted to my surroundings. It takes five days every time."

There are ways to combat loneliness. One of the best is to keep busy, and this is not difficult for the singlehander, because there is always something that needs doing aboard a boat. Many singlehanders find it helpful to imagine that they have company. Bill Homewood imagined his recently deceased father was on board, watching out for him and telling him what to do. The boat can become an intimate companion, and the pets carried by a few solo sailors provide a kind of outlet for affection and communication. Tania Aebi said that her cat Dinghy became her "best little buddy." Gerbault's books became his "best friends." Slocum conversed with the moon, and he made "the porpoises leap" and the turtles "poke their heads up out of the sea" when he sang *Johnny Boker* and *We'll Pay Darby Doyl for his Boots*. Sharon Sites Adams also fought the loneliness problem with imagined conversations and vocal outbursts. She wrote, "I talked and talked. I talked to the boat, to the gooney birds, to the moon and all the time to my tape recorder—it became my friend. I said 'hello' to a lovely star every night. I even screamed."

Incidentally, modern electronic devices such as tape recorders, radio-telephones, and even receiving radios may give the modern singlehander some form of temporary relief from loneliness. Aside from Sharon Adams, others have made good use of tape recorders. For example, Robin Lee Graham constantly recorded his own voice and played it back, and H. G. Hasler, who carried no radio, used his recorder to play tapes of jazz pieces "whenever morale needed boosting." Gerry Spiess in his 10-foot *Yankee Girl* carried cassette tapes of comedy programs. He said they were a godsend, and he played them over and over. Spiess believes "there is no better cure for loneliness than being able to laugh."

Two-way radio communications between shore or other boats have afforded some relief from loneliness for modern singlehanders, especially those in ocean races where there are congenial competitors nearby. As a matter of fact, radios have been of real practical value in some cases, as for example, when Chichester, in 1964, obtained advice over his radio phone from a boatbuilder on how to repair a serious leak, and when Chay Blyth received soldering and engine repair instructions in a similar manner during his circumnavigation. Thus electronic communications can afford the kind of contact that can bring real security as well as easing loneliness, a psychological advantage the old-timers didn't have. Navy psychologist Dr. Benjamin Weybrew, in considering the advantage of radio contact for men in space, has said, "The fact that astronauts can communicate with the outside world may be what holds them together in the long run."

Sealed in his tiny cabin, Gerry Spiess vividly described his anxiety and respite through his radio during a lengthy gale: "I was terrified. And at night it was even worse. It was like a medieval torture chamber with a wild cacophony of noise. It was like nature had gone mad. The whole world was a spinning, shrieking blackness. I remember in the middle of this four days of perpetual battering glancing out the four-inch porthole. There was a Dutch ship passing close by. I was so despondent my heart leapt with joy at the sight of the ship that, to my tormented mind, was a symbol of civilization. I scrambled from my bunk to call them on the radio. I prayed someone on board would be listening to my frequency. I was so anxious to talk to somebody—anybody. When a voice in broken English asked if I was a very little sailboat, I was so happy to hear another person I simply broke down and cried. Tears flowed down my cheeks and I was so choked up with emotion I couldn't reply immediately."

Fear, to some degree at least, is experienced by most singlehanders. Dr. David Lewis, in collaboration with the Medical Research Council in London, made a study of the medical and psychological factors affecting the singlehanders competing in the 1960 transatlantic race. His findings showed that only one out of five contestants never felt "acute fear," although the degree varied with each individual. In general, there were two types of fear: initial tensions and anxieties lasting for the first few days, and then a very rational apprehension resulting from potentially dangerous situations, such as during a gale or when approaching a coast in bad visibility. Interestingly, Dr. Lewis found that quite often the singlehander does not remember the extent of his fears. He concluded: "Observations noted *at the time* are the only valid ones." Of his own reactions, he wrote, "I honestly forgot that I had been frightened at all during one gale, until I looked up my notes."

Dr. John C. Lilly, in his studies of the mental aspects of singlehanding, noted that a critical period of fear during a solo voyage often occurs near the "point of no return" (PNR). This is the point beyond which it is easier to go on than turn back. It would not necessarily come near the middle of a passage but might come early if, for example, the vessel were running before the trade winds and when turning back would mean a difficult beat to windward. Actually, the point is likely to come very early, because it is really a state of mind, a mental PNR, when the singlehander considers such matters as the effort he has expended in planning and preparing for the cruise and the possible humiliation of turning back for no very good reason. At any rate, whenever it occurs, the mental PNR is a significant moment for the cognizant sailor. Often he has a powerful feeling of anxiety and indecision. Donald Crowhurst agonized over whether to continue or not. In his logbook he wrote, "Racked by the growing awareness that I must soon decide whether or not I can go on in the face of the actual situation. What a bloody awful decision—to chuck it in at this stage—what a bloody awful decision!"

Continuing beyond the PNR may bring some relief in the sense that a difficult decision has been made, but this is the time when many a singlehander will have the strongest feeling of being entirely on his own, when he will have the fullest realization that he cannot count on receiving any outside assistance. Thereafter,

Complex psychological
pressures caused the voyage of
Donald Crowhurst to end in
tragedy. (Photo by Peter
Dunne/*Sunday Times*)

barring storms or emergencies, this kind of apprehension may gradually subside as
the sailor becomes increasingly habituated and the passage nears its end.

Fears in one form or another are perfectly normal for the solo voyager. The
danger is in letting fear turn into panic, which could seriously hamper judgment.
According to studies made by Doctors Bombard and Lindemann and others, panic
and loss of morale are the chief causes for the perishing of castaways adrift at sea.
Bombard wrote, "Statistics show that 90 percent of the survivors of shipwreck die
within three days, yet it takes longer than that to perish of hunger and thirst."
Some psychologists even think that it is possible to literally die of fright. Most of
the time, however, castaways who do not survive simply give up and stop fighting
for life or perhaps kill themselves by jumping overboard. Actually, experienced
seamen are rarely troubled by extreme panic, although I have heard of a few cases
where fear caused greenhorns or slightly experienced sailors to lose their sense of
reason.

It is not easy to fight fear, but a major weapon is self confidence. This is best
assured by careful preparation, attention to one's health, seeing that the boat is
sound and well equipped, learning all one can about the proposed route and
weather conditions, polishing the techniques of singlehanding, preparing for all
possible emergencies, and gradually building experience.

Another weapon is prayer and faith in God, or at least a belief in an exterior
force which, to some extent, controls one's destiny. Some singlehanders become

superstitious, but usually this affords far less comfort than religion. Chay Blyth, whose circumnavigation was one of the most strenuous, had this to say: "Ten months of solitude in some of the loneliest seas of the world strengthened every part of me, deepened every perception and gave me a new awareness of the power outside man which we call God. I am quite certain that without God's help many and many a time I could not have survived to complete my circumnavigation." The religion of most singlehanders is not overly fatalistic, however. It is decidedly not a conviction that God or a superior being will protect the solo sailor no matter what blunders are committed in seamanship. It is more a belief in the adage, "The Lord helps those who help themselves." As Robin Knox-Johnston put it, "If you are trying to do a particularly difficult job, and failing time and again, the knowledge that the Lord will assist you if you help yourself keeps you going at it, and in my experience the job usually gets done."

Less grim than fear, but sometimes as much of a problem for the voyager are psychological frustrations caused by any circumstance that interrupts his ability to control his own destiny. This kind of emotional stress can be caused by gear failure or physical problems, but such difficulties often can be corrected through repair or convalescence. For a sailor, perhaps the ultimate frustration may be day after day of calm weather. During this time the boat cannot move, and she rolls endlessly, slatting her sails and chafing her gear. This may not sound serious to one who has not done much sailing offshore, but it can cause severe exasperation. Dodge Morgan said that being becalmed is the most difficult of all problems. When he had no wind for a lengthy period in the desolate Southern Ocean, he confessed, "I am just about ready to lose my mind. It is devastating."

There is little a sailor can do to combat the frustrations of a flat calm, except try to keep busy, lower the sails, and tighten up the running rigging to prevent chafe. It may help to run the engine if practical, and search for wind. Needless to say, the passage should be planned whenever possible to avoid regions having a high percentage of calms.

It is not at all unusual for singlehanders to suffer from hallucinations. These are imaginary perceptions or sensations—"tricks of the mind" such as hearing voices that don't exist or seeing visions that are not real. Just how many solo voyagers have hallucinations is hard to estimate, since not everyone is willing to admit having them, presumably for fear people might suspect serious mental disorders. Actually, there is no reason to feel abashed by such experiences, because completely normal people can hallucinate under certain conditions, and the environment of the singlehander can be quite conducive to illusions, false impressions, and even the false beliefs known as delusions, which are closely associated with hallucinations. Dr. Lilly, who made a study of this subject with respect to singlehanders, set up controlled experiments whereby he could cause normal people to hallucinate in a matter of a few days or even hours.

Many singlehanders have frankly admitted to having hallucinations and a few have been very explicit on the subject. Dr. Gilin Bennet, who has studied the psychological aspects of singlehanding, wrote that half of the 1972 OSTAR racers reported one or more illusions or hallucinations. Slocum described in some detail his imaginary Spanish pilot from the ancient caravel *Pinta* who took charge of the *Spray* while her captain was ill. Dr. Lindemann told of his feeling of traveling backwards, of an imaginary Negro servant, and a black horse that pushed his boat.

Robert Manry described a phantom hitchhiker and a wild search for an imaginary island. The interesting but frightening illusion of levitation was described by Fred Rebell when he became disassociated from his boat and found himself "floating in the air" as much as a hundred or more miles away from his actual location. During one of these "flights" of fancy, he spotted a vessel which he later actually saw.

Incidentally, it is interesting that more than a few singlehanders have reported dreaming about or imagining a steamer approaching their boats, and shortly after this warning, the real ship, identical to the one in the dream, has made its actual appearance. One singlehander who experienced this told me he thought the explanation lay in pure coincidence. In other cases, the experience might be some form of hallucination, but a psychiatrist-sailor friend offered still another possible explanation: that it might be the phenomenon known as *déjà vu*, the illusion of having already experienced something actually experienced for the first time. In other words, when the sailor saw the ship in actuality, it could possibly be that he imagined he saw her previously. Dr. Bennet verifies the *déjà vu* phenomena are not at all unusual.

Although many singlehanders have survived hallucinations with no ill effects, there is no question that such mental disturbances are potentially dangerous. They can seriously impair judgment and cause fear and irrational behavior that could prove fatal. Dr. Lindemann mentioned that several times he had the urge to jump overboard to reach some imaginary food, and others have turned over the helm at critical times to a phantom crewmember. One castaway walked off his life raft into the sea thinking that he was walking down to the corner drug store.

As a result of considerable scientific research in recent years, a lot more is known now than before about the nature and causes of hallucinations. In the normal, mentally healthy person, hallucinations can be a kind of substitute for dreams. Psychologists tell us that dreams are important for mental health, since they help us get rid of tensions and frustrations, resolve certain conflicts, and perhaps fulfill some secret wishes. If we are denied dreams through lack of sleep, we are subject to an alternative in the form of hallucinations, which are very near relatives of dreams. So close is this relationship, in fact, that Dr. Calvin S. Hall, director of the Institute of Dream Research, has written, "Dreams are pure and simple hallucinations. They are the hallucinations of a sleeping person." The difference between dreams and hallucinations is that the former are normal and restorative, while the latter are not normal and can be damaging. Thus adequate sleep is a necessary element in the avoidance of hallucinations. Mere rest will not suffice; it must be sleep, which, whether we realize it or not, produces dreams. Gerry Spiess wrote, "My sanity was saved by minutes of sleep and dreams."

Dr. Lilly has told us that there are two types of hallucinations experienced by the singlehander: the first is the "fatigue" type caused by exhaustion and lack of sleep, and the second is what he calls the "surplus-energy" type, caused primarily by monotony. In reference to the latter type, psychiatrists may use the term "stimulus deprivation." There is no doubt that certain activities on a small boat at sea can be extremely monotonous for a singlehander. Hour after hour of steering is one of those activities, and Dr. David Lewis has suggested that self-steering devices have been most helpful to modern solo sailors in minimizing hallucinations. Of course self-steerers not only alleviate monotony, but also reduce fatigue. It may very well be that rhythmic motions produced by wave action can contribute to a tendency to hallucinate. Dr. Lewis wrote, "Possibly the rhythmic effect of monotonous activities tends to induce auto-hypnosis." At any rate, controlling the boat's motion as much as possible (with anti-rolling and anti-yaw measures) and especially varying activities seems to be helpful in minimizing hallucinations that are due to the effects of monotony.

Even the repetition of monotonous sounds can affect the mind to some extent through perceptual deprivation, according to Dr. Michael Cohen. In his *Dr. Cohen's Healthy Sailor Book*, he wrote, ". . . the monotonous sound of the wind in the rigging, and the steady noise of the waves ensures that at least some degree of perceptual deprivation can be expected on every blue water cruise." Those repetition sounds were described so colorfully by William Andrews when he wrote about his little sneakbox *Sapolio* poking through the waves, "splashing, dashing, whang-it-ty-bang: with a "cachunk, swash, ripple-ripple, cachunk, cachunk, for hours and sometimes days." In a calm his boom chafed against the mast "squeaking most plainly 'Right arm, r-i-g-h-t-a-r-m-m-m, left arm, l-e-f-t-a-r-m-m-m.'" It might pay the singlehander to control those sounds when possible. Halyards can be tied off, booms vanged, gear belayed, etc. Doing so will not only be beneficial to the psyche, but may prevent harmful chafe.

One of the most striking examples of a fatigue hallucination was told by the South African boating writer Frank Robb. According to Robb, who claims the story is completely true, a singlehander making a passage in the Caribbean Sea encountered rough weather that lasted four days and denied him much-needed sleep. When the weather moderated, he was unsure of his position but soon spotted a fishing boat and an island with a protected harbor. He sailed in, passing a launch full of sightseers, and found a snug spot to anchor. After dropping the hook, he furled his sails, went below, and collapsed on the cabin sole into a deep sleep. Twelve hours later the singlehander awoke, went on deck, and found that, although the boat was anchored in eight fathoms of water, there was no land or boats in sight. His mind had simply invented the island and harbor in order to allow his body to sleep. His physical actions were completely controlled by powerful fatigue hallucinations.

The utter necessity of sleep for singlehanders was learned by Dr. Hannes Lindemann not only from medical research, but also from unique, first-hand experiences. During his transatlantic crossing in a 17-foot rubber foldboat, he was often unable to sleep except for brief periods. At certain times when he could not make his boat steer herself safely before the large seas produced by the blusterous trade winds, he could only try to accumulate brief snatches of sleep between waves. He practiced a form of self-hypnosis called autogenesis, which was helpful, but still he hallucinated frequently. He found out that sleep was a "vitally important factor." He wrote, "The castaway should try to sleep, if only for a few minutes at a time. Seconds of sleep may save his life."

In summary, experts seem to agree that illusions, delusions, and hallucinations in the normal person are primarily caused by fatigue, especially lack of sleep, and by monotony and solitude. Other contributing factors may be improper diet, certain illnesses (abnormal physiological conditions, for example), certain drug poisonings, and perhaps autohypnotic types of motion. Thus hallucinations are best avoided by getting plenty of sleep (eight hours a day if possible), resting, varying one's activities, keeping busy, relieving monotony as much as possible, keeping mentally active, possibly relieving or varying hypnotic sounds and motions, maintaining good health, avoiding drugs, and eating proper meals. The one factor a singlehander can't do much about is eliminating solitude, but a radio, tape recorder, pets, or simply talking to oneself my help.

Of course, a great many singlehanders have never been troubled by psychological problems, but others on particularly strenuous voyages have had considerable troubles with abnormal behavior of the mind. Thus it makes sense to know what one might expect and what preparations and preventive measures can be taken. One compensation for a difficult passage is the perfect right of successful singlehanders to be extremely proud of themselves. By their accomplishments they have proven to themselves that they can withstand alone not only awesome exterior forces of nature but also the more potent internal adversaries in the mind. The rewards of inner satisfaction and self assurance can be very great and everlasting.

PART II

The Vessels

Steven Callahan sails his *Napoleon Solo*. (Courtesy of Steven Callahan)

4

Good Designs
for Singlehanding

BOATS SPECIFICALLY DESIGNED FOR solo ocean crossings have varied in length from just under 6 feet to 236 feet, and singlehanded offshore passages have been made successfully (and unsuccessfully) in every kind of craft imaginable. Thus it is evident that there are many and varied opinions regarding the choice of an ideal vessel for singlehanding.

The most important criterion for choosing a design is its suitability for the fundamental purpose for which it is intended, such as solo racing, leisurely cruising, or perhaps an attempt at breaking a record. Regardless of the intended purpose, however, virtually all singlehanders seek, in varying degrees, the following characteristics for their boats: safety and seaworthiness, handiness, seakindliness, comfort, and speed. To some degree speed is needed on any boat, because even if she is not racing, she will have to make port during the time of favorable weather and before her supplies are depleted. The dilemma is, of course, that many of these desirable qualities are in opposition to each other when they are translated into design parameters. For example, speed necessitates largeness, but handiness suggests compactness; seakindliness is associated with heavy displacement, but the fastest passage-making suggests light displacement. Thus one characteristic will have to be emphasized at the expense of another, and major compromises or trade-offs must be made.

Design Parameters

Size

With the exception of highly specialized craft intended to win races or break records, the proper size for a solo or shorthanded offshore cruising boat should be

Hugo Vihlen in his tiny *April Fool*, one of two boats under six feet to cross the Atlantic. (Courtesy of Hugo S. Vihlen)

determined primarily by two considerations: 1) how much the owner can afford, and 2) how large a boat he or she can handle. Generally speaking, the larger the boat, the safer, faster, and more comfortable she is; so it makes sense, in my opinion, for the singlehander to get the biggest boat he can afford and can handle with ease.

Just how easy a boat is to manage depends on such factors as the size of her sails, how she is laid out and equipped in labor-saving gear, her maneuverability, auxiliary power, and hull draft. The skipper's age and physical condition are also considerations. Carleton Mitchell once said that he determined the *Finisterre*'s size by how large a headsail he could carry forward. Since those times labor-saving gear such as reliable and effective roller-furling jibs have greatly extended the size limitation for a boat sailed with a small crew. But it is well for the ocean-going singlehander to bear in mind that complicated equipment, especially that which is electrically operated, can break down in heavy weather at sea. So the boat should not be so large that her skipper cannot handle her easily with manual backup systems.

On the subject of ultimate seaworthiness and survival, many offshore sailors will tell you that a very small boat is just as safe or even safer than a much larger vessel in a storm at sea. Their arguments usually bring up the example of the fragile corked bottle which will survive the worst possible storm in open waters. While there is some truth in this reasoning, and a small boat has the greater proportional strength for a given construction material, there is little doubt that a cockleshell is more roughly handled by the elements over a broader range of conditions. Although glass bottles and perhaps even electric light bulbs are not broken by the waves, they are tumbled and rolled, and the cockleshell had best be prepared for the same kind of treatment. Furthermore, the midget seagoer will be violently treated much earlier than a larger craft when the weather deteriorates. Being adversely affected by the scaling laws, the small boat will be subject to a knockdown or roll-over sooner, and she must heave to earlier. Additionally, she will most likely have a difficult time beating away from a lee shore in a real blow.

On the other hand, a large vessel handled by one person can also have many problems in heavy weather. She is difficult to handle; her gear is heavy and can cause injuries; her weight and size detract from maneuverability and cause crew fatigue; her deep draft makes her more subject to accidental groundings. Thus it seems that the medium-sized cruiser has many more safety advantages, for she is easily handled yet able to cope with a wide range of adverse conditions offshore or along a hostile coast. And just what is medium size? Exact dimensions are, of course, impossible to set. For a lower limit we might suggest the approximate overall length of 25 feet, but John Guzzwell made a very successful circumnavigation and weathered some extremely bad weather in a boat just over 20 feet long, and obviously there are many seaworthy and unseaworthy boats in every size. The upper size limit is even more difficult to set, because it depends on the weight and design of the boat, the capabilities of the person handling her, the extent of her cruises, the character of the waters she will be sailing in, and her labor-saving gear.

The very smallest cockleshells are seldom chosen for offshore passagemaking because they are considered the safest craft for the job. They are nearly always chosen for economic reasons or for the purpose of breaking a record.

Displacement

The best weight for a singlehanded boat depends on how she will be used. When she is not used for racing or record setting, I tend to favor moderate displacement, as this allows a reasonable parameter for strength, ease of motion, and the ability to carry weight without excessively sacrificing speed and buoyancy. Weight carrying is important for a long-distance cruiser, even one sailed with a small crew, in order that she can take along ample fuel, water, and stores.

Weight is not necessarily a requirement for strength when modern materials are properly used, but the vessel should have an exterior skin sufficiently thick to resist abrasion from accidental groundings and collisions with sea life or flotsam. One should think in terms of hitting a floating container while sailing at high speed. A few years ago, I declined an invitation to crew aboard a new ULDB (ultralight displacement boat) in a Bermuda race. How lucky for me that I couldn't go, for the boat was stove in while crossing the Gulf Stream and quickly sank. Fortunately, all her crew were rescued after spending a most unpleasant time in a life raft.

To some extent, displacement depends on how much time the boat will be expected to sail upwind. As a general rule, light boats are easily managed and fly

Dodge Morgan's *American Promise*, light but not ultralight, was able to carry considerable water and supplies. (Courtesy of *Cruising World* magazine)

downwind, but against the wind they tend to pound and make slow progress. Some well-designed ultralights can sail to windward reasonably well, but their motion is hardly pleasant in a choppy sea. Hal Roth raved about his lightweight *American Flag*, but then he sailed the vast majority of the BOC race with the wind and seas astern. It should be pointed out that heavier boats are not necessarily slow downwind. Dodge Morgan set records with his *American Promise*, which was light but not ultralight, and without unduly affecting performance he was able to take ample supplies for a non-stop circumnavigation and carry enough water to take hot showers. On the other hand, an excessively heavy boat will more often be swept by seas, and she may need a large, less handy rig for sufficient power in light airs. For your average shorthanded offshore cruiser, it seems that extremes of displacement should be avoided. Some people may consider moderation a "copout," but it provides far more plaudits than debits.

Hull Form

A solo cruiser needs a hull form that offers maximum strength, seaworthiness, seakindliness, directional stability, maneuverability, weatherliness, and speed. The strongest hull shape for a given weight is one that is well rounded (observe the strength of an egg shell). Flat areas, particularly those forward where they receive the full brunt of the seas, should be curved or at least well braced when the boat is built of thin wood, fiberglass, or aluminum. The cabin house should be well rounded and have maximum crown commensurate with non-slip safety. Another important factor regarding strength is a lack of vulnerable appendages, such as fins, skegs, or rudders that could break off or crack surrounding hull areas and cause flooding. This is not meant to condemn modern designs that have fin keels, but a lot of thoughtful engineering should go into the support and strengthening of underwater appendages. An integral fin rather than one that is bolted on is usually stronger.

Seaworthiness and seakindliness are related, but there are differences in that the former has more to do with safety and the latter more with comfort. In my opinion, the most important requirement for the seaworthiness of an offshore solo monohull cruiser is a high range of stability (perhaps 130 degrees or more), because it may very well be necessary for the singlehander to lie ahull in heavy weather, and without sufficient reserve stability there is considerable danger of capsizing. A high range is obtained primarily with ample keel ballast, reasonably heavy displacement, and narrow to moderate beam. I favor moderate beam, because a narrow boat may sacrifice seakindliness by rolling rhythmically when sailing downwind and heeling excessively upwind.

After the disastrous Fastnet Race in 1979 when a gale caused about half the fleet of racers to be severely knocked down or to capsize, the danger of excessive beam combined with light displacement became painfully apparent. Recently, a simple rule-of-thumb, known as the Capsize Screening Formula, was developed by the United States Yacht Racing Union to serve as a rough guide in determining a boat's resistance to capsizing. Take the boat's beam in feet (and tenths of feet) and divide it by the cube root of her displacement in cubic feet (divide her weight in pounds by 64 to obtain cubic displacement). The result should be 2 or less for the boat to pass the screen.

Some features that enhance both seaworthiness and seakindliness are minimal overhangs to inhibit slamming, a reasonably fine entry to discourage hobbyhorsing, and sufficiently low ballast (and height of mast) for a favorable effect on the vessel's roll inertia. A feature I consider important to seaworthiness, even though many early voyaging boats did not have it, is weatherliness, because it may be particularly difficult for a singlehander to claw off a lee shore. He needs a reasonably deep keel (or centerboard) with ample lateral plane so that leeway can be minimized even when the keel is stalled. And incidentally, I like a swept forefoot with raked-back keel to lessen impact in the event of collisions with flotsam.

The importance of directional stability is obvious for a singlehander. Even with an excellent self-steering gear, there are times when it will not be used. Directional stability can be obtained with a long keel but at some sacrifice to maneuverability. A good compromise is a moderately long fin with prominent skeg and the rudder far aft. For a long-distance cruiser I like a fairly long fin, so that draft need not be excessive to prevent leeway and for easy hauling on a marine railway.

A vessel's course-keeping ability is also affected by the symmetry of her hull. Generally speaking the extremely wedge-shaped hull (fine forward and full aft) is a poor course keeper, because her helm changes at various angles of heel. The symmetrical hull better keeps the same helm at all heeling angles, but it is apt to hobby horse and fall short in performance before the wind. Here again a compromise is advisable, and consideration should be given to how much time the boat will be sailing off the wind. Designer/author/singlehander Steve Callahan (Chapter 2) wrote me that he now feels the afterbody of his *Napoleon Solo* was a little too fine and next time he would fill it out a bit. This would give her more power, particularly with a full crew, but on the other hand her symmetry (for a dinghy-type hull) provided good helm balance for singlehanding.

A few of the legendary singlehanders, Jean Gau for instance, were not at all interested in speed, but most sailors whether racers or not want a reasonably fast boat. They want to sail well in the company of others, and they don't want an offshore passage to take forever. The primary form requirements for a fast hull are maximum sailing length, minimum wetted surface area, fairness, power, and prismatic coefficient (designer's jargon for the degree of fullness at the ends). Power, or the ability to carry sail, is obtained both from beam and a high prismatic (full ends). Here again, a compromise is needed with beam to produce power without excessive head resistance or unduly compromising the stability range. Wetted surface can be lowered without trading off too much tracking ability by shortening the keel and using a kicker or long skeg with rudder far aft.

While on the subject of power, I might stray slightly from the specific subject of hull design to say a few words about water ballast, which is increasingly being used by singlehanders racing monohulls. A properly designed water ballast system in a hull with plenty of flare can produce tremendous power, and I think it makes sense for any long-distance shorthanded boat provided safety is not compromised. The risk of capsize is minimal if: the boat is given high reserve stability with ample keel ballast, water ballast is no more than that sufficient to give the boat a 10-degree heel, and the singlehander is conscientious about jettisoning his ballast before heavy weather to avoid the possibility of being caught with it on the wrong side. It seems safe to say that water ballast is here to stay so long as it is approved by the racing rules.

Another innovation that is being seen with increasing frequency is the use of twin rudders. In my view they should not be necessary unless the hull is extremely unbalanced with a very broad stern or unless the rudders are needed for "drying out" (used as props to hold the boat upright in areas of extreme tide). The main disadvantage of twin rudders is their added resistance in form drag and wetted surface. If the hull is reasonably balanced and the rudder axis properly raked, a single rudder should serve very well. Since the fetish for spade rudders in the 1960s, some of us have decried the practice of raking the axis so that the head of the rudder post is far forward of the heel. This practice causes unnecessary drag and the tendency for the rudder to stall easily when the boat is well heeled. At substantial heeling angles the rudder is acting more like an airplane's wing flap, pushing the stern upward. With a vertical axis or preferably one raked the opposite way, the rudder's force is more lateral when the boat is heeled. More will be said about special rudders and water ballast when specific boats are discussed later in the chapter.

Classic Types

Outstanding singlehanded voyages have been made in almost every kind of craft imaginable, yet there are a few favorite standard types. First of the circumnavigating vessels, of course, was the *Spray*, and she inspired many replicas. This is not surprising, because Joshua Slocum gave high praise to his vessel, and it is true that she had some good qualities for ocean cruising. Some of these are: an easy motion due to her heavy displacement, large volume and deck space for comfort, the ability to carry large quantities of stores with little harm to performance, and very good directional stability for self-steering. On the other hand, the old boat, which probably began her life as an oyster sloop in the early 1800s, had some shortcomings for singlehanded voyaging. She had gear of considerable size and weight for one man to handle; she was somewhat lacking in windward and light-air sailing abilities; and although she was exceedingly stiff, she had a relatively small range of stability as compared with the average modern monohull. Even her greatest contemporary champion, Kenneth E. Slack, who wrote the fine book, *In the Wake of the Spray*, admits that she was "slow, clumsy, and unhandy beside the modern yacht. . . . To sail such a craft amid congested harbors and steamer-ridden shores of these modern days requires a degree of skill far greater than the usual owner possesses. After all, there are few of us able to measure up to the standard of Captain Slocum."

Another popular early type was the *Sea Bird* yawl, a 25^1/$_2$-footer designed for *Rudder* magazine at the turn of the century. Several people had a hand in her design, including C. D. Mower, L. D. Huntington, and Thomas Fleming Day, the editor of the *Rudder*. As Day wrote in his magazine, "I am not a designer, but I claim to be the author of this craft." Many seamen felt that the *Sea Bird* was not the most suitable type for offshore work, because she had hard chines and flat bilges. For given scantlings, flat sections are not as strong as curved ones, and boats with hard bilges can pound under certain conditions, but, despite this characteristic, the *Sea Bird* proved a very satisfactory offshore boat. In 1911, Day, together with two companions, sailed her across the Atlantic from Rhode Island to Gibraltar and from there to Rome. One of the *Sea Bird*'s crew, Frederick B. Thurber, told me that she had two main faults, insufficient area of her lateral plane for windward ability, and a high, square cabin trunk that caused some anxiety, as it took a battering from the seas. Incidentally, Robin Knox-Johnston had a similar problem with his *Suhaili*'s slab-sided cabin house, which was damaged by boarding seas. The *Sea Bird*'s freeboard was quite low by today's standards, and Thurber said that she was swept several times, but Captain Day claimed the chines were helpful in keeping spray off the deck in a moderate chop.

One of the *Sea Bird*'s outstanding features was ease of construction due to her V bottom, which minimized bending frames and planks. Several of these boats

Figure 4-1. *Above* The Seagoer class *Islander* was a larger version of the famous *Sea Bird* type. This craft, under the command of Harry Pidgeon, sailed two and a half times around the world. (Photo courtesy of *Yachting* magazine) The plans *opposite* show her hard chines, low deadrise, and cutaway forefoot. (Courtesy of *Rudder* magazine, part of Fawcett Publications)

---

were homebuilt, and the most famous of them, Harry Pidgeon's yawl *Islander*, was sailed around the world 2¹/₂ times (two circumnavigations being made single-handed). Actually, Pidgeon's boat was a larger version, 34 feet long, known as the Seagoer class. The famous circumnavigator liked his *Islander* so well that after she was finally wrecked on a South Pacific island during her third voyage around the world, he built another but slightly smaller Sea Bird type. Another homebuilt boat of this type that was sailed around the world, for the most part singlehanded, is William Murnan's *Seven Seas II*. She was built of stainless steel and was very heavy when fully loaded. She was 30 feet long and, being a centerboarder, drew only 3 feet. Although she had very little freeboard, she weathered much heavy weather and often rode with a tire drogue over her stern (see Chapter 10). Both Murnan and Pidgeon claimed their boats would run off very well in heavy weather, although they would sometimes take water over the stern.

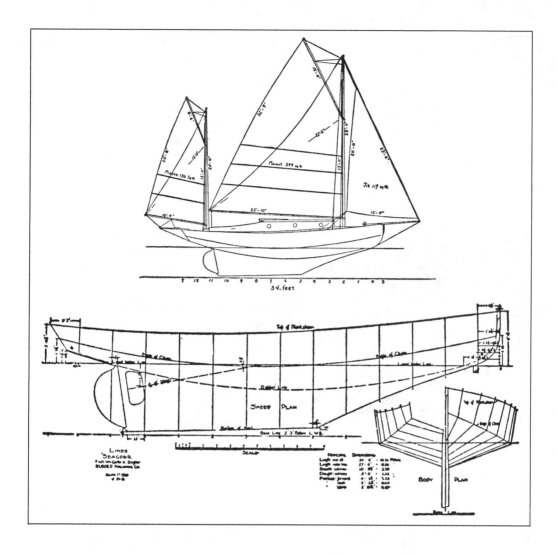

At one time during his voyaging Harry Pidgeon met up with Alain Gerbault in his *Firecrest*. The two circumnavigators inspected each other's vessels, and each admitted definite preference for his own. The *Firecrest*, an English racing cutter quite typical of the early 1900s, was an interesting contrast to the *Islander*. The 39-foot cutter, designed by Dixon Kemp, was narrow and deep with a plumb stem, prominent forefoot, and a long, overhanging counter. She was weatherly, could quite easily be hove to in heavy weather, and, although she had a strong weather helm when heeled, was fairly steady on her helm in consistent winds; yet she had some disadvantages for offshore singlehanding. Among her faults were initial tenderness that caused her to "sail on her ear" when it blew and a tendency to bury her bow and hollow entrance. Furthermore, she would sometimes tend to gripe when running before heavy seas; and her long bowsprit was not conducive to maximum safety when it was necessary to work forward.

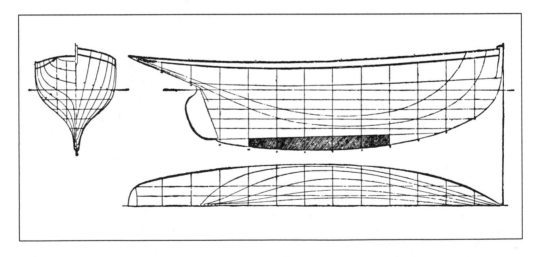

Figure 4-2. The photo shows Alain Gerbault's famous cutter *Firecrest* in Le Havre, France, after her circumnavigation. (Courtesy of *Yachting* magazine). The plans of *Firecrest*, which was designed by Dixon Kemp, show her narrow, deep hull with plumb bow and overhanging stern, typical of the "plank on edge" English cutter type. She was 39 feet long overall, and had a beam of only 8 ¹/₂ feet. (Hawthorn Books, Inc.)

Other favorite vessels for offshore singlehanding include the double-enders. These vary from the heavy, full-ended Norwegian sailing lifeboats (Redningskoites) designed by Colin Archer, to the somewhat more fine-ended, canoe-stern types. An example of the latter was Edward Allcard's 34-foot yawl, *Temptress*. Famous Colin Archer types sailed singlehanded around the world are Al Peterson's 33-foot, gaff-rigged cutter, *Stornoway*, and Frank Casper's 30-foot, Marconi-rigged cutter, *Elsie*. And let's not forget Al Hansen's gaff-rigged *Mary Jane*, probably the first boat to be sailed by one man around Cape Horn from east to west (unfortunately she was later wrecked on the coast of Chile). Other craft that have circumnavigated singlehanded, which are quite similar to Colin Archer designs, are J. Y. Le Toumelin's 33-foot cutter, *Kurun*; Vito Dumas' 31-foot ketch, *Lehg II*; and Robin Knox-Johnston's 32¹/₂-foot ketch, *Suhaili*. The latter is said to be one of the William Atkin Eric designs based on the Colin Archer type. Other famous heavy-displacement double-enders with generous beam and long, shallow keels are the Carol and Tahiti cruisers designed by John G. Hanna. The most famous of these used for solo voyaging is Jean Gau's 30-foot ketch, *Atom*, which was sailed twice around the world and about a dozen times across the Atlantic.

Some offshore sailors feel that the pointed stern is the safest type for running off before following seas, because there is no flat surface for an overtaking wave to strike when it comes from dead astern. The majority of designers today, however, seem to think that almost any kind of stern can be seaworthy if it is properly shaped. Overhang should not be excessive, and if the stern is a counter type, it should not be excessively flat, or it may pound. A vital feature of a proper stern is its buoyancy. An overly buoyant stern combined with a fine bow and deep forefoot may lead to broaching to or even pitch-poling in steep following seas, while a stern

Figure 4-3. The Tahiti ketch, designed by John G. Hanna, captured the imagination of a generation of home builders. (Taken from *A Ketch Called Tahiti*, by John Steven Doherty)

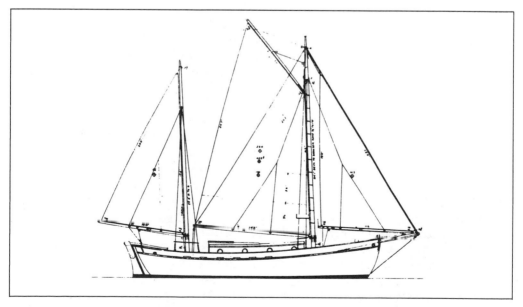

that lacks buoyancy may fail to damp pitching, or it may squat and be pooped by an overtaking wave. It is especially important that a double-ender be fairly full aft, because there is normally less volume in a pointed stern than in a counter or transom stern. Edward Allcard was pooped in his *Temptress* even though she had more volume in her stern than some double-enders, such as the Tumlare type. One advantage of either a pointed stern (but not an extreme canoe stern) or a transom type is the allowance of an outboard rudder, which is a good feature on a deep-sea boat, because it permits some accessibility for inspection and repairs, and a rudder trim tab is easily attached for self-steering.

The heavy-displacement, double-ended type has a good reputation as a sea boat, but perhaps this is due primarily to its unusually robust construction and seakindliness. Disadvantages of the design are mediocre sailing ability, especially in light airs and to windward, lack of maneuverability in crowded waters, although the hull is usually quite well balanced for self-steering, and a less-than-desirable range of stability as compared to the typical modern yacht. Several of the double-enders have turned turtle, including *Atom* (see Chapter 10) and *Lehg II*. Granted, they were in extreme conditions that could have capsized any other craft of similar size, but where safety in ultimate storms is concerned, the higher the range of stability the better. A more recent healthy development is the production of classic double-ended designs in fiberglass, which allows very strong construction but with a saving in hull weight that can be consigned to extra keel ballast. Four such designs are the Westsail 32, produced in California; a 40-footer produced by the Colin Archer Club of Stockholm, Sweden; the Saga 34 of Norfolk, England; and the Hans Christian line.

Two other designs for singlehanding that might be considered classics are the Folkboat and Vertue classes. Both these boats are slightly over 25 feet long with a moderate beam of little more than 7 feet, transom sterns with outboard rudders, and moderately long keels. The Vertue is heavier, intended as a sea boat, but the Folkboat has repeatedly proven herself offshore and might be considered the smarter boat on most points of sailing. She has considerable aft rake to her rudder, which results in less lateral plane and less wetted surface. There was a time when some sailors thought this feature was detrimental to self-steering, but this thinking is not so much in evidence today. As I intimated earlier, a considerable rake aft often causes the rudder to operate more efficiently when the boat is heeled or rolling, at which times the resultant of force components working on the rudder is acting in a more lateral and thus more effective direction. It is also true that gravity tends to keep such a rudder amidships when the boat is unheeled. The really important concern with regard to self-steering is the directional stability of the hull, which is generally achieved through a reasonably symmetrical shape with somewhat balanced ends and an ample, but not necessarily extreme, length of keel, or at least a long skeg aft. Vertues and Folkboats have good directional stability, and in addition their rounded underbodies with slackish bilges and short ends make them comfortable sea boats for their size.

The Vertue was designed by J. Laurent Giles shortly after World War II and was closely based on his design of the gaff-rigged cutter *Andrillot* of 1936. Many of this class have made celebrated passages. Among those sailed singlehanded are *Salmo* and *Speedwell of Hong Kong*, skippered respectively by A.G. Hamilton and John Goodwin; David Robertson's *Easy Vertue*; Dr. Joseph Cunningham's *Icebird*;

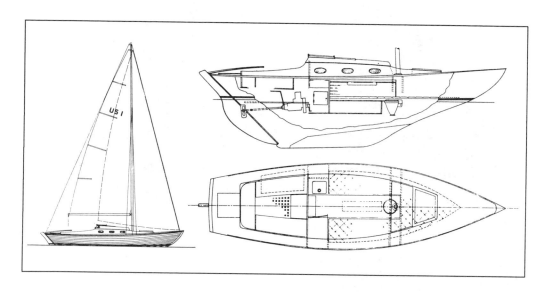

Figure 4-4. The handsome Folkboat, which has made so many offshore passages. Her dimensions are: LOA, 25 feet, 2 inches; LWL, 19 feet, 8 inches; beam, 7 feet, 3 inches; draft, 3 feet, 11 inches; displacement, 2.15 tons; sail area, 262 square feet. (Courtesy of *The Skipper*)

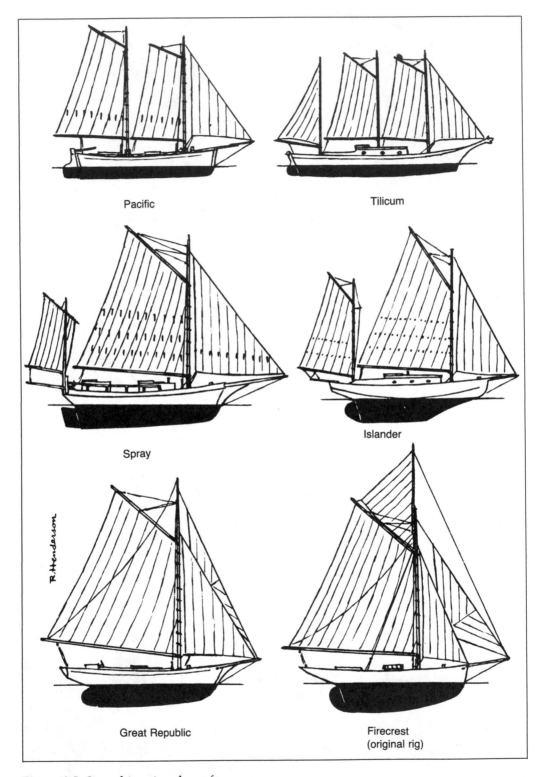

Figure 4-5. Some historic solo craft.

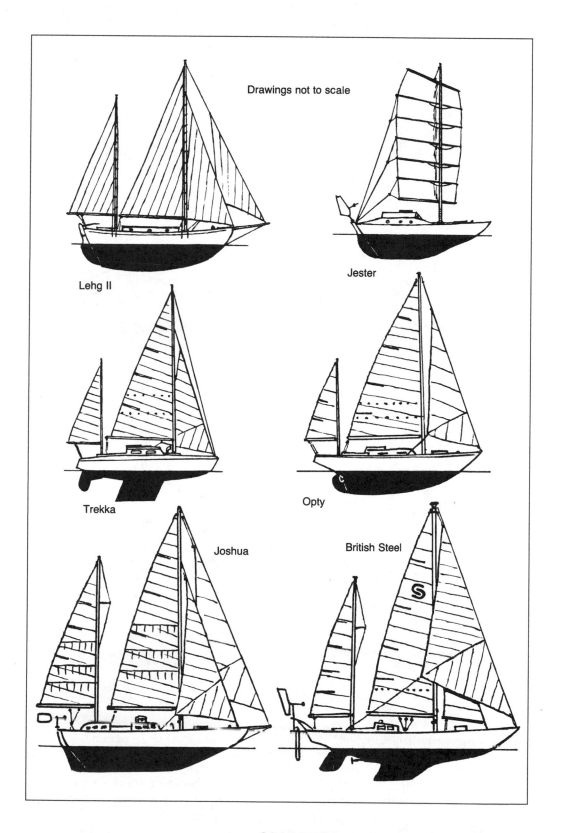

Drawings not to scale

Lehg II

Jester

Trekka

Opty

Joshua

British Steel

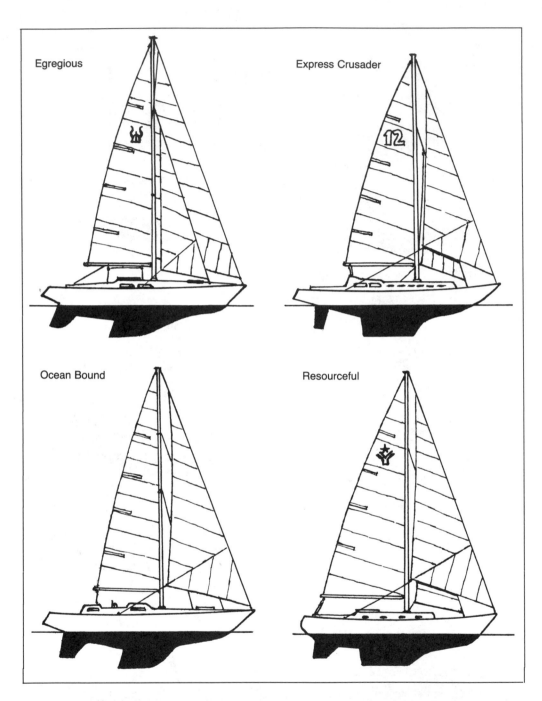

Egregious

Express Crusader

Ocean Bound

Resourceful

and Ed Boden's *Kittiwake* which recently completed a circumnavigation. But the most famous of all is *Cardinal Vertue,* described in Chapter 1, which was twice sailed across the Atlantic in 1960 and later taken around the world via the Roaring Forties and Cape Horn by Australian Bill Nance. A wealth of detail about this class is given in Humphrey Barton's book *Vertue XXXV,* which tells the story of his doublehanded Atlantic crossing and heavy weather experiences in *Vertue XXXV* during the spring of 1950. Barton, who was a yacht surveyor, former partner of Laurent Giles, and founder of the Ocean Cruising Club, suggests several ways of improving the standard boat for rugged offshore work. These modifications include a stronger doghouse and smaller unbreakable windows. The book shows plans of a Vertue intended for extended ocean cruising. She has slightly more freeboard than the standard boat, a lower, longer cabin trunk, and small round portholes rather than windows.

The Folkboat was the result of a Swedish design competition held in the early 1940s. The original concept had a long, overhanging stern, but later it was chopped off a bit to make a more seaworthy raking transom stern. Tord Sunden was responsible for the final design. Famous boats of this class include Valentine Howell's *Eira*, Adrian Hayter's *Valkyr*, Ann Gash's *Stella Ilimo*, and Mike Bale's *Jellicle*, which was sailed from England to New Zealand mostly singlehanded, and of course, Hasler's highly modified *Jester*.

On *Jester*, Hasler carried the central-control-point concept, developed by Marin-Marie, to a new level of efficiency and in this respect his boat (which recently completed her seventh solo transatlantic passage) might be considered a real breakthrough in ease of handling and protection for a solo crew. *Jester* is a standard Scandinavian Folkboat below the water, but from the waterline up she is not quite like any yacht that preceded her. She is flush-decked, without a cockpit well, and with a kind of turtle-backed cabin trunk. The central control point is a circular hatch fitted with a folding pram hood, and from this position the boat can be steered and completely handled. Her one sail can be hoisted, trimmed, reefed or unreefed, and handed without ever the need of leaving the hatchway. From 1952 to 1959, she carried what Hasler called a "lapwing rig," but she was converted to a Chinese lug rig for the 1960 OSTAR. (These rigs and others will be discussed in Chapter 5.)

Jester's crew can operate the boat from either a high standing position in the control hatchway, which allows the upper torso and arms to be above deck, or a seated or low standing position, which allows the head only to be above deck. Lines for the sail adjustments are handled from the high position. The pram hood (similar to that on a baby carriage) is mounted on a rotatable ring around the edge of the circular hatchway, and the raised hood can be turned in any direction to give maximum protection or visibility. Normally, of course, it would be turned to windward in rough weather. Steering can be done with either steering lines or a whip-staff which works athwartships. A vane gear steers the boat most of the time on passages, and its control lines can also be handled from the hatchway.

Two large access hatches are on either side of the cabin trunk, but these are normally closed when underway. There is also a hatch in the foredeck, which is opened only in calm weather or when moored. Additional ventilation is supplied by 10 small opening ports. The main accommodations, consisting of bunks, galley, and head, are located in the after half of the hull. This makes good sense when there is no cockpit well to restrict space below, because there is far less motion from pitching abaft amidships. The hull's forward half is used mostly for stowage.

Molded Stock Boats

Although many stock production boats make good singlehanders with a bit of modification, the most extreme ocean racers, designed for maximum advantage of a handicap rule such as the IOR (International Offshore Rule) are not always ideal. The basic reasons for this are that such boats are designed for speed with a full crew, and quite often the hull is distorted or wrapped around measurement points that yield the best possible rating at the expense of optimal overall performance. Quite often the most extreme racers lack directional stability, seakindliness, sufficient buoyancy forward, an adequate keel sump for bilge water, and a decent range of stability. Moreover, standard racing rigs are seldom set up for easy handling by one person.

Despite this general indictment of certain IOR-type boats for offshore singlehanding, there are some notable exceptions. One boat that comes quickly to mind is the Ericson 37 *Egregious* sailed around the world via Cape Horn in record time by Webb Chiles (Chapter 2). Disregarding the leak that almost sank her, Chiles' "beautiful bitch" was a sweet sailing boat, fast, manageable and with some healthy features such as a swept-back forefoot to lessen impact in the event of a collision with flotsam.

An even more wholesome IOR boat was *Ocean Bound*, the Sparkman and Stephens-designed Huisman 41, which completed two opposite direction circumnavigations under the able hand of David Scott Cowper. This boat was a direct descendent of Prime Minister Edward Heath's *Morning Cloud*, which had such a fine racing record in British waters. A smaller cousin is *Perie Banon*, the S & S 34 that Jonathan Sanders sailed twice around the world non-stop.

Another 34-foot IOR champion that proved a successful solo ocean crosser was the Aloa class sloop designed by J.M. L'Hermenier. Two Aloas, one sailed by a woman, Marie-Claude Fauroux, and the other by a 62-year-old man, Yves Olivaux, made good showings in the 1972 OSTAR and had few problems, even though Olivaux was handicapped with an injured arm.

It should be said that the above-mentioned models were early IOR boats and were not as extreme as some of the newer designs. These earlier models generally have more weight, longer keels, more balanced hulls, rudders attached to skegs, and smaller, less complicated rigs, all of which contribute to ease of handling by a shorthanded crew.

The majority of successful stock boats with proven records were not designed to the IOR or any other rating rule. Some that have made outstanding singlehanded or shorthanded passages are the Valiant 40, Ohlson 38, Contessa 32, Seawind, Ericson 30, Arpege, Vega, Alberg Triton, and Catalina 27. Even smaller stock boats such as Tania Aebi's J. J. Taylor 26 and the 15-foot West Wight Potter have crossed oceans, but for a reasonable margin of safety and comfort, I wouldn't want a boat much smaller than the Triton or Catalina 27. Some brief comments on the boats listed above might be of interest to those looking for a well-proven, reasonably priced, and, for the most part, readily available cruiser for shorthanded passage making.

The Valiant 40 is a modern double-ender with a contemporary but conservative underbody and a distinctive canoe stern. Designed in 1974 by Robert Perry, this 40-foot cutter has made numerous voyages and is now considered a bluewater classic. The well-known singlehander Dan Byrne sailed his *Fantasy*, the first-built Valiant, solo around the world in the first BOC Challenge. Another solo circumnavigating Valiant was *Resourceful*, sailed by Mark Schrader, who became the first American to sail around the world below the five southern capes. Some of the

An early, more balanced IOR design, *Aloa VII,* was sailed by Marie-Claude Fauroux and Yves Oliveaux in the 1972 OSTAR. (Photo by Karina Paape)

Valiant's attractive features for offshore singlehanding are good directional stability, due in part to her long fin keel and prominent skeg, a buoyant, pointed stern for effectively running before high seas, ample sheer and freeboard for dryness, small ports for safety in heavy weather, and the cutter rig with large inner staysail allowing good performance with the jib lowered or roller-furled. About the only caveat is that the Valiant 40s were built of fiberglass using a fire retardant resin, and I have heard of some boats (not all) with serious blistering; thus a condition survey is certainly in order before purchasing this or any used boat. In 1980 designer Robert Perry wrote me: "The Valiant remains my personal favorite design, and I have to admit to being rather emotionally involved with the whole project. I have sailed the Valiant under every conceivable condition including survival conditions and I continue to use the Valiant as the benchmark in evaluating my newer designs."

The Ohlson 38 is an amazingly versatile boat with speed, seaworthiness, maneuverability, and traditional good looks. I have owned one of these boats for 15 years and so can speak from firsthand experience. Clare Francis demonstrated the boat's handiness, seaworthiness, and speed in the 1976 OSTAR, when she weathered several gales and yet established a speed record for women singlehanders in her *Robertson's Golly.* Presently the O-38 *Toucan* is being sailed around the world singlehanded by American Keith Sedwick. Designed by the great Swedish designer Einar Ohlson in 1967, the O-38, which is really a small 37-footer, was molded to Lloyd's specifications by the Tyler Boat Company of England. Of moderate dis-

The Valiant 40 *Mooneshine* being singlehanded by Francis Stokes. She is well balanced under reefed main and forestaysail. (Photo by Brian Harrison)

placement, she is built of solid (non-cored) fiberglass but with 14 full-length, foam-filled fiberglass stringers to stiffen the hull. Advantages of this boat for shorthanded offshore sailing are: a good stability range (134 degrees) for reasonable safety when lying ahull, a large foretriangle so that an inner staysail can be rigged when going to sea, a well-balanced hull with small, skeg-hung rudder providing an easy helm, a swept forefoot for collision resistance, and phenomenal upwind abilities for a cruiser. About the only possible disadvantage I can think of is that the boat heels fairly easily up to about 15 or 20 degrees, but then she stiffens tremendously and it takes a real blow to submerge her rail. My cousin put it best when he described our *Kelpie* as being the "sweetest" boat he had ever sailed.

The Contessa 32, designed by British naval architect David Sadler in 1969, is also built to Lloyd's standards, and she too is an extremely versatile boat. She is fast, weatherly, maneuverable, well balanced, and has an exceptionally high stability range. Calculations have shown that she will heel to 157 degrees before capsizing. Testimonials to the Contessa 32's seaworthiness include a solo circum-

Exceptionally seaworthy, the Contessa 32, designed by David Sadler, was the only boat of her class to complete the disastrous Fastnet race of 1979.

navigation, a doublehanded rounding of Cape Horn against the wind, and finishing the disastrous 1979 Fastnet Race when a Force 10 gale caused every other competitor in her class of 58 boats to drop out. The Horn-rounding *Gigi* once suffered a 150 degree knockdown, but she promptly righted and kept her rig intact. Wholesome features include a swept forefoot, moderately long integral fin keel, prominent skeg reaching the rudder's heel, ballast-displacement ratio of 45 percent, moderate beam, and a fairly short sloop rig that can be converted to a cutter. The Contessa 32 was used as the benchmark boat for an investigation of the Fastnet disaster by the Royal Yachting Association.

The Seawind, a 30-foot ketch designed by Annapolitan Tom Gilmer in 1961, is said to be the first fiberglass boat to circumnavigate the world. This voyage took place in 1963–68 when Alan Eddy made an east-to-west rounding via the Panama Canal in his *Apogee*. A traditional boat with full keel and outboard rudder hung on a transom stern, the Seawind is a wholesome, conservative type. Although not a racer, she is capable of good sailing performance and very respectable passage times. *Apogee* once averaged 160 miles per day for eight consecutive days. Some good features for shorthanded cruising are good directional stability due in part to her long keel, swept forefoot, pronounced sheer for dryness at the ends, moderate displacement for an easy motion, modest draft and keel configuration that allows easy hauling, and a handy rig that allows versatile sail combinations in heavy weather. She is also heavily constructed, and *Apogee* once withstood an aggressive attack by a school of pilot whales (see Chapter 11). On the negative side, a self-steering vane may be hard to rig because of the mizzen boom, and her upwind performance is slightly inferior by modern standards. Still, she has very many more good than bad qualities.

An entirely different 30-footer is the French-built Arpege, designed by Michel Dufour in 1967. These boats still are seen cruising everywhere. One notable single-handed voyage was a passage across the Pacific, a non-stop distance of 5,600 miles, by Jean-Yves Terlain in *Blue Arpege* during the 1969 solo transpacific race. The Arpege is well built, but she is much lighter than the Seawind, and she is a faster boat considering all points of sailing. Her pretty hull is fitted with a bulbed fin keel and deep rudder on a very narrow skeg. Advantages of the design for solo work offshore are: a very well-balanced hull, ease of rigging a steering vane, fairly light displacement that allows use of a small rig, excellent windward ability, and accommodations that allow a chart table aft and berths that are near the pitching axis. Disadvantages are a rather vulnerable skeg and nearly vertical keel plus a stern that may be somewhat lacking buoyancy and power.

Still another 30-footer that might in some respects be considered a compromise between the Seawind and Arpege is the Ericson 30. Like the Seawind, the Ericson has a fairly buoyant stern, and the early model has an outboard rudder. As with the Arpege, the Ericson has a fin keel, but its leading edge has considerably more rake. The newer model, called the 30+, has an optional triangular-shaped deep fin for optimal windward performance, but the shoal draft version with longer keel bottom is better for cruising and hauling out on a marine railway. Designed in the early days of the IOR by Bruce King, the Ericson 30 makes few concessions to the rule. These boats have proven to be very successful passagemakers, with circumnavigations by Richard B. Sweat in *My Honey* and Andrew Urbanczyk in *Nord IV*, a 30+. Some of the Ericson's good qualities include excellent performance with good windward ability, reasonably high freeboard for dryness, ease of attaching self-steering vanes, and a very buoyant hull. The rigs are generous for good light air performance, but perhaps a bit too generous for offshore work. Urbanczyk shortened his mast by six feet, while Sweat added 1,200 pounds of ballast to *My Honey*. Both rigs were beefed up also—a wise precaution on most stock boats that will be sailed extensively offshore.

As are most boats designed by Carl Alberg, the Triton has always been a favorite of mine. At 28 feet, she is a bit small and her freeboard on the low side for a 'round-the-world voyage, but James Baldwin successfully circumnavigated alone in his *Atom*, which was named after Jean Gau's famous Tahiti ketch. Designed in 1958, the Triton was one of the first stock racing cruisers to be built of fiberglass, and like many of the early boats made of the material she was heavily constructed. It is also interesting that the early boats rarely suffer from the osmotic blistering that has plagued many modern craft of almost every make. The Triton has a conventional underbody with a full keel, rudder attached to the keel, and a swept forefoot. She has a well-balanced, stable hull, and sails to windward very well. Her three-quarter rig allows easy handling by a singlehander. Among her few disadvantages are a rather low stern, a high doghouse that blocks visibility from the helm, and a cockpit well that needs modification for watertightness. Jim Baldwin inserted slides in his cockpit to make it watertight and reduce its volume.

Another small boat with an outstanding offshore record is the 27-foot Vega, a Swedish sloop designed by Per Brohall in 1964. Thousands of these craft are sailing all over the world. Probably the best known Vega voyage was made by John Neal, who wrote a fairly popular book about his adventures called *Log of the Mahina*. Lesser-known voyages include a mostly solo circumnavigation by Dima Grinups in his *Sandra II*, and a very fast doublehanded Atlantic crossing by *Little My III*. The latter sailed from the Cape Verde Islands to Barbados in 14 days, 16 hours, which is remarkable time for such a small boat. She reportedly surfed in the trade winds at speeds up to 13 knots, yet was dry, comfortable, and easily managed. Her excellent downwind behavior might be attributed to her well-balanced hull with flattish run, modest displacement, and moderately long full keel. Despite her rather shoal draft, the Vega's windward performance is adequate for a cruising boat. She is well built, and great attention is given to details. One flaw in both the Vega and Triton is the deck-stepped mast with inadequate support underneath. Both Baldwin and Neal had to beef up the under-deck mast-supporting structure. The Vega is fairly narrow and therefore a trifle tender initially, but she's quite stiff at moderate angles of heel.

Frankly, the Catalina 27 would not be my choice for extended offshore work, but Patrick Childress made a 2½-year solo circumnavigation in his *Juggernaut* with very few problems. I am including the boat here because it is quite easy to singlehand, is readily available, and offers more boat for the money than almost any other I know. Designed by Frank Butler in 1970, the Catalina 27 is an inexpensive craft but one that is attractive looking and sails very well. Advantages for coastal singlehanding are a buoyant hull with moderately high freeboard, a fairly long fin keel, swept forefoot, good hull balance, maneuverability, and a simple rig. Disadvantages include light construction, an accommodations arrangement that is best for harbor living, and a raked spade rudder that makes the helm a bit too quick for singlehanding. The boat can be beefed up and modified, of course, and the first thing I would do is to replace the cast aluminum spreader sockets with those made of stainless steel.

Monohull Racers

The primary requirement for a solo racing boat is length, because a heavy, non-planing hull can rarely be driven faster than 1.35 times the square root of its sailing waterline length. Thus, in a fresh breeze, the longest boat should be the fastest. Not until after 1976 was there a size limitation on OSTAR racers, so prior to then the question of a boat's size boiled down to how large a boat one man could handle.

Determination of the largest size has usually been derived from an estimate of the largest sail a man can handle. In the early 1930s, the British designer-sailor Uffa Fox wrote that one man "could reef or stow a 500-square-foot mainsail in all weathers but not a larger sail." After completing the 1960 OSTAR, Francis Chichester decided that his mainsail of 380 square feet and genoa of the same size was more than he could manage in heavy weather. It is interesting that today this hypothetical limit has grown considerably higher, for Jean-Yves Terlain, skipper of

It is astonishing that one man could handle the enormous *Vendredi 13* let alone the 236-foot *Club Med.* (Courtesy of *Yachting* magazine)

the 128-foot *Vendredi 13,* handled working staysails of 930 square feet, and after the race he reckoned that he could have managed more. Leslie Williams, who did well in the 1968 singlehanded race, wrote that he thought he could conveniently handle a sail up to about 1,200 square feet in light winds. Maximum sail size was pushed up to over 2,000 square feet when Alain Colas sailed his mammoth *Club Mediterranee* in the 1976 OSTAR.

With a sail size limitation, the way to get the longest hull with the most sail area is obviously with a multi-mast arrangement, each mast carrying sails of maximum size according to a predetermined limitation. *Vendredi 13* was rigged with three boomed staysails of 930 square feet each on three masts of equal height, while *Club Med,* which was inspired by *Vendredi 13,* was given four similar masts, each having mast-attached sails of 1,035 square feet and staysails up to 2,205 square feet. A major reason for *Club Med*'s extreme length was to put sufficient space between her masts to minimize backwind and blanketing of the sails on each mast by those on adjacent masts. The arrangement might be compared to four sloops sailing in tandem, one behind the other. On *Vendredi 13* the attempt was made to reduce sail interference by having a single sail on each mast and attaching their luffs to stays only in order to obviate the air flow disturbance problem associated with mast-attached luffs.

Despite the limited success of the monster boats in solo transatlantic racing, the concept has definite drawbacks. These are lack of maneuverability, expense, low speed in light airs, unsuitability for normal use after the race, and general unhandiness. Furthermore, having a 250-ton steel hull such as *Club Med*'s travelling at 12 knots or so, much of the time unmanned while her master sleeps, can present a very real menace to navigation. This is one of the main reasons why a size limitation of 56 feet was put into effect before the 1980 OSTAR. (It was extended to 60 feet for the 1984 race.)

As for the slow speed of monster boats in light airs, the problem is that when there is little wind, speed primarily depends on the ratio of sail area to wetted surface. Although wave making is the main form of resistance when the boat is moving fast and her sail area/displacement ratio is a critical factor in a breeze, the surface area of her hull is what really slows her down in light weather. The wetted surface of the monster solo boats is enormous, yet sail areas are relatively small. Dick Carter, designer of *Vendredi 13*, expressed the fear that when there was little wind his creation would be "glued to water." In an effort to shorten the keel for less wetted surface (and to lower the center of gravity) Michel Bigoin, the designer of *Club Med*, specified keel ballast of spent uranium 238, a material with much higher density than lead.

Another difficult aspect of an extremely long boat is her construction. Her hull has to be kept reasonably light yet strong, rigid to prevent panting, and stiff to resist longitudinal flexing. Of course, expense is also an important consideration. The hoped for solution in the case of *Vendredi 13* was foam-core fiberglass sandwich construction, but the hull turned out to be a bit heavier and more flexible than expected. In fact, there were some rather alarming reports (perhaps exaggerated) about *Vendredi 13*'s hull whipping to such an extent that it once acted like a springboard, catapulting her skipper upward, knocking his head against the overhead. Fortunately, he was wearing a crash helmet.

The hull flexibility problem was solved with *Club Med* by building her of steel. Although this material is heavy for a racer, steel becomes progressively more weight-acceptable the larger the size. The 236-footer was built in 16 separate sections which were then welded together. Because she was assembled upside down, it was necessary to launch her that way and then roll her right side up in the water.

A lot of preplanning went into the creation of *Club Med*. She was designed on the computer using math formulas to derive her shape. Scale models of her hull were then tank tested in rough as well as smooth water, and her rig was developed after extensive wind tunnel testing. To simplify handling, she was loaded with alarms, sensors, computers, and other gadgetry. There were even TV cameras at the base of each mast so that skipper Colas could monitor the sails from his central control station, where he had 24 winches assembled to adjust the running rigging. Colas admitted to being a "slave of technology." Some of his equipment, however, such as the SatNav and radar, was sealed before the start of the 1976 OSTAR, as it was banned by the rules at that time. The problem with electronic gadgets is that they can fail all too easily in a wet environment. For the race, electricity was generated with solar panels, wind generators, and a free-wheeling variable-pitch propeller. *Club Med*'s electrical equipment was quite well protected and caused few serious problems, but ironically, a simple mechanical flaw that was not detected in trials led to her downfall (actually, the downfall of her sails). Her Achilles heel was a sheave-lead arrangement at the mastheads that caused severe chafe when the masts moved in a seaway. Colas suffered the ultimate frustration of having 20 halyards part.

Aside from resorting to super size, there is another direction the designer can take to achieve unusual speed. He can make the boat super-light and fairly flat-bottomed so that she will partially plane or, to some extent, seem to lift up and skim over the water's surface rather than plow through it. With this approach, the boat can often partially escape from her restricting wave system, and then speed is not quite as dependent on length. Semi-planing types include multihulls and some canoelike monohulls of very light weight with ballasted fins.

This concept of achieving super speed—by drafting a very light, narrow monohull—has also been tried several times for solo ocean racing. A good example of this type, which has a canoelike hull with a small but deep fin keel, is the Michael Pipe-designed *Strongbow*, sailed by Martin Minter-Kemp in the 1972 OSTAR (see accompanying plans of *Strongbow*). She combines light displacement with long sailing length and a reasonably high sail-area-to-wetted-surface ratio, while offering the advantage of high resistance to capsizing. In the words of designer-author Douglas Phillips-Birt, she is "a highly specialized but basically healthy type of yacht." Although she did not finish better than seventh in the race, which is by no means bad for a boat of moderate size, she was hampered by the lack of adequate trials and time for tuning. At any rate, she has a great potential for speed, and indeed was said to have been clocked at over 20 knots on one occasion. Her speed is due not only to her length, 65 feet overall, and her light hull, whose depth (excluding keel) is a mere $1^1/_2$ feet, but also to her narrow beam, which is only 10 feet, 5 inches. Windward performance is enhanced by a very deep, narrow keel tipped with a streamlined bulb of ballast weighing 5 tons. Minter-Kemp praised the boat for her maneuvering ability, quickness in stays, stiffness, and seakindliness, although she did pound under certain conditions. Such a design demands a very high strength-to-weight ratio, and *Strongbow* achieved this with cold-molded plywood construction consisting of five laminations, some of which were laid diagonally. In addition, she was built with a steel structure nearly amidships which supported and connected the mast, keel, and shrouds. Nevertheless, it was reported that she broke a stringer, loosened a bulkhead, and took in water around her keel bolts. Such a hull can be under very considerable strain, especially at each end during heavy weather when moving at high speeds. Minter-Kemp described the motion of his boat as being "like driving a fast car on bad roads."

A somewhat similar but more extreme example of the light-displacement canoe type is *Sea Gar*, shown in Figure 4-7. This boat was never built, but she was designed by Frank R. MacLear before 1960 to compete in the singlehanded transatlantic race. She anticipated some of the modern developments with respect to solo racing despite the fact that she is based on an ancient craft, the gaumier, or Carib Indian dugout canoe.

The *Sea Gar*'s dimensions are length on deck, 60 feet; length on the water line, 47 feet; beam at the deck, 8 feet; and draft, 12 feet. Her extremely narrow beam, only 6 feet at the waterline, will allow great speed to windward in steep seas, provided she is stiff enough to stand up to her modest sail area. Stability with little outside ballast (2,000 pounds) is derived from the leverage of her extremely deep

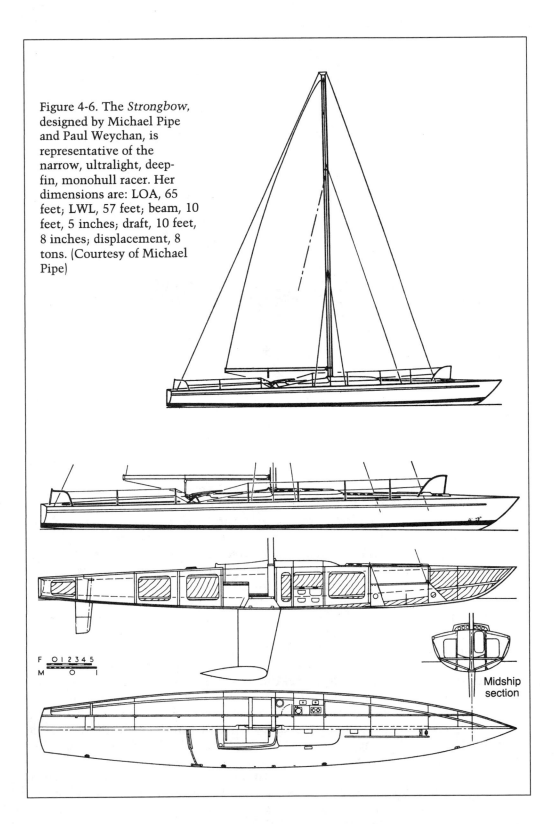

Figure 4-6. The *Strongbow*, designed by Michael Pipe and Paul Weychan, is representative of the narrow, ultralight, deep-fin, monohull racer. Her dimensions are: LOA, 65 feet; LWL, 57 feet; beam, 10 feet, 5 inches; draft, 10 feet, 8 inches; displacement, 8 tons. (Courtesy of Michael Pipe)

Midship section

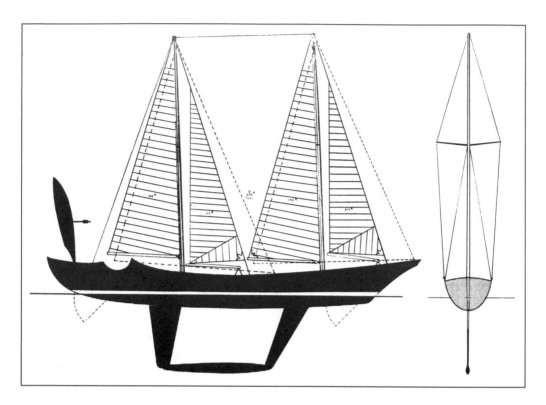

Figure 4-7. The *Sea Gar*, designed by Frank MacLear, is a more extreme example of the light displacement canoe type.

keels. As can be seen in Figure 4-7, the keels are two high-aspect-ratio tandem fins joined at the bottom by a streamlined bulb of ballast. This keel concept has also been suggested by the hydrodynamicist and publisher for the Amateur Yacht Research Society, John Morwood, and it anticipated recent experiments with similar configurations on America's cup racers. Such fins minimize wetted surface while providing high lift, and if the connecting ballast is properly shaped, it will mitigate "end losses" at the after fin, according to Morwood. In order to enhance stability during long tacks at sea, movable ballast in the form of sand bags would be placed on racks on the windward side, and as a safeguard against being caught aback with the bags to leeward, they are rigged to slide overboard during an unlikely knockdown to windward.

For self-steering, *Sea Gar* would have a wind vane gear, but, in addition, she would have tandem centerboards, one at the bow and the other at the stern, which could be trimmed for nearly perfect balance on any point of sailing. Her two-masted rig would also contribute to balance flexibility. Should the boat develop a weather helm, corrections could be made by trimming in the forward sails while easing off the after sails and/or raising the forward board while lowering the after one. This system allows almost infinite variations of trim.

As for sailing performance, MacLear estimates that *Sea Gar* might be driven to windward at 10 knots, reach at 14 knots, and surf before high seas and strong winds at 20 knots. He estimates that the maximum speed-length ratio (speed divided by the square root of waterline length) for this type of boat should range between 2.2 and 3.5. The obvious disadvantages of such a design concept are the extreme draft, which limits the boat to fairly deep harbors, and the restriction on accommodations and side deck space due to the narrow beam. Furthermore, she might be initially tender, and of course, with any boat requiring shifting solid ballast, there may be some risk in getting caught with the weight on the wrong side. Even if that risk is minimized with an automatic jettison plan such as that envisioned for *Sea Gar*, exhausting physical effort would be required to move the sand bags to the windward side.

An early boat that used shifting ballast quite effectively was Eric Tabarly's monohull sloop, *Pen Duick V*. She was somewhat similar to the light-displacement, deep-fin, canoe-body concept but for the fact that her beam was very much greater and her length was limited to 35 feet by the rules of the 1969 singlehanded transpacific race. Movable ballast was in the form of water pumped to tanks on the windward side, and with the proper pumps, the time, if not effort, required to shift the water was not too great. In early trials, it took over 12 minutes to move the water, but after the installation of a large rotary pump, the pumping time was greatly reduced. Of course, most of the water might be allowed to flow by gravity to the leeward side just before tacking, but with that method there is a slight risk of being caught by an unexpected gust. It is safer to balance the movable ballast more or less equally immediately prior to coming about. One annoyance to Tabarly was that his rotary pump leaked and there was no bilge sump in the flat-bottomed boat, which meant that water was often flowing up the sides of the hull and wetting his supplies at even small angles of heel.

Pen Duick V was capable of high-speed planing in favorable wind and sea conditions, but at some sacrifice to comfort and range of stability. Although her broad beam of 11 feet, 4 inches allowed roomy accommodations in one dimension, the shallow depth of hull limited headroom, and her flat bilges caused severe pounding in head seas. Apparently her strong aluminum construction could withstand the slamming, but at a cost in discomfort and anxiety for the crew. One day during the transpacific race, Tabarly wrote in his log, "I've never known a boat to shudder like this before. Everything is vibrating, as though the whole rig will come down at any moment." As for stability, the boat was very stiff, especially when her water ballast was being used, but she lacked the reserve stability and self-righting capabilities of a more normal monohull. This was mainly due to her considerable beam and light keel ballast of only 900 pounds.

A more modern, state-of-the art monohull using water ballast was the 60-foot sloop *Thursday's Child*, built and sailed by Warren Luhrs, president of Hunter Marine. This boat was so fast in the 1984 OSTAR that she stayed close with the giant multihulls and actually finished only 10 hours and 2 minutes behind the first boat. She sometimes exceeded 20 knots, and on a few occasions was clocked at 30 knots, according to one report. These phenomenal bursts of speed were made possible by ideal wave and wind conditions propelling a very light-displacement hull with an exceedingly long waterline and ample water ballast contained in outboard, under-the-deck tanks. The following photograph shows her water ballast schematic diagram displayed on a plate in the cockpit. There is a forward retractable scoop for taking on over 4,000 pounds of ballast in four tanks on either

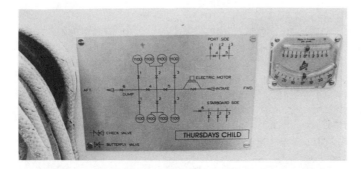

A schematic diagram of the complex water ballast system of *Thursday's Child* is mounted in the cockpit for ready reference by the skipper. (Photo by Karina Paape)

The navigation station of *Thursday's Child* is gimballed, greatly contributing to comfort and efficiency. (Photo by Karina Paape)

side and a number of valves for shifting the water, normally through gravity flow before changing tacks.

A beamy hull with outboard water ballast located above the center of gravity not only increases initial stability and sail-carrying power, but also beneficially affects the boat's pitching motion when the keel ballast can be reduced. A trade-off, however, is a reduced stability range and increased vulnerability to capsizing. A good safety rule of thumb is that the weight of the water ballast (when all of it is carried on one side) should cause a bare-poled boat in calm conditions to heel no more than 10 degrees.

Although not extremely wide at the waterline, *Thursday's Child* has a lot of flare and considerable beam at the deck. Fine at the bow and broad aft like a dinghy, she has an unbalanced hull that is not conducive to steady steering when the heeling angle changes. This problem is counteracted not only with the water ballast, but also with an outboard rudder that swings from side to side like a pendulum. Such an arrangement allows the rudder to remain vertical regardless of heel and thus greatly increases its efficiency by keeping side force directed to the side rather than upward. A similar effect has been achieved with twin side-by-side rudders canted outward, but the upper, non-vertical rudder increases drag.

One of the disadvantages of *Thursday's Child* for everyday use is her lack of accommodations, but she does have a few unusual comfort features for a singlehan-

The fast aluminum cutter *Skoiern IV*, sailed by Jacques de Roux in the second BOC, was found drifting without her skipper during the second leg of the race. (Photo by Herb McCormick)

der. Both the navigation station and galley are gimballed so that they always remain level (see accompanying photo). Also, there is a small deck shelter with a means of steering inside and a couple of observation bubbles. Two features that don't really appeal to me are the open stern, which can allow following seas into the cockpit in heavy weather, and the low companionway sill, which can allow downflooding into the cabin in the worst conditions unless storm slides are used. Granted, the deck shelter acts as a sort of buffer zone and protects the cabin to some degree. Her rig was too light for the rigors of the southern seas, and she was dismasted during the 1986–87 BOC Challenge.

Still another variation on the monohull solo-racer theme is the 50-foot aluminum cutter *Skoiern IV* sailed by Jacques de Roux in the second BOC. Until her skipper was lost overboard, the French cutter showed her heels to the other racers. At least, she won the first leg and was among the leaders during the second, when it was assumed she hit a floating object and subsequently lost de Roux.

Designed by Dominique Presles, *Skoiern IV* was intended for ease of handling as well as speed. Easy handling characteristics were considered an important part of the formula to get there first, since complications and capricious behavior can lead to crew exhaustion and/or inefficiency, which is bound to slow the boat. The long, shallow hull was given good directional stability with a sharply raked fin keel and fairly symmetrical lines. As compared with the dinghy shape, her entry was fuller and her run much finer for better hull balance.

Jacques de Roux aboard *Skoiern IV*. (Photo by Herb McCormick)

Although she carried some water ballast, there were no complicated features such as swinging rudders, daggerboards, or auxiliary rudders, but just a skeg-mounted rudder with vertical axis placed as far aft as possible. A second steering station inside the cabin made it easier on the helmsman in foul weather offshore. She was given a well-proven masthead rig with only one full-length batten and a roller jib backed by an inner staysail. Running backstays are a complication, but it was reasoned that tacks are seldom changed on long downwind ocean races, and runners with check stays supply needed support for a tall mast with large fore-triangle.

Multihull Racers

Quite a different approach to speed is the multihull concept, which provides sail-carrying power with extraordinary beam rather than with keel ballast. Multihulls, used successfully for centuries by the South Pacific islanders, avoid the excessive wetted surface and head resistance of an extremely wide single hull by using two or more narrow hulls. Widely separated, side-by-side multiple hulls eliminate the necessity for ballast as a means of holding a tall rig upright, and this allows much lighter displacement than would be necessary for a ballasted monohull. The most common multihulls seen today are catamarans and trimarans, the former having twin hulls and the latter one main hull with a secondary hull called an "ama" on each side. Related to the catamaran is the proa, which has two hulls with the rig on one of them rather than on a platform between hulls as on a cat.

Some advantages of multihulls over monohulls are tremendous speed off the wind when lightly loaded, relatively level (unheeled) sailing, the potential for unsinkability, often great deck and accommodations space, spirited acceleration, and shallow draft or beachability. Disadvantages are a low range of stability and susceptibility to capsizing, inability to self-right after a capsize, extra stress on the rig as a result of inability to heel, inability to carry ballast or heavy stores without harming performance, sluggishness in stays, and difficulty of entering slips due to broad beam. Comparing cats to tris, cats are usually faster downwind but slower upwind (there are exceptions, of course); depending on the amount of beam, cats are usually stiffer but have a lower stability range than tris; and cats are normally less expensive when both hulls can be made from the same mold.

The multihull concept has merits, and it has proven highly successful in many of the singlehanded transatlantic races, but it has at least one serious drawback for the heaviest weather offshore. As is often pointed out, an unballasted multihull can capsize, but what is far more important, it normally can't self-right. Of course, a monohull having a ballast keel can capsize too (though not as easily as a multihull), but with moderate beam, keel depth, and weight of ballast, she will right herself unless badly holed. On the other hand, the normal catamaran or even trimaran may be far more stable in the inverted position than when upright.

A lot of thinking has gone into solving the multihull capsize problem, but as yet no entirely satisfactory system has been worked out. Some of the systems tried or suggested have included masthead flotation tanks or inflatable masthead bags, sponsons above the rail, V-shaped hulls to inhibit heeling beyond the point at which the leeward side of the V becomes horizontal, ballast or ballasted fins, ballasted swing keels or lever arms that can be hauled out from the hull to cause a righting force when the boat lies on her beam ends, a method of hauling a float attached to the head of a hinged mast downward to turn the boat upright, and system of flooding one hull of an upside-down boat to make her lie on her side and then, after attaching masthead flotation, clearing the flooded hull to allow righting.

We are even beginning to see the use of stabilizing hydrofoils to cause lift acting upward in the interest of preventing excessive heeling. One trouble with hydrofoils, however, is that they require heavier-than-normal hulls and connecting members to resist possible damage caused by the upward lift of the foils. *Paul Ricard*, a foil-stabilized trimaran, enjoyed considerable success after her hull was lightened, but she broke up under the able command of Eric Tabarly during the 1986 Route du Rhum Race. Furthermore, underwater foils cause extra drag that can be very detrimental in light airs unless they can be retracted. The use of ballast on multihulls has not been very successful because of the adverse effect of weight on performance. Masthead flotation is highly desirable, but solid tanks may cause considerable weight and windage aloft, and, furthermore, such floats can break off or even cause a dismasting in heavy weather unless the rigging is extremely strong and well engineered.

End-over-end righting, which has been used successfully on small racers and daysailers, also has been tried effectively on large scale models of offshore multihulls. The system developed by Carlos Ruiz uses two spinnaker poles rigged to the bottom of the capsized boat to form a bipod overhanging the bows, and a water bag is attached to the apex of the bipod. The bows are then flooded, and after they sink, the crew attempts to hoist the water bag, which causes the boat to stand on her head while the sterns rise and then fall over the bows, thus restoring the boat to an upright position. Finally, the bow compartments are pumped dry.

Donald Crowhurst, who was an inventive electronics technician, devised a clever scheme for righting his trimaran, *Teignmouth Electron*, which he entered in

In these four photos, Rob Wright demonstrates a modified "Ruiz system" self-rescue of his 21-foot Tremolino trimaran. (Photos by Jim Morse)

the 1968–69 Golden Globe Race (Chapter 2). The system, which was never fully completed, consisted of a buoyancy bag lashed to the masthead that would be inflated automatically by a cylinder of carbon dioxide when the boat was heeled to a certain angle. The method devised to activate the CO_2 was to fasten electrodes on the upper topsides so that they would complete an electrical circuit when they became submerged as a result of heeling. Actually, the system was quite complex, for Crowhurst used a bank of electrodes rigged and positioned in such a way that

they could distinguish between spray or temporary immersion and a truly dangerous angle of heel. Mercury switches might have been an alternative to using the electrodes. At any rate, the inflated bag would prevent the trimaran from turning turtle during a capsize, but she would still have to be righted from the position of lying on her side. For this part of the operation, a pumping system was devised that would flood the upper float, theoretically pressing the boat downward and then turning her upright. Other gadgets used by Crowhurst were alarms that monitored unusual stresses on the rigging and sheet releases activated by abrupt changes in wind speed registered on his anemometer.

Donald Crowhurst's trimaran *Teignmouth Electron* was loaded with sophisticated gadgetry to minimize risks in heavy weather. (Devon News/Sunday Times)

The unique proa *Cheers*, designed by Dick Newick and raced successfully across the Atlantic by Tom Follett. (Courtesy of Dick Newick)

Designer/builder/solo sailor Walter Greene capsized in his 60-foot trimaran *Gonzo* on his way across the Atlantic for the start of the 1982 Route du Rhum Race. For a while after his unfortunate experience, Greene swore off sailing offshore multihulls, but then he dreamed up a righting system that convinced him he would be able to recover from a capsize. The system that was built into his catamaran *Sebago* utilized hull flooding to position the capsized hulls one above the other and then airbags to lever the boat upright. One hull has buoyancy and the other one, designed to be flooded, has no buoyancy. The air bags are winched down to the submerged hull. There was nothing radically new about this concept, but before the 1984 OSTAR, veteran trimaran sailor (and winner of the 1980 OSTAR) Phil Weld called *Sebago* "the first proven self-righting multihull ever to enter the race." Incidentally, Weld knew from firsthand experience about multihull capsizing, as he and a crew member spent several days on (and in) the bottom of his trimaran *Gulf Streamer* after she turned turtle in the Atlantic while on his way to the 1976 OSTAR.

Ingenious as these anti-capsize systems may be, they have some drawbacks. It is seldom advisable to rely too heavily on electricity at sea on a small boat during heavy weather because of the possibility of power failure or short circuits from wet wiring. Also, pumping and flooding methods that look fine on paper are often difficult if not impossible to operate when capsized in the worst weather offshore. Very generally speaking, it might be said that the more complicated a system is, the less practical or reliable it becomes.

Another interesting type of multihull is the proa, as exemplified by *Cheers*, designed by Dick Newick. This boat finished third in the 1968 OSTAR and once was sailed 250 miles in 24 hours by her solo skipper, Tom Follett, yet she is only

Tom Follett on the bow of *Cheers*, casting off for his solo passage from St. Croix to England in 1968. (Courtesy of Fritz Henle)

40 feet long. She is actually quite similar to a catamaran, with two almost identical double-ended hulls, except that one carries the rig, accommodations, and lateral resistance appendages, while the other hull is merely the outrigger or "ama," and it is considerably lighter in weight. The ama is always kept to leeward, and to change tacks the booms of her stayless, two-masted rig are swung through arcs of up to 180 degrees, so that, in effect, she is tacked by sailing forward and then "backwards." The lateral resistance appendages are two tandem dagger boards with rudders attached. If half lowered, a board acts purely as a lateral resistance appendage, but when fully lowered its rudder is exposed and can steer the boat. The rudders are linked to a whipstaff, which is controlled from amidships by the helmsman. The two masts and tandem dagger boards enable the boat to be balanced quite easily (especially so, since she does not heel very much). Thus no vane gear is required, and this at least partially alleviates the problem of self-steering on a planing multihull.

With her ama to leeward, *Cheers* has considerable resistance to capsize because of her low rig, heavy main hull, buoyant ama, and beam of over 16½ feet. But if she should get caught by a sudden wind shift that puts the ama to windward, she could flip over with comparative ease. In fact, she once did this during early sailing trials. To safeguard against such an eventuality at sea, a sponson, or flotation chamber, was added above the rail of the main hull on the side away from the ama. In addition, her masts are sufficiently buoyant to discourage her from turning turtle. If she should happen to turn bottom side up, however, she has greater self-righting capabilities than the average tri or cat.

The obvious drawbacks of a boat like *Cheers* are lack of accommodations and lack of maneuverability in crowded waters, mainly due to her inability to come

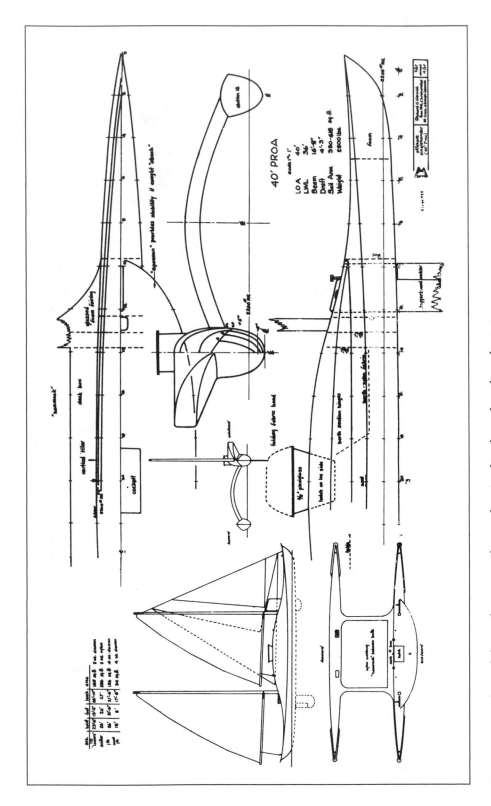

Figure 4-8. Plans of the 40-foot proa *Cheers*, showing her daggerboards and sponson, a flotation chamber to windward that guards against capsize due to a sudden wind shift. (Courtesy of Dick Newick)

about through the eye of the wind. In fact, her designer admitted that she needed a motor to be suitable for congested waters.

Modern, state-of-the-art multihulls are capable of incredible speeds. In the heavy-weather 1986 Route de Rhum, hydrofoil-assisted tri *Fleury Michon VIII*, skippered by Philippe Poupon, averaged just under 11 knots over the entire distance sailed. In breaking the transatlantic record from Sandy Hook New Jersey, to The Lizard in England, in 1984 (crossing in 8 days, 16 hours, 36 minutes), the 60-foot catamaran *Jet Services*, skippered by Patrick Morvan (with crew), averaged better than 15 knots for more than a week, and at one time was clocked at a steady 30 knots for more than two hours. Later, in 1986, Loic Caradec's 85-foot catamaran *Royale* broke the transatlantic record by crossing in 7 days, 21 hours, 5 minutes at an average speed of 15.54 knots and with one 24-run of more than 19 knots. *Formula Tag*, an 80-foot cat skippered by Mike Birch (with crew), once sailed 518 miles in 24 hours. Despite such exciting speeds, however, ocean racing multihulls are definitely not for everyone. Adding extra weight by overloading can ruin their performance, and windward ability with the capability of tacking smartly is often less than desirable, while self-steering may present more problems as compared with a monohull.

In addition, the large, high-tech multihulls can be difficult to handle, and solo racing at such high speeds involves a relatively high degree of risk. Not only is there the possibility of a capsize, but also probability of damage if the boat should happen to collide with flotsam or sea life. *Jet Services* was damaged three times after striking whales (she also struck a shark) and had to be abandoned after colliding with a tree trunk.

To obtain top speed from a catamaran it is often necessary to fly one hull (lift it from the water) to decrease drag. Regarding his learning process with *Jet Services*, Morvan said, "At the beginning, when we saw half of the weather centerboard out of water, we got worried and reduced sail. Now we know that to go fast, we should sail with only one hull in the water, and we're getting there." This practice certainly increases the risk of capsize for an offshore singlehander, but highly paid professional sailors backed by big business sponsors are often willing to take such chances. Wizard multihull designer Dick Newick put it this way: "Multihulls excel in high performance, which attracts those who want to win races; sometimes these speed demons don't have the discretion to know when to stop pushing their boats. Their disasters can be expensive lessons, showing us where the limits are, if we have the wits to learn."

Compared with some of the high-tech boats, the rig of *Jet Services* was easy to handle, for it was fitted with a fixed-pole mast, fractional rig, and had no running backstays. Others have masthead rigs with large headsails, rotating wing masts, and complicated rigging that needs continual adjusting. The primary advantage of a rotating wing mast is that it eliminates mast interference with the air flow and increases lift, but there is no easy way of reducing its area in a real blow. Loic Caradec, who was lost in the 1986 Route du Rhum, was overpowered by the 700-square-foot wing mast on his record-setting catamaran *Royale*. He had a heel alarm to warn him when the heeling angle became dangerous, but there was no way he could shorten down, and he reported that the alarm was sounding continuously. Not very long after his last radio report, the big cat was found upside down with Caradec missing.

An extremely complicated rig is the one used on the catamaran *Elf Aquitaine II*. Her entire sail plan is mounted on a huge aluminum boom called a balestron, which swivels at the center of her x-shaped cross beams. The arrangement increases slot efficiency and avoids blanketing when sailing downwind, but the rigging needs constant adjusting, and during the 1984 OSTAR skipper Marc Pajot reported sailing backwards seven times after his rig became backwinded.

Before the start of that same race, BOC winner Philippe Jeantot stated that his 60-foot catamaran *Credit Agricole II* was "very, very fast," but he admitted that "maybe she is too much boat for one man." Later, near the Azores, he turned turtle in only a Force 4 wind. It seems that the cat had an overly tall rig with a very high center of effort, which made her particularly vulnerable to capsizing.

Most of the hottest racers, whether wing-masted or not, carry fully battened mainsails with enormous roaches, and they must be partially lowered and then rehoisted to change tacks when the boats have permanent backstays. Otherwise, the sail's leech will foul the stay. Another problem with many of the most sophisticated rigs, especially on catamarans, is the difficulty of keeping the jibstay properly tensioned for the best windward performance.

On the positive side, with sophisticated construction using computers to analyze stress, and with high-tech materials (such as Kevlar, carbon fiber, Nomex core, wood/epoxy saturation, etc.), hulls are becoming lighter, stronger, and more widely separated to increase stability. Of course, there are trade-offs in extreme beam, including greater susceptibility to pitchpoling and, from a purely practical standpoint, difficulty in docking.

One unexpected handling benefit from very high speeds is that the spinnaker, which Chichester called "a lubberly sail," is seldom needed for optimal performance. The fact is that the large racing multihulls move so fast that the apparent wind draws forward in iceboat fashion, allowing the genoa or a reaching jib to be more effective than a spinnaker. During the 1986 Route du Rhum, winner Philippe Poupon in his Nigel Irens-designed trimaran *Fleury Michon VIII* flew his 'chute for only three hours, and that was in light air when the balloonlike sail was easy to handle. (Spinnaker flying in light weather on a modern multihull can be simplified because the boat's broad beam eliminates the need for a pole).

Desirable Features

Let us review some of the desirable features for a solo cruiser. All of them may not be possible, or perhaps certain of them might have to be de-emphasized if the craft will be used for special purposes, such as racing, record setting, or cruising in extremely heavy weather, but most features are nevertheless desirable and should be designed into the boat whenever possible, especially when she is intended for normal singlehanded cruising. For the sake of discussion I have sketched a composite cruiser, shown in Figure 4-9, that might be considered a happy compromise for solo passage-making at reasonable speed, in comfort, and with considerable emphasis on safety. The boat is not highly specialized, because she may be used for a variety of purposes. She will not be sailed singlehanded all of the time, and some of her life will be spent on inshore waters as well as at sea.

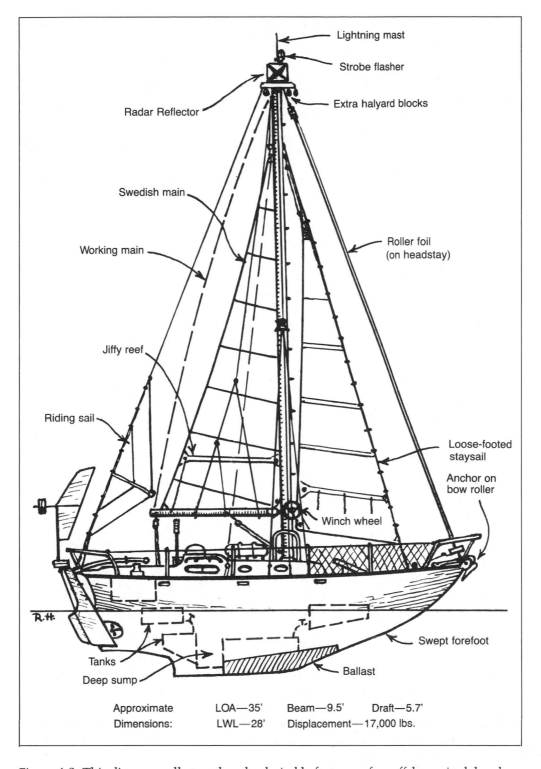

Figure 4-9. This diagram pulls together the desirable features of an offshore singlehander.

This cruiser is of medium-size, about 35 feet long overall, because this size is not only reasonably economical, but also allows a good turn of speed with minimal handling difficulties, and she is large enough for ample stores, adequate comfort, and a high degree of safety over a wide range of conditions. She is of moderate displacement, not so light that her motion is excessively quick, nor so heavy that she lacks buoyancy or requires a lot of sail and heavy ground tackle that could be burdensome for one person to handle. Incidentally, I feel that a vessel's motion is of great importance to a singlehander, because it causes or at least adds to fatigue, and it increases the risk of falling (perhaps overboard). This boat's beam is fairly narrow by today's standards to increase her range of positive stability and inverted self-righting ability while allowing an easier motion when she is rolling. The beam is not so narrow, however, that the boat is tender or overly subject to accumulative rolling.

She is fairly short-ended, because long ends tend to pound and may at times lessen directional stability, while a long waterline is essential to speed. Her overhangs are nevertheless sufficient for reasonably good looks and reserve buoyancy. The stern is a raking transom type, but the boat could be a full-sterned double-ender. Her rudder is outboard for good steering control (due to having a long arm between the rudder and the boat's turning axis), accessibility, and ease of using a rudder tab for self-steering. A rudder tab is highly effective yet causes minimal drag. Her keel is moderately long for directional stability, but not so long as to produce an unresponsive helm. The keel's leading edge is swept back to lessen impact in case of a collision with a submerged object, but its bottom is fairly horizontal so that the boat will not pitch forward too much when grounded or slipped on a marine railway. Wetted surface is kept moderately low and maneuverability well balanced with directional stability by means of the medium length of the keel and the cutaway lateral plane aft. This cutaway also affords some protection for the rudder heel during a grounding. Keel ballast is about 45 percent of displacement, which should be ample for stability, but not so much as to cause an overly quick roll, since the boat has moderate beam and fairly slack bilges. Notice that some tanks are in the keel and that they are connected with higher tanks, so that at times, with a pump or gravity flow, the center of gravity can be moved slightly to modify, to some extent, stability and motion. There is also a deep sump in the keel for bilge water.

Freeboard is enough for reserve buoyancy, but not so high as to detract seriously from windward performance in a blow or make it too difficult for the singlehander to climb aboard the boat from the water. For this purpose, it is a good idea to secure permanent steps to the transom, rudder, or elsewhere aft. The cabin trunk is well rounded, has small, unbreakable windows or ports, and there is a Plexiglas observation dome in the companionway hatch that slides into a cut-out section in the hatch scabbard. The side decks are wide, uncluttered, and have a high toerail. The cockpit well is small, but is as deep as efficient drainage will allow, because a singlehander needs all the security possible on deck. There are numerous hand grips at strategic points and two pipe rails for security at the mast. Lifelines are high and they support nets forward to protect the crew and prevent headsails from washing overboard when they are lowered. Although not shown, there are weather cloths or dodgers aft, open at the bottom for good drainage, and with heavy Mylar windows for visibility. As can be seen, the boat will have an engine, because it can be most handy for battery charging and for maneuverability, particularly for a singlehander in crowded waters. The helm will be forward near the companionway so that the sailor can easily get below and reach equipment stowed just inside the hatchway.

Not a great deal will be said about the boat's rig, because this subject is discussed in Chapter 5, but a few comments may be appropriate here. It can be seen that the rig is what might be called a Bermuda cutter with the mast stepped almost amidships. This location inhibits pitching and provides a relatively safe location for working at the mast. A storm trysail with its own track is shown hoisted, and the sail is dyed yellow for maximum visibility, particularly at night. The small staysail is self-tending, but boomless, because it is not prudent for the singlehander to risk being struck by a low boom. The main boom is quite high and short. It has a gallows frame, and its outboard end is well clear of the permanent backstay. A riding sail that will not interfere with the boom can be set on the backstay. There are mast steps and bright spreader lights useful for sail changes at night and which can be used for flare-up lights in the presence of ships. Notice, also, that there is a permanent radar reflector mounted at the masthead. Most halyards are led back to the cockpit, and there are lazyjacks to simplify lowering the mainsail. The winch wheel on the mast is not necessary if the new low-stretch all-rope halyards are used.

Below, the boat has an L-shaped galley near the companionway, because this location has minimal motion and its shape permits the singlehander to wedge and strap himself in. A chart desk is on the boat's opposite side, also near the companionway, with a quarter berth abaft it which can double as a seat. Just forward of the galley and navigation areas, there is a low bunk on each side of the boat. Of course, the leeward berth will always be used, but even so, it should be fitted with a bunk board, lee cloth, or safety belt. The area forward of the bunks contains the head, a workbench, and stowage space for sails and other gear. There could also be a couple of folding pipe berths forward for occasional guests or crew.

Many of the features discussed are obviously desirable for any boat, but they might be considered especially important for singlehanding. Extra care and thought should be used when designing, constructing, and rigging a solo boat. Of course, she should be strong, watertight, buoyant, and stable; but in addition, it is highly desirable that she have good directional stability, an easy motion, the ability to lie-to comfortably, a layout that allows accessibility to gear from the cockpit, every possible safety device to avoid any kind of accident, and arrangements that make handling by one person as simple and easy as possible.

Alec Rose aboard his yawl *Lively Lady*. Note the long external chainplate straps, and how the mizzen boom has been omitted so as not to interfere with the self-steering vane. (Courtesy of *Yachting* magazine)

5

Rigs for Singlehanded Sailing

Comparison of Rigs

THE SUITABILITY OF A VESSEL'S rig for singlehanding will depend on a number of factors: the size and displacement of the vessel; the purpose for which she will be used (i.e., racing, inshore cruising, normal offshore cruising, extremely difficult passage-making, etc.); and the size, strength, and age of the singlehander. A large, heavy boat will naturally require a lot of sail for respectable sail-area-to-wetted-surface and sail-area-to-displacement ratios. Such a boat will normally have a divided rig, since there is a limit to the size of a sail one person can handle. Of course, modern gear such as the multi-speed, self-tailing winches can extend the size limit considerably beyond the 500-square-foot maximum-sized mainsail conceived by Uffa Fox in the early 1930s. Nevertheless, heavy boats longer than about 45 or 50 feet will usually need to have their sail plans divided into three sails. The most popular sail plans are the ketch and cutter rigs.

The larger boats having a basic three-sail rig will often be rigged as ketches, because with this rig the largest sail can be a manageable size without diminishing total sail area. In addition, the ketch rig offers the advantages of a low center of effort for stability, ease of balancing the helm, ease of shortening sail in a sudden squall, a spar aft for setting a riding sail, and perhaps ease of setting up a jury rig in the event of dismasting. Disadvantages are relatively poor windward ability due to the mizzen being backwinded when close-hauled, blanketing of the mainsail by the mizzen when running, poor performance in ghosting conditions (unless, perhaps, the boat is very light or has a bowsprit that will allow an ample foretriangle for large headsails), greater maintenance of spars and rigging as compared with a one-masted rig, and often interference of the mizzen boom with a practical, high-aspect-ratio self-steering vane.

Concerning the latter problem, Robin Knox-Johnston's ketch *Suhaili* had a complicated vane gear that looked as if it were designed by Rube Goldberg. It consisted of an elaborate metal frame supporting a vane on the boat's port side and another on her starboard side opposite the mizzen. Once during *Suhaili*'s circumnavigation, the gear on one side was seriously bent as a result of a knockdown. Sir Alec Rose solved the mizzen-versus-steering gear problem on his *Lively Lady* by omitting the mizzen boom and using the mizzen mast only to support a mizzen staysail. Of course, many large ketches have very short mizzen booms that do not interfere with the self-steerer. Light-displacement boats such as Bruce Dalling's old *Voortrekker* need only modest sail area to drive them at high speed; consequently a miniscule mizzen with a short boom will suffice.

There are many advantages to the cutter rig for general-purpose singlehanding. The cutter provides a three-sail rig for easy management, but with only one mast. Sail is more centralized or concentrated amidships as compared with other rigs. This increases safety, because there is a wide working space with minimal motion near the mast, and the crew seldom has to venture onto the boat's extremities in heavy weather. Also, the mast amidships provides a wide base for efficient staying, while its weight in that location has a favorable effect on the moment of inertia to help alleviate extreme pitching.

Another consideration that is seldom mentioned is the relationship of the centralized rig with boat's keel length. Very generally speaking, a spread-out rig seems more appropriate for a long keel and a centralized rig seems more appropriate for a short keel. At least the boat with a very short fin keel may have problems with overly sensitive balance for singlehanding when her rig extends far forward and aft, especially if she has a bowsprit and overhanging mizzen boom.

Other plaudits for the cutter rig are windward efficiency due to high-aspect-ratio sails with effective slots between them, light-air ability because of the height of the rig and the large foretriangle for light-weather jibs, and heavy-weather ability for sustained beating against rough seas due to slot efficiency, pitch damping, and better mast support provided by the sails. Although the ketch rig enables sail to be shortened quickly in a sudden squall without sacrificing balance by simply dropping the mainsail, many experienced seamen feel that it is not safe to sail very long in heavy weather with a large headsail and no sail attached to the after side of the mainmast because of vulnerability to mast breakage. If the headsail and mizzen were dropped instead of the mainsail, then the mainmast would be better supported by the mainsail, but then power and ability to go to windward would be seriously impeded. In contrast, the cutter can reduce sail quite effectively and safely by dropping or rolling up her jib, and the staysail with a slightly reefed main usually provides an efficient rig for prolonged windward sailing in a blow. Of course, the same would apply to a double-head-rigged ketch, but her center of effort would normally be moved quite far forward.

A cruising cutter's staysail is often rigged on a boom so that it is self-tending when tacking. As has already been mentioned, however, it may be advisable for an offshore singlehander to dispense with the boom because of the possibility, slight as it may be, of being struck by the spar. With a proper sheeting and traveller arrangement, it is possible to make a boomless sail self-tending, but this may require an overly short, low foot on the staysail and perhaps a curved traveller. An ordinary double-sheet arrangement may be best for offshore work, because a boat is

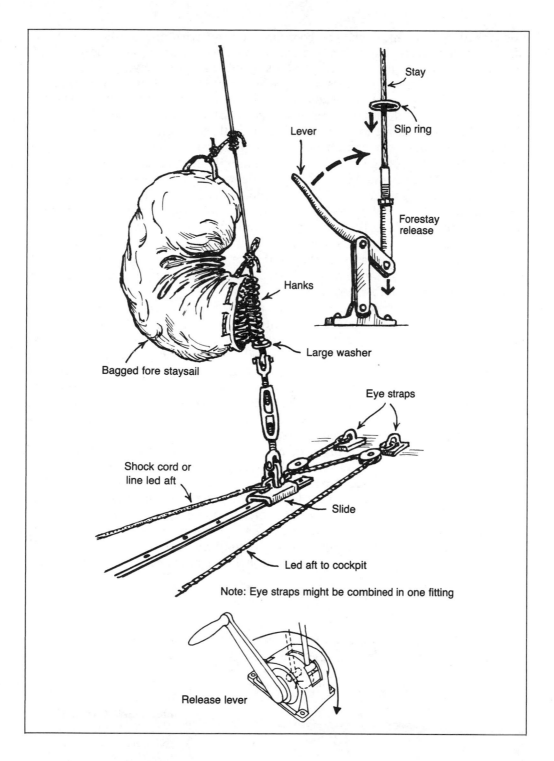

Figure 5-1. Sliding forestay, Merriman release lever of the pelican hook type, and a Schaefer Rotary release fitting.

not tacked very often at sea. The boomless staysail with double sheets not only offers advantages in shape and fine-trim capabilities, but it will allow a slight amount of overlap, which will increase its power and efficiency.

For light-weather, inshore sailing where frequent tacking is involved, the singlehander will probably want to use a fairly large jib alone, without the staysail. In this case, it is well to have a removable staysail stay that can be released from the deck and brought aft to the mast where it will not interfere with the jib when tacking. This might be accomplished with a quick-release lever or with a slide on a centerline track (see Figure 5-1) if the boat has a flush foredeck. One advantage of the sliding arrangement is that the singlehander can control the operation from the cockpit. A line leading from the slide to a block just forward of the forward end of the track and thence back to a winch near the cockpit pulls the stay forward to set it up taut, and a backhaul line is rigged to pull the stay aft when the forehaul is slacked. A disadvantage of this plan is that there is a fair amount of clutter on the foredeck over which the sailor could possibly trip when going forward in the dark. In addition, such an arrangement must be securely through-bolted to the deck, ideally with a full-length backing plate.

The quick-release lever necessitates a trip to the foredeck when the stay is released or set up, but the deck is less cluttered when the lever can be held to the stay with a slip ring (like a pelican hook) or a deck lever can be housed in a scuppered well. A Merriman release lever of the pelican hook type is illustrated in Figure 5-1, as is the Schaefer rotary lever. Another alternative is to attach the forestay with a trigger snaphook that can be released under load by inserting a marlinespike or fid through the hole that houses the trigger (Figure 5-2). Tension is quite easily applied with a turnbuckle that has folding handles that lock down to prevent unscrewing once the tension is set.

Two famous cutters of my acquaintance used for singlehanding are Frank Casper's *Elsie* and James Crawford's *Angantyr*. The latter is over 60 feet long, displaces 35 tons, and carries 1,647 square feet of sail, and she demonstrates how handy the cutter rig can be even for such a large, heavy vessel. Crawford sailed his boat solo across the Atlantic, and he occasionally managed her alone with apparent ease on crowded inland waters. I once saw *Angantyr* with only one man aboard beat to windward under full sail through a small, crowded anchorage during a popular regatta. She seemed to weave her way through the anchored fleet of yachts and

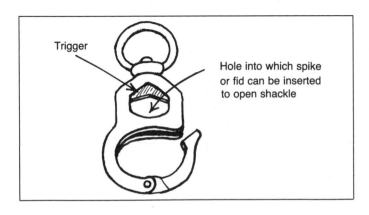

Figure 5-2. A trigger snapshackle may be released under load by inserting a marlinespike or fid through the hole that houses the trigger.

In the rather special case of the Nootkan canoe *Tilikum,* sometimes singlehanded by John C. Voss, the three-masted rig made a good deal of sense. (Courtesy of Provincial Archives, Victoria, B.C.)

come about between them with no trouble at all. Of course, such boat handling is as much due to the skill and experience of the skipper as it is to the qualities of the vessel, her rig, and her gear.

Elsie is much smaller, less than 28 feet on the waterline, but she is quite heavy for her size, and Frank Casper found her cutter rig, with the mast nearly amidships, a very handy arrangement. He liked the large foretriangle for light-air jibs, and he once told me that he found the staysail very useful for self-steering.

The sloop rig is probably more suitable for small coastal boats of light displacement, however, because in the smaller sail sizes two sails are normally more efficient and manageable for a singlehander than are three sails. Furthermore, the sloop rig avoids the backwind problem associated with mizzens and staysails and it also avoids the problem of the staysail stay interfering with shifting large jibs when tacking on a cutter.

Extremely large boats may need three or more masts in order to divide the total sail area into sails of manageable size. Prime examples are *Vendredi 13,* which carried three masts supporting three boomed staysails, and the mammoth *Club Mediterranee,* which carried four masts with two sails per mast. These rigs have certain practical advantages for one person handling a very large boat, but they certainly lack aerodynamic efficiency. In fact, OSTAR founder H. G. Hasler called *Vendredi 13*'s rig "desperately inefficient, even to windward, with a quite excessive amount of mast and rigging for her sail area." Of *Club Med,* Eric Tabarly said she was "merely an enlarged version of *Vendredi 13* with all her defects as well, multiplied by two. It is even more under-powered than *Vendredi 13* was, and this presupposes that she will sail poorly in light and moderate winds. A boat rigged with eight sails set one behind the other cannot sail into the wind at the right angle, and this weakness against the wind threatens to be particularly awkward in the OSTAR which generally enjoys westerly winds for most of the time."

John C. Voss used a three-masted rig on his small Nootkan canoe, *Tilikum.* In the vast majority of cases, the three-masted schooner rig is most unsuitable for small boats, but for the *Tilikum* there were some special advantages. She was very narrow and relatively unstable; thus she needed a sail plan with the lowest possible center of effort. In addition, she was the type of boat that would lie to a sea anchor streamed from her bow, and this often necessitated a riding sail that could conveniently be set on the aftermost mast. Another consideration was that she carried no self-steering gear, and so her spread-out rig provided a versatile sail plan for varying the boat's balance.

A rig that is especially suitable for singlehanded cruising is the ancient Chinese lug rig, as adapted by H. G. Hasler and Jock McLeod. Hasler's folkboat *Jester* and the central-control-point concept were discussed in Chapter 4. The type of rig he developed (illustrated in Figure 5-3) is basically a lug sail with full-length battens and multiple sheets to lessen sail twist and assist in reefing. It is a balanced sail; that is to say, its leading edge is somewhat forward of the mast, which keeps the center of effort inboard to prevent weather helm when the sheets are started as shown in Figure 5-3. The sail illustrated is a more modern version than that used on *Jester*, as the battens are all about the same length and the upper spar is peaked up higher for better efficiency to windward. Some of Hasler's and McLeod's later sails have less balance, but they are usually used on two-masted schooner rigs, which minimize the problem of the center of effort moving outboard with well-started sheets, because the sails for the two-masted rig are narrower than that for the one-masted rig, and because a schooner sometimes can be sailed downwind wing-and-wing.

With the modern Chinese lug concept, the singlehander can hoist, trim, reef, and lower his sail by adjusting four lines led to his control station (see Figure 5-3). The normal procedure for reefing is to slack the halyard, which drops the lower battens down on the boom. The reefed portion of the sail is collected by lazyjacks, and the battens are held securely by tightening the downhaul and sheet. In some cases it may be necessary to adjust the parrel line also.

Despite the great convenience of this rig for singlehanding, there are some drawbacks. It lacks the speed in light airs and the weatherliness of modern Marconi rigs, and it might not be desirable for a singlehander who will sail his boat alone only part of the time. Another possible disadvantage is that the Hasler rig lacks stays and shrouds, which permits the mast to whip a great deal in some conditions. Although the lack of standing rigging prevents compression loading, a few of these masts have broken (see Chapter 11). Thomas Colvin, an American designer who uses the Chinese rig, prefers standing rigging carried fairly slack on his boats as a safeguard against mast breakage. It seems that the longer unstayed masts have had the most problems with failures. *Jester's* relatively short wood spar has survived a dozen Atlantic voyages over the past 25 years.

It now seems that modern technology has provided the answer for large unstayed masts in the form of carbon fiber spars. When *Lady Pepperell* pitchpoled during the 1982–83 BOC Challenge her carbon fiber masts, which were engineered to withstand 14 inches of deflection without breaking, remained intact. These spars are not as well suited to being supported by stays, as they are relatively weak in compression and they do not hold screw fastenings well, but carbon fiber seems ideal for freestanding masts.

A minor problem with the Chinese rig is that there is an enormous pile-up of rope tails when the sheets are trimmed, and these can get under foot and possibly become fouled. One offshore singlehander, Colin Darroch, solved the problem by installing spring-loaded anchor rode reels for his sheets, and they would not only

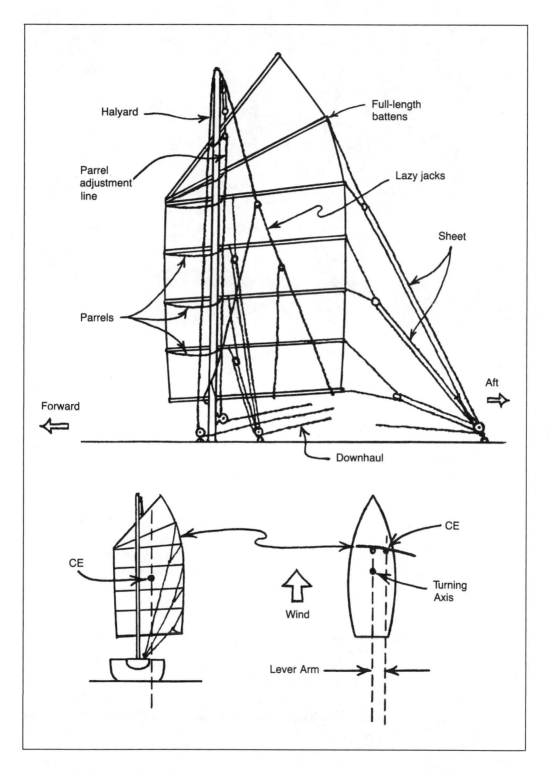

Figure 5-3. The modified Chinese lug rig, as developed by H. G. Hasler and Jock McLeod.

Although *Lady Pepperell* pitchpoled in the Southern Indian Ocean in 1983 during
the BOC Challenge Race, her carbon fiber masts remained intact. (Courtesy of West Point
Pepperell)

stow the slack line, but also, with the sheets cast off their cleats, would automatically slack and trim the sheets in gusty winds.

Before Hasler developed the Chinese rig he used in the 1960 transatlantic race,
he also experimented with the Ljungstrom rig, which was patented in 1938. This
rig uses a rotating mast having twin sails that lie together when beating and
reaching but which spread apart and can be wung out on opposite sides of the boat
when running. The sails are boomless, and they are wound up on a rotating mast
when they are furled or reefed. Hasler modified the Ljungstrom plan to what he
called a "lapwing rig" by adding two identical cantilevered booms to the twin sails.
The system had some merits, but he finally rejected it for extended offshore work,
primarily because of air becoming trapped under the sail and consequent balloon-
ing when it was wound up on the mast in a strong wind.

A more modern variation on the Chinese lug rig is the so-called Gallant rig
developed by Jack Manners-Spencer in England. This is actually a soft wing sail
with full-length battens bent around and enclosing the mast. In theory it has many
of the handling advantages of the Chinese rig but is aerodynamically more efficient, improving windward performance and speed when reaching. The Gallant rig
has been endorsed by sailmaker/author Jeremy Howard-Williams.

In America the most popular freestanding rigs in recent years have been used
on the Garry Hoyt-developed Freedom boats. These craft are cat-rigged, either with
one or two masts, and with wishbone booms or full-length battens. A Freedom 25
was sailed halfway across the Pacific, from San Francisco to Hawaii, by David
Schaal, and another Freedom 25 was sailed across the Atlantic by Michael
Bohmann. Blind singlehander Jim Dickson sailed a Freedom 36 from Newport,
Rhode Island, to Bermuda. The patented gunmount spinnaker, which uses a spin-

Jim Dickson at the helm of his Freedom 36. (Photo by Susan Thorpe)

naker pole attached at its middle to a swivel fitting on the bow pulpit, was managed effectively by Schaal, and it was even carried by Dickson. A major disadvantage of cat rigs is that they cannot be hove to in the conventional way with opposing sails (see Chapter 10); nevertheless, Bohmann successfully weathered a Force 11 gale during his ocean crossing. Personally, I prefer what Hoyt calls a cat-sloop rig, which has one large mainsail but also a small self-tending jib that is carried upwind in light to moderate winds. This improves light air speed and windward performance with little sacrifice to handiness.

Sail Construction

Offshore cruising sails should be a compromise between strength, stability, and ease of handling. Ease of handling is especially important for the singlehanded sailor—and this characteristic is most often found in sails made of soft cloth with a conservative shape that requires a minimum of adjustments. The degree of a sail's softness is a balance between the stability and the pliability of the cloth. A very soft, easily handled material may lose its shape more easily and require frequent adjustments in a fresh breeze, but it greatly facilitates furling, bagging, and stowing. A good compromise is unbalanced polyester cloth (Dacron in the U.S.A.), which is lightly filled with a relatively flexible stabilizing resin. An unbalanced cloth is one having the threadline heavier in one direction than in the other. Threads running the length of the cloth are called the warp, and those running across the cloth at right angles to the warp are called the fill (or weft in England). The normal crosscut sail, with seams running at right angles to the leech, would need an unbalanced cloth having heavier fill. A conservative shape requiring few adjustments is one with moderate camber, luff round, foot round, and roach. For long distance sailing, consideration should be given to an ultraviolet sunscreen coating.

Strength and longevity are important to every long-distance cruiser, whose sails should be of slightly heavier-than-normal cloth with ample chafing patches wherever they touch the spreaders or rigging. Sails usually come apart at the seams, so these should be triple stitched using a dark thread, which has proven more resistant to sun rot than white thread, as well as more noticeable where it breaks. Stitched areas subject to chafe that cannot easily be covered with patches should be treated with a polymeric coating. Extra multilayered reinforcing patches and heavy straps are advisable at the head, clew, and reef grommets. Nylon sail slides are not likely to stick, but be sure they are extra hefty and are attached with shackles or webbing in such a way that they cannot jam in the track.

Batten pockets need special attention, as they are vulnerable to damage in heavy weather. Pockets should have a layer of cloth between the batten and sail, be located between seams, and have patches to keep the battens from poking through the sail. I prefer that the outboard ends of offset pockets be handstitched and coated to prevent chafe from the topping lift and that the offset openings be fitted with eyelets and lashings. Some cruising sailors prefer hollow leeches that eliminate the need for battens, but I like the extra area afforded by a modest roach and feel that battens better control leech curl and reduce flutter even if there is no roach. Use plastic protectors on the inboard ends of all battens.

Visibility is a prime consideration for a shorthanded boat, so deck-sweeping headsails are not recommended. Every headsail should have a luff length that allows the fitting of a tack pendant long enough to allow the helmsman to see under the foot. This will also help reduce foot chafe on the bow pulpit and lifelines. It is well to have a high-cut clew for the sake of visibility, but it should not be so high that a lone sailor cannot easily reach the clew to inspect the sheet attachment or adjust the leech line. An exception might be a high-cut Yankee jib. Speaking of leech lines, be sure that every battenless sail has a substantial leech line with an easily operable cleating device, because nothing fatigues the leech (and the single-hander) faster than a continual noisy flutter.

Be sure that all sails and bags are well labeled with waterproof magic marker or the equivalent. Both sides of the bag should be marked to show what sail it contains, and each corner of the sail should be labeled not only with the name of the sail but also the name of the corner—"tack," "clew," and "head." Mark all reef grommets with numbers corresponding to the depth of reef, and number all battens and batten pockets. Bear in mind that it is easy for a tired singlehander to make careless mistakes when changing or reefing sails.

Even if the boat will never be raced, I like sturdy telltales at the luffs of all headsails and at least one telltale window in the luff. These greatly assist the singlehander in achieving proper sail trim at a glance. The telltales should stream straight aft without twirling on each side of the sail. The mainsail should have ribbons of UV-resistant cloth at the outboard end of each batten pocket.

Tips on handling spinnakers alone are given in Chapter 12.

Deck Layout and Sail Handling Gear

Just how the deck is laid out for singlehanded sailing will depend on the boat's size and design, her rig, and the skipper's personal preference. The ideal is a balance between comfort, handiness, efficiency, and safety; and like most aspects of yacht design, trade-offs are almost always necessary. For instance, you may want the helm near the companionway for comfort and convenience but often at a cost in range of visibility.

The first requirement for singlehanding is that all sheets be within easy reach of the helm. If the helm is near the forward end of the cockpit, the mainsheet might be trimmed most conveniently from the bridge deck, or if there is no bridge deck, from the after end of the cabin trunk. When the helm is near the after end of the cockpit, the mainsheet traveller might best be mounted across the cockpit well. It is better by far to have the mainsheet come down almost vertically near its outboard end, with the sheet raked slightly aft of the vertical to prevent the traveller slide from binding. If it is raked forward or is attached to the middle of the boom, power and efficiency are lost, or the boom may be permitted to ride up and require constant use of a vang. Be sure the sheet tackle has sufficient purchase power and that the sheet can be quickly and easily released from its cleat. Harken makes very satisfactory tackles with ratcheting blocks for heavy winds and easy releasing cam cleats. Headsail sheets should be within easy reach of the helm but also readily available when the boat is steering herself and the singlehander is not at the helm. Winches must be mounted so that the line leads slightly up to the winch (95 or 100 degrees to the winch axis) in order to prevent overrides.

Opinions are mixed on the merits of leading halyards aft to the cockpit. Some singlehanders prefer that everything be led aft, while others like the conventional system of belaying halyards and reefing lines at the base of the mast. Certainly the main halyard and reef earings should be at the same location whether aft or forward (reefing will be discussed in the next section). Arguments against leading halyards aft are that extra blocks at the base of the mast and fairleads increase friction on the line and cause chafe or fatigue. Also, it is often necessary for halyards to perforate the dodger or its coaming, and these holes can let through a lot of water in heavy weather. In some cases there may be a high doghouse that prevents running lines over the top of the cabin trunk. Then too, it is often necessary for the singlehander to go forward regardless of where the halyards are led, in order to tie stops or reef points around lowered sails. The big advantage of having all lines led to the cockpit is obviously to cut down on the number of trips forward.

My personal preference is that when the cabin trunk design allows, and sails are fitted with lazyjacks, especially when there are full-length battens, the main halyard and its reefing lines should be led back to the cockpit. The same goes for most spinnaker control lines. On the other hand, I prefer that the jib halyard be cleated at the mast, because the singlehander usually must go forward when changing or just lowering a headsail in order to gather it in, keep it from washing overboard, and tie it with stops or bag it. Normally the singlehander will slack the sheet just enough so that the clew can be pulled forward to the mast if it is an overlapping sail; then he will go forward and slack the halyard gradually, leading it around its mast winch and forward where he can control it, while he lifts up the foot of sail (if it is low cut) and pulls it inboard while the sail is being lowered. Brian Cooke on *British Steel* actually had his jib halyard led forward to a bow winch to facilitate handling the jib when it was being lowered.

Some singlehanders think it is a good idea to rig downhauls to aid in lowering headsails. A good way to help muzzle the jib is to run the downhaul from the head to a ring seized to a hank slightly lower than midway up the luff, then through the clew grommet or a ring at the clew and forward to a block at the tack as shown in

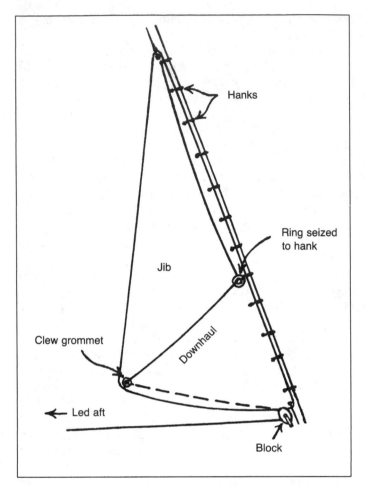

Figure 5-4. A slight variation of a Gerr downhaul.

Figure 5-4. This kind of downhaul, often called a Gerr downhaul, will automatically pull the clew forward if the sheet is released as the sail is pulled down. The downhaul, together with the halyard, can be led back to the cockpit, but the singlehander may still have to go forward to stop or bag the sail in fresh winds and when seas are coming over the bow. Disadvantages of such a downhaul system are the possibility of the line fouling on lifeline stanchions, binding in such a way as to adversely affect the jib's camber, or the jib's filling with water and ripping in heavy weather if it is not well stopped. In my opinion, roller furling is a better alternative, especially when the boat is cutter-rigged and has a large forestaysail that will provide effective power when the jib is furled. Roller furling and reefing will be discussed in the next section.

Winches are all but essential on a modern boat to tension her running rigging quickly and properly, and they are especially important for the singlehander. For maximum efficiency, self-tailing winches obviate the need to haul on the line as it comes off the winch drum. Self-tailing winches hold the line in jaws or in a cleating device on top, but I would certainly have a conventional backup cleat nearby for use in heavy weather. Nearly every winch manufacturer now makes self-tailers, some with electric and hydraulic options. Some features to look for are ease of disassembling for servicing, variability of the line gripper for different size lines, and positioning of the line guide lifting arm or stripper to allow an almost full turn of line around the gripper to decrease the chance of line slippage. For a shorthanded boat over about 30 feet, I like two-speed self-tailers with a ratcheting winch handle.

Of course, winches are expensive, but it is often possible to economize by using line stoppers or lockoffs which work like cam cleats but are opened and closed manually with handles. If two different lines use the same winch, they are led through two stoppers just forward of the winch. When one line uses the winch the other is locked off. This system also avoids the clutter of having too many winches clustered together at one spot and the problem of handles hitting nearby winches. When installing any deck fittings, consider not only the handiness of the location but also whether or not it will cause a serious tripping hazard for the singlehander moving about in the dark. Hal Roth had high praise for his Lewmar halyard stoppers after the second BOC Challenge. With almost any clutch stopper, however, there is some compromise between gripping ability and wear on the line.

Lazyjacks are the traditional mechanism for controlling sails during the lowering and furling process, and they were commonly seen when the gaff rig was predominant. With the advent of the tall Marconi rig, lazyjacks gradually died out, but today they are making a comeback. They consist of lines that hang down on either side of the sail to guide and contain the sail as it is lowered, thus simplifying the job of furling and stopping. There are two basic ways of rigging lazyjacks, and each system has it proponents. One system hangs vertical lines looped under the boom from double topping lifts; the other system uses non-vertical jacks suspended from a line on each side of the sail running from the boom near its after end to a point on the mast more than two-thirds of the way up. Some disadvantages of traditional systems are chafe on the sails and the jacks tangling or otherwise fouling. The non-vertical system, which has the advantage of being most easily adjustable, needs fairleads under the boom to prevent the looped lazyjacks from slipping along the boom; thus roller reefing can't be used.

In recent years modern variations on traditional lazyjacks have been developed to avoid some of the problems associated with the older systems. The best-known modern systems are the Doyle Stack-Pack®, using non-vertical lazyjacks and the Dutchman, using vertical jacks. The latter system, produced by Martinus Van Breems, Inc., of Westport, Connecticut, is said to be effective with modern, stiff sail cloth. It uses coated wire jacks suspended from a single topping lift with the vertical wires woven through a series of grommets in the sail. Advantages of this patented method include the reduction of chafe and entanglements, neat stacking, and the elimination of double lines (one on each side of the sail). Trade-offs are the difficulty of properly tensioning the jacks so as not to affect sail camber or create slackness that could cause fouling (like on the spreaders!), wearing of the plastic coating on the wires, adjustments of the topping lift to keep the jacks precisely vertical, and the difficulty of putting on a waterproof sail cover. (An alternative system, using dacron cord and a continuous topping lift, allows easy adjustment from the deck.) Doyle Sailmakers has alleviated the sail cover problem with a pouchlike cover into which the sail drops as it is lowered. The Stack-

The Dutchman® (above) features lazyjacks attached to the topping lift and woven through grommets in the mainsail so that the sail automatically flakes itself on the boom when lowered. (Courtesy of Martinus Van Breems, Inc.)

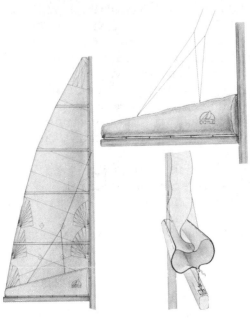

Doyle Sailmakers offers a Stackpack® that combines a fully battened mainsail, integral lazyjacks, and a built-in sail cover.

Pack® uses full-length battens that run parallel to the boom, and they help make a neat stack, but still the sail usually must be manually helped into the cover.

 With any kind of lazyjacks, full-length battens can assist in lowering and reefing and often eliminate the need for reef points except perhaps in extremely heavy weather. Other benefits of full-length battens are that they prevent the sail

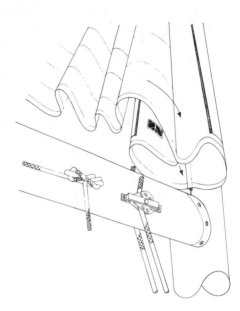

The Zip-Stop® mainsail from Zip-Stop, Inc. has a two-ply luff with zippers on each side. To furl the battenless sail, a special halyard pulls a scoop down from the masthead. This gathers the sail along the luff and zips the cover behind it.

from flogging, hold camber in light airs, extend sail life, and allow a large roach for extra sail area, although the roach must be limited when there is a permanent backstay. On the negative side, full-length battens add weight aloft, provide a greater chance of fouling or causing slides to bind, and make it more difficult to change or remove the sail. BOC winner Philippe Jeantot thinks fully-battened sails are fine for light winds, but he used a battenless main with slightly hollow leech in the strong westerlies of the Southern Ocean.

Another mainsail-furling system that is appropriate for singlehanding is the Zip-Stop® system, developed by Bill Stephens of St. Michaels, Maryland, and sold by North Sails and Ulmer-Kolius. This system uses a furling sock/slider that travels up and down the luff on a boltrope zipper. When the sock is pulled down from the head after the outhaul is released, it gathers in the sail and encloses it in a two-ply luff, which forms a protective cover just abaft the mast. Unfurling is accomplished by hoisting the sock and pulling out the clew with the outhaul. Reefing is accomplished with the conventional jiffy method which will be described in the next section. An early form of Zip-Stop® used no battens, but later short battens installed at less than right angles to the leech were used. Now there is even a so-called "wing" which makes it possible to zip up a special, fully-battened sail by hauling on a looped line, which causes external rod battens to turn vertically so that they will fit into the sock. I am a bit wary of the system in very heavy weather when the deeply reefed sail must be rehoisted to be enclosed, and also some zippers have been known to bind or jam.

A wishbone boom can also make life easier for the singlehander, as it is normally carried with the forward end raised higher than the after end, preventing the boom from riding up and excessively twisting the sail, and eliminating the need for a boom vang. Furthermore, it is possible to rig cradle lines under the wishbone to catch the sail when it is lowered. With a wishbone, the singlehander is less likely to be hit on the head by the boom. Such a system is used by designer Mark Ellis with his Nonsuch rig. A half wishbone has been devised by Bierig Sailmakers for self-tending headsails. A curved aluminum spar is fitted inside a large pocket, and the spar inverts in order to change camber when tacks are changed. The device is marketed under the name Camberspar®, and it has been used effectively on some of the Garry Hoyt Freedom boats. An obvious drawback of any self-tending sail is that it can't overlap the mast, and therefore falls short on power in light weather.

Reducing and Changing Sail

Two of the greatest problems for the singlehander are reefing and changing sails. Even casual cruising requires that different headsails of suitable size and cut be set for various strengths of wind, and, of course, mainsails and mizzens must be reduced or changed in heavy weather.

In current vogue, in American waters at least, is the jiffy (also called slab) reefing system. This is merely a simplified, quick version of conventional points reefing made possible by today's superior sail cloth and relatively short booms. With jiffy reefing the primary load-carrying line is a clew earing, which is led from a point near the outboard end of the boom up through a reef grommet in the sail's leech, then back down to a cheek block on the boom (or to an internal sheave), and then forward to a winch. The reef grommet at the tack is often attached to a hook or horn near the gooseneck. Only a few reef points or a lacing line rove through eyelets are needed to hold up the bunt (loose part of the sail that hangs down). Some boats use none at all. If the sail has slides at the foot, shock cord rove through the eyelets can be secured to specially-made hooks attached to the sail slides (see Figure 5-5).

A handy jiffy-reefing system for singlehanders uses a single reefing line to haul down the clew and tack cringles (grommets), and this line, along with the halyard, is led back to a winch at the forward end of the cockpit. If there are lazyjacks to contain the bunt and keep it from hanging down, the singlehander need not leave the cockpit (unless, perhaps, the weather were so severe that the bunt required extensive securing with points or a lacing line). Single-line jiffy reefing is illustrated in Figure 5-5, which shows the earing tackles inside the boom. To reef, the singlehander slacks the sheet, slacks the halyard enough to compensate for the reduced luff length, and hauls in on the earing until the tack and clew cringles come down to the boom. Winching the earing taut tensions the foot to help provide a flat sail for heavy weather. Finally, the halyard is winched taut to tension the luff and pull the draft forward where it belongs. Of course, the topping lift must be set up to support the boom during the operation. Incidentally, I would recommend a topping lift of low-stretch rope (that cannot chafe the leech or fatigue at the masthead sheave), operable from the deck. It is also valuable as a spare halyard.

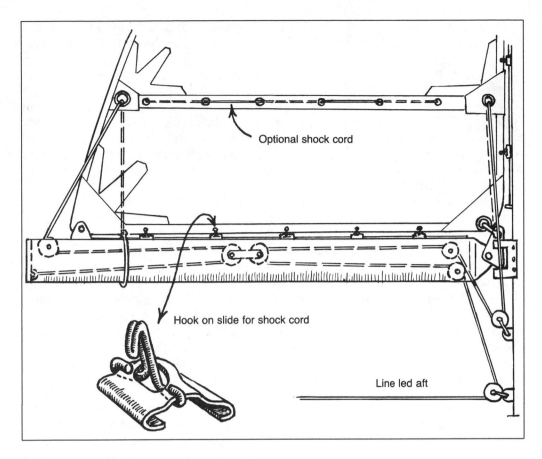

Figure 5-5. Multipurchase one-line jiffy reefing.

Although roller reefing is not as popular as it was at one time, the system is far from dead. Clare Francis used it successfully on her solo Atlantic crossing in 1973. The only trouble she had with her gear came from its binding as a result of saltwater corrosion, but this problem was all but eliminated with lubrication. Of course, roller-reefing systems should be properly designed, and often they are not on stock boats. Common deficiencies are undersized gear, an inadequate flange to hold the luff of the sail aft, a handle that slips off, too great a boom diameter near the gooseneck to allow for the build-up of luff rope when the boom is turned, and, especially, an incorrectly shaped boom to allow a proper sail shape after it is reefed. The best-shaped boom (seldom seen) has a wider diameter aft than forward to prevent excessive droop of the boom's after end when a deep reef is rolled in. If the boom is not made this way, its diameter aft can quite often be increased by fastening tapered wood strips to its after end. Marcel Bardiaux, who used roller reefing so effectively on his *Les 4 Vents*, had a bulge on the lower side of his boom so that after a reef was rolled in he could leave the boom turned with the bulge downward to flatten or remove camber from the sail, which usually is highly desirable in heavy weather. Another disadvantage of roller reefing is the inability to apply foot tension with an outhaul, but this can be alleviated with the use of full-length battens.

With roller reefing, a long track for the gooseneck slide is helpful because the singlehander can then ease the halyard until the slide is at the bottom of its track, and then turn the boom, winding the sail around it, until the boom reaches the top of the track. Next, the halyard is slacked again until the boom is down, and the process is repeated. In this way, the singlehander does not have to slack off the halyard at the same time he is cranking the boom around. Of course, the lower sail slides should be on a relieving line, and they should be removed before the reefing operation begins. The reefed sail's boom should be left fairly high on the gooseneck track in order that the luff can be easily tightened with a downhaul tackle. A taut luff will not only flatten the sail, but also will keep the camber forward for efficiency and to minimize heeling.

Reel winches which self-store a wire halyard are slow when hoisting, and they can be dangerous, especially so for a singlehander. More than a few experienced sailors have been injured by a spinning handle as a result of the brake slipping or the handle slipping out of the operator's hand. In most cases, a lone sailor should not use reel winches, despite their handiness. Nevertheless, in the case of internal halyards, where the mainsail will be deeply reefed, it may be desirable to have an all-wire halyard that is self-storing on a reel, rather than a wire halyard with a rope tail, because, with the latter system, the reefed sail must be supported by the relatively weak linkage of a wire-to-rope splice. With external halyards, however, the wire and rope can be joined by the stronger arrangement of two eye splices over thimbles. I once had a wire-to-rope splice pull apart inside the mast, and so I am a bit sensitive on this point. If reel winches are used, it is advisable to use a toggle-screw type (such as that made by Barient) by which the pressure on the halyard can be released gradually and/or use a winch wheel to eliminate the need for a handle that can strike the operator. With the toggle screw, it is often possible to release the brake just enough that the boom can be turned while the halyard is eased automatically when roller reefing. A further suggestion for offshore sailors is to frequently wash the salt out from under the brake band for smooth, easy operation. (Oil should never be used on the band.)

Internal halyards have their good and bad points. They reduce windage and noise resulting from slapping the mast, and they help prevent fouling, but they are less accessible for inspection and repairs and large halyard exits allow the mast to fill with water rapidly in rainy weather or in the event of an extreme knockdown.

A handy arrangement for the singlehander is drum roller reefing whereby the boom is turned by a wire wound around a drum on the forward end of the boom. The wire is led from the drum to a block at the base of the mast and thence back to a winch accessible from the cockpit (Figure 5-6). With the halyard also led back to the cockpit it is possible for the lone sailor to reef without having to go forward. A variation of this system is being used by Richard Wilson on his trimaran *Curtana*.

A very deep reef of any kind has its drawbacks, because extreme reduction results in an undesirable sail shape, boom droop, or excessive bunt that can fill with water and be difficult to secure. Furthermore, in a real blow, it is not always desirable to have the mainsail attached to a boom that can swing about and possibly cause damage or injury. Quite often a battenless, loose-footed storm trysail is the best choice in a prolonged storm, especially if the boat will be hove to (see Chapter 10). The trysail should be slightly smaller than a triple-reefed main, should

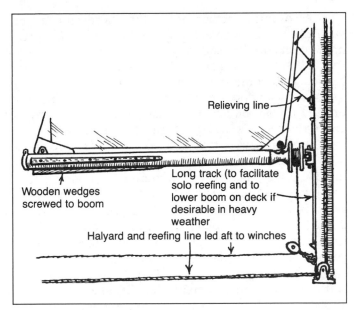

Figure 5-6. Drum roller reefing.

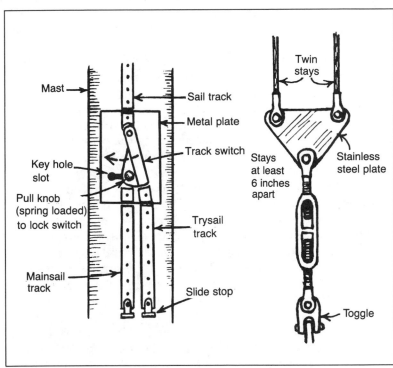

Figure 5-7. Sail changing systems.

have its own sheets to avoid attachment to the main boom, and should have its own full-length track on the mast. A less desirable arrangement than the full-length track is a short track on which the trysail can be bent and a switch that routes the sail slides to the main track as illustrated in Figure 5-7.

A common method of handling headsail changes on a singlehander's boat is with the use of twin side-by-side headstays. This rig allows two headsails to be hanked on simultaneously, and it is a relatively easy matter to lower a jib, transfer the halyard to the new jib, and hoist away. Of course two jib halyards can be carried, and sometimes, when it is desirable to keep the boat balanced or keep maximum way on, the new jib can be hoisted before the old one is lowered. The unused jib can be left permanently hanked on, stopped to the pulpit, or bagged. Often the bags are sausage-shaped and closed with zippers. Another possible advantage of twin stays is that there is a spare in case one should happen to break.

In theory, twin stays sound very workable, but in practice they have certain disadvantages, such as the difficulty in obtaining equal tension on each stay, sag and inefficiency caused by the luff not being on the boat's centerline, extra weight and windage, and the problem of getting the stays far enough apart so that they don't interfere with each other. Quite often when a jib is set on the windward stay it will sag to leeward and the luff will chafe against the leeward stay. There have even been cases of the jib hanks (even piston hanks) clipping themselves to both stays. This happened to Clare Francis, and she decided to do away with the twin-stay system. With sufficient practice, she found that sail changes could be made almost as easily with a single stay. Of course, with one stay, a replacement jib can be hanked on beneath the lower hank of the jib that is already hoisted, so that if a change is required, the hoisted jib can merely be unclipped as it is lowered; and then the new jib can be hoisted immediately after the halyard is transferred. Then, too, very-light-weather sails can be hoisted flying on their own wire luffs.

The problem of unequal tension on twin stays might be alleviated with the use of an inverted triangular plate with each stay attached to the top corners and a turnbuckle from the stemhead attached to the triangle's bottom corner (see Figure 5-7). A "U" bolt was used in a similar way by Mike McMullen in the 1972 OSTAR, but it broke and had to be replaced during the passage.

Strongbow (see Chapter 4) had an interesting arrangement for simplifying jib changes. She had two widely spaced headstays secured some distance abaft the stem, and directly under the stays was a large, self-draining locker that could be closed with a sliding hatch cover. The jibs were tacked down inside the locker so that they could be lowered directly into it. The claim was made that a jib could be hoisted and sheeted without leaving *Strongbow's* cockpit.

A fairly recent development in yacht racing is the headsail luff support systems containing double slots. The best of these systems, first popularized in America by Tim Stern and Ted Hood, use a streamlined aluminum extrusion, which either fits over an existing headstay or stands on its own (depending on the particular system), having two full-length grooves into which the bolt ropes of the jibs are fed. The arrangement is handy on racing boats, because headsails can be changed without the need of lowering the sail to be taken off until its replacement has been hoisted, but the system has also proved useful for the singlehander when the foil is used with roller furling (to be described later). With proper feeders, one at the bottom of the foil and a lower feeder attached by a lanyard to the tack fitting, it is possible for the lone sailor to hoist the sail from the cockpit or mast without the need to hank or unhank a jib. The side-by-side, double-slot arrangement also allows two headsails to be set simultaneously for running downwind.

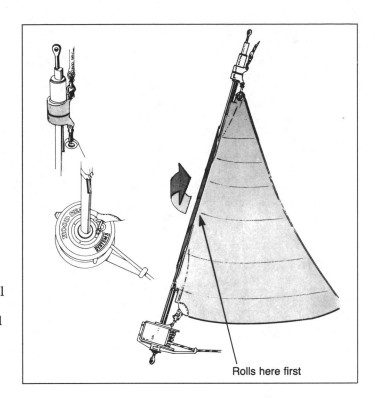

Figure 5-8. The Sea Furl system with double swivel action permits the foil to turn ahead of the tack and head, thereby removing a slight amount of camber. (Courtesy of Hood Yacht Systems)

Rolls here first

Undoubtedly the greatest drawback of a slotted-foil-stay system, aside from occasional feeder jams, is that when a sail is lowered there are no hanks to hold the luff on board, and the sail can slide overboard, although it will not be lost entirely because of being secured at the tack. The singlehander can alleviate the problem by having ample nets rigged from the forward lifelines. With some foils, sturdy slugs (cylindrical sail slides) that fit inside the groove can be sewn to the jib luff to retain advantages of hanks, but then automatic feeding will be sacrificed unless perhaps the slugs could be stored in an attachable magazine.

There is a special problem in lowering a jib that is tacked to the end of a long bowsprit because of the danger that the singlehander might fall overboard. Of course, there should be a sturdy safety net rigged from the bowsprit shrouds, but even so, a long sprit is precarious to work on. Alain Gerbault once fell from his but was lucky enough to catch hold of the bobstay and haul himself back aboard. In the old days, boats with long bowsprits were often fitted with traveller rings by which the tack of a hankless jib could be hauled inboard for sail changes. The same thing might be accomplished by the more modern method of using a slide on a track.

Robin Knox-Johnston used the simpler arrangement of leading a line from the jib's tack through a block on the end of the bowsprit and then aft. Of course, this method failed to hold the tack close to the sprit when tension on the tack line was released, but apparently that was no great disadvantage. Robin wrote in his log, "The procedure for changing sails was as follows: Let fly the tack. This allowed the storm jib to come inboard and I unshackled it. Next slack away the halyard until

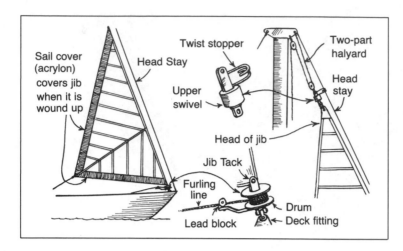

Figure 5-9. Standard roller furling.

the sail is on deck and unshackle it, and lastly unshackle the sheet. I then shackle up the peak, tack, and clew of the 'Big Fellow' and hoist it up halfway on the halyard. This is to keep it clear of the water once I haul it forward on its tack. With the tack made fast I haul the sail up taut and then trot aft to adjust the sheet." It should be said that this was not all there was to the procedure, because *Suhaili* had a triple-head rig, and the "Big Fellow" was actually a large flying jib forward of a working jib, which in turn was forward of a boomed staysail. The working jib could be released from the bowsprit with a Highfield lever, and it was usually taken in when the large flying jib was set. Robin wrote that he always set one jib before handing the other in order to provide a lee and also to maintain balance throughout the operation.

An obviously valuable arrangement for a singlehander is the roller furling concept, whereby a sail can be rolled up on its own luff. Standard rigs utilize a head swivel and roller drum below the tack which stores a furling line (see Figure 5-9). Casting off the furling line and hauling on the sheet causes the sail to unwind; the reverse procedure furls it up again. Quite often, sail can be reduced by partially rolling up the sail, although some manufacturers of the gear do not encourage this. The primary disadvantages of sailing with a partially rolled sail are that there are severe strains on the foot and leech, the rolled sail's shape is not ideal, and there is no way to tension the luff to flatten the draft and pull it forward where it belongs. Nevertheless, partially rolled jibs can be used sailing well off the wind where strains and the harmful effects of distortion are minimized. All but two of the finishers in the second BOC Challenge, mostly a downwind event, used roller furling headsails.

Roller furling comes in a variety of forms: unsupported wire luff, grooved foils (already described), twin headsail gear, and internal (inside spar) furling. The latter system, devised by P. T. Jackson and marketed by Hood as Stoway® furling, proved extremely useful to Dodge Morgan on his circumnavigation and even to Phil Weld on the mostly upwind OSTAR. Most types of roller furling can be operated electrically and even hydraulically, but there should always be a manual means of operation, because electricity often fails in heavy weather and hydraulic seals can leak. Drawbacks of internal furling are some sacrifice to sail shape (no battens nor roach,

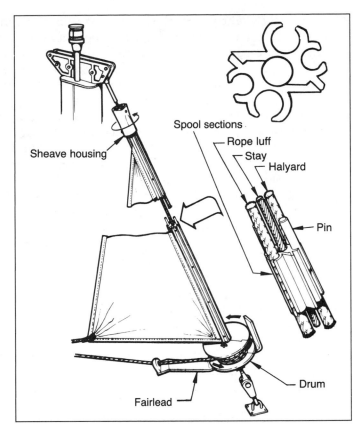

Figure 5-10. Famet Marine roller furling (*right*).
Figure 5-11. (*below*) The Hood Stoway System proved its worth in the circumnavigation of Dodge Morgan, as well as to Phil Weld in the 1980 OSTAR. (Courtesy of Hood Yacht Systems)

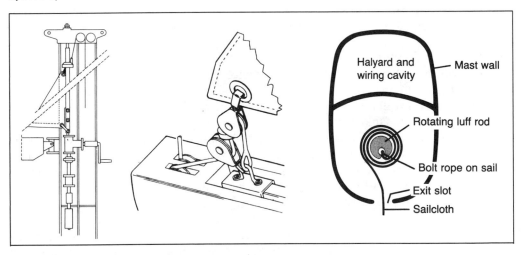

for example), occasional jams, and often a wailing sound from the wind when the sail is furled.

Each type of furling system has its advantages and disadvantages. Unsupported wire-luff furling, such as the systems made by Schaefer and Blue Water

Marine, is set slightly abaft the forestay as illustrated in Figure 5-9, and winds up around an internal luff wire that is not connected to a stay. This allows the furled sail to be lowered to the deck when it is desirable to hank on a heavy weather jib or full-hoist light air jib to the forestay. The trouble with this system is lack of torsional stiffness (compared with a foil) in the roller-furling jib and the difficulty in obtaining adequate luff tension for good windward performance.

Grooved foils, described earlier, have much greater torsional strength (resistance to twisting) and can better keep the luff straight, but again there is the problem of the sail being unattached by its luff when it is being lowered and thus some danger of it being blown or washed overboard. For shorthanded offshore work where considerable sail changing may be necessary, I lean toward a system that accepts slides or sturdy slugs in the luff groove, as with Famet Marine's Reefurl® or Supermarine's Superfurl®. The Mariner Company produces a roller jib that uses hanks, but although this system is in most respects praiseworthy, there is a problem with chafe on the hanks when sailing with the jib partially rolled. Heavy chafing patches on the jib are a help. Another alternative is to use luff stops, lashing lines that secure the sail to the foil, such as those made by North Sails. These require grommets spaced about 30 inches apart in the luff through which the stops are threaded. With the North arrangement each stop is tied by slipping a loop in its end over a button on the stop.

All roller systems suffer to some degree from lack of proper draft and shape when the sail is used partially rolled. Since there is no way to tension the rolled sail's luff as the wind increases, the draft is generally too full and too far aft. Partial solutions to this problem are to use a very flat-cut sail, and use a system that reduces draft as the sail is rolled, such as North Sail's Aeroluff® (a mid-luff, rotating boltrope), foam luff (a foam-padded luff), or a double-swivel drum (a drum with double-swivel action, allowing the tack and head to lag slightly behind the foil as it turns). The latter system is illustrated in Figure 5-8. These solutions are not very effective except for the first several turns of the roller jib. Most of the BOC racers used foam-padded luffs.

Jib roller furling seems most appropriate when there is an inner forestay or staysail stay that can carry a sizeable staysail. This plan provides a backup headsail in the event of a roller jib failure. Although many offshore solo racers carry roller staysails, I prefer a hanked-on staysail for ocean sailing. There is some chafe on the jib from the staysail hanks when coming about, but there is seldom a need to short tack offshore. Hal Roth warns against using Wichard hanks, which are modern snaphooks, because his jib sheets would snag on them when coming about. However, these hanks do allow snapping and unsnapping with one hand.

Roller-furling twin headsails were used for singlehanding as early as 1930, when Otway Waller devised the system, primarily for self-steering in following winds. Paul Hammond, on his Starling Burgess-designed *Barnswallow*, later modified the rig, and, in recent years, Wright Britton has improved on the system with his "Roller Jeni Wings." Britton's rig seems to be a well-engineered and versatile arrangement, for the twins—two identical headsails sewn to the same roller luff wire—can be carried with their clews locked together, and their tacks fastened together near the stem to produce, in effect, a single, roller-furling jib; or the tacks can be secured to a point just forward of the mast to produce a balanced wing-and-wing rig for downwind sailing (see Figure 6-8 in the next chapter).

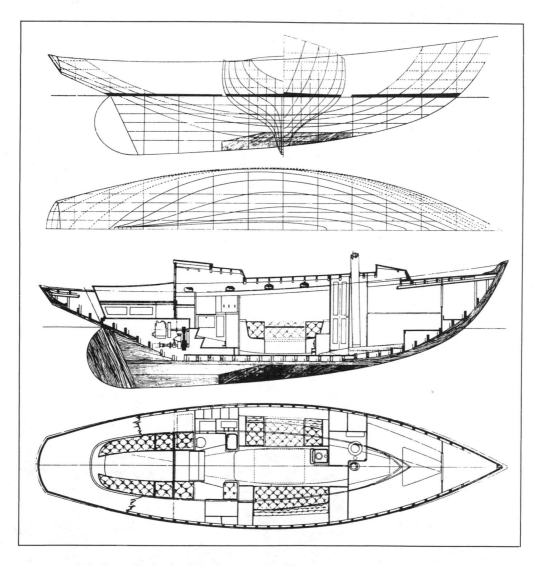

Figure 5-12. Paul Hammond's *Barnswallow*, built especially for singlehanding, anticipated the central control concept. She has a long keel of moderate draft for good directional stability and ease of entering shallow harbors. (Courtesy of the executors of Uffa Fox, deceased)

Much of the modern gear that has been discussed can improve efficiency and simplify operations on any yacht. Innovations and refinements, such as head foils, internal halyards, roller-furling mainsails, and so forth, may be advantageous for the singlehander who cruises short distances in relatively protected waters, but those who make distant passages offshore should be extremely cautious about fitting out with gear that is very complex and sophisticated. If such equipment is used, it is important that the singlehander use the specific brand that has proven most reliable and learn how to service and repair the gear. Back-up systems should be provided in the event of failures or irreparable breakages.

Galway Blazer, skippered by Peter Crowther in the 1976 OSTAR. (Courtesy of Jonathan Eastland)

6

Self-Steering

A<small>N ESSENTIAL REQUIREMENT FOR</small> long-distance singlehanding is the ability to make the boat steer herself. It is obvious that the lone sailor must be able to leave the helm to perform necessary chores and satisfy essential body demands, most especially to sleep.

Natural Ability

In the early days, natural course keeping was not quite the problem it is today, because, if I may be allowed a sweeping generality, most well-balanced cruising boats of former times had more consistent directional stability than modern stock boats of low wetted area. Men like Slocum, Blackburn, Tom Drake, and even William Andrews could very often get their vessels to steer themselves on most points of sailing by simply adjusting the sheets and/or securing the helm, whereas this technique is seldom possible with fast, modern designs except for relatively short intervals while sailing close-hauled. Good course keepers like the *Spray* and Drake's *Pilgrim* derived their steadiness, for the most part, from their long keels, relatively symmetrical waterlines, favorable longitudinal relationship of the center of gravity to the true center of lateral resistance, high initial stability, and longitudinally spread out low aspect ratio rigs. In contrast, the latest racing-cruiser has a short fin keel, either a wedge-shaped or diamond-shaped hull, a very fine entry, a tall rig concentrated over the load waterline, and initial tenderness for the sake of a favorable handicap rating, and these characteristics discourage natural course keeping.

Easy heeling affects the steadiness of the helm in modern boats for several reasons. First, there is a wide separation in the transverse direction of the sail's

The schooner *Pilgrim*, sailed solo across the Atlantic by her creator Thomas Drake, proved to be a natural course keeper. (Courtesy of *Yachting* magazine)

center of thrust and the hull's center of resistance, especially when the rig is tall and the draft is deep, and thus a strong turning moment is created, which varies with the angle of heel. Second, the waterlines on many modern hulls become highly asymmetrical with heeling. Third, wedge-shaped or fine-ended boats will often change their longitudinal trim when heeled, thus changing the relationship of the center of lateral resistance with centers of gravity and effort.

Singlehander and yachting editor Alain Gliksman, who won the under-35-foot award in the 1972 OSTAR, described the difficulties of balancing a heeled boat designed to the International Offshore Rule with the remark: "I don't like the modern IOR boats because when they heel it is like trying to drown a cat—it keeps wanting to come up again; it gets wild and you are getting nowhere." The increasing use of skegs and rudders with some rake aft (rather than the usual forward rake of the typical spade rudder) has helped some of the newest boats, but still, most modern racing-cruisers need special assists for self-steering. Certainly the new breed of boat is a far cry from such naturally stable course-holders as the 35-foot schooner *Pilgrim*, which Drake claimed would steer herself by the trim of her sails alone "for days and days and days on any point of sailing." Self-steering assists needed by the modern boats take the form of wind vane gears, autopilots, special self-steering sails, and sheet-to-helm connections.

Vane Gears

There are a number of vane gear systems, the most common being: (1) the trim tab type, with the wind vane driving a tab on the main rudder; (2) auxiliary rudder types, with the vane driving its own separate rudder; (3) the servo-pendulum type, whereby the vane twists a vertical pendulum paddle, causing the waterflow to swing the paddle laterally and thus control the helm; and (4) above-water types, whereby the vane controls the helm directly and the self-steering device has no underwater parts.

Although vane steering had been used on model boats for some time previously, Marin-Marie is credited with being the first to use this kind of self-steering on a full-sized yacht, when the Frenchman made a transatlantic solo crossing in the motorboat *Arielle* in 1936. The boat was fitted with an electric automatic pilot, but this was seldom used except in flat calms, and most of the self-steering was accomplished with the use of a V-shaped wind vane connected to an auxiliary rudder mounted on the transom. A significant contribution to the art was made in 1955 when English designer Michael Henderson fit his midget ocean racer, *Mick the Miller*, with a vane gear, which some observers claimed could sail the boat to windward better than could a good helmsman. The gear consisted of a small vane with a nearly vertical axis linked to an auxiliary semi-balanced rudder. Then in 1956, Ian Major made a doublehanded Atlantic crossing in the 25-foot *Buttercup*, a twin-keel boat fitted with many innovations including a vane gear of the trim tab kind. Another pioneer, who reportedly was working on vane gear designs as early as 1953, is H. G. Hasler. He used a trim tab on the outboard rudder of his *Jester*, and later he developed a servo-pendulum gear manufactured by M. S. Gibb Ltd. in England.

The simplest, or at least the most easily understandable, vane steering is the kind that has previously been designated as Type 4, the above-water gear. This controls the helm with the vane alone, and there are no underwater parts. A simple gear of this kind and its operation is illustrated in Figure 6-1. To put the gear in operation, the plywood vane is weathercocked into the wind, and the steering lines are crossed and attached to the tiller. When the boat strays off course, the vane changes its angle to the boat and pulls on the appropriate steering line to make the course correction as illustrated. Notice that there is a counterbalancing weight on the vane that offsets the effect of gravity when the boat is heeled or rolling. The V-flaps at the vane's trailing edge are not necessary, perhaps, but some authorities claim they add greater torque at low angles of attack and cause quicker response.

The simple vane gear shown in Figure 6-1 is probably only suitable for a quite small, well-balanced boat. For a large boat using this system, the area of the vane would have to be very large in order to generate sufficient power, but the large size would be difficult to manage in heavy weather. When Francis Chichester used this type of gear in 1960 on his *Gipsy Moth III*, he alleviated the difficulty to some degree by making his vane, which he dubbed "Miranda," from cloth so that it could be "reefed," in effect, in a blow. As compared with plywood, cloth is not as durable, but it can have a bit of camber to increase the power. More recently the power of the above-water vane gear has been increased without the need for an extremely large vane area by such innovations as the dual-axis, vertically-pivoted vane acting as a pantograph, wedge-shaped or V-shaped vanes, similar to that of the *Arielle* (with the apex of the V pointing into the wind), and vanes with horizontal or nearly horizontal axes.

The latter types are especially popular, and one of the simplest gears, similar to the QME (Quantock Marine Enterprises) vane, designed by Peter Beard, is illustrated in Figures 6-2 and 6-3. It can be seen that the vane is weathercocked, and when the boat strays off course the vane will tip over on its horizontal axis, exerting a considerable force on the appropriate steering line. Notice in Figure 6-3

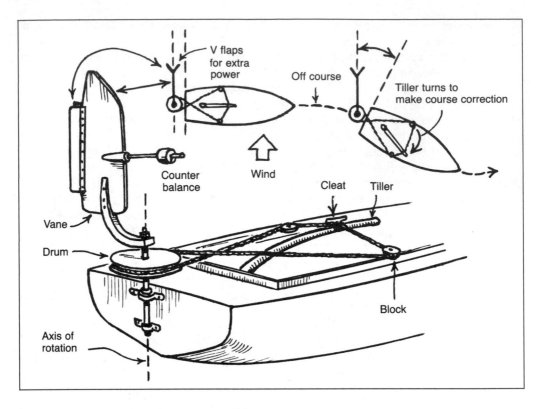

Figure 6-1. Simple vane gear for a small boat.

that when the counterbalance weight is to windward on the starboard tack, the steering lines are crossed and we have what is called a reverse linkage, but when on the port tack with the weight to leeward the lines are rigged directly (uncrossed) to the tiller. The steering lines are changed over quite easily with a pair of snaphooks.

We used a QME gear on our well-balanced fin-keel, spade-rudder Cal 2-30 sloop and later on our Ohlson 38, which has a full keel but with a small rudder separated from the keel and mounted on a small skeg. The device worked quite well on both boats in steady conditions when reaching and beating, but it was not successful in light, shifty winds or when running. As a matter of fact, many types of vane gears fail when running, because of the weakening of the apparent wind on that point of sailing and also because of quartering seas slewing the stern off course and/or heeling the boat and because of the sudden acceleration when the boat begins to surf. Incidentally, a spade rudder often causes greater friction than a well-engineered rudder hung on gudgeons, but many spades are semi-balanced (with the turning axis somewhat abaft the leading edge), and this design partially alleviates the problem. Some real advantages of a small, above-water vane gear are that it is light in weight and easily detachable, there is no need to deface the boat's stern with heavy, ugly brackets or special boomkins to support underwater parts, and most important, there is no additional drag to detract from speed. On the other hand, the above-water gear on a large boat will not normally be as effective or powerful as a well-designed gear having submerged appendages.

Francis Chichester's *Gipsy Moth III* being steered by "Miranda," a large, reefable vane having no special appendages underwater. (Courtesy of *Yachting* magazine)

When the position and installation of the rudder allows it, the main rudder trim tab (Type 1) turned by the wind vane is an effective self-steerer. This type has been used successfully by Hasler, Howell, Nance, and many others, and a standard gear of this type of Hasler's design is made by Gibb Ltd., in England. The system seems best suited for outboard rudders hung on double-enders or transom-sterned boats. The basic principle of operation is quite simple. The vane turns a tab attached to the trailing edge of the rudder. Water flow on the tab forces the rudder in the opposite direction to which the tab is turned. In other words, if the tab is turned to port, the rudder is forced to starboard. In practice, the system is more complex, since there are many subtleties in the engineering of a particular rig that can affect the performance. A direct vane-to-tab linkage has been used successfully on occasion, but in many cases such a linkage can cause oversteering and yawing problems. Quite often, reduction linkage is used to reduce the tab response, such as the simple, slotted-bar linkage shown in Figure 6-4, which creates a mechanical advantage and angle differences between the vane and tab. Ordinarily, of course, the helm is left to swing free with the main rudder trim tab simply initiating the

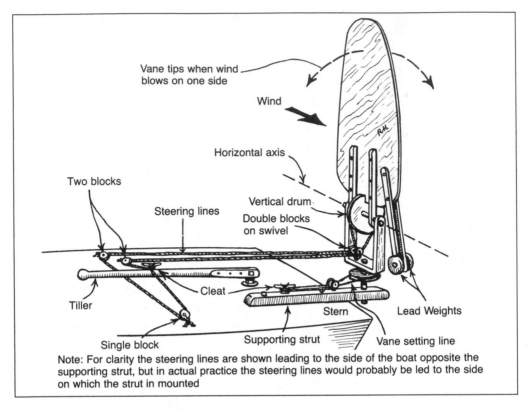

Figure 6-2. Horizontal axis vane (similar to the QME gear).

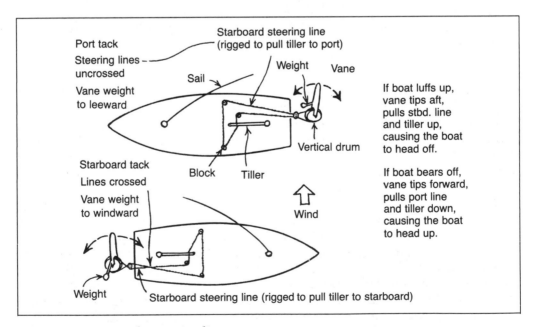

Figure 6-3. Crossing the steering lines.

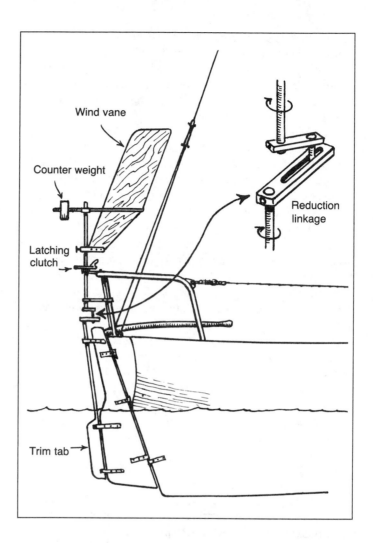

Figure 6-4. Trim tab gear.

Slotted bar reverse
linkage on OSTAR racer
Bollemaat IV.

steering, but in certain cases, when sailing at high speeds, the helm might be lashed, leaving the steering to the tab alone.

When a standard make such as the Gibb cannot be found, it may not be difficult to fabricate the trim tab gear if the boat has an outboard rudder. In Jimmy Cornell's *Ocean Cruising Survey*, based on interviews with nearly 200 small boat voyagers, Cornell reported on self-steering that "best results were achieved by those able to fit a trim tab to their main rudder." Such a system causes minimal drag as compared with other underwater gears, although a tab normally cannot be lifted out of water when it is not in use. Also, this method requires no complicated system of lines and blocks. A currently-made gear of this type is Saye's Rig made by Scanmar Marine Products in California.

Auxiliary rudders (Type 2) are sometimes used when the main rudder is inboard and difficult to fit with a trim tab. In this case a secondary rudder, controlled by the vane, is often mounted outboard, generally on the transom and/or stern pulpit. Occasionally, an auxiliary rudder is permanently mounted inboard on its own skeg, as in the case of *Mick the Miller*, and this system can be very effective. It has at least one drawback, however, in that a non-removable auxiliary rudder always adds somewhat to the underwater drag, even though it can be kept quite small when semi-balanced. On the other hand, a stern-mounted auxiliary rudder, if it is not too heavy, can be designed for easy raising or removal when not in use, eliminating drag, harmful weight aft, unsightliness, and possible vulnerability to damage in heavy weather. An additional advantage of any auxiliary rudder is that it can serve as an emergency back-up in the event that the main rudder should fail. Some authorities recommend that auxiliary rudder self-steering gears be fitted only on smaller boats (perhaps under 40 feet long), but power can be increased by balancing the rudder blade or adding a trim tab to the trailing edge.

Some well known gears of the auxiliary rudder type are Automate and RVG (Riebant Van Gear). Currently in production is the tab-controlled Auto-Helm made in Los Angeles, California.

It seems that most of the well-known modern singlehanders sailing sizeable boats, including circumnavigators Chichester, Rose, King, Blackwell, Baronowski, and others, have used servo-pendulum self-steering gears. The reason for this is that in recent years these gears have been made highly reliable, they have great power and sensitivity, and they can be readily fitted to the popular counter sterns. Furthermore, most standard types are not outrageously expensive, nor does the boat require modifications, as in the case of a permanent inboard auxiliary rudder with skeg.

Figure 6-5 shows a simple, step-by-step diagram of the gear in operation. This illustration shows no structural supports, as are customarily shown in manufacturers' drawings, because these often add to the complexity and make it difficult to visualize the operation. In step A, the vane turns because of the boat straying off course or the wind shifting (the vane always tries to point into the wind). The turning motion is transmitted through a reverse linkage, in this case a crossed belt or slotted bar, as illustrated, connecting the vane to the underwater pendulum suspended over the stern. The pendulum is twisted (step B), and since it is hinged on a longitudinal axis, the water flow forces it to swing to one side (step C). This motion turns the quadrant at the top of the pendulum and thus pulls the appropriate steering line, which leads to the tiller (step D). Although the procedure may

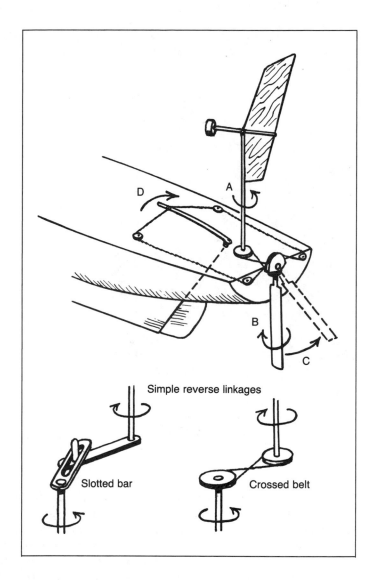

Figure 6-5. Operational principle of the servo-pendulum vane gear.

Simple reverse linkages

Slotted bar

Crossed belt

seem like a Rube Goldberg arrangement, it is really quite efficient. I have been sailing with an Aries vane gear, which uses a servo-pendulum controlled by a small, horizontal-axis vane, and I was quite impressed with the way it steered a heavy 36-footer and a 40-footer (both with moderately long keels) under a variety of difficult conditions. There have been many good reports over the years about the Aries, which is made by Nick Franklin (Marine Vane Gears) in England, and also about the Hasler-Gibb gear (previously mentioned), which uses a vertical-axis vane similar to the one shown in Figure 6-5. Still another popular and relatively inexpensive pendulum gear is produced by Gunning in England. Its vane axis is horizontal, and there is the unusual feature that several different sized vanes can be fitted for different strengths of wind. Indeed, Noel Bevan is said to have carried seven vanes (some spares) on his *Myth of Malham*, but Clare Francis tells us that she used a

The reliable Aries wind vane. (Courtesy of John Rock)

general-purpose vane on her Gunning gear, which eliminated the need for frequent changes. Her gear was badly smashed during a gale in the 1976 OSTAR, but she managed to haul it on board and make repairs with a cat's cradle of lashing lines. Servo-pendulum gears used successfully part time by the BOC racers were the Aries, the exceptionally rugged but heavy Fleming, the Navik, which uses a trim tab on the pendulum, and the highly praised Monitor, which touts low maintenance Delrin ball and roller bearings. According to the *Ocean Cruising Survey*, the Aries is the most commonly used vane gear, but the Monitor seems to have some advantages such as less vulnerability to galvanic corrosion from the mixing of dissimilar metals.

Some specific self-steering gears with their operational details can be seen in the Amateur Yacht Research Society's book, *Self Steering*, edited by John Morwood, and also in John Letcher's book *Self-Steering for Sailing Craft*, Gerard Dijkstra's *Self Steering for Sailboats*, and B. Belcher's *Windvane Selfsteering*. Not all of these books, however, consider in much detail the various alternative ways of attaching the gear to the vessel or the matter of linkage with wheel steering. Attachments must be made in the strongest possible manner, but many sailors rightfully object to boring more holes than necessary and weighing down their sterns with supporting structures that resemble a child's jungle gym. A lot of planning should go into the attachment of the gear, not only for strength, freedom of movement, neatness, and simplicity, but also for flexibility of adjustment after trial and error. It is a wise plan, if possible, to mount the gear in a temporary way in order to test it before the final installation. Many of the individual manufacturers will have ideas about methods of attachment and also about rigging for wheel steering. Marine Vane Gears, for instance, makes a special drum with a clutch that is secured to the wheel for the acceptance of steering lines (see Figure 12-2). The lines may be easily disengaged in a moment by simply pulling a knob to free the wheel for normal sailing, an important feature when sailing in crowded waters. On some boats an emergency tiller might be rigged when the vane gear controls the helm, but unless the wheel steering system works very freely, excessive friction might cause a problem.

A vane gear's power and sensitivity is very much dependent on the mitigation of friction. Whenever possible, it is advisable to use ball bearings and plastic bushings where this is commensurate with strength. Constant lubrication is needed also, because of the saltwater environment. I have heard about and seen quite a few cases of vane gears malfunctioning because corrosion or salt deposits jammed the moving parts. Of course, steering lines, too, must be led fair and run through firmly attached blocks of suitable type and size.

Autopilots

An entirely different approach to self-steering is with the use of an autopilot, which uses an electric motor or hydraulic drive unit to turn the helm or rudder directly. After the boat strays off course, she is turned back to her proper heading when a compass-sensor compares heading with rudder angle and directs the motor or drive unit to move the rudder in the direction that reduces the heading error. The main differences between vane steering and autopilot steering are that the former uses wind and water power to turn the rudder, while the latter uses electric power; and vane gears hold courses in accordance with wind direction, while autopilots normally steer compass courses. Actually some autopilots offer tiny, optional wind-vane attachments so that the boat can be steered either by wind or compass, but these small motor-operating vanes are generally considered inferior to a proper, full-sized, servo-pendulum wind vane.

Formerly, vane steering was considered best for a sailboat under sail, as it could effectively steer the boat to windward, playing the shifts like a helmsman, and especially because it uses no electricity. Nowadays however, most singlehanders—at least those sailing large, fast boats on downwind passages—prefer autopilots, since electro-mechanical efficiency has been improved in recent years, and there are now a variety of means of keeping the batteries charged. Furthermore, autopilot self-steering creates no underwater drag, and it is much more effective for large boats or even small racers when running in steep following seas. The majority of the BOC racers used autopilots as their primary means of steering and vane gears as secondary or back-up means. Sometimes vane steering was used when the wind came from ahead, or at times when conditions were particularly favorable for the vane, or when the batteries were down.

Autohelm 3000. On a well-balanced boat, this small, on-deck autopilot creates a minimal electrical drain.

Just how great the electrical demand of an autopilot will be depends on many factors, such as the model design and power of the particular pilot, the size and weight of the vessel, her balance and yaw characteristics, sea conditions, other electrical equipment, and so forth. A large vessel that is difficult to steer will require an autopilot with considerable torque output, but a small, well-balanced boat might use one of the small, inexpensive, low-powered, on-deck models such as the small Autohelm, CPT Autopilot, First Mate, or Tiller Master. We use an Autohelm 3000 on our Ohlson 38 and figure that in ideal conditions the electrical drain is little more than one light bulb, but our boat is exceptionally well-balanced and easy to steer.

One factor to consider on a long, tough voyage is the vulnerability of the autopilot to water. Many of the small on-deck models are said to be quite vulnerable, particularly those that operate a tiller with a piston arm. On the other hand, some wheel-operating pilots are quite resistant to water. Our Autohelm 3000 survived a filled cockpit, and the CPT pilot is said to run underwater, but belts can break or slip in heavy weather. For maximum safety from water damage and generally better performance, a below-decks installation is best, but this will be more complicated and the pilot much more expensive. Although the highly respected Shannon Boat Company has reported problems with the below-decks Autohelm, the company admits that the pilots may not have been installed correctly.

The technology of autopilots is changing and generally improving all the time. Some of the theoretical improvements are the use of fluxgate compasses, proportional rate correction, and digital feedback. The latter feature uses a microprocessor in sending information between rudder and compass and is allegedly less likely to fail than the old-fashioned mechanical feedback or even the more modern analog feedback. Proportional rate correction is touted as an improvement over the older dead band/proportional correction, whereby the motor is off within a narrow zone of courses and the pilot moves at a steady rate in proportion to the number of degrees off course. With proportional rate, however, pilot speed variation is introduced, and the rudder rate of change is proportional to the heading rate of change. The fluxgate compass is an electronic compass that uses a magnetometer to sense position relative to the earth's magnetic field. As compared with the conventional magnetic compass, the fluxgate is less affected by the boat's motion, and its efficiency is claimed to reduce power consumption. Another feature with the newer autopilots is that they can be interfaced with Loran or other radio navigation systems to provide a course that considers leeway and current. A good source for unbiased information on autopilots is *Practical Sailor*, in Newport, Rhode Island.

On long passages autopilot motors can burn up and parts can wear, so it is important to carry spares. For the second BOC Challenge, winner Philippe Jeantot carried six Autohelms (three 3000s and three 6000s), while Jean Luc van den Heede had nine pilots (mostly Autohelms and Plastimos). Other brands carried and for the most part esteemed by the BOC racers were the Alpha Marine and Course Master pilots. The Alphas have been highly praised by the likes of Dan Byrne, Francis Stokes, and Mark Schrader.

Dodge Morgan carried a pair of Wagner autopilots that became ineffective in heavy weather soon after he started his record breaking circumnavigation, forcing him to put into Bermuda. According to *Cruising World* magazine, the small pilots drew 3.5 amps but became overloaded and failed to control the rudder in the worst conditions. Morgan was forced to trade off electrical economy for power in rough weather by replacing one of the units with a larger pilot that drew 20 amps. Both these consumption figures sound high to me, but I suppose the 60-foot *American Promise* with her big rig was a real handful in a blow.

The disadvantage of battery drainage has become less of a problem as a result of modern experiments with charging devices that use such readily available energy sources as the sun, wind, and water. Attempts have even been made to utilize the vessel's motion and heat from the stove, but better results have been obtained from solar panels, wind generators, and free-wheeling underwater propellers.

The latter system can utilize through-hull shafts with propellers that drive alternators. Although the rotating props cause some drag, they have been used with at least moderate success by transatlantic racers such as *Vendredi 13*, *Second Life*, and *Gazelle*. Also, the BOC racer *Legend Securities* made good use of a similar scheme that utilized a backward-mounted propeller. A variation of this system is a rotator, towed some distance astern from a long line that turns a generator, operating much like a patent log. Towed water generators can be satisfactory for some displacement cruisers but less so for racers because of the rotator's drag and the fact that water generators can burn up at surfing speeds. Despite these drawbacks, however, several BOC racers carried Neptune generators. Ian Kiernan devised a method of preventing burn-ups by altering the length of the tow line so that the rotator would jump out of the water at "red line" revolutions when the boat would begin to surf.

More satisfactory results have been obtained from solar panels. Bill Homewood enthusiastically endorsed his Solarex panels saying that they even "worked in fog and cloud cover." However, his electrical demands on the 31-foot *Third Turtle* were modest compared to those on the large, sophisticated racers that were loaded with electronic gear. (Even so, Hal Roth said that 80 percent of his electric power was generated by solar panels during the second BOC Challenge.) Drawbacks of solar charging are vulnerability of the panels to waves breaking aboard, corrosion, low efficiency with a low sun angle, and reduced output in cloudy weather. On the plus side, solar charging is light, quiet, automatic, and highly reliable when the sun is shining.

Windmills have been used with some success, but wind generation, like any other electricity-producing system, has certain disadvantages. Fan or propeller-type windmills can be dangerous if they are large and located in an exposed area (my cousin was killed by one), and they can be damaged by exceedingly strong winds. OSTAR racer *Strongbow* had her three-foot-diameter aluminum fan blown away during a squall, and BOC racer *Biscuits Lu* lost several blades from her windmills in heavy weather. Windmills need to weathercock and so require a fair amount of space in which to operate. One idea, as yet unproven, for a safe, space-saving wind generator is the Savonius rotor, conceived by my friend Irving Groupp. A cluster of wind-rotated scoops turning an alternator is mounted on a stay or shroud, as shown in Figure 6-6. The advantage of this arrangement is that it requires little room in

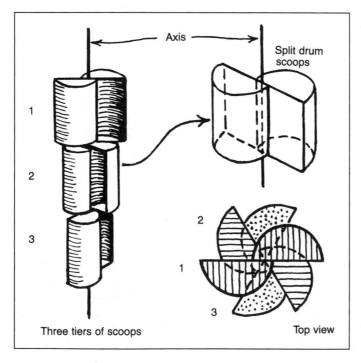

Three tiers of scoops   Top view

Figure 6-6. Savonius-type rotor.

which to operate, is safe and secure, and can be activated by the wind from any direction without weathercocking.

Those sophisticated racers with power hungry communications, navigation, and self-steering systems also need gasoline or diesel-powered generators. Many BOC racers used gasoline-powered Honda or diesel-powered Kubota generators. The drawbacks of such generators are noise, the need for fairly level operation, non-automatic operation, the possibility of mechanical failure, and the need to carry fuel. With respect to the latter, I would much rather carry diesel because of the explosive nature of gasoline. To solve the problem of operation at high angles of heel, some singlehanders mount their generators on gimbals, while others mount them on an angle to be used on one tack only.

Of course, the normal auxiliary-powered cruiser can use her engine to generate electricity. On our boat *Kelpie* the engine drives an alternator and a generator that charge two 12-volt, 95-amp batteries. I have a battery condition meter to show the state of charge of each and a switch that allows each battery to be charged by either the generator or alternator or both. The generator is slower but perhaps more reliable, while the alternator charges much faster but with some sacrifice to longevity. *Kelpie* has very modest electrical equipment, and I find that I only need to run the engine about a half-hour every other day to operate her Autohelm 3000 autopilot.

Steering Sails and Sheet-to-Helm Connections

Many singlehanders have worked out completely satisfactory self-steering arrangements with special steering sails and/or by rigging sheets of special or standard sails to the helm. Although these methods forego a few of the advantages of vane or

Designer and self-steering innovator Frederic A. Fenger singlehanding the 17-foot canoe *Yakaboo* through the West Indies. (Courtesy of Wellington Books)

auto-pilot steering, they can avoid the use of expensive, complicated, and cumbersome equipment, and, of course, there is no electric power drain. Furthermore, with sail self-steering, trial and error experiments are often possible without the need of investing in costly mechanical gear that might prove less than entirely satisfactory.

The innovative singlehander Otway Waller is given credit for inventing self-steering with twin headsails when he sailed the 26-foot yawl *Imogen*, designed by Albert Strange, from Ireland to the Canary Islands in 1930. Shortly thereafter, Frederic A. Fenger, Marin-Marie, and Paul Hammond devised different variations of the same system. More recently, twin-headsail steering has been improved, standardized, and marketed by Wright Britton of Britton Yacht Systems. Even in this age of highly-developed vane gears, twin headsails are a viable form of self-steering, partly because they work so well when running long distances—during tradewind passages for instance—when vane steering is least successful.

The basic principle of the twin-headsail rig is quite simple. Typically, two identical headsails (sometimes called twin staysails, or twin spinnakers, or twin wings) are boomed out on opposite sides of the boat, and their sheets are led back through quarter blocks to the tiller. When the boat strays off course, one twin pulls on its sheet harder than the other twin, which makes the helm correction and returns the boat to her proper course. (See Figure 6-7a). It is desirable to have the twins angled slightly forward so that their outboard edges are somewhat forward of their inboard edges, as illustrated. Waller used an angle of only 10 degrees, but Fenger claimed, as a result of experiments with models, that 23 degrees was ideal. With this wider angle, and some space or gap between the luffs so that some wind can flow between the two sails, Fenger found that it was not necessary to secure the sheets to the helm (see Figure 6-7b). The gap between twin headsails may not be essential for course-keeping, however, because the Britton rig has the luffs of both twins sewn to a common wire with no gap, yet I was told by Wright Britton that a sheet-to-helm connection should not be necessary when the wind is aft.

John Letcher reported negative results in self-steering with his twins unconnected to the helm using a gap and the 23-degree angle, but he conceded that

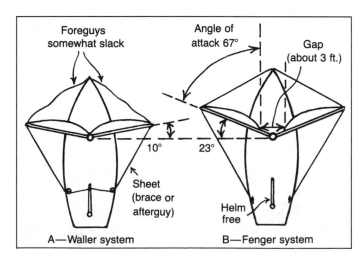

Figure 6-7. Twin headsails.

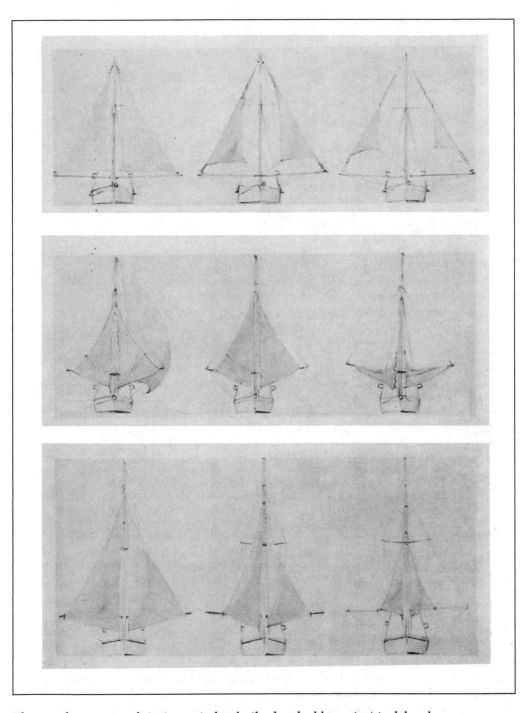

Three early systems of rigging twin headsails sketched by artist/singlehander Marin-Marie. His method used on *Winnibelle* is shown in the middle, while Otway Waller's on *Imogen* is at the top and Paul Hammond's on *Barnswallow* is at the bottom. The latter two systems use roller-furling gears to reduce sail. (From *Wind Aloft, Wind Alow* by Marin-Marie)

A dramatic painting by Marin-Marie of *Winnibelle* running before a storm with her twin headsails set. (From *Wind Aloft, Wind Alow* by Marin-Marie)

angling the twins forward to form a wedge configuration contributes to stability. John feels, however, that the stability is gained at the sacrifice of considerable driving power. It is certainly true that with the 23-degree angle the thrust of the sails is not working in exactly the same direction in which the boat is moving with the wind dead aft, but on the other hand, this configuration with its 67-degree angle of attack causes some aerodynamic lift, which adds to the magnitude of the thrust even if it is from a less-than-optimal direction. Shroudless racing boats often ease their sheets so that their booms are well forward of athwartships with good results, and Fenger claimed that this practice increased directional stability on sailing canoes without loss of speed. As a matter of fact, Marcel Bardiaux made satisfac-

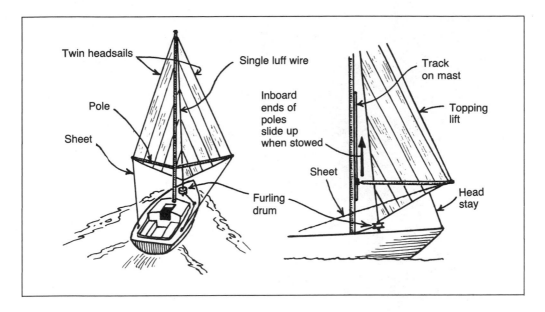

Figure 6-8. Britton twin-headsail system.

tory speed in the trade winds with his twins angled as far forward as 45 degrees, and he claimed his *Les 4 Vents* sailed a steady course with the helm left free.

One of the major differences among the various twin-headsail arrangements is the manner of their setting and handing. The Waller, Hammond, and Britton systems make use of roller-furling gear. Waller had the luffs and furling drums at the outboard ends of the poles, while Hammond had the tack of each twin and two drums located near his *Barnswallow*'s stem. The Britton arrangement has a single roller drum controlling the luffs of both twins tacked down to the foredeck just forward of the mast (see Figure 6-8). With the roller gear, sail is reduced or furled by rolling the twins up on their luffs. Marin-Marie, however, found no need for roller furling; he simply hoisted and lowered the twins with halyards in the conventional way. In some cases, the poles secure at fairly low points on the mast, and their outboard ends are hoisted aloft with their topping lifts so that they lie alongside the mast for convenient stowage when the twins are not being used. Other poles are secured to the mast quite far aloft so that the outboard ends may be dropped to the chainplates for convenient stowage. John Letcher's poles secure to the mast at the lower spreaders, which seems like a good idea, because the mast gets some bracing at that point from the lower shrouds. There is a neat arrangement with the Britton system whereby the inboard ends of the poles are fitted to vertical mast slides, and the inboard pole ends are down, perhaps about seven feet above the cabin top, when in use, but are up at the top of the slides so the poles may be stowed alongside the shrouds or mast when not in use (see Figure 6-8).

Some sailors who use twin-headsail rigs report severe rolling in following seas; thus the outboard ends of the poles must be kept high to prevent the possibility of dipping them in the sea. Of course, this requires that the sails be cut with high clews, and the inboard pole ends not be carried too low, or else the poles will have a tendency to ride upward. In general, it seems best to keep the poles about

Wright Britton's 40-foot yawl *Delight* using Britton "twin wings topsail" for greater speed in light airs. (Courtesy of Wright Britton)

horizontal or cocked upward very slightly. Occasionally, a storm trysail is hoisted and sheeted flat amidships to help damp rolling, but since the true wind is from astern the damping will be minimal. Incidentally, Captain Waller alleviated the rolling of his *Imogen* by hoisting an anchor some distance up the mast, where it was secured to stop it from swinging. Evidently, this raised the center of gravity somewhat and increased the roll inertia to affect the motion beneficially. John C. Voss once used the same trick with some success.

Self-steering with twin headsails works well when the wind is aft or slightly on the quarter, but other systems are needed when the wind is farther forward. Some of these systems are illustrated in Figures 6-9, 6-10, 6-11, and 6-12. Figure 6-9 is an easily-rigged method used by singlehander Tony Skidmore as his "sole means of self-steering" on a 17,000-mile voyage in a 24-foot, fin-keel sloop. As can be seen in the diagram, a small staysail, a storm jib in Skidmore's case, is held slightly aback by a windward sheet led through a block at the shrouds, thence to a quarter

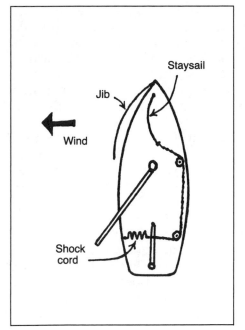

Figure 6-9. Backed staysail
(Tony Skidmore).

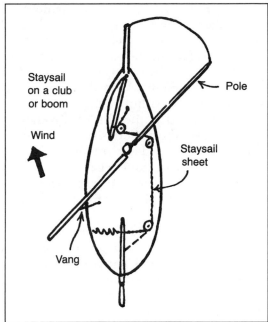

Figure 6-10. Staysail and poled-out jib
(Frank Casper).

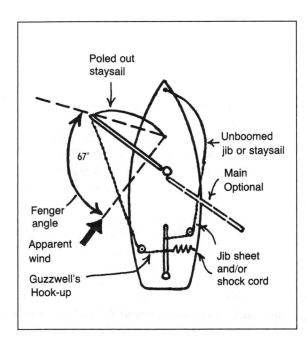

Figure 6-11. Weather twin.

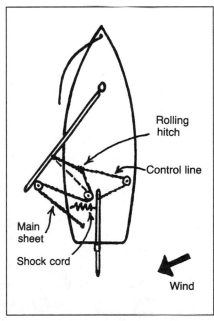

Figure 6-12. Mainsheet control
(John Letcher).

block, and finally to the tiller, which is held almost amidships by elastic cord. When the boat wanders off course toward the wind, the weather sheet pulls harder than the elastic cord and pulls the tiller up to put the boat back on course. If she falls off too far, the staysail exerts less pull on the sheet, and the cord pulls the tiller down to make the course correction. In an article written for *Yachting Monthly* magazine, Skidmore claimed that the system worked for all points of sailing "from a close reach to within 15 degrees of a dead run." The magazine's editor also tried the method and verified its effectiveness.

Many of the modern sheet-to-helm arrangements for self-steering make use of elastic lashings, and it is interesting that this wrinkle was used by Captain Waller back in 1930. He is said to have used rubber straps for exercising the muscles called "Sandow Developers," named after the popular strong man. Nowadays most sailors use elastic shock cord, although John Letcher writes that he prefers surgical tubing.

A somewhat similar method to Skidmore's was used by Frank Casper aboard his cutter *Elsie,* and Figure 6-10 is based on a diagram that Frank sketched for me. The *Elsie's* staysail is fairly large and is set on a permanent boom. The windward sheet has an extra purchase, and sometimes the sheet is shifted aft on the tiller as shown by the dashed line in the diagram. In light weather when the wind is quite far aft, a jib is poled out to weather. Under these conditions, the circumnavigator carries his mainsail vanged down and trimmed flatter than normal to help prevent rolling. A vane gear is carried in addition to steady the boat in very rough seas.

A single staysail poled out on the windward side is often referred to as the weather-twin method of self-steering. With this system, the weather-twin's sheet is usually led to the tiller as shown in Figure 6-11. This windward sheet pulls the tiller up when the boat luffs, and the pull is counteracted by the strain of either shock cord and/or a jib or unboomed leeward staysail sheet attached to the tiller's opposite side, as illustrated. John Guzzwell, who used this latter kind of arrangement on his *Trekka,* secured the weather-twin sheet farther aft on the tiller than the leeward headsail's sheet to balance evenly the strain on the helm.

Frederic Fenger theorized that the angle of attack of the weather twin should be about 67 degrees (see Figure 6-11), so that the wind flow is reversed, moving from leech to luff, and Stanley Bradfield tried this trim successfully on his double-ender *D'Vara.* On this boat, the weather twin's sheet was secured to the tiller in the customary manner, but its pull was counteracted by an elastic rubber strap. Bradfield could carry full sail in addition to the twin, and he found that the system worked well in a variety of wind strengths on all points of sailing, from a dead run to nearly a beam reach. The *D'Vara* was hardly a typical boat, however, for she had an unusual main-trysail ketch rig, and she was designed by Harrison Butler to the metacentric shelf theory, which some designers still think produces an exceptionally well-balanced hull.

For brief periods of solo sailing, an ordinary staysail boomed out to weather with a standard spinnaker pole and carried with the mainsail broad off is a very simple means of self-steering before the wind. The staysail's sheet is led to the tiller's weather side, and its pull is counteracted with shock cord. I have even used a jib (rather than a staysail) successfully, which normally means that the headsail is not angled forward. Even so, with careful adjustment of the shock cord, the method can be made to work on many boats, because a change of course into

Frank Casper at the helm of his sturdy double-ender *Elsie*. Casper's sheet-to-helm self-steering arrangement is shown in Figure 6-10. The vane gear helps to steady the boat in rough seas. (Photo by Harold Chasalow)

the wind causes extra pull on the sheet and a change away from the wind causes less pull, as the jib becomes partially blanketed by the mainsail. It is important, however, to rig a boom vang or preventer to avoid an accidental jibe.

Figure 6-12 shows still a different kind of sheet-to-helm self-steering, the connection of the mainsheet to the tiller. This method was used successfully by John Letcher on his solo and doublehanded Pacific voyages. It can be seen that a line, which John calls the control line, leads from the tiller to a windward block and thence to one part of the mainsheet tackle where the control line is secured, normally with a rolling hitch. Notice that the part of the mainsheet holding the rolling hitch is bent or pulled away from being a straight line. The dashed line shows the sheet as it would be if the control line were not attached. This pull by the control line on the mainsheet is counteracted by shock cord or elastic led from the tiller to the leeward coaming. The system is based on the premise that most well-balanced boats will hold a steady course when close-hauled in a steady breeze. An increase in wind velocity will normally cause heeling and luffing up toward the wind, while a lull will cause bearing away. With the mainsheet-to-tiller system, a puff will put more pressure on the mainsail and pull on the control line via the mainsheet, thus pulling the helm to weather and correcting the course; while a lull will do just the opposite, increase the bend and allow the shock cord to pull the tiller to leeward. The method takes a good many trial-and-error adjustments, but John has used it on points of sailing from beam reaching to close hauled on a variety of boats in various strengths of wind, and he has written that "it has never failed."

It should be evident that there are many ways to skin the cat as far as self-steering is concerned. Other sail methods are to use a riding sail, set on the back-stay with its sheet attached to the helm, or to secure the mizzen sheet to the helm on a yawl or ketch. A very simple method for temporary use, which need not take any extra sails or equipment, is to rig the jib sheet from its leeward winch to a quarter block to windward and thence to the tiller, which is held almost amidships by shock cord. This arrangement will be discussed in more detail in Chapter 12.

Self-steering is not the only challenge the singlehander faces, but its importance is illustrated by the remark made by Clare Francis when a reporter asked her a question concerning her motivations and the increasing popularity of the sport. She said simply. "People are sailing the Atlantic because of self-steering devices."

PART III

Singlehanded Seamanship

Krystyna Chojnowska-Liskiewicz aboard *Mazurek*. (Courtesy of PA Interpress Photos)

7

Solo Techniques

SUCCESSFUL SINGLEHANDING REQUIRES the highest caliber of seamanship. Not only must the solo skipper be a generally proficient sailor, but he or she should have, or at least develop, a good sense of order and care, extra vigilance, a high degree of patience, and considerable forehandedness.

The sense of order and care leads to an awareness of details in cruise organization, the recognition of correct procedures and proper sequence in boat handling, and immediate realization when any piece of gear is faulty, out of place, or subject to damage. Stowage and upkeep of all gear should be systematic and consistent.

Such orderliness and attention to detail, of course, must be accompanied by constant vigilance. The accomplished seaman has an ever-roving eye. He or she continually observes the sky, inspects boat, rigging, and gear, and scans the water for boat and ship traffic and for flotsam.

Patience is important for a singlehander, because haste and lack of patience may lead to carelessness or oversights in boat management or navigation. Certain lapses in seamanship that might be inconsequential when there is a full crew aboard could well be serious for one who sails alone. A solo sailer should learn to take all the time needed to do a job right. R. T. McMullen, the famous British yachtsman who singlehanded a heavy gaff-rigger in the 1870s, once declared in no uncertain terms that if an hour more were required "to take a perfect reef, another hour it should have."

Forehandedness has to do with the ability to anticipate, to know what might or probably will happen. I don't mean to imply that the successful singlehander must be clairvoyant, but rather that he or she should have sufficient knowledge, experience (which can be built up gradually), and familiarity with the vessel to perceive what problems could possibly develop. Then, of course, thought can be given to avoiding the problems and to coping with them if they should occur.

Forehandedness is essentially planning ahead: laying out all gear that will be needed; stowing all supplies securely where they will be readily available; changing sails somewhat ahead of time; keeping well fed, fit, and rested in order best to cope with any crisis; and in general preparing the boat and oneself for any eventuality.

W. S. Kals, boating writer and occasional singlehander, has given the sound advice that the best seamanship calls for an alternate plan. A good seaman thinks ahead and follows a plan, but envisions an alternative just in case some unpredictable circumstance upsets the original plan. It is quite easy to see how this principle would apply to singlehanding in coastal or inland waters. If the sailor is headed for a certain port, for instance, and the weather deteriorates or headwinds and a choppy sea delay his time of arrival until after dark, he should pick a secondary, more easily accessible anchorage as an alternative. Another example would be that when sailing into a difficult harbor entrance where the sails might be blanketed or strong currents could create a problem, the engine should be readied for instant use and gear organized for the possible need of dousing sails. Conversely, if the engine is running but might not be entirely reliable, the sails should be ready for instant use. The anchor and rode and even docking lines should also be prepared, for they could well be needed if something were to go wrong with the original plan.

At sea, the alternative principle also applies. The offshore seaman carefully considers what change of course or tactic should be made in the event of illness, major gear failure, or dangerously heavy weather. These cases could possibly justify such alternative actions as heading for the nearest port or steamer lane or scudding before a storm rather than heaving to. As Kals reminds us, the great Captain Slocum changed his plan from an eastabout to a westabout rounding of the world after he had already crossed the Atlantic (which meant that he had to recross the ocean) because he was warned of pirates along his intended route.

A quality that every solo seaman should have is a healthy amount of wariness. Most singlehanders, especially those who cruise extensively, are bold and adventurous, for the occupation by its very nature takes a certain degree of courage, but the very best seamanship demands considerable caution. I remember once when Eric and Susan Hiscock called at our home port, they stayed a day or so longer than they had intended because of a spell of threatening northeasterly weather. Actually, the weather was somewhat wet but quite mild, and most local sailors including myself would not have had any qualms about leaving for the next port at which the Hiscocks intended paying a visit. Yet the famous circumnavigating husband and wife team stayed put, not just because the weather was unpleasant and they were enjoying their stay, but because they were in strange waters in fairly uncertain conditions, and laying over was the sensible thing to do. There are probably few sailors who have covered as much of the earth with so few difficulties as the Hiscocks on their three circumnavigations. Though Eric passed away in 1986, Susan, well into her seventies, continues to live aboard *Wanderer V* in New Zealand and takes occasional singlehanded sails.

Watch Keeping and Routine

The singlehander who cruises in coastal or inland waters from port to port may very often feel that such passages are relatively easy and insignificant compared to the feats of the solo voyagers. This feeling may lead to his underrating the problems involved. In many respects, however, coastal and inland singlehanding is more difficult than sailing offshore. The former activities normally require a much higher degree of vigilance and attention to the helm because of boat traffic and the imminence of shoal water. Then, too, the coastal sailor must be ever mindful of the possibility of being caught on a lee shore in heavy weather. Of course, the offshore singlehander also encounters these problems, potentially at least, when he makes a landfall, but he has much less exposure to them for a given amount of time under way.

When sailing alone on inland waters, it is important to keep a constant lookout. The helm can be left unattended while the sailor goes forward to sit in the shade or attends to one of the many chores that always needs doing on a boat, but he must condition himself to look around constantly for converging vessels, especially fast motor boats and steamers, which can approach so rapidly. He should not go below until well clear of all traffic and never remain in the cabin for more than a few moments when there are other boats in his vicinity. This kind of proper caution all but eliminates the possibility of sleep, and so it is advisable to make short runs from port to port when well rested. Of course, it is possible to stand watch all day and night when alone, and many singlehanders have sailed for 24 hours or considerably longer without any sleep, but this greatly increases the risk. Not only is there the danger of falling asleep and colliding with another boat or running aground, but lack of sleep produces fatigue, which is perhaps the major enemy of the singlehander.

Fatigue not only causes errors in calculations and judgments, but also leads to lethargy, carelessness, and downright laziness. The lazy sailor who neglects caution and attentiveness, who delays taking action when it should be taken, and who fails to doublecheck his seamanship and navigation, is simply asking for trouble. Aside from weariness and lack of energy, other symptoms of fatigue are forgetfulness and irrational behavior. The bone-tired sailor might, for example, strap on his safety harness and go forward to do a chore and then forget completely what he was going to do; he might struggle to stuff the large genoa into the spitfire's bag; or wonder what's wrong when he tries to put his left shoe on his right foot. Very deep fatigue was discussed in Chapter 3, and it was seen that this can possibly lead to alarming and sometimes dangerous hallucinations. Stay-awake drugs may only increase any hallucinatory tendencies.

Although the inland sailor on protected waters with an abundance of harbors can make short runs and need not be seriously deprived of sleep, the coastal singlehander quite often is faced with longer distances between ports. In this case, he must sleep during an offshore tack or when hove to, if there is sufficient sea room. Although some singlehanders disagree, it is generally considered safer to sleep during the daytime than at night when there is a lot of ship traffic. Ships' officers repeatedly point out how difficult it is to see the usual small boat navigation lights, and it is often true that lookouts are more lax at night.

Naps for singlehanders should be brief, perhaps no longer than an hour at a time, depending, of course, on the proximity of land, wind direction, weather, and so forth. A reliable alarm clock is a vital piece of equipment. As Bernard Moitessier can testify, failure of an alarm can lead to the loss of one's vessel (Chapter 11). Of course, one has to wake up after the alarm sounds. It was reported that during the 1972 OSTAR, one singlehander carried three alarm clocks to go off in succession as a precaution against oversleeping. Gunther Milowsky, during a solo Atlantic crossing in 1978, actually had four successive alarms and he wrote during one stressful period, "I rarely heard the first two of my four alarm clocks ringing, although I normally wake up before the first one starts to ring." Bill Homewood has another solution to oversleeping. He wrote, "The best way to wake up is drink two pints of liquid before going to bed. Your bladder will wake you." It seems that prolonged periods of sleep are not really essential, and serious fatigue can be avoided with sufficient accumulation of short periods, when they include sound sleep and not merely rest.

When tacking offshore to snatch some sleep or rest, it is imperative that the boat not change her course. Bernard Moitessier, Jean Gau, Harry Pidgeon, Vito Dumas, Gary Mundell, Desmond Hampton, Richard McBride, Howard Smith, and other famous loners have grounded on coasts because they were below when the wind shifted, or their boats failed to follow their intended courses for some other reason, such as the set of an unpredicted current. Wind shifts can be a real problem when vane gear steering is being used. Several partial solutions are self-steering by sails (rather than vane) rigged to flog or perhaps become blanketed and make a noise that will wake up the singlehander; an off-course alarm that sounds a buzzer when the boat strays too far from her compass course; an adjustable depth sounder alarm that warns of shoal water; and an autopilot that operates from the compass. None of these means, however, is a substitute for periodically waking up and having a look around. During the waking moments, there is the opportunity to check the compass course and lights, scan the horizon, read the taffrail log, check important gear, and observe the weather.

If the singlehander heaves to for sleep, it is important to know just how the vessel will behave and how much drift or leeway she will make. Of course, this knowledge is gained from experience and trials in a variety of conditions. Heaving to is normally accomplished by shortening sail, perhaps reefing the main or setting a storm trysail, and carrying a small jib aback (trimmed to weather) while the helm is lashed down. An easier method is to put the wind a little forward of abeam and then slack all sheets right off, but this causes the sails to flog, which is very harmful to them over a lengthy period of time, especially in a fresh breeze. Some singlehanders simply lie ahull; that is, they lower all sail and let the boat drift beam on (or nearly so) to the wind and seas, usually with the helm lashed down. An average boat lying ahull might make as much as 1½ knots of leeway in moderate weather, but a modern boat with an abbreviated lateral plane might drift considerably faster in a blow. Lying ahull in our Ohlson 38 for 15 hours in a Force 8 to 10 gale, we made about two knots of leeway.

When the drift is toward a shore that is not extremely far away, naps should be brief, and it may be advisable to put over a sea anchor. In fair weather, there is little reason for not using a type that holds the boat quite firmly, such as the parachute drogue, or a large conic type such as the old-fashioned cornucopia (see Figure 7-1). The famous small boat voyager and occasional singlehander John C. Voss invented a conic sea anchor that could be folded up for easy stowage, and this is also illustrated in Figure 7-1. For heavy weather, unless dangerously close to a lee shore, it may be advisable to use a drogue that allows more drift and affords more give to relieve shock loading, because a boat that is firmly tethered in such conditions may not be able to yield properly to the smash of the seas. This matter is discussed in Chapter 10.

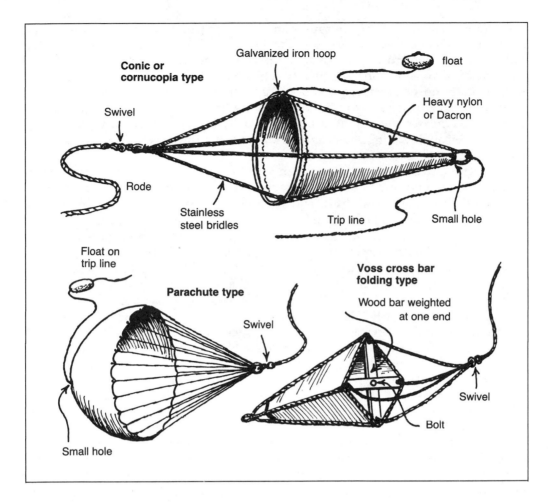

Figure 7-1. Sea anchors.

Offshore, the singlehander can usually enjoy a more relaxed routine when he is far from transoceanic steamer lanes. In remote areas of an ocean it is reasonably safe aboard a well-lighted boat to lead a more nearly normal life, sleeping at night and staying awake throughout the day. Although solo racers will awaken themselves quite frequently for the primary purpose of checking their course and the trim of their sails to maintain the best possible speed, the ocean cruising singlehander may sleep for lengthy periods at night, waking up only when there is a change of motion, unusual sound, or unwanted angle of heel. Seamen well acclimated to their way of life can often count on the alarm system of their own senses to arouse them when sails or gear urgently need attention. Many consider it safe enough to forego the alarm clock when far away from ships, but there should always be a radar reflector hoisted and bright navigation lights turned on.

Aside from the matter of sleep and watch keeping, another vital part of the shipboard routine is meals. They must be nourishing and adequate to sustain strength and good health. Many singlehanders eat very little for the first few days at sea, presumably because of nervousness, incomplete adaptation, or seasickness.

Bill Homewood writes, "I eat hardly anything for (the first) two or three days. Sometimes I feel a wee bit seasick. After five days my appetite is good." It often takes a few days to grow accustomed to the vessel's motion and to become used to the idea of being alone and completely self-dependent. Nevertheless, it is important to keep up one's strength and energy with adequate food. Also, if one is actively seasick, it is vital to continue drinking liquids in order to avoid dehydration. Seasickness remedies are a help, but it is particularly important that the singlehander avoid taking a remedy that makes him drowsy before he has had time to sail clear of coastal waters.

For the sake of stimulating the appetite, it is a good idea to carry a great variety of food supplies. Aside from a wide assortment of canned goods, freeze-dried stores and even many fresh fruits and vegetables can be carried on extended passages. Provisioning is discussed in Chapter 9. Robin Knox-Johnston said of his stores: "If I were to do another voyage like this I would take a much greater variety of food. I relied far too much upon basics like bully beef and tinned vegetables, thinking that as long as I kept myself well fed I would not be too worried about variety. This was a mistake. I got fed up with the run of stews and bully and baked bean salads, and for several months ate less than I ought to have done through sheer lack of interest." Many BOC racers raved about the "Yurika" brand of "boily bags" which are made in Canada, according to a report in *Practical Sailor* magazine. Another favorite is the French canned foods sold under the label "Sportfood," but they are hard to get in the U.S.A.

Food should not only be nourishing and varied, but there should be some high-energy producers, such as high-protein cereals, honey, candy, and other sweets, because the singlehander is very apt to be extremely tired at times. Also, many singlehanders feel that there should be at least one hot meal a day and periodic hot drinks in cold weather. This is important for morale as well as the digestion. In rough weather, the single-burner swing-type stoves that are gimbaled two ways and burn Sterno or lamp oil are a real blessing. An unbreakable thermos bottle or two are indispensable. Regular meals, with a breakfast, lunch, and dinner, seem to suit many singlehanders, but others prefer to eat only when they are hungry. Apparently an irregular schedule seems to do no harm; the really important matter is a sufficient quantity, and especially quality, of food intake.

The rest of the daily routine for the passage-making singlehander relates mainly to hygiene and seamanship chores. Good health depends not only on food, rest, and sleep, but also on care of the body, which, of course, is vitally important for anyone entirely alone and beyond the reach of medical help. Minor ailments such as small cuts or boils should not be neglected because of the chance of a serious infection that could leave the loner partially incapacitated. Treatments should always be started early, and all preventive measures for possible illnesses should be taken.

Dr. Hannes Lindemann had a daily ritual (when weather permitted) consisting of what he called his "hygiene hour." At these times, he would strip himself of all clothing, expose his whole body to the sun for a short while, clean himself and remove all salt, treat himself for any afflictions, such as salt-water boils, massage and exercise any muscles that were not being used, dry his clothes, dust himself with talcum, and so forth. In regard to exercise, normal activities on a boat usually require ample use of most muscles, but certain muscles, especially on a cockleshell, may become partially neglected. John Letcher, who is an athletic singlehander and whose passages were made in boats larger than cockleshells, told me that he occasionally had problems with the weakening of unused muscles after a considerable time at sea, and he sometimes practiced calisthenic and isometric exercises.

The modern sailor has to be particularly careful about overexposure to the sun, as the protective ozone layer in the atmosphere is thinning (there's a hole in it over Antarctica), and incidents of skin cancer are increasing. It is important to wear protective clothing, use awnings when possible, and apply sunscreens to exposed areas of the skin.

Offshore sailors always have a great number of chores to do each day. Aside from regular checks of all parts of the boat and her gear, there is the normal cleaning, tidying up, putting things in order, and the inevitable repair and maintenance of equipment. Singlehanders often make a list of checks and jobs that need doing. A typical list would include such items as oil fittings, whipping or splicing lines, replacing a chafed line, taping cotter pins, drying out gear, replacing telltales, checking the bilge, water tanks, and batteries, rigging chafe preventers, repairing a flashlight, freeing up a sticking drawer, checking the steering vane, replacing a broken fitting, and so forth. In his book *Gipsy Moth Circles the World* Francis Chichester reproduced a typical work list—he called it his "agenda"—which contained 71 chores. He wrote, "This list is nowhere near a complete record of the work done on *Gipsy Moth*—it is rather a list of merely extra jobs. It omits all sail changing, radio work, adjustments to the self-steering gear, navigation, all regular work in the galley . . . Nevertheless, incomplete as it is, my agenda may give some idea of the human effort needed for singlehanded ocean sailing." Chichester's agenda may also convey the importance of self-discipline in solo passagemaking. Carrying out all the necessary jobs promptly and in a careful manner not only is vital for sound seamanship, but also keeps one busy and provides therapy against anxiety, depression, and loneliness. Naomi James also found that a written agenda not only improved her seamanship but had a very good effect on her psychologically. When difficult decisions were necessary she often wrote down the alternatives with arguments for and against.

Difficult Operations and Heavy Gear

Many operations involved in singlehanding a boat are difficult or strenuous, and anything that can be done to make them easier will not only make sailing more enjoyable, but also will make it safer and reduce the hazards of fatigue. Some of the tasks that can be arduous or complicated when alone are docking, picking up a mooring, breaking out the anchor and bringing it aboard, bending sail, and bringing the dinghy on board.

Most jobs that are difficult for one person to handle can be simplified if they are well thought out. As said earlier, planning ahead is the key to successful singlehanding. Take the job of bending on a mainsail, for instance. It might seem impossible for one person to feed a foot boltrope into a grooved boom near the mast while he simultaneously pulls aft on the clew at the other end of the boom. Ordinarily, this is a two-person operation, but it is simple for one person to perform if he ties a line to the clew and runs it through a block at the outboard end of the boom and back to the mast. Such a solution would seem obvious, but it is all too easy, when one normally sails with a crew, to overlook what can be done alone with simple devices such as blocks, purchases, fairleads, Spanish windlasses, and so forth.

When self-steering gear is not used during a short cruise or day sail, tasks often become difficult because the helm cannot be left unattended for very long. Of course, the helm can be lashed or otherwise secured, and a boat that is reasonably well-balanced under sail or that carries a consistent torque under power will hold a steady course for a short while; but a singlehander who is working a long distance from the helm will often have to make many trips back and forth from the working station to the cockpit to readjust the helm. One solution to this problem, without resorting to self-steering arrangements, is to rig steering lines that can be led to any work area. With a tiller, this is usually a simple matter of running the lines from the tiller through snatch blocks on each side of the cockpit and then forward. Wheel steering makes the problem more complicated, but most boats have (or at least should have) a means of rigging an emergency tiller. On our present boat, the square head of the rudder post, which accepts the emergency tiller, is just abaft the wheel (under a screw-on deck plate); thus there is a problem with the wheel interfering with the tiller. There is plenty of room abaft the rudder post, however, so it is a simple matter to put the tiller on backwards and then rig steering lines to it. With this arrangement, the helmsman has to remember to steer the opposite way to which he ordinarily would with tiller-steering, but this is not difficult because the backwards tiller works the same as does a wheel. One has merely to think of turning the helm the way he wants the bow to go.

An auxiliary engine is invaluable for a singlehander cruising on inland or coastal waters, despite the fact that a few purists refuse to use any power but sail. Peter Tangvald, for instance, once unbolted his balky engine from its bed, hoisted it on deck, and pushed it overboard. He claims that engines often give a false sense of security, and he cites the example of a boat that was wrecked because her engine failed in the middle of a dangerous pass leading to a harbor near Tahiti. There is great truth in what Tangvald says, but if the skipper understands the failings and limitations of his auxiliary power and learns not necessarily to depend on it in a crisis, then the engine can be extremely helpful. Of course, the boat that was wrecked should have been motorsailing through the pass, or at least had her sails ready for hoisting, but she had her sail covers on and so was helpless immediately after her engine quit.

A properly used and cared-for engine is a tremendous convenience in bringing a boat up to her mooring, maneuvering in tight places, docking, breaking out the anchor, motorsailing against rough seas to reach port before dark, charging up the batteries, and, of course, supplying power in a calm. For lack of a reliable engine, circumnavigator John Sowden spent two days drifting around in a calm when only 15 miles from his destination at Suva, Fiji, where there was a dangerous pass that had to be negotiated. In my opinion, it is not sissy or unseamanlike to use auxiliary power when it is helpful. On the contrary, proper use of the engine in certain conditions can be the most seamanlike action to take. The important matter, however, is not to become overly dependent on the auxiliary and to learn to handle the boat in all conditions under sail alone.

The engine greatly simplifies breaking out a heavy or well dug-in anchor. The singlehander can haul his boat up to short scope, belay the rode, then go back to the cockpit and drive the boat ahead under power until the "hook" is broken out. He can then put the gear in neutral and go forward to pull up the anchor and bring it on board while the boat drifts slowly to leeward. If too much effort is required to shorten scope, the anchor line often can be led aft near the engine controls, so that the solo sailor can take in slack as he slowly drives the boat ahead under power. It is interesting to note that *Barnswallow* had her anchor rode permanently led aft to the cockpit, and her standard anchor, a large Danforth, was stowed in a low hawsepipe, so her skipper seldom had to go forward.

Under sail, hauling in the anchor line is more difficult, since the sailor will often have to beat up to his anchor if he cannot haul his boat up to it. For this, it is often best to use a small, high-cut headsail that can be backed but will clear the head of the singlehander kneeling on the foredeck. Normally, the sailor will sheet in his mainsail and control the headsail from the foredeck while he gathers in slack from the anchor line or chain. This seems like a formidable operation, but it is not quite as difficult as it sounds, because the boat will all but come about by herself when she fetches up on her anchor line, which will become taut and pull the bow around through the eye of the wind. When she sails off on the opposite tack, the sailor can gather in slack, but he has to be extremely careful not to get his fingers pinched when the line becomes taut again. Remember that even seamen as great as Alain Colas and Eric Hiscock have suffered serious anchor handling injuries.

Very often, after the anchor line has been heaved on and the boat begins to move, her momentum will reduce the effort of hauling in the remaining line and it can be pulled in hand-over-hand. Once the rode is at a short stay it is usually not too difficult to break out the anchor under sail, but if it is really dug in, a windlass, powerful winch, and/or tackle might have to be used. A windlass is a wonderful piece of machinery for a heavy boat, an all-chain rode, and deep anchorages.

Lifting the "hook" on board is not as much of a chore as it once was, because the most commonly used anchors today, such as the plows, Bruces, and Danforths, have more holding power and thus can be lighter than those of former times. In a good holding bottom with ample scope, a 20-pound, "hi-tensile" Danforth can hold a boat up to 40 feet long in all but storm conditions. There will be times, however, when heavy storm anchors or old-fashioned fisherman types for use in thick weed or rocky bottoms will have to be hefted on board, and then the singlehander may want some help in the form of mechanical advantage. He will seldom need such formerly used devices as anchor davits and catheads, but he may want to use a boom with a winch, or cat his anchor under the bowsprit, if the boat has one. Increasingly popular is a roller chock at the stem head, which allows a plow anchor to be pulled up with its shank over the roller. When it is necessary to bring a heavy anchor on board with a boom, the spinnaker pole, reaching strut, or staysail boom can be used. The pole is secured to the mast (or stay or pedestal in the case of the staysail boom) and supported with a lift. A tackle or line leading to a winch is rigged from the outboard end, and the pole is swung out over the water so that the anchor can be lifted clear of the topsides. After it is lifted above the deck level, of course, the pole is swung inboard so that the anchor can be lowered to the deck.

The same principle may be used to bring a heavy dinghy on board. Quite often the main boom is used with a tackle, perhaps the vang, rigged from the boom's end or middle. The dinghy can be lifted with a bridle rigged between its bow and stern. With a lightweight dinghy, the boom is not always necessary. I have brought our Dyer Dhow onboard singlehandedly by hoisting it with the main halyard after fenders have been rigged to protect the topsides.

A laborious task for a singlehander is freeing his boat after a grounding. For the most part, the same actions would be taken aboard a solo boat as on one fully crewed, but, of course, more effort is required by one person, who cannot use methods that involve crew weight, such as putting people on the bow to lift the after end of the keel, or putting them on a broad-off boom to make the boat heel. The boat might be made to heel without too much effort, however, by lifting the swamped dinghy from the end of the boom. Kedging off may be difficult for one person, but it helps to use an anchor no heavier than necessary and a long, light anchor line that is neatly coiled on the after thwart or stern sheets of the dinghy, so that it will pay itself out easily when the boat is being rowed away from the grounded vessel for the sake of setting out the kedge. If there is no dinghy or raft, a light anchor might be swum out after it has been lashed temporarily to a number of life jackets or buoyant cushions.

For boats with short keels or a lot of draft aft, it is often helpful to have a very light Danforth that can be thrown a good distance off one side of the bow so that the boat can be turned toward deep water. Then she can be heeled by sail or weights and be driven ahead and hopefully off the shoal under power and/or sail. It usually pays for the singlehander to take his time, plan ahead carefully, and be sure where the deep water is through soundings or a careful study of the chart. There are times when a lone sailor might want to wait for a rise in tide rather than exhaust himself trying to free the boat immediately. Obviously, the urgency will depend on whether the boat is being damaged, the state of the tide, and other factors.

If the singlehander does not have a windlass, he should have a powerful winch with suitable chocks and fairleads as well as proper ground tackle. Powerful self-tailing winches are handy for the singlehander, as electric and hydraulic-powered winches. Marcel Bardiaux had one very powerful winch that he could move to different advantageous locations, and once he found it indispensable for extricating his boat from a dangerous coral reef (the incident will be described in Chapter 11).

After a hard grounding on rocks or coral, the hull should be inspected carefully to see that it is not holed, so that the vessel will not sink in deep water after she is freed. Bardiaux's *Les 4 Vents* nearly sank after she was pulled free of the reef despite the fact that she was fitted with some flotation.

Other operations that can sometimes present problems for the singlehander are docking and picking up a mooring. Picking up a mooring is seldom difficult with an engine, because the boat can be turned into the wind (or current when that dominates), and the approach speed can be controlled by backing down when close to the mooring. Then the singlehander puts his gear in neutral, walks forward quickly, and picks up the mooring float with a long boathook.

Under sail, however, the procedure is more difficult, because speed cannot be controlled so easily. In most cases, where the current is not extreme, it is best to make the approach under mainsail alone (if the boat is maneuverable under this rig) while sailing on a close reach and aiming a few boat lengths to leeward of the pick-up float. Speed can be controlled by slacking or trimming in the mainsheet,

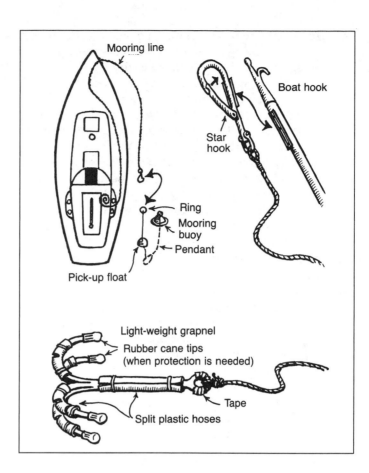

Figure 7-2. Mooring and docking aids.

and some control can be obtained by the degree and speed that the rudder is turned. The shoot into the wind just to leeward of the pick-up float must be almost perfectly timed, because if the boat has too much speed, she may overrun her mooring before the sailor has a chance to pick it up; or else if he does pick it up, he may not be able to hold it. On the other hand, if the speed is too slow, the boat may stop short, beyond the reach of the singlehander, or she might lose steerageway as a result of her slow speed. Obviously, this maneuver takes practice and one must know the vessel. Heavy boats carry more way than light ones, and in fresh winds, boats with tall rigs and a lot of windage stop more abruptly than those with clean, short rigs.

A method for picking up the mooring advocated by at least one experienced singlehander is as follows: A line, which will be called the mooring line, is run from the cockpit to a bow chock, then aft to the cockpit again outboard of the lifeline stanchions and rigging. The line's returning end is fitted with a large snaphook (see Figure 7-2). When the boat is brought up to her mooring, she is made to overshoot slightly so that the pick-up float can be grabbed from the cockpit. The snaphook on the mooring line is snapped into the eye on top of the float, and then the float is cast off. The boat is snubbed by hauling in on the hookless end of the mooring line; then she is allowed to drift back to leeward of the float, where slack is taken in on the mooring line. The singlehander then walks forward, picks up the float, and properly secures the mooring pendant. It will be helpful if the pick-up float is fitted with a vertical staff that can be grabbed easily.

One disadvantage of this system is that when the boat has such a long distance to drift back, her bow will most likely blow off, despite tugs on the mooring line, and if the pick-up is made under sail, the sail may fill and drive the boat ahead. Obviously, the sheet must be well slacked and kept from fouling. Also, it may pay to drop the mainsail promptly while the boat is still head to wind, but only after the pick-up has been made. One occasionally sees a self-confident skipper shoot for his mooring and drop sails before the mooring is picked up, but in my opinion this should never be done when there is only one person aboard. Special hooks, one called the Happy Hooker® and another the Mooring Hook® (formerly Star Hook) which is closed with a spring gate controlled by a lanyard, can simplify the mooring pick-up. The latter device, illustrated in Figure 7-2, can easily be attached to the boat hook. Both hooks are sold by West Products and other chandlers. A similar device is the Grab Boat Hook® sold by the Jay Stuart Haft Company.

Another pick-up method is to make fast a short line with a buoy to the pick-up float. The singlehander reaches for it in the conventional way, with a boat hook from the bow, but having the extra buoy attached allows more room for error. The singlehander shoots for the pick-up float but errs very slightly toward having too little speed. Then if he finds he cannot quite reach the pick-up float, he can probably reach the extra buoy, assuming it has drifted a short distance to leeward of the float. Of course, one has to be careful that the line linking the extra buoy to the pick-up float is not too long, as it could be an obstruction to boat traffic. Also, the buoy should be a prominent size and color so that it can be easily seen. Reflective tape (such as that made by 3M) stuck on the top of the buoy is a great aid to visibility at night.

Docking under sail in a large, heavy boat can involve considerable risk for a singlehander. It is far better to dock under power if the engine is reliable. Ordinarily, when the current is not a major factor, it is best to bring the boat alongside to leeward of the dock in order that the wind will keep her a short distance away from rough pilings, concrete, and so forth, which could mar her topsides. A recommended method, when there is no one on the dock to take a line, is as follows: A line is belayed at the bow, led through the bow chock on the side that will face the dock, and then led aft outboard of everything to the cockpit where the line is neatly coiled and hung on a winch or stanchion near the helm. Another line is belayed at the stern on the same side. This stern line should have an adjustable loop in its end and be fairly short, perhaps 8 to 12 feet, from the cleat to the loop, which also will be hung near the helmsman. After the bow and stern lines and fenders have been rigged, the boat is brought in almost parallel to the leeward of the dock, and the engine is reversed just before the cockpit is opposite a cleat, bollard, or piling on the dock. When most of the way has been lost, the singlehander shifts into neutral, steps to the side of the boat, and puts the loop of the stern line over the piling or dockside cleat. With the other hand he takes the coiled bow line, jumps ashore, runs forward, and takes a turn around another piling near the bow. It is important that the bow line be secured promptly before the bow is blown off by the wind.

One often hears arguments that a single spring line should be rigged from amidships leading aft to the dock in order to bring the boat close alongside parallel

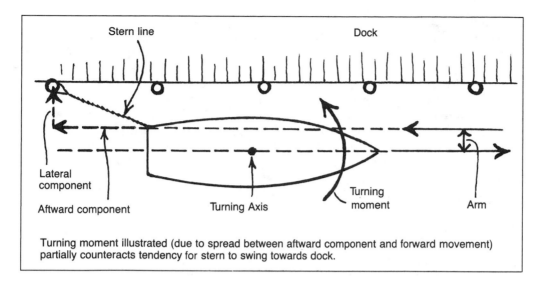

Turning moment illustrated (due to spread between aftward component and forward movement) partially counteracts tendency for stern to swing towards dock.

Figure 7-3. Forces when docking with a stern line.

to the dock, but this line can create extra complications for a singlehander. Contrary to what has been written by some advocates of the amidships spring line, a stern line of proper length will not swing the stern into the dock with any great force, because the lateral component of the stern line's pull will be at least partially counteracted by a turning moment caused by the stern line's aftward component pulling from the boat's quarter (see Figure 7-3).

It is usually not difficult to leave from the leeward side of a dock. One method for a boat that is to be backed away is to have one turn of the bow line around its piling and both ends of the line leading back to the cockpit. After the engine is started and spring lines and fenders taken in, the stern line is cast off, and then one end of the bow line which leads to the cockpit is let go. The bow line is hauled around its piling to fall free, and the engine is put in reverse, and the boat backs away. The singlehander takes in the line from the cockpit before he shifts into forward gear, because otherwise he might overrun the line and possibly foul the propeller when the boat goes ahead. Some modern boats do not back very well in a strong breeze, as their bows tend to blow off and the stern tends to round up into the wind, especially before there is sufficient sternway. If this is the case, it may be well to let the stern blow off a bit before casting off the bow line. Another alternative is to warp the boat around so that she can leave bow first.

Small, light boats can be brought in on the windward side of a pier when it is very well padded and the boat is protected with fenders. This is a simple operation in a weak current, for the boat will blow against the dock. Departing is then a bit more difficult, because the boat will have to be pushed far out from the dock before she backs away. A commonly used method is to go forward on a spring line which forces the stern away from the dock. This usually works well unless the boat has a very cutaway forefoot with a lot of windage forward and her bow is easily blown off. A fender or so should be placed forward to protect against this, and the rudder may have to be turned toward the dock initially to keep the bow clear.

If it is necessary to sail up to a dock, the operation will be somewhat similar to picking up a mooring, but the approach should be made in such a way that the boat can always be turned aside at the last minute in case the speed is too fast. It is safer to err on the slow side, and quite often a line can be thrown to a person on the dock if the boat stops short, but speed should never be allowed to drop to the point where the boat loses all maneuverability and gets in stays. It is usually a good plan to make the approach with a small jib (high cut for visibility) so that it can be backed for the best possible maneuverability at low speeds. It takes real skill and familiarity with one's vessel to emulate Captain Slocum when he docked his heavy *Spray* in Gloucester's harbor so gently that "she would not have broken an egg," yet even Slocum could have occasional problems maneuvering in close quarters under sail, for in the same harbor he later "scratched the paint off an old fine-weather craft in the fairway."

In the event that there is no one on the dock to catch a tossed line, a useful tool for the singlehander is a small, lightweight grappling hook covered with split plastic hoses and rubber tips on its prongs to prevent it from scarring the dock. The device can be used after the boat is brought to a stop close to a narrow pier, at which time the grapnel, attached to a light line, is thrown over the far side of the dock so that it hooks onto the edge or some other projection, and the boat is hauled in and made fast. Another useful tool is the Dock Grabber (made by Davis Instruments) consisting of two wires at the end of a pole that holds open a looped dock line. It allows you to drop the loop over a distant dock piling or cleat. Then too, a sturdy crab net can be used to grab a distant piling or cleat, but it is best to have a line made fast to the net's ring.

Navigating Alone

Navigation can present some problems for the singlehander, especially when close to shore. In crowded waters, it is often too risky to spend any time below at the chart table, so the chart and all essential equipment must be available near the helm. A clear plastic case that is watertight and can hold a folded chart or chart book is invaluable. It may also be helpful to have a grid of parallel lines, printed on clear plastic sheet, for placement over the chart (obtainable from leading chandleries or navigation supply companies) to eliminate the need for parallel rules or protractors, as these can be difficult to handle while steering. Courses or bearings can be drawn on the plastic case with a grease pencil, and its markings can be rubbed off quite easily with a rag or paper towel. The preferred dividers are the bowed kind that are designed to be operated with one hand.

There should be a locker easily accessible from the helm where binoculars and navigation gear can safely be stowed. Shelves inside the companionway can be used when the helm is near the forward end of the cockpit. Quite often the chart case can be held up vertically against the after end of the cabin house with a piece of shock cord stretched between two eyes. On some boats with the helm near the companionway, the sliding hatch can serve as a chart table. The chart in use is taped or otherwise fastened to a piece of plywood or masonite on top of the hatch, and it can be slid in and out of the hatch scabbard in wet weather.

Sometimes the sailor who cannot leave the helm must make very rough checks without proper navigation instruments. A pencil with some notches might be used instead of dividers in an emergency and a couple of rubber bands around the pencil (so that it can be rolled across the chart without slipping) will yield a crude substitute for parallel rules. Robin Knox-Johnston wrote of a trick he used at times as a rough means of measuring distance off from a lighthouse or other tall landmark of known height when it appeared to be about one finger's width above the horizon. Ordinarily, of course, the distance-off by vertical angle method requires a sextant, but Robin could get a crude approximation by using his finger held horizontally at arm's length, which he found subtended an angle of about one and a half degrees. Also, a wide-spread thumb and little finger held at arm's length subtends an angle of about twenty degrees, while the hand's width subtends about ten degrees.

When a singlehander takes bearings, it is preferable that the instrument used contain its own compass when the main steering compass cannot be used for sighting, because it is obviously impossible to receive the boat's heading from a helmsman at the same moment the bearing is read. Of course, a hand-bearing compass can be used, and this instrument is also handy to stow below near the skipper's berth so that he can check the course from his bunk, although an old-fashioned telltale compass hung from the overhead above the bunk is a still better arrangement. It is also highly desirable that the lone sailor's radio direction finder (RDF) have its own compass, because the instrument usually cannot be brought very close to the ship's compass without inducing serious deviation errors. Likewise, the RDF can be affected by deviation, and it should be operated from a consistent location where errors have been recorded. Some offer the added convenience of having their own compasses.

Although some veteran sailors, such as Peter Tangvald, claim they can sense shallow water by their vessel's change in motion and by visual and audible differences in the waves, a depth sounder can be very useful for sailing on-soundings when the instrument is working properly. The arrangement that has the indicator below and a repeater in the cockpit is a convenient one for singlehanding. A less costly arrangement is to have the indicator mounted on a hinged arm just inside the companionway so that it can be swung outside the cabin for visibility from the helm or inside the cabin for viewing from below. Pointer or digital indicators are probably easier for the singlehander to read than the flashing light indicator, which often has to be interpreted to some extent and can be obscured by direct sunlight. As said earlier, an audible alarm that can be set to sound off at a given depth can be valuable for the lone sailor making a landfall.

Accurate dead reckoning is difficult on any vessel, but it is especially so when one sails alone, because the boat may sail an erratic course when there is no one at the helm, and very often, temporary course changes, from a windshift, for instance, will go unrecorded. The course must be checked and the log read as often as possible. The singlehander has to become intimately familiar with his self-steering device in a variety of wind and sea conditions in order to estimate accurately its ability to hold a steady course. Averaging yaws may not suffice, since the boat may swing in one direction and remain there for a longer period than she does in the opposite direction. An off-course alarm (described earlier) for major course alterations can be invaluable. Also helpful, as mentioned before, is a telltale or extra conventional compass below which is rigged in conjunction with a mirror so that a course change can be seen from the bunk. For quick reading, it is preferable that the compass have a five-degree card with only a few numbers and the cardinal points marked in large, bold letters. A hand-bearing compass with edge-reading facilities can also be satisfactory.

Speedometers may be used to measure distance on short runs, but they require time keeping, of course, and so are not as convenient or accurate as distance-recording logs. Many offshore sailors tow a taffrail log from the stern. These are quite accurate, and they use no electricity, but their rotors are occasionally fouled with weed or bitten off by large fish. An extra rotor or two should be carried, and they are said to be less attractive to fish when painted black. Some experienced sailors can "guesstimate" without instruments the speed of their boats with surprising accuracy, but hull speed can be particularly deceiving at night.

Onboard computers such as the Brookes & Gatehouse Hercules or Hornet Systems can be very helpful with dead reckoning and other calculations (such as finding distance off course, VMG (velocity made good), true wind speed and direction, etc. However, there were a good many failures of B&G as well as other makes of electronic instruments on the rugged BOC races. Winner Philippe Jeantot was quite happy with his Danavigate 7000, which had many of its functions rigged up to a fire alarm to wake him from a sound sleep.

Nowadays most singlehanders, at least those who are financially endowed or sponsored, use electronic navigation systems such as Loran C, SatNav, Omega, or Decca (the British developed system). Loran is more suitable for U.S. and European coastal waters, and SatNav is the system to use for worldwide coverage. The latter does not provide continuous position fixes as does Loran C, but must wait for a satellite pass to provide a fix. This wait can vary between 30 minutes and four hours, but DR can be used between fixes or the SatNav can be linked with Omega or Loran for continuous position finding. Offshore, of course, a sailor may only need to know his position once or twice a day. In foggy regions some singlehanders are equipped with radar, which also may be ordered with optional alarms signifying that a target is within a specified range. Every boat should carry an RDF, which is relatively inexpensive and easy to operate, and can be used worldwide.

Modern electronic systems are most useful and normally very accurate. In fact, they are so good that they may tend to spoil the singlehander and lull him into a false sense of security. Electronic navigation should never be the only means of position finding. The electronic aids mentioned are fairly expensive, most are subject to errors (from thunderstorms, altitude of a satellite, land effects, powerful radio transmitters on shore, etc.), and they may use considerable electricity. Furthermore, electronics are subject to failure from wetness and/or salt water corrosion. One expert wrote regarding SatNav that it is best run almost continuously to keep it dry, but this would create an excessive electrical drain for most singlehanders.

The point I am trying to make is that the lone sailor must be proficient at piloting and dead reckoning; if going offshore, he should know the basics of celestial navigation and carry a sextant, accurate timepiece, and *Nautical Almanac*. Even if not well versed in the subject, the singlehander should at least know how to obtain latitude from Polaris (in the Northern Hemisphere) and how to take a noon sight which provides a rough means of obtaining longitude as well as latitude. Celestial navigation will always be needed if only for back-up purposes.

A glimpse at the future navigator's station? Right now, this is what you see aboard a 60-foot super high-tech ocean racer for French singlehander Jean Yves Terlain. *Top shelf, left to right:* electrical panel; ICOM M-700 single sideband; Furuno 1700 digital radar; Shipmate RS5100 SatNav; engine gauges. *Middle row:* electrical panel; Magnovox MX 2400 integrated Satcom terminal, hooked to an antenna dish in a dome on the boat's stern; ICOM M5 VHF and printer for the Satcom; two Apple Macintosh displays for a navigation program called MacSea, which integrates performance and weather data to select a course for the next 24 hours; battery gauges. *Bottom row:* amp gauge; keyboard for the Satcom terminal; Robertson AP40 autopilot; Brookes & Gatehouse integrated instrument control units. Below the autopilot is a good old-fashioned barometer. The phone is left ashore when Terlain puts to sea. (Photo by Roger Kennedy)

Although it takes practice to make an observation with the sextant from the deck of a small boat, the method is reliable in clear weather, and calculations have been greatly simplified with modern systems such as HO 214, HO 229, and HO 249. There are also tiny computers such as the Sharp Merlin, Navcom, and Celesticomp that do away with laborious arithmetic, but once again, know how to reduce a sight without electronic calculators in case of failures from battery exhaustion, corrosion, or dampness.

Slocum often talked, tongue in cheek, about his chronometer, an old tin clock which he bought for one dollar and later "boiled," but the Captain could check his time from the early method of lunar observations. Ann Gash (Chapter 2) navigated with a kitchen clock after her chronometer was stolen. Nowadays, the offshore singlehander can obtain accurate time with an electric watch, which operates from a tuning fork or quartz crystal, and a good portable radio, which gives time checks from the BBC (London), WWV (Colorado), WWVH (Hawaii), CHU (Canada), or other stations. WWV and WWVH, operated by the National Bureau of Standards on 2.5, 5, 10, 15, and 25 MHz, also broadcast high seas storm information for the offshore mariner.

During the 1960 transatlantic race, Valentine Howells lost power for his radio, and therefore proper time checks, because his battery straps shrank, crushing a huge battery, and, incidentally, dangerous chlorine gas was formed when the acid ran into the bilge. The lessons seem clear: carry a proper battery holding box and a portable transoceanic radio that can receive time signals with dry cell batteries and adequate spares. It is also advisable to carry a spare timepiece.

There seems to be a variety of opinion on the most suitable sextant for the singlehander. Some favor small, lightweight models for their ease of stowing and because they can be held a long time without tiring the arm, while others prefer heavier models (but seldom over five pounds) on a small boat, because they can be held steadier in a wind and the larger models are usually easier to read and operate. Micrometer screws for fine adjustments, rather than vernier scales, are generally preferred. More than a few singlehanders have used cheap plastic sextants successfully, but I have heard of slight distortion of the frame in the tropics and a few problems with mirrors and filters. One has to be careful that the cheap plastic sextant has proper sun shades to block out damaging rays, not always in the visible spectrum; otherwise, serious eye damage could result. The rotating, variable-density, polarized shades found on some of the newer sextants allow any shading variations with one simple adjustment.

Some sailors claim that sextants with bubble attachments are handy when the horizon is obscure, but even in weather that is quite calm it is difficult to hold the bubble steady on a small boat. Furthermore, one can get false readings from wave slope gravity. It is helpful to use an averaging device or to plot the sights on graph paper. In purchasing a bubble attachment, one should be sure the bubble is damped for marine use. There are unusual conditions where a bubble might be useful as a check. Such a condition could be the one experienced by Francis Chichester in 1964, during his Atlantic crossing in *Gipsy Moth III*. One day Chichester's sun observations were wildly erratic, up to 90 miles in error, he said, although he was an expert navigator, having written several textbooks on the subject. He finally came to the conclusion that there was a huge undetectable ground swell, due perhaps to a distant storm, that was giving him a false horizon.

A great aid in taking a sight alone is a stop watch that can be clicked at the instant the celestial body kisses the horizon. Some singlehanders, however, find it sufficiently accurate to count off the seconds. Brian Cooke described his method as follows: "My drill is to take the sight then immediately count the seconds to myself while putting the sextant in a safe place; then looking at my watch and recording the time; then picking up the sextant and reading the altitude and noting this . . ." Ann Davison, on the other hand, found the counting method difficult, for she wrote: "Lurching through the companion hatch, clutching the sextant, I would murmur, 'One and two and oops and three, no four, and oh-oh, and six, where was I? and oh-damn,' and climb out again to take another sight." She resolved to buy a stop watch at the first opportunity.

Singlehander Jean-Claude Protta designed a very sophisticated chronometer that is attached to the sextant. A button, pushed at the moment of a sight, will stop the second hand, and after time has been recorded, another button will restart and

Fred Rebell trying out his home-made sextant. (From *Escape to the Sea* by Fred Rebell)

automatically reset the hand. I find it not too difficult to hold a stop watch and start it when the celestial body kisses the horizon. Then I later read the chronometer time and subtract from it the time shown on the stopwatch to obtain the GMT (Greenwich mean time) of the sight.

Solo sailors vary tremendously in their proficiency as navigators. Some set off on a voyage with little if any knowledge of celestial navigation and hope that they will learn en route, while others are masters of the art and insist on pinpoint positions. Naomi James said on a radio program that she got half way around the world and realized she had been confusing longitude with latitude. On the other hand, Frank Casper was such as expert that he used lunars (à la Slocum) for time, and he once got a letter of thanks from the U.S. Naval Observatory for finding an error in the tables of the *Nautical Almanac.* John Letcher has also worked out a reasonably accurate method of figuring time from lunars without use of the lunar tables, which are no longer published in the *Nautical Almanac.* Then, in contrast, there is the case of Fred Rebell, who not only did not know celestial navigation before he set forth to cross the Pacific in a semi-open boat, but even attempted to make his own instruments. His sextant was constructed from a Boy Scout tele-scope costing one shilling, an iron hoop, and a hacksaw blade bent into an arc with the teeth serving as the degree scale. A taffrail log was made by inserting some twisted strips of aluminum into a broom handle, which served as the rotor, while the indicator was fashioned from a geared-down clock. This kind of equipment can hardly be recommended, but amazingly enough, it did work to some extent, and it illustrates the ingenuity of some singlehanders.

Mast steps on *Thursday's Child*. (Photo by Susan Thorpe)

8

Safety Considerations

SAFETY IS A VITAL CONSIDERATION on any boat, but there is a somewhat different emphasis for the singlehander. On a fully crewed vessel, for instance, horseshoe buoys, man-overboard poles, and water lights should be hung aft near the helmsman for the sake of a crewmember who might happen to fall overboard. But such safety gear has limited value for one who sails alone, for if he goes over the side, there is obviously no one on board to throw the equipment. There is also no one at the helm to bring the boat back for a rescue. A great deal of self-discipline is required to prevent overly hasty movements, dashes to the foredeck, the performance of tasks without safety lines in heavy weather, and casual or careless behavior in general.

To begin with, the singlehander should be aware of the risks involved in sailing alone and develop sound, seamanly habits that minimize the chance of an accident. Sound habits include wearing skidproof deck shoes, using a safety harness, carrying a knife, going below to use the head, keeping inboard of the lifelines, going aloft only when conditions are favorable, taking extra precautions when using the stove, handling running gear with great care, and in heavy weather remembering the old adage "one hand for yourself and one for the ship."

Safety Precautions and Equipment

- A life jacket or buoyant vest should be worn in heavy weather when close to shore or other vessels. Offshore in remote regions, some singlehanders feel that a flotation device will just prolong dying, but others would rather remain afloat in hopes of a miraculous rescue or to die of hypothermia instead of drowning.

● Safety harnesses can be invaluable, despite the fact that some singlehanders never wear them. A harness consists of a belt, with shoulder straps usually, and a moderately short, heavy lanyard with a large, strong snaphook that may be clipped to the rigging or a bolted eye to allow working with both hands in rough weather. There should be a hook on each end of the lanyard so that the singlehander can free himself if held underwater during a knockdown or capsize. The singlehander should practice using his harness properly; otherwise, a harness can be more of a liability than an asset. Incidentally, there are jackets on the market, such as those made by International Sailing Products, Mustang, and Henri-Lloyd, that have retractable, integral harnesses. There should be plenty of convenient places where one can clip on. Some singlehanders use a jack wire or line that runs from the cockpit to the foredeck so that the lanyard's hook will have an uninterrupted fore-and-aft travel. Welborn Marine offers a Latchway® system consisting of a small turnstile (accepting a lanyard's hook) that allows movement along a cable without the need to unhook and rehook when passing an obstruction such as a stanchion.

● Decks should be kept as clear as possible, and all smooth surfaces anywhere on the boat (especially varnished surfaces and the companionway ladder) should be skidproofed with abrasive strips or by some other means. Treadmaster® is a commonly used non-skid deck covering. It may be advisable to mark obstructions that could be tripped over with reflective tape for night work.

● There should be a substantial toerail all the way around the boat. Some traditional boats have bulwarks, and these give a great feeling of security, but they must be well scuppered to allow quick drainage, and if they are below knee level there should be a lifeline above for maximum safety.

● Double lifelines should be fitted from bow pulpit to stern pulpit, running through closely-spaced stanchions that are through-bolted. Upper lifelines should be a minimum of 24 inches high or well above a tall sailor's knees. A lifeline below the knees could be a tripping hazard. Lower lifelines should also run the full length of the boat about midway between the upper lifeline and the rail. Lifelines should be routinely inspected, especially if they are composed of stainless steel wire running through plastic tubes, as they could possibly be affected by shielding corrosion (from lack of oxygen). Do not trust the average pelican hooks found on standard lifeline gates; I have seen these break on two occasions. Nets around the foredeck increase safety and serve to contain wayward sails.

● An easy means of climbing the mast is all but essential to the singlehander, who on long-distance passages may have to go aloft for inspections, to make repairs, and to look for shoals or distant landmarks. (Examples of such incidents will be given in Chapter 11.) Permanent mast steps or ratlines are preferable, but a hoisted ladder or bosun's chair with a suitable tackle may suffice. There are several hoistable mast ladders on the market, and some, such as the Quick-Step® or Mast Mate®, attach to the mast along the sail track or groove to minimize movement.

Slides or a short length of luff tape in a mast groove can also be used to hold a bosun's chair close to the mast as it is being hoisted. Dodge Morgan

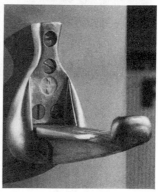

These folding "mast walkers" feature a turned-up end, which provides a firm foothold. (Courtesy of Innovations P.B. Canada)

used such a system on *American Promise*. He took the precaution of feeding the fall of his hoisting tackle into a bag secured to the bottom of his chair so that there would be no possibility of the line fouling on deck.

Some sailors might wonder why all singlehanders don't have permanent mast steps. The reason is that steps have a few drawbacks including extra windage and weight aloft, a tendency for some types to sing in the wind, and a real potential for fouling halyards and even sails. Some of these objections can be eliminated by using folding steps, but they may compromise a little security, since the climber's foot can more easily slip off. The accompanying photograph shows a folding step from Innovations P.B. Canada that has a turned-up end to minimize foot slippage.

- Booms should be eliminated where they can be, and they should be kept as high as possible.
- Headsail sheets are best secured with bowlines rather than snap shackles that could strike a singlehander in the head.
- Sails should never be allowed to lie spread out on the deck. Not only are modern synthetics very slippery to walk on, they also can cover unseen obstacles, as John Biddlecomb learned when he stepped on a headsail and fell through his open foredeck hatch in the 1986–87 BOC Challenge, resulting in a severe groin injury.
- Accidental jibes are particularly hazardous for the singlehander, and a jibing preventer should always be rigged when running. One device that

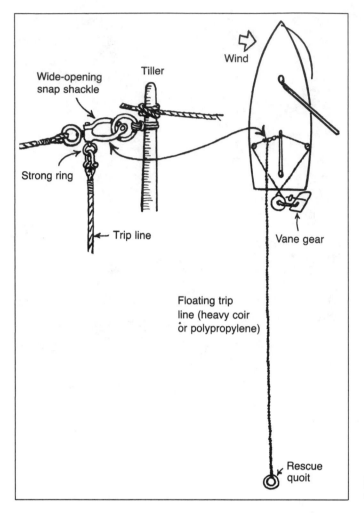

Figure 8-1. Tripping the vane gear

Philippe Jeantot and others found effective is the Walder Boom Brake, a small drum mounted under the boom with lines led to each side of the boat for control during a jibe. A drawback of the device is the possibility of its lines tripping the singlehander when walking forward or aft from the mast to the cockpit.

● In the event a lone sailor does go over the side, some take the precaution of towing a floating line with a rescue quoit or a small, brightly painted buoy at its end. When the boat is rigged for self-steering, the towed line should be rigged to trip the steering vane or free the helm so the boat will round up into the wind when the line overboard is pulled. A very simple method utilizing a wide-opening snap shackle is suggested in Figure 8-1.

● The boat should be balanced to have a slight weather helm (most boats naturally have such a balance) so that she will automatically round up when the self-steering gear is released. It has been suggested that a singlehander can clip on his safety line to release the self-steering in the event that he should fall overboard. This plan would be satisfactory provided the sailor could not accidentally trip the gear when moving about on deck and provided the attachment was to a solid part of the gear or boat that would keep the connection in the event of a fall overboard.

● Boats with high freeboard need some permanent means of boarding, such as transom steps or perhaps footholds on the self-steering gear. In some cases a rail-secured, rolled-up stern ladder that has a weighted lower rung and a release line hanging overboard may suffice. A better arrangement, however, is a permanently mounted metal ladder on the transom that has a lower section hinged to fold down so that it can be extended well below the water's surface. A floating pull-down line should be rigged so that it can be reached easily by a person overboard.

● There should be two large-capacity, preferably diaphragm-type, bilge pumps, one operable from the cockpit near the helm and the other from below. The deck pump should be usable without the need of opening a cockpit seat locker. In addition, it is advisable to have a portable pump and a couple of sturdy buckets.

Radar Reflectors, Detectors, and Alarms

A good radar reflector is especially important for the singlehander as a defensive measure when he cannot stand watch. These devices, which are small geometric structures made of light metal or wire mesh with multiple, right-angle corners, reflect signals back to vessels using radar. A reflector can be hoisted in the rigging or preferably mounted at the masthead, but experts say that for greatest efficiency, the usual octahedral type should not be mounted or suspended with one point up. A recommended reflector is the Firdell Blipper®, which is encased in a radar-transparent plastic case that protects against chafe.

Radar detector alarms afford considerable protection against being run down when there is no one on watch. Their function is to sound a loud alarm when they are swept by the radar beams of approaching ships. Noel Bevan, the ingenious solo seaman who sailed *Myth of Malham* in the 1968 OSTAR, invented an omnidirectional masthead radar receiver that sounds an alarm in the cabin and can detect a ship as far away as 10 miles. Bevan also devised another gadget, a hand-held device that he called a passive radar receiver. Resembling a small square megaphone, it produces hooting sounds with the use of a radar crystal and amplifier that can indicate the position of an approaching ship in fog or darkness. This is not like the portable "Whistler" radar that sends out its own signal, but it is similar to and evidently anticipated the Hepplewhite detector made in Suffolk, England.

When I recently wrote to *Practical Sailor*, the modern consumer's report for sailors, to inquire about radar detectors, editor Nick Nicholson wrote: "We've never evaluated radar detectors, but I've never found one that worked well." According to Bill Homewood, some singlehanders using the "beeping type" found that they were "constantly going off and becoming a nuisance." Norton Smith, who won a solo race from California to Hawaii and a Mini Transat, feels that a radar detector is a real help at sea, but his would sound off constantly within 70 miles of San Francisco. Norton attributes this to television and other microwave pollution. He wrote that far offshore his detector once alerted him to a ship about two miles away, which he learned through radio contact had not picked him up on radar even though Smith was displaying a radar reflector.

Francis Stokes had a similar experience during the 1976 OSTAR. His log entry for June 17 reads: "I was sitting wondering whether to eat breakfast or go back to bed when the radar check beeped. When that thing goes off the source has to be close because of its low sensitivity. I rushed to look out, and there was a brightly lit freighter bearing down on me less than a quarter-mile off. We were approaching obliquely, and I passed a couple of hundred yards off his stern. Actually, there was almost no time to take evasive action had it been necessary. The whole thing was over in what seemed like moments. I raised him on the radio . . . He didn't see me on radar which isn't very reassuring."

Some radar detectors work better than others, and when I took a sail with Stokes on his OSTAR racer his detector wasn't working well close to shore. I have seen good reports about the Escort radar detector and the Watchman, made by Lokata in England and Combi in the U.S.A. There is also a sonar detector that can pick up the sound of a ship's propeller from many miles away. This device is the Soniar 112 made by Soniar Electronics in New York.

Other alarms that can be of considerable value are audible depth finders and off-course alarms. I use a simple digital Impulse depth finder with an alarm that can be set to go off at 4 feet, 8 feet, or 20 feet. More elaborate models have alarms that can be set for any depth up to nearly 100 fathoms. Off-course alarms such as the Hestia model produced by Brookes & Gatehouse can be set to sound off when the boat departs from her proper heading by an angle greater than 20, 30, 40, 50, or 60 degrees. It is probably best not to set too small an angle at sea when it is rough or the wind is shifty when the boat is steering herself. It was stated that the off-course indicator used by Noel Bevan was one of many "good alarms which nearly drove [him] mad."

Radio Transmitters

Radiotelephones are carried by many modern singlehanders, for they provide a contact with the rest of the world, which is a great help psychologically, and provide a means of calling for help in the event of trouble. Furthermore, most races and individual sponsors require two-way radios. The trouble is that VHF (very high frequency) equipment has a very limited range, little more than line-of-sight. Long-range SSB (single sideband) equipment is quite expensive in addition to being a drain on the batteries and requiring complicated installation with a relatively long antenna and a ground plate. Ham radio has about the same drawbacks as SSB and also requires the operator to learn Morse code and pass an exam.

Singlehanded sailors who venture offshore should carry an EPIRB (emergency position-indicating radio beacon), which is a small portable transmitter that sends out distress signals over the aircraft emergency frequencies 121.5 and 243 MHz. There are now EPIRBs that can contact an international satellite tracking system. In most of the major solo races nowadays, the racers use the Argos transmitters described in Chapter 2. These are very expensive but increase safety immeasurably. Another alternative is a portable emergency radiophone that transmits and receives on 2182 kHz, the international distress frequency. Jock McLeod used one of these sets, a Safetylink, in the 1972 OSTAR to check his position occasionally from a passing ship, although, as he wrote, "One is not encouraged to have social chats on 2182."

Navigation and Emergency Lights

Proper navigation lights are an obvious safety requirement, yet there is little question that the standard legal running lights on small yachts are difficult if not impossible to see from a large ship, especially when those lights are obscured by sails. One night when a steamer passed close to my small yawl, I heard a voice from the bridge call down, "You'd better get bigger lights than that, buddy." The International and Inland Rules of the Road now allow a boat under sail alone to carry, in addition to normal side lights, an all-round red light over an all-round green light at the masthead. Another option for a sailboat under 65.6 feet long is the masthead tricolor combination light that uses one bulb for the red, green, and white stern light. Such arrangements help solve the problem of side lights being obscured by sails, and the options seem highly appropriate for singlehanders.

When the solo sailor is awake and spots an approaching ship, he may want to use a "flare-up" light to attract the ship's attention by shining a searchlight on his sails. A few experienced sailors claim that white sails are often less visible when lighted at night than those colored yellow, orange, or red, but white normally offers the greatest contrast.

Although of dubious legality, it may be desirable to have a flashing strobe light, preferably carried at the masthead, which can be used as an emergency flare-up light allowed under the Rules of the Road. There are masthead units such as the Mars-I lamp made by Asimo Engineering Co. that combine running lights and a strobe flasher.

Jerry Cartwright carried a flashing, 360-degree, buoy marker light (Guest, No. 561) lashed to his boat's backstay, and the light was allowed to flash continually every night when he was asleep (it is said to last about 100 nights on the same battery). Although Jerry was not sure about the light's legality, he reasoned that the extra safety it afforded justified its use, and he felt that on the high seas there is little chance that another vessel will mistake the blinker for a buoy. In checking into the matter of legality, he obtained unofficial opinions from two different Coast Guard station commanders, who said they would prefer that a small boat be seen and that such a flasher could qualify as a flare-up light allowed by the Rules of the Road. Since the early 1980s when the Rules of the Road were modified, there seems little doubt that a strobe flasher is illegal except for distress (see Rules 36 and 37 in the Coast Guard's *Navigation Rules*). Nevertheless, I would not hesitate to turn on my flasher if I were about to be run down.

An interesting point was brought up by solo transatlantic sailor Clare Francis, who believes in turning off her running lights and displaying a single white light when asleep. She reasons that if you are a sleeping singlehander and show running lights that indicate to the other vessel that he has the right of way, then you must be able to get out of his way. Of course, this situation would seldom arise unless the other vessel were a privileged sailing craft, a slow-moving vessel that you were overtaking, or a vessel fishing, laying cables, and so forth, or your boat were displaying an additional forward white light indicating she was under power. Nevertheless, Francis hopes that a single 32-point white light would lead the ship to assume the boat is "at anchor, fishing, or at least stationary" and thus take evasive action early. Actually, the legally correct lights for a singlehander off watch (under Rule 27) would be the running lights plus not-under-command lights, two 32-point red lights in a vertical line, one over the other. One well known singlehander who used these lights was Sir Alec Rose. The problem of designating that a boat is not under command will be discussed further in Chapter 13.

One possible hazard of using unconventional lighting is the chance of attracting a ship by arousing her master's curiosity and then possibly being damaged by the ship. This happened to Howard Blackburn several times during his solo Atlantic crossings. He usually carried white instead of colored sidelights because of their better visibility, but on several nights he was approached by steamers that came dangerously close. Even in the daylight, it is not unusual for ships to come right alongside. Harry Pidgeon, Francis Brenton, Francis Chichester, Bernard Moitessier, Tania Aebi, and others have had their rigs damaged by ships standing by.

Emergency Precautions

Visual distress signals such as hand-held flares and those shot from a Very pistol should be carried by every boat.

Collision mats are seldom carried, but as W. Leslie King and others have found out, they can be invaluable to the singlehander after a collision or serious grounding. Although some sailors like circular mats, the typical mat is triangular or square-shaped with lead weights or a piece of chain and corner lines that can be used to position and hold it over the damaged area of the hull and thus slow the rate of leaking (see Figure 11-1). A square mat is usually placed in the diamond position and is hauled beneath the water with the hogging line attached to the lower corner. Jock McLeod carried on his *Ron Glas* a mat made like a "pillow case" so that it could be stuffed full of blankets and the like. It had grommets all around the edges to accept multiple lashings. Collision mats have been out of vogue in recent years, but they could well come back into style because of the difficulty in performing emergency repairs on many of the modern boats with their fiberglass construction and liners that make it difficult to reach a damaged area from the inside of the hull. It could be worthwhile to carry a Simpson damage control gear, which will be described in Chapter 11. Other equipment relating to damage control will also be mentioned in that chapter. Tools and spare parts will be listed in Chapter 9.

Two other methods of controlling damage and reducing the likelihood of sinking in the event a boat is holed are the use of watertight collision bulkheads and/or foam flotation. Both of these safety measures are best installed at the time a boat is built, but can be retrofitted to most boats with some labor and sacrifice of space.

A life raft is important on any offshore boat, but there is no need for a singlehander's raft to be large unless there are times when he will be carrying crew. A two- or three-man raft should suffice for most singlehanders. It should be com-

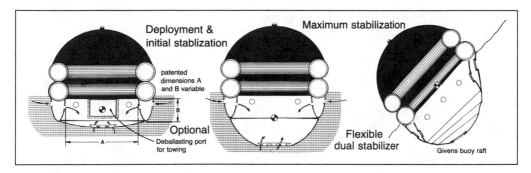

patented
dimensions A
and B variable

Optional
Deballasting port
for towing

Flexible
dual stabilizer

Givens buoy raft

Figure 8-2. (*Above*) This inflatable Givens life raft has a huge water ballast bag and is the most stable type, but not the most mobile. (Courtesy of Naval Institute Press)

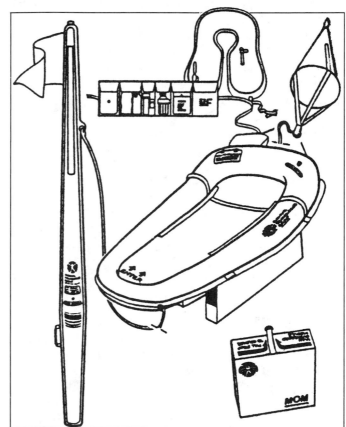

Figure 8-3. The MOM VII Man Overboard Module. All gear, including the inflatable raft and man-overboard pole, is packed in the canister at the lower right. (Courtesy of Survival Technologies Group)

partmentalized, have a canopy, and have water pockets for stability. Just how much stability a life raft should have is open to debate. Some sailors prefer maximum stability with a huge bottom water bag, but such a system compromises locomotion unless there is a deballasting port such as that used with the Givens raft (Figure 8-2). Other sailors such as Steve Callahan prefer maximum locomotion, which trades off stability to some degree. One such highly mobile raft is the Elliot, which can be outfitted with a sail. An ordinary inflatable dinghy is usually a poor substitute, primarily because it lacks proper pull-tab or hydrostatic CO_2 inflation, a canopy, and stability pockets.

One minimum life raft that is suitable for singlehanding is contained in the MOM (Man Overboard Module) made by the Survival Technologies Group. Although this raft is small and does not have a canopy, it is water ballasted and well equipped with emergency gear including a blanket to defend against hypothermia. The MOM consists of the raft with sea anchor, inflatable man-overboard pole, life jacket, and other equipment stowed in a compact canister that can be hung from the stern pulpit. The module's contents are deployed by pulling one strap, and a long line can be attached to the strap and towed. In the event a singlehander falls overboard, he stands a chance of grabbing the towed line. Tony Lush worked with the Survival Technologies Group and even devised a radio-controlled module that could be deployed instantly when triggered by a transmitter that he carried on his body.

As far as a conventional life raft is concerned, I favor carrying it in a fiberglass canister that is secured to the cabin top or some out-of-the-way area that is easily accessible. In addition to the standard emergency gear that is contained in the canister, I would have a "grab bag" with extra gear such as water stills, portable VHF radio, emergency transmitter, your favorite seasickness medication, a survival manual, lifeboat sextant, small speargun, spare blanket, and extra water. Rafts should be inspected by qualified examiners at least every two years.

Multihull Safety Measures

Most safety considerations pertaining to multihulls were discussed in Chapter 4. To reiterate briefly, a multihull may need sturdily attached masthead flotation with extra strong mast and rigging, automatic sheet releases, and some means of self-rescue in the event of a capsizing. Of course, all sponsons and amas must be very strongly attached, and for obvious reasons there should be nets or webbing covering open spaces between hulls. Sheet releases vary from simple cam-action jam cleats, which are mounted on hinged planks held down by shock cord, to the sophisticated electronic gadgetry devised by Donald Crowhurst for *Teignmouth Electron* and by Hugh McCoy for his 60-foot catamaran *Fury*. The latter used an aircraft gyrocompass electronically connected to a heel indicator to release a mainsheet at a set angle of heel.

A simple, swiveling cam cleat can be held by shock cord or a thumb screw (see Figure 8-4). The screw may provide a somewhat more easily adjustable means of altering the resistance to sheet tension needed for releasing. A frequently used automatic release is the one made by Hepplewhite, which utilizes two mercury switches, one for port heel and the other for starboard, and may be set to free a sheet at any heeling angle. A disadvantage in electric gear, of course, is that there is some drain on the battery and perhaps some risk of a short circuit from wet wiring. Furthermore, Michael Ellison, who sailed *Tahiti Bill* back to England after the 1972 transatlantic race, complained that the Hepplewhite would often release due to wave action rather than angle of heel from the wind. The jerking of the boom in rough weather can be a problem for mechanical-type releases.

If a multihull should happen to turn turtle in heavy weather offshore, rescue might be considered a two-step operation. The first is simply to survive on the bottom of the upturned boat until the blow abates, and the second is to right her.

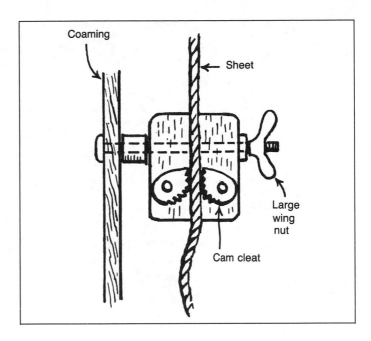

Figure 8-4. A simple, flip-up cleat.

Conditions must be ideal to right the typical multihull, especially a catamaran, because of her tremendous stability in the inverted position. Righting systems were described in Chapter 4.

Despite a relatively low range of positive stability and a very high range of negative stability, most multihulls make adequate life rafts when capsized. In 1973 two people survived for two months on the bottom of a capsized trimaran in the Pacific. Every oceangoing multihull should be provided with enough flotation to float the inverted hulls reasonably high, a hatch in the bottom or other means of entering and exiting the boat, EPIRBs and/or a transponder to call for help, and safety gear and supplies that are accessible when capsized. Steve Callahan even envisions the possibility of mounting a mast and sail on the bottom of the capsized multihull for limited locomotion when it can't be righted.

British Airways II (foreground) and *Sebago* at the start of the 1984 OSTAR. (Courtesy of Bill Homewood)

9

Passage Planning
and Preparation

A VITAL ELEMENT IN SUCCESSFUL solo cruising is careful passage planning. This starts with selecting the ideal route and time of year for optimal weather and minimizing hazards. Considerations concerning the route and time of a passage are the odds of encountering storms, the percentage of calms and fair winds, the avoidance of ship traffic, navigation aids in coastal and inland waters, currents that can help or hinder, shoals or obstructions, fog and ice, the availability of good anchorages, and so forth.

Important Publications

Major sources of information for route planning are as follows: *Coast Pilots*, published by the National Ocean Survey, which covers U.S. coastlines; *Sailing Directions*, published by the U.S. Naval Oceanographic Office, which cover foreign ports and coasts (or the British Admiralty *Pilots*, having a very similar coverage); *World Port Index*, giving port information, published by the U.S. Naval Oceanographic Office; the U.S. *Pilot Charts*, issued monthly (or periodically in atlases) by the U.S. Naval Oceanographic Office, which show the average ocean winds, currents, storm tracks, and other important information; and the British Admiralty publication *Ocean Passages for the World*, which gives recommended routes, weather, winds, currents, and so forth. *World Cruising Routes*, by Jimmy Cornell, is an invaluable reference source that covers much of the same information as *Ocean Passages* but in a very readable form, concentrating on routes plied by modern sailors. The *Atlantic Crossing Guide*, produced by the Royal Cruising Club Pilotage Foundation and published by International Marine Publishing Company, is another good

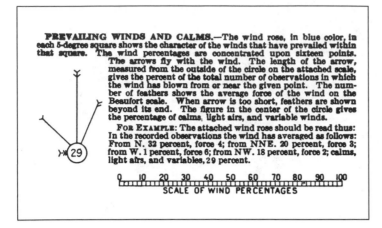

PREVAILING WINDS AND CALMS.—The wind rose, in blue color, in each 5-degree square shows the character of the winds that have prevailed within that square. The wind percentages are concentrated upon sixteen points. The arrows fly with the wind. The length of the arrow, measured from the outside of the circle on the attached scale, gives the percent of the total number of observations in which the wind has blown from or near the given point. The number of feathers shows the average force of the wind on the Beaufort scale. When arrow is too short, feathers are shown beyond its end. The figure in the center of the circle gives the percentage of calms, light airs, and variable winds.

FOR EXAMPLE: The attached wind rose should be read thus: In the recorded observations the wind has averaged as follows: From N. 32 percent, force 4; from NNE. 20 percent, force 3; from W. 1 percent, force 6; from NW. 18 percent, force 2; calms, light airs, and variables, 29 percent.

SCALE OF WIND PERCENTAGES

Figure 9-1. Pilot chart wind rose.

source of information for anyone plying the Atlantic. Obviously, charts and cruising guides of the places to be visited should be carried also. Two interesting and helpful charts for extended passages are the Admiralty charts 5308 and 5309, entitled respectively *The World-Sailing Ship Routes* and *Chart of the World Showing Tracks Followed by Sailing and Auxiliary Powered Vessels*. Of less value in the planning stage, but important once the route has been determined, are such publications as *Notices to Mariners* (prepared by the National Ocean Survey and U.S. Coast Guard), *Light Lists* (published by the Coast Guard and Defense Mapping Agency Hydrographic Center), *Tide Tables* and *Worldwide Marine Weather Broadcasts* (both published by the U.S. Department of Commerce), and *Radio Navigation Aids* (published by the Defense Mapping Agency Hydrographic Office).

Especially valuable are the pilot charts, for they divide the sea into five-degree squares and show the percentage of calms and gales, and the wind velocity and direction within each square. This information is based on many thousands of observations made during a period of more than 125 years, since the idea for pilot charts was originated by Matthew Fontaine Maury, the American pioneer in oceanography. Wind characteristics are shown graphically with the use of a wind rose in each five-degree square (see Figure 9-1 for a complete explanation). Short arrows of about equal length detached from the wind roses show the direction of the current, and numbers beside them show average current strength. Long, fine, unbroken, red lines show the tracks of some representative storms; while other red lines, made up of small circles, dashes, jagged marks, or dots, have to do with the limits of ice. Other lines and symbols on pilot charts show areas of fog, steamer lanes, lines of equal magnetic variation, lines of equal atmospheric temperature, location of ocean station vessels, lines of equal barometric pressure, limits of prevailing wind areas, reported icebergs, and more. Despite its great value in optimal routing and voyage planning, however, the pilot chart is not entirely a panacea for predictions, because it only gives percentages and averages of conditions that have occurred in the past. Offshore sailors should bear in mind the wisdom of H. G. Hasler, who made a remark to the effect that the winds do not read the pilot charts.

In congested shipping areas such as the English Channel or the approaches to New York City, the singlehander should carefully study traffic separation routes.

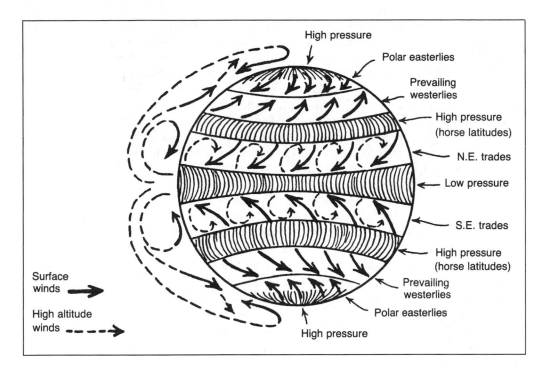

Figure 9-2. Simplified global winds.

These routes, which are recommended but not mandatory for ships, are found on standard charts and in navigation-related publications such as *Reed's Nautical Almanac.*

Global Weather and Currents

Most readers probably know about the general circulation of winds around our planet, but, for those who are uncertain of the basic pattern, a brief study of Figure 9-2 should be helpful. The illustration gives a generalized and simplified picture of the winds shown as they would be blowing if there were no land masses. The shaded bands are areas of high or low atmospheric pressure, with the concave hatch marks representing low pressure and the convex marks representing high pressure. The basic system results primarily from temperature differences and the earth's rotation. At the equator, where the globe is hottest, the air rises, leaving a belt of low pressure and calms corresponding to what meteorologists call the intertropical convergence zone (ITCZ) or equatorial trough, but more commonly known as the doldrums. Air that has risen in that region moves north and south, and much of it sinks to form high-pressure belts of light, variable winds, known as the horse latitudes, so called (according to one theory) because early ships carrying horses to the New World were often becalmed in those areas, and the animals were jettisoned when they died of thirst or starvation. The sinking air at the horse latitudes splits in two, with portions returning to the ITCZ to form the northeast and southeast trade winds. These are fairly consistent, strong, steady winds that were long used by commercial sailing vessels for trade, and hence their name. North and south of the horse latitudes the portion of sinking air that didn't return to the equator forms winds that move in the opposite direction to the trades, called the prevailing westerlies. Air that escaped sinking in the horse latitudes continues toward the poles, where it cools and sinks to form a high-pressure area and the polar easterly winds. The east-west components of the various wind belts are due to the Coriolis force, the deflection of a moving body to the right in the northern hemisphere and to the left in the southern hemisphere due to the earth's rotation.

The preceding description of global winds is highly idealized and simplified, but in actuality, the systems are greatly altered by the existence of land masses and the seasonal effect caused by the earth being tipped on its axis. The land not only blocks the flow of wind, but, more significantly, it causes uneven heating. As a result, fast-changing high and low pressure systems form inland, interrupting the continuity of the oceanic high pressure belts in the middle latitudes. These pressure systems add a circular, swirling motion to the winds in the region of the westerlies, and the wind tends to rotate clockwise around large highs in the North Atlantic and North Pacific Oceans, while rotating counterclockwise around highs in the South Atlantic, South Pacific, and southern Indian Oceans. The circulation of surface winds for the half year from approximately May to November is shown in Figure 9-3, while the half year from approximately November to May is shown in Figure 9-4.

These illustrations also show in a very general way the location of semi-permanent highs and lows over the oceans, the major wind systems, areas of variable winds, the position of the ITCZ, and regions of tropical storms. The most noticeable differences in wind patterns between Figures 9-3 and 9-4 are the development of a closed (circular) and intense low-pressure system near the Aleutian Islands (the Aleutian low) during the northern winter and the strengthening of a low near Iceland (the Icelandic low) at the same time; the shifting northward of the ITCZ in the northern summer; and the reversal of winds in the Indian Ocean, China Sea, and north of Australia, which are known as monsoons. The latter are striking examples of wind systems produced by alternate heating and cooling of the land. In the northern winter, a high forms over southern Asia, and the monsoon blows northeast toward the ITCZ north of the equator; in the northern summer, the heat forms an inland low, which draws the wind from the Indian Ocean high, causing the southwest monsoon north of the equator. South of the equator the monsoons have a westerly component in the southern summer and an easterly component in the southern winter (although at the latter time they are usually considered part of the southeast trades) due to the Coriolis force mentioned earlier. It is also plain to see that the westerlies of the southern hemisphere are unblocked by land masses; thus they are much stronger and more consistent than their counterparts in the north.

Some other, less noticeable differences between Figures 9-3 and 9-4 are the upward shift of the southern hemisphere westerlies during the southern winter; the building of the North Atlantic (Azores) high and the building (with a tendency to shift westward and somewhat north) of the North Pacific high in the northern summer; and a weakening of the southeast trades in the western South Pacific in the southern summer partly due to opposition from the northwest monsoon east of

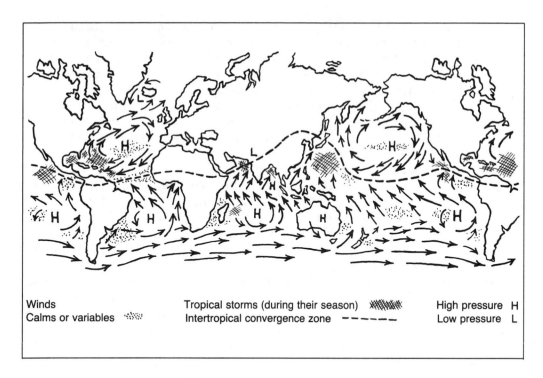

Figure 9-3. General pattern of weather and wind circulation: May to November.

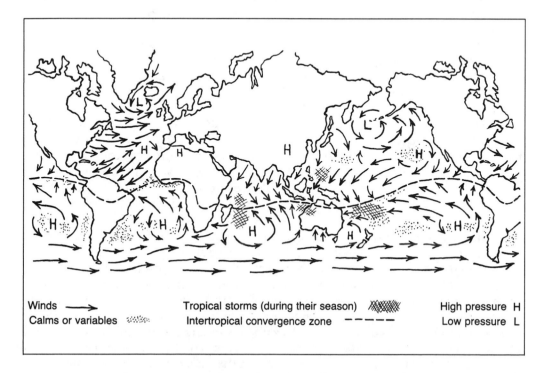

Figure 9-4. General pattern of weather and wind circulation: November to May.

Australia. It can also be seen that along with the seasonal shifting of the ITCZ, the trade-wind belts shift in a similar way. Their average limits in the higher latitudes shift from 25°N in January to 30°N in July for the northeast trades and 30°S in January to 25°S in July for the southeast trades. The trade-wind limits closest to the equator shift from about 2°N in January to 10°N in July (Atlantic) and 4°N in January to 12°N in July (Pacific) for the northeast trades. The southeast trade-wind limits nearest the equator shift from the following average positions in January: 0° (Atlantic), 4°N (Pacific), and 15°S (Indian Ocean) to July positions of 5°N (Atlantic), 8°N (Pacific), and 0° (Indian Ocean).

Cross-hatched areas in Figures 9-3 and 9-4 show the regions affected by tropical storms. They normally begin to occur in the early summer and become most frequent in the late summer or early fall of their hemisphere. These storms, which can be extremely dangerous, form over the ocean in or near the ITCZ. They drift westward, usually curve toward the pole of their hemisphere, and very often continue curving (or recurving) until they move in a westerly direction due to the Coriolis force and the prevailing westerlies. It should be emphasized that the illustrated regions by no means show the limit of areas subject to these disturbances, for individual storm tracks often proceed a considerable distance poleward, and they are sometimes very erratic. They are best avoided by cruising in the affected regions during the proper season only. Tropical storms are known as hurricanes in the West Indies-Gulf of Mexico-North Atlantic region and in the area just west of the Mexican coast; but they are known as typhoons in the western North Pacific and cyclones in the Arabian Sea-Bay of Bengal-Indian Ocean regions. In the general vicinity of Australia and in the western South Pacific, they are called cyclones, but they are known as willy-willies off the Australian northwest coast. Although most of these storms reach their peak in the late summer or early fall and are almost nonexistent during the winter and spring, those in the western North Pacific can occur at any time of the year, but they reach their peak in August. The South Atlantic is free of tropical storms because the ITCZ in that area does not move south of the equator. Nevertheless, there are very strong winds called *pamperos* off the Argentine coast from July to September and sometimes later.

Although not as important to the offshore sailor as the winds, ocean currents are another factor to be considered. In a very general way these currents follow a pattern similar to the wind systems. North and south of the equator are the west-flowing north equatorial and south equatorial currents, which correspond to the trade winds. They are divided by a weaker easterly flow called the equatorial countercurrent in the very approximate vicinity of the doldrums. Farther toward the poles, there are great current swirls that rotate clockwise north of the equator and counterclockwise south of the equator, roughly similar to the way the winds swirl around the oceanic highs. We might consider that the North Pacific current and the Gulf Stream correspond with the prevailing westerly winds in the northern hemisphere; while a worldwide current called west wind drift corresponds roughly with the prevailing westerly winds in the southern hemisphere. The portion of the great current swirls that move toward the equator from the middle latitudes are the Canary and Benguela currents on the east sides of the North and South Atlantic Oceans, the California and Peru (Humboldt) currents on the east sides of the North and South Pacific Oceans, and the West Australian current on the east side of the

Indian Ocean. Those parts of the swirls that move away from the equator toward the middle latitudes are the Gulf Stream and Brazil current on the west sides of the North and South Atlantic, the Kuroshio and East Australia currents on the west sides of the North and South Pacific Oceans, and the south equatorial current joining the Agulhas current on the west side of the Indian Ocean. In the northern part of the Indian Ocean during the northern summer, there is a monsoon current forming a large clockwise swirl that is a reversal of the circulation in that area during the northern winter.

Route Planning

The basic principle involved in route planning is to be in the right place at the right time for optimal winds and weather. The primary considerations are to avoid sailing into the regions affected by tropical storms during the dangerous seasons and to make passages in the higher latitudes during the warmer months (prior to or just after the end of the tropical storm season) when gales and extra-tropical lows, producing stormy weather, are at a minimum.

The classic routes around the world followed by most singlehanders (except for those who want the challenge of exceedingly difficult voyages) are the east-to-west trade winds route, via the Panama Canal-Torres Strait-Cape of Good Hope; or the west-to-east route following the westerlies in the southern hemisphere. The latter is a lot faster but much rougher than the typical trade wind route. In fact, a track that passes through the South Pacific in the latitudes of the Roaring Forties or Furious Fifties and passes south of Cape Horn can be positively dangerous for a lone sailor in a small boat. Nevertheless, the eastward solo passage has been made successfully by such small craft as the 31-foot *Lehg II*, sailed by Vito Dumas; the 25-foot *Cardinal Vertue*, sailed by Bill Nance; and even a 20-foot plywood yawl, the *Ahodori*, sailed by a Japanese sailor, Y. Aoki. The latter, I understand, suffered two capsizes. Of course, Bardiaux deliberately rounded the wrong way in his 31-foot *Les 4 Vents*. More recent eastward circumnavigations via the Horn by very small craft include the 25-foot *New Penny*, sailed by Israeli Gidaliahu Shtirmer in 1977, and the 29-foot *Mermaid III*, sailed by Kenichi Horie in 1974 (see Chapter 2).

If one were to attempt the easiest possible small-boat circumnavigation with a starting point on the U.S. East Coast, one would leave for the West Indies in early June after the spring gales but before the hurricane season. It would be a good idea to hang around the West Indies, where there are some protected harbors until after the hurricane season and then, in early November before the boisterous winter trades begin, to head for the Panama Canal.

Departing from England, a safe plan is to leave in early or mid-summer, well before the autumnal gales, when the notoriously rough Bay of Biscay is relatively calm. It's a good idea to make a bit of westing past Biscay, but then keep far enough east to pick up the fresh northerlies known as the Portuguese Trades. When these are in effect, they'll carry the voyager in minimal time to the Canary Islands, where he can wait until well after the end of the hurricane season before making a trade wind passage to the West Indies and Panama Canal.

The recommended time for departing the Canaries is late in November so that one can reach the West Indies, cruise there, and cross the Caribbean Sea during a relatively placid season. From the Panama Canal there is the fairly short, but often windless, passage to the Galapagos Islands. Moitessier and others recommend making the passage between December and February for the best use of winds and current, but a main consideration is to reach the South Pacific islands after the hurricane season, which tapers off at the end of March. Many voyagers stop at the Marquesas and then Tahiti, reaching them by way of the trade wind "milk run." The southeast trades are normally fresh and steady in the eastern part of the Pacific, but in the western part unsteady winds are likely during the northwest monsoons from about December to March.

Starting the voyage from the U.S. West Coast, some sailors might sail down the coast and thence to the Galapagos, but most will sail out to the Hawaiian Islands, taking care to stay in the southeast sector of the North Pacific high. After a stay in Hawaii, the circumnavigators will usually head southward for the South Pacific Islands before or after the South Pacific tropical cyclone season, which is approximately from mid-November until the end of March. In the vicinity of Fiji the southeast trades are most reliable in June and July. Many voyagers with plenty of time wish to cruise through the South Sea islands and perhaps visit New Zealand and East Australia, as was done by John Guzzwell and others. The most important consideration is either to avoid the areas affected during the worst of the cyclone season (during January, February, and March) or stay close to well-protected anchorages. It is also desirable to avoid the southernmost localities during the southern winter. Guzzwell recommended a February crossing from New Zealand to Australia for favorable winds in the Tasman Sea, but one must stay below the zone affected by cyclones. A common route from the lower east coast of Australia to Torres Strait is inside the Great Barrier Reef, but it requires very careful piloting.

It is important to pass through the tricky Torres Strait when the monsoons are favorable, and, of course, where there will be minimal threat from the willy-willies, which can form in the vicinity of the Timor Sea and northwest Australia during the months between December and April. If one figured on an approximate three-month crossing of the Indian Ocean, a departure from the strait in July would provide the combination of southeast winds with the avoidance of Indian Ocean cyclones, which may begin as early as October. Although John Sowden reported an easy October passage through Torres Strait despite having no auxiliary power, he had a lengthy stay in Indonesia and thus avoided exposure to cyclones at sea.

The circumnavigator will have to decide whether to travel 1,200 miles up the Red Sea or round the southern tip of Africa. The decision is sometimes a trade-off of a longer, rougher trip around South Africa's Cape Agulhas for a shorter, more tedious beat up the Red Sea, an area notorious for political unrest. Among others, Al Peterson, Walter Koenig, and Webb Chiles had extremely difficult trips up the Red Sea. Chiles was even captured and jailed in Saudi Arabia. Tania Aebi wrote favorably of the Middle Easterners she encountered along the Red Sea route, but she suffered from head winds and heat. Even when conditions are most favorable, between November and the end of February, when winds are often fair in the lower part of the Red Sea, they are calm or northerly in the upper part. In addition, there are unmarked reefs and strong currents, plus the heat and ever-present danger of political unrest. Thus a passage across the Indian Ocean (normally via Christmas

Island, Cocos-Keeling, Rodriguez and Mauritius) to Durban is most often preferred when the southeast trades are strong and when cyclones are minimal in the western Indian Ocean, from about June to October.

Rounding the Cape of Good Hope is seldom easy. Singlehander Jean Gau, who survived a capsize in that area (see Chapter 11), described the difficulties very well in an article published in *The Spray*. He wrote:

> There is a reason for the bad weather in the neighborhood of jutting land masses. The greater the land mass, the greater the turmoil. As a result one can expect the worst off the "Cape of Storms." Moreover, in this region the presence of two currents, each one sweeping with great velocity in opposite directions, makes the southernmost tip of Africa one of the most difficult headlands to navigate. The westerly current along the shore is known as the Agulhas current. Nearer to the South Pole the Antarctic drift (west wind drift) runs eastward, pushed by the never ceasing westerly of these regions. It is amongst these perpetual storms that the highest waves in the world are to be found, particularly at the limit of the two oceanic currents where they reach the maximum height of 45-50 feet. By comparison, waves in the Pacific and Indian Ocean seldom reach more than 30-35 feet, those in the Atlantic 25-30 feet, while in the Mediterranean they do not exceed 15-20 feet. Fifty miles south of Cape Agulhas, in bad southwesterly weather the wind goes against the current and creates a very dangerous sea. The waves then have a tendency to become very steep when they meet an obstacle such as a ship. They break and fall on deck as heavy masses of dead water which can cause tremendous damage. It is one of those giant waves which on the night 26/27 February 1966 broke across *Atom*, causing it to capsize and lose its masts.

Despite Gau's gloomy description, the passage around Cape Agulhas and the Cape of Good Hope is relatively short, and a great many sailors have made it safely. Nevertheless, it is essential to be well rested and prepared, and a singlehander would do well to sign on a crew for the brief passage, although many have made it alone. The easiest time of the rounding will most likely be near the middle of the southern summer in January or February when the weather is warm, there are good chances for favorable winds, and the westerlies, being farther south, are least likely to oppose the Agulhas current and create steep, dangerous seas. Favoring southeasters are common in the summer, but they can be extremely boisterous at times.

The passage from the Cape of Storms up the South Atlantic toward the eastern bulge of South America is relatively easy. Once the southeast trades are reached, it is, in the modern vernacular, "a piece of cake" until the doldrums. There are no tropical cyclones in the South Atlantic, as the ITCZ does not invade that area. A singlehander might want to break the isolation with stops at St. Helena and Ascension Islands, or he might take a more westerly course if bound for the West Indies and skirt the coast of Brazil. Jean Gau, who sailed the latter course, warns of the danger from floating trees near the mouth of the Amazon during the rainy season (November–June). Of course, the West Indies should be reached well before the start of the hurricane season. A good time to head north for the U.S. east coast, or for Bermuda if one is going to England, is in May or preferably June when the winds have a southerly component and the American spring gales have diminished.

From Bermuda to England, an initial course north of the rhumb line is advisable, because it is similar to a great circle track (the shortest distance) and gets one most quickly into the prevailing westerlies. Many stop at the Azores, but they face the probability of some head winds from there to England.

Race Strategy

One of the most common passages for singlehanders is that from Plymouth, England, to Newport, Rhode Island, not because it is an easy passage, but because it is the course for the OSTAR (or C-STAR, as it is now called), held every four years and starting in early June (see Chapter 2). The principal difficulty of the course is that it runs against the prevailing westerlies. There might be considered seven possible routes: (1) the far-northern, (2) great-circle, (3) rhumb-line, (4) Azores, (5) corner-cutting southern, (6) northern trade-wind, and (7) southern trade-wind (see Figure 9-5).

The far-northern route is the one advocated and followed in 1960 and 1964 by H. G. Hasler after considerable research into the routes of early square-riggers and a study of the theories of Captains Hare and Becher. Hasler learned that many sailing ships leaving from Scotland and keeping north often beat those vessels sailing from the English Channel on early summer Atlantic crossings. Normally a procession of lows move across the upper North Atlantic from west to east, and they rotate in a counterclockwise direction. Hasler reasoned that if a ship could pass to the north of many lows, she would have a good percentage of favorable winds. His planned route in 1960 went as high as 55°N in mid-Atlantic, and he actually sailed even farther north. The strategy seemed to work quite well, as *Jester* finished second in the first race and fourth on corrected time (fifth on elapsed) in the second race (see Chapter 2). This was not bad considering that *Jester* was only 25 feet long and carried a single Chinese lug sail, which is not the most suitable for windward work. There are, however, many drawbacks to the route, because it is considerably longer than a direct course; a fair amount of heavy weather may be encountered; there is often fog, especially in the vicinity of Newfoundland; the temperature is cold; and there is greater exposure to drift ice. Thus it is not surprising that the far-northern route is not popular, especially for boats that have good windward ability.

The great-circle, or orthodromic, route is the next most northerly course, and is the shortest distance between two points on a globe, even though it appears as a curved track on a Mercator chart (the usual chart projection). The major drawback of a great-circle course from England to America is the high percentage of head winds. In fact, the Admiralty chart for sailing ship routes shows a route just south of the great-circle course that is labeled "seldom possible." Despite this discouragement, however, many of the racing singlehanders, including those who have done well, have made passages that follow fairly closely to the great-circle route. In actuality, a true great-circle course from Plymouth to Newport is not possible, because of the necessity of passing south of Newfoundland. Furthermore, the danger in that area from drifting icebergs makes it advisable to keep far south, perhaps as low as 45°N latitude or lower when nearing Cape Race, to reduce the

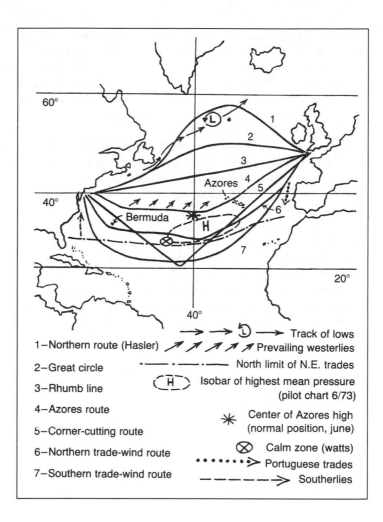

Figure 9-5. Possible routes for OSTAR racers.

1—Northern route (Hasler)
2—Great circle
3—Rhumb line
4—Azores route
5—Corner-cutting route
6—Northern trade-wind route
7—Southern trade-wind route

→ → ⓛ → Track of lows
↗ ↗ ↗ ↗ ↗ Prevailing westerlies
— · — · — North limit of N.E. trades
⟨ H ⟩ Isobar of highest mean pressure (pilot chart 6/73)
✳ Center of Azores high (normal position, june)
⊗ Calm zone (watts)
•••••⟩ Portuguese trades
— — — ⟩ Southerlies

risk. The average limit of drift ice actually reaches slightly farther south than 38°N in June.

The rhumb-line, or loxodromic, route is the one next farther south, and it is the straight-line course on a Mercator chart. This course, too, gives a high percentage of head winds, but it is the next-shortest distance across, being only slightly over a hundred miles longer than the great-circle route. One minor advantage in sailing along the rhumb line (when winds permit) is that it is possible to hold a steady compass course, whereas with the great-circle route, the course must be changed continually. The usual means of determining one's course changes by the great-circle route, incidentally, is by using a gnomonic projection chart, which shows great-circle routes as straight lines.

The Azores route naturally passes near the Azores, usually between Flores and Fayal, then down about to latitude 36°N, then straight across, until turning more northward when northeast of Bermuda. Although this route is about 600 miles longer than a straight course on the Mercator chart, it has fewer head winds on the average. One problem with the Azores route is that more calms are apt to be met. Actually, this will depend on the location of the Azores high, the center of which should be avoided, as the winds there are apt to be very light and flukey. According to the *Mariner's Weather Log* (published by the U.S. Department of Commerce), the normal position for the Azores high is centered near 35°N and 40°W during the time of the race. Sailor-meteorologist Alan Watts, however, mentioned a "zone of maximum calm at about 26°N and 48°W" in an article he wrote for *Yachting World* just before the 1972 race. Watts' calm area is considerably south and west of where one would expect to find the normal Azores high, but the high often shifts its position a great deal from month to month and also from year to year. Moreover, the isobar of highest pressure often covers a considerable area. Thus it seems that the chances of meeting some calms along that route are fairly high.

The trade-wind routes are, of course, much farther south, which adds a great deal to the distance but assures a much higher percentage of favorable fresh winds and advantageous currents. Eric Tabarly described what he thought was the most northerly practical trade-wind route as passing south of the Azores, down to about latitude 28°N, and then passing south of Bermuda before proceeding northward. This track, however, still passes into or near the horse latitudes, and so the risk of meeting calms is not a great deal less. A more southerly trade-wind route, down to about 24°N or a few degrees farther south, as recommended by the Admiralty *Sailing Ship Routes* chart, gives much greater assurance of fresh, favorable winds. The trouble with this plan is that the favorable conditions seldom justify the extra distance that must be sailed. It is a relatively pleasant passage and makes sense for cruising, but usually not for racing.

Meteorologist Alan Watts suggested the possibility of a corner-cutting, trade-wind course, whereby one would depart from the southern trade-wind route near the Azores and sail directly for a point at about 22°N, 46°W, and then directly for the finish. This course would theoretically get one below the mid-Atlantic zone of calms, and a distance of almost 900 miles would be cut from the deep southern route, but there are other areas of light winds, part of the horse latitudes, such as one near Bermuda, that might be difficult to avoid. In addition, the winds are not as fair and the current not as favorable when corner-cutting.

Simply put, those are the most essential factors relating to the weather that the OSTAR contestants must consider in planning their courses. The choice is not easy, because there are a great many variables. Although we tend to think of the prevailing westerlies as zones of somewhat steady winds, they can be extremely fickle in the northern hemisphere, as individual alternating low and high pressure systems and fronts move across the Atlantic from North America upsetting the regularity of the system. Quite often, there is a fair percentage of favorable winds where there are supposed to be head winds. For this reason, as well as the distance factor, the more direct routes seem to have paid off the majority of times thus far. Winners Chichester and Tabarly followed courses between the great-circle and rhumb-line routes in 1960 and 1964, while winner Williams was slightly below the great circle, and runner-up (on elapsed time) Dalling kept fairly close to the rhumb line in 1968. Winner Colas and runner-up Terlain were near the great circle in 1972, but the third-place finishers in 1968 and 1972 stayed closer to the Azores route. In the stormy race of 1976 the leading boats were either close to the rhumb line or great circle, and winner Weld followed the rhumb line in 1980 except for a 500 mile southwesterly detour to avoid a storm. Ice warnings kept most of the top boats farther south in 1984, but the top monohull sailed a near straight-line course.

In recent times, commercial ships and naval vessels often use what is called optimal track routing, whereby estimates are made of the most desirable routes that will avoid adverse conditions and minimize time for passage. These estimates are based on long-range weather forecasts translated into prognostic wave charts, showing the direction of waves, as generated by the winds, and isopleth lines, showing mean wave heights within bounded areas. Of course, wave information is of greater importance for powered vessels than sailboats, which are primarily concerned with the wind, but weather forecasts and storm conditions are obviously important to sailors also. An OSTAR racer might profit enormously, for instance, by advance notice of an approaching low and its probable track, so that he could skirt its north side to get favorable winds, or perhaps head farther south to avoid it. Today's yachtsmen are making increasing use of optimal routing from private commercial services since these high-tech, computer-based services are now readily available at a reasonable cost and most transoceanic racers have effective radio communication. Routing services available to American yachtsmen include the Bendix Corporation of New Jersey, Weather Routing Inc. of New York, and the highly recommended Oceanroutes, Inc., of Palo Alto, California with offices around the world. These services normally provide a long-range forecast with optimal routing at the beginning of a passage and then numerous updated weather reports with course change advisories en route.

Another alternative to using a shore-based routing service is for the yachtman to plot his own optimal route based on updated information obtained from weather facsimile equipment. Because this equipment was once bulky, expensive, and power hungry, it used to be practical only for large vessels, but now relatively inexpensive radiofax recorders the size of a small typewriter can supply updated weather charts with little drain on the batteries. Some recorders such as the Alden Marinefax IV have self-contained radios designed to receive radiofax charts worldwide. This equipment can be valuable to any seagoer, racer or not. It has proven reliable not only for route planning, but for forecasting and avoiding bad weather along the way.

Condition of the Vessel

After thoughtful passage planning, the next important steps in successful solo voyaging are preparing the vessel for sea and ensuring that she is properly equipped. A failure in gear, rig, or some part of the hull that might be considered a mere inconvenience aboard a fully-crewed vessel could possibly be a very serious problem for a singlehander. It is therefore the safest policy that the solo sailor's boat be given a thorough condition survey by a well-qualified surveyor before she sets forth on a hard voyage. In addition to technical competence, the surveyor should have sea experience, because only then can he have a full appreciation of the problems involved. As the blue-water singlehander/surveyor Ian Nicolson wrote in his book *Surveying Small Craft*, "Anyone who has been through a big gale in a small boat is unlikely to make a slovenly surveyor."

Rigging Checklist

It is essential that spars and rigging get a thorough going over. Rigging failures and dismastings are all too common, and these accidents are especially devastating for an offshore singlehander. Before putting to sea, check the following:

1) There should be toggles at the bottom of all shrouds, as well as the top and bottom of the jibstay and the permanent backstay if it is to carry a riding sail.

2) Standing rigging should be a size larger than that found on the typical stock boat.

3) Turnbuckles should be of the reinforced, open-barrel variety uniformly installed for ease of adjustment. They should be fitted with cotter pins rather than lock nuts or cotter rings.

4) Halyards should have fairleads and keepers to prevent them from jumping out of their sheaves, as well as stops to prevent their eyes from being pulled into the sheaves. Halyards ends should be secured to prevent them from going aloft.

5) Clevis pins, cotter pins, and rigging fittings should be large enough to prevent deformation, point loading, and shearing. All nuts and screw pins should be secured with peening or cotters.

6) The mast should have a minimum number of holes drilled in the same vertical position. Large holes (such as abandoned halyard exits) should be plugged whenever possible.

7) Tangs should be of sufficient weight and bent to align with shroud or stay.

8) Spreaders should be positioned to bisect the angle they make against the shrouds, with spreader tips securely lashed and wrapped to prevent chafe. Spreader sockets should be extremely strong and preferably not made of cast aluminum. Wood spreaders should be free of rot and protected with ferrules to prevent splitting.

9) All metals on spars should be compatible or else carefully insulated against galvanic corrosion.

10) Sheaves should be a proper size, their diameters at least 20 times the diameter of the wire rope they accept.

11) Eye splices and tail splices, (especially those running inside the masts) should be inspected for kinks, corrosion, and "meat hooks" (wire snags). All eyes should be formed around thimbles.

12) All rigging fittings (turnbuckles, toggles, swages, terminals, tangs, etc.) should be inspected with a magnifying glass and, if possible, with a dye penetrant and developer to reveal any possible hairline cracks from stress or corrosion or manufacturing defects.

13) Reel winches should be fitted with screw pin brakes and preferably winch wheels instead of handles. Today's low-stretch rope halyards eliminate the need for reel winches, which can be dangerous (see Chapter 5).

14) All running rigging should have proper leads to avoid chafe.

15) Sail tracks should be through-bolted or otherwise securely fastened near the heads of storm sails. All sail tracks should have stops. The mast should be fitted with a double track or switch for the storm trysail.

16) Standing rigging should be designed to prevent compression bends (a minimum 12-degree shroud-to-mast angle is preferable).

17) Rigging should be reinforced as necessary to prevent excessive mast whip through the use of double lower shrouds, forestay, baby stay, and/or running backstays.

18) The gooseneck fitting should be heavy-duty, designed to take stress when the boom is broad off.

19) There should be a proper main topping lift, adjustable at the mast and able to double as a spare halyard. A boom crutch or better yet, a gallows frame, should be fitted.

20) The reefing system should be effective and manageable. Jiffy (slab) reefing is a good way to reduce the area of the mainsail. If the boom is equipped for roller reefing, it should have a built-up diameter aft to prevent droop (see Chapter 5).

21) Chafing gear such as baggywrinkle should be installed near spreader tips and other offending parts of the rigging.

22) All blocks should be extra strong and strapped. Pay particular attention to turning blocks, which must take double strain.

23) Backstay insulators should have interlocking shroud eyes for safety in the event of insulator breakage.

24) Spars should be inspected for dents, cracks, rot, or corrosion. Hollow masts should have adequate drains at the bottom. The mast step should be deep enough to prevent the mast from jumping out or shifting. The mast heel should have an adequate tongue and should be exactly square and fair to avoid unwanted mast hook. Any electric wires running aloft must be well secured and protected; preferably they should run inside the spars.

25) On multihulls or other craft that can capsize and turn turtle, the masthead should have sturdily attached flotation with appropriate rigging (some multihull sailors would disagree on this item).

26) Headsails with less than maximum luff length should be fitted with head pendants if they are hoisted using rope-tailed wire halyards in order to allow at least three full turns of wire around the halyard winch when the sail is fully hoisted.

27) Welds, rivets and bolts securing mast components should be inspected for cracks, corrosion, looseness, and erosion. All masthead fittings should be of substantial strength regardless of their weight and windage.

On a fiberglass boat, some of the important hull features that should be checked are the centerline joint (if the hull is made from two halves), the hull-deck connection, rigidity of the topsides up forward, sturdiness of bulkheads, security of chainplates, stern and rudder tubes, thickness where fittings are secured, attachment of fin keels and skegs, through-hull fittings, and areas of flexibility, especially flat areas in way of hard spots. Continued flexing in an area against which the hard edge of a structural member is pressed can fatigue and crack the fiberglass.

Take the case of singlehander Barry Nelson, who in 1970 took a brief shakedown cruise in preparation for a solo circumnavigation in a stock 28-footer. Nelson had not gotten far, fortunately, when he heard the fiberglass crack, and soon afterwards his boat began to fill with water. He called for help and was promptly found by a Coast Guard helicopter, which lowered him a large-capacity pump. Later, a Coast Guard cutter took him in tow, but that action caused too much stress, and there was a massive failure of the towed boat's bottom. She sank so fast that Nelson had time only to save his wallet. Along with the boat, about $7,000 worth of gear bought for the circumnavigation was lost. The fiberglass failure was due to cheap, light construction, and considerable flexibility near a hard spot under a forward

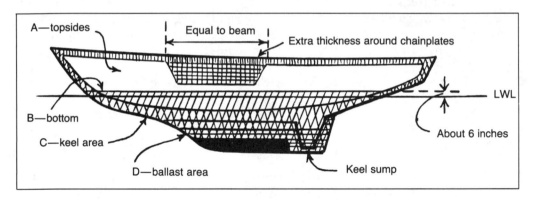

Figure 9-6. *(Above)* Fiberglass hull reinforcement (suggestive of Lloyd's recommendations). The hull is gradually thickened from areas A to B, B to C, and C to D. The weight per square foot of D should be about 2½ times that of A.

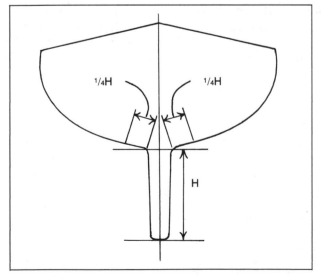

Figure 9-7. Keel reinforcement in the ¼ H areas (suggestive of ABS scantlings). Area where reinforcing laminates may be needed equals approximately one quarter of the keel's height.

bulkhead. It is my understanding, also, that the boat's hull thickness was built up with liberal use of the "chopper gun," which simultaneously sprays chopped glass and resin onto the hull.

Let's face it, a lot of the cheap, stock boats, especially the smaller ones produced today, are not built for extended, hard use offshore. In most cases, however, standard boats that are not too poorly constructed can be suitably strengthened by some of the following means: adding stiffeners in flexible areas; glassing over the bilge in way of thin, hollow skegs that could possibly break off and cause flooding; bolting all fittings and connections; beefing up thin, vulnerable areas of the hull; strengthening the hull-deck joint; adding floor timbers, web frames, and stringers in areas subject to great stress; strengthening and better securing the bulkheads; adding knees in the vicinity of chainplates; installing backing blocks under deck and through-hull fittings where needed, and so forth. Some details of fiberglass construction are illustrated in Figures 9-6, 9-7, 9-8, and 9-9.

As for boats built of other materials, it is important to inspect fastenings and welds; sound thoroughly with a hammer for rot, voids, or wasting; examine carefully for corrosion and electrolysis; look for evidence of stress, unwanted movement, and leaks; examine for cracks, fractures, bulges, or dents; investigate any suspicious areas where there are misalignments, paint blisters, stains, or surface irregularities, and so forth.

Figure 9-8. Fitting attachment.

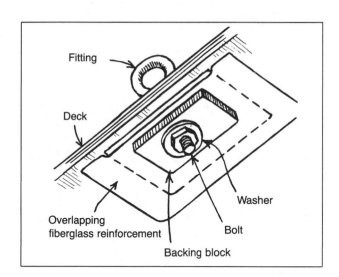

Figure 9-9. (*Below*) Hard spots and two possible remedies

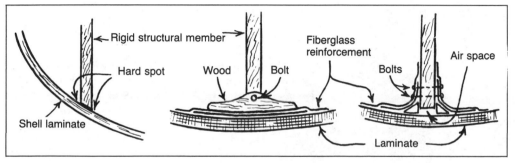

Regardless of the construction material, such components as the rudder, centerboard, mast step, partners, steering system, and all deck fittings should be thoroughly checked.

Special attention should be paid to watertight integrity. Check through-hull fittings to see that they are properly installed and that the valves are easily workable (plug-type seacock valves are preferable). Hoses should be attached with not one, but two, stainless steel hose clamps whenever possible. Diaphragm bilge pumps are most often recommended, and they ought to be sturdy, large-capacity types, operable from below and from the helm.

Cockpit well drains must be large, and it is important that there be a high companionway sill and heavy storm slide to keep water from a flooded cockpit out of the cabin. The importance of a self-draining cockpit well of small volume cannot be overemphasized. On two occasions, I have seen keel boats with open cockpits fill and founder after knockdowns. Even if a cockpit is self-draining, when the volume is large and the drains small, many boats can sink alarmingly low in the water when their wells are flooded. Commander R. D. Graham in 1933 made a singlehanded passage across the northern Atlantic and then from Newfoundland to Bermuda in the keel cutter *Emanuel*, which lacked a self-draining well, but he survived through exceptional seamanship, having an otherwise very able boat fitted with an effective pump, and having a great deal of luck. As the noted seaman-surveyor, Humphrey Barton, observed ". . . with her open cockpit there is no doubt that *Emanuel* was for a period in danger. A few heavy seas in succession bursting over the after part of the yacht would have sunk her."

Windows must be of "unbreakable" glass, Lexan, or Plexiglas able to withstand the smash of solid water on the leeward side during a knockdown. If they are

Commander R.D. Graham's *Emmanuel*, which made a fast singlehanded crossing of the North Atlantic in 1933. *Emmanuel* was a splendid sea boat, but she lacked the important safety feature of a small, rapidly self-draining cockpit. (Courtesy of Wm. Blackwood and Sons, Ltd.)

questionable or overly large, storm shutters should be fitted and used at sea. Be sure the cabin roof is sufficiently crowned and/or supported to resist inversion, which could (and has been known to) pop out windows. Hatch covers, dogs, and hinges must be capable of withstanding the heaviest weather. I believe that flush hatches are the safest kind. Be sure there are sturdy dogs on cockpit seat covers. There should be a means of blocking off all ventilators, even Dorade types, in the worst conditions. More than a few boats have faulty engine exhaust systems that allow water to enter the exhaust manifold from the outlet in heavy following seas. There should be a high loop in the line and preferably a cutoff valve at the outlet to prevent this.

A design feature that contributes to both comfort and safety is some sort of shelter for the cockpit that offers protection from the elements. A certain amount of compromise between shelter and visibility is usually necessary because some shelters can block the sailor's view. The accent should be on visibility when the boat is used in coastal waters where there is a lot of traffic, but offshore in cold remote areas, the singlehander needs all the protection he can get commensurate with reasonable visibility.

One way to satisfy both requirements without undue sacrifice to either is to fit a sturdy, folding dodger that has ample windows for reasonable visibility, yet can be folded down when maximum visibility is needed. A number of offshore solo boats have been fitted with plastic observation domes from which the singlehander can look out or steer while below decks. Some small boats have rounded or angular domes allowing use of sturdy Lexan installed in their companionway hatches to afford visibility from below when the hatch is closed; however, this arrangement makes rigging a dodger difficult or impossible. For the coldest and most rugged kind of long distance sailing it is best to have a permanent shelter over the entire forward end of the cockpit with plenty of Lexan windows. A number of BOC racers had such arrangements. Terlain's *UAP-Pour Médecins Sans Frontières* even had a Buckminster Fuller-style geodesic deckhouse, but that would not be very practical or appealing for the average all-purpose boat.

One often-neglected aspect of fitting out for offshore work is the matter of securing heavy gear. A major problem associated with the disastrous Fastnet Race of 1979 was that loose gear flying around below forced many of the crews of the racing craft to abandon the security of their cabins for the exposed decks or life rafts. Items such as anchors, batteries, stoves, tanks, and ballast should be fastened so that they cannot shift or come loose, even if the boat capsizes. As Edward Allcard has said, "Assume that one day the boat will turn upside down." When Eric Hall capsized in the Roaring Forties in December 1970 while singlehanding his sloop *Manuma*, he narrowly escaped serious injury by a falling storm anchor he had stowed in the bilge. Batteries should be encased in ventilated, acid-resistant boxes. A lesson can be learned from Valentine Howells not to lash the battery with lines that can shrink and crush the casing. There is a double reason for seeing that tanks are well secured, because a gasoline or LP gas tank breaking loose could cause a dangerous fire hazard, whereas a water tank could lose its precious contents. Incidentally, baffling in the tanks is important to keep the sloshing liquid from bursting a seam. Take particular care with forward tanks, which are especially vulnerable to violent motion caused by the boat's pitching. A forward water tank on Francis Stokes's *Mooneshine* came loose in the 1976 OSTAR. Metal plumbing or fuel lines subject to fatigue or cracking from moving or flexing should have their connections or vulnerable areas replaced with securely clamped flexible hoses.

All loose gear ought to be capable of being stowed inside lockers whose doors have secure latches (not friction or magnetic fasteners). Fiddles around shelves are seldom high enough. If the boat has ballast in her bilge, it should be secured there, not simply wedged. Even ballast inside the keel cavity on some boats is subject to slight shifting, which in time can cause erosion. When the ballast is not bolted and consists of small pieces, it is a good idea to roll the boat violently to hear if there is any movement in the keel. Care should be taken to stow gear in lockers or the stern lazarette where it cannot fall under the handles of seacocks, fall against hoses or wires and possibly pull them loose, or become entangled in the steering quadrant and jam it. Cabin soles should be secured, but not so thoroughly that one can't gain access to the bilge at a moment's notice. Even icebox tops should be latched.

Wiring ought to be carefully inspected, because electricity is very often the first thing to fail during heavy weather at sea. Usually the problem is due to short circuits from wet wiring. See that the wiring is well secured, covered with waterproof insulation, and installed high out of the bilge where it is least subject to moisture. It is vital that the wiring be protected with fuses or non-self-resetting circuit breakers to avoid overheating, which could possibly cause a fire or explosion if there is gasoline or LP gas aboard. Be sure that all switches are sparkproof. Incidentally, all wiring, piping, bolts, and, indeed, every part of the hull interior should be accessible. Quite often a ceiling or liner prevents accessibility, and if so, access holes should be cut, or else the liner or ceiling should be easily removable by loosening a few screws or with the use of a wrecking bar in a sudden emergency. See that the boat is properly bonded and grounded for lightning protection and the avoidance of electrolytic corrosion.

Further details of preparation for sea and boat inspection can be found in my earlier books, *Sea Sense; Heavy Weather Guide*, 2nd edition (with William J. Kotsch); and *Sailing in Windy Weather*. Two excellent sources of boat safety standards are The American Boat and Yacht Council and The American Bureau of Shipping, which publishes the *ABS Guide for Building and Classing Offshore Racing Yachts.*

Provisioning

In provisioning for a voyage, a singlehander has an advantage over a large crew in that he need not carry a tremendous quantity of stores. Nevertheless, he must figure on taking longer to reach his destination than a fully-crewed boat would take, and it is of far greater importance that he is adequately nourished for the sake of good health, stamina, and physical fitness. It is probably better to overstock than understock, unless overloading will be very harmful to speed, because the lone sailor is less able to keep to a definite timetable. He might be delayed by a number of eventualities that would not so seriously affect a fully crewed vessel.

Even in these days of vitamin pills, there is the danger of some ill effects from a long, steady diet of canned foods. Symptoms of scurvy are not as rare as one would think aboard small offshore boats that travel long distances. In his book *Along the Clippers' Way* Francis Chichester tells how one of England's most experienced yachtsmen, John Illingworth, developed more than a mild case of the disorder, and Chichester speculated that the first of the women solo voyagers, Ann Davison, also had symptoms of scurvy, despite the fact that she took vitamins. Likewise afflicted was Vito Dumas, who claimed that he might not have reached port had he not been able to dose himself with vitamin C. In more recent times Solomon Parker, a participant in the 1979 Mini Transat suffered from scurvy and anemia resulting from lack of vitamins even though the race was not extremely long. Singlehander Michael Richey wrote, "I have often wondered how much morale is bound up with nutrition, whether times of depression and lethargy are not the result of vitamin deficiency or even scurvy rather than psychological pressures."

Preventive measures against scurvy and other forms of malnutrition include not only vitamins and minerals, but also raw fruits and vegetables. Of course, the old anti-scurvy standby was lime juice for British sailors (hence the reason for their being called "limeys"), but lemons have more anti-scorbutic value, and, according to Chichester, the customary ration of lime juice was the result of a mistake in language, because the West Indians called a lemon a lime. A small-boat voyager without ice is obviously limited in the kind of fresh foods he can take, but some excellent sources of nutrition that will keep well are potatoes, onions, hard squash, cabbage, carrots, celery, garlic, oranges, lemons, grapefruit, and fruit or vegetables that will ripen after being picked, such as apples, tomatoes, and bananas. Dr. Hannes Lindemann, who made two Atlantic crossings, first in a dugout canoe (1955–56) and then in a rubber-and-canvas foldboat (1956–57), strongly recommends raw onions for the prevention of scurvy. Garlic is also valuable, he claims, for it keeps well under the worst conditions, and as compared with onions, garlic is a greater aid to digestion, although it contains fewer vitamins. Lindemann is also a great believer in the restorative powers of honey and red wine, while he thinks evaporated milk and beer are very important for calories and energy.

Clare Francis is one of many singlehanders who stresses the importance of high-energy foods. On her first solo Atlantic crossing, she lost weight and became very weak until she began increasing her normal intake of carbohydrates. She recommends cake, honey, canned puddings, candy, and bread. Most bread will not keep for very long, but putting it in plastic bags with a desiccant will help a great deal. Of course, flour and yeast will keep a long time, and several singlehanders have baked their own bread, even in simple folding ovens. Some BOC racers praised the "quick-fix" type high-protein cereals used by runners. "Eat a cup of it and you're ready to climb the mast," claimed Hal Roth.

Patrick Childress, who solo circumnavigated on a Catalina 27 in 1982, stresses the value of eggs, which will keep at least six weeks if previously unrefrigerated and oiled with vegetable shortening. He also recommends dried beef jerky and pancakes containing nutritionally valuable wheat germ, oatmeal, and raisins.

Most singlehanders do not want to use refrigeration because of the electric power drain and the need to run a generator, which, of course, may use considerable fuel. Nevertheless, there are efficient holding-plate systems that can be operated by a compressor belted to the auxiliary engine, requiring that the engine be run as little as a half-hour every other day. Another refrigeration system that requires no electricity but only a small flame to boil ammonia has often been used in rural houses, but it is seldom suitable for boats at sea because of the motion and heeling. Despite this, however, Marcel Bardiaux successfully used this type of refrigeration during his eight-year circumnavigation. His refrigerator's heating element, using kerosene fuel, was mounted in gimbals to minimize inefficiency caused by motion. From a safety standpoint, the arrangement should be satisfactory when only diesel and kerosene fuels are carried, but there could be risk of explosion when there is a continual flame low in the hull of a boat carrying gasoline or LP gas. Well-insulated iceboxes are perfectly satisfactory for short cruises. In fact, a large, portable, well-insulated, fiberglass chest with a gasketed top that is taped shut in such a way that the tape runs entirely around the seam will keep ice up to two weeks in temperate climates.

Aside from the picked fresh vegetables and fruits already mentioned, there are other nourishing foods that will keep for long periods without ice. Some of these include nuts, cheese, rice, macaroni, beans (especially soy beans), lentils, cereals (wheat germ and granola), margarine, eggs, and dried fruits such as dates, figs, raisins, apricots, and prunes. Cress and mustard have been grown by several single-handers, but even easier to grow are bean sprouts, which can be kept in glass jars. BOC racers used boil-in-bags retort pouch foods that need no refrigeration.

Fresh meat poses a problem, but animal protein can be supplied by powdered, canned, or ultra-high-temperature processed milk; salted butter, fresh eggs that have been greased or previously boiled for about 30 seconds for preservation; or canned meats, even though some nutritional value may be lost in the canning process. In addition, some smoked, cured, salted, or dried meats may be taken, such as certain smoked bacons, dried Burgundy ham, chipped beef, Lebanon bologna, meat immersed in brine, and so forth. Many voyagers take along a supply of Long Life milk, a whole milk processed at ultra-high temperature that keeps many months without refrigeration. It is packaged in waxed cardboard boxes.

Fresh fish can be caught, of course, and some fish can be eaten raw after being marinated in lemon juice or vinegar and onions. The plentitude of fish in the sea will depend on where one is sailing. Sometimes flying fish can regularly be picked up off the deck (a low light in the rigging will attract them at night), but trolling at sea is often not effective. Tristan Jones has some good suggestions for fishing at sea in his book *One Hand For Yourself, One Hand For the Ship*. Robin Knox-Johnston says that a speargun is "essential," and one of them all but saved Steve Callahan's life when his boat sank, forcing him to drift for 76 days in a life raft. A novel means of catching fish is the method used by Alain Gerbault, whereby the circumnavigator used his own toes as tempting bait. He described dragging his foot in the water to attract a dorado and then spearing the fish as it struck at his toes. The method could hardly be recommended for anyone with slower reflexes than world champion tennis player Gerbault.

As for the water supply, the old rule of thumb is half a gallon per person per day, which is really sufficient when beer, soft drinks, and canned juices are taken. But carry enough water for generous drinking, which doctors say is very important for good health. Singlehander Gary Mundell, who was wrecked on a Pacific island in 1985, found that drinking quantities of water even alleviated his mental depression. A really important matter is to have the water supply divided between two tanks or portable containers such as jerry jugs in case some of it should go bad or one of the tanks should happen to leak through a rivet hole, seam, or elsewhere. Many voyagers have a catchment system that utilizes a groove on the main boom. This might be the groove that holds the slides at the mainsail's foot or a special channel made of wood strips secured to the boom. Usually the boom is topped up slightly so that rainwater falling on the sail will run into the groove and forward to a bucket hung at the gooseneck. In some cases, however, a watertight hollow boom is allowed to fill and a plastic tube is led from an outlet directly to a water tank. It is important to let some rain wash the salt off the sail before beginning to collect drinking water.

Fitting Out

Gear and portable equipment for long-distance cruising will, of course, include a very complete inventory of spares and tools. With the advantage of having more space for a given size of boat, the singlehander in anything larger than a cockleshell will have room for stowing almost anything that might be needed.

Portable gear and spares should include heavy weather sails; fittings of every kind, especially winch handles, blocks, shackles, pins, turnbuckles, chains, and toggles; lines, sheets, rodes, and warps; emergency tiller, steering cable, rudder head fitting, and perhaps a substitute rudder; a stay or shroud of the longest length and an extra spreader; miscellaneous hardware and fastenings of every kind; spare anchors, including a drogue; sail stops, shock cord, and short lines; tackles, vang gear, preventers, and chafe guards; horn, lights, radio, and signal gear (such as flags, Aldis lamp, loud hailer, etc.); pumps, buckets, and bailers; bodily-comfort equipment, such as hats, sunglasses, awnings, warm clothing, foul-weather gear, etc.; and, most especially, spare parts kits. These include a sewing and sail repair kit (with thread, twine, marline, needles, fiddle, spike, palm, tapes, patches, beeswax, sail slides, hanks, sail shackles, leather, etc.); an electrical repair kit (with bulbs, fuses, electrical tape, copper wire, batteries, circuit tester, solder and soldering tool, radio parts, etc.); a plumbing kit (hoses to fit any through-hull fitting, hose clamps, spare parts for the head and all pumps, syphon hose, gaskets, nipples, packing, grease, diaphragms, flap valves, and tapered wooden plugs); a hull-repair kit (caulking cotton, bedding and seam compound, foam rubber, plywood sheets, common putty, cup grease, soft metal sheets, plastic steel, self-curing urethane putty, fiberglass tape and resin, canvas, epoxy adhesive, etc.); and engine-repair kits (gasoline engine: points, condenser, rotor, water pump, seal, impeller, distributor cap, coil, spark plugs, belts, etc.; diesel engine: injectors, starting-motor, solenoid, fuel filters, fuel pump, injector feed lines, etc.; and engine tools, such as gauges, spanners, and crank handle, a starting booster fluid, and lube oil). It is also important to carry spare parts for the stove, a patch kit for the inflatable raft, and, especially, extra parts for the bilge pumps and self-steering vane gear.

Some essential tools include assorted sizes of screwdrivers, pliers, wrenches, hammer, wood saw, hack saw with spare blades, wire cutter, bolt cutter, wrecking bar, hatchet, brace and bits, drill and bits, tin snips, chisels, files, plane, surform, clamps, vise, crimping tool for compressing sleeves on wire cables, etc. Pliers should include a large-channel type with adjustable jaws, needle-nose, and Vise-Grips. Important wrenches are: monkey, Stillson, end, socket, spark plug, and chain wrench. It is essential to have an end-wrench of sufficient size to fit the largest nut on the boat, and be sure to try the wrench to see that it will fit. One day I was caught out with a badly leaking stuffing box and found that my brand new, largest adjustable end-wrench would not fit, even though it was an identical size and make as a wrench used previously to tighten the gland. Later the new wrench had to be modified to make it fit. Apparently, there is sometimes a slight discrepancy between tools of identical make and model.

The ingenuity of some singlehanders can often overcome the lack of a needed tool or spare. Robin Knox-Johnston, for instance, made a clever roller-reefing handle from a turnbuckle, and he made a feeler gauge for setting the spark on his generator by measuring off one inch of thickness of a writing-paper pad and counting the pages within the measurement. He found that 200 pages made an inch; thus three pages gave him the required thickness of 15/1000 inch.

Safety equipment and certain basic deck gear have already been discussed.

Health and Survival Aspects

No less important than a well-found vessel is the singlehander's own fitness and preparedness for eventualities affecting his or her health. Although some fit young sailors set off with scarcely a thought about their health, it is certainly advisable for everyone to have a medical and dental check before leaving on a lengthy offshore passage. There may be considerable risk involved if there has been a past history of heart trouble, serious stomach ulcers, gallstone disease, suspected appendicitis, and so forth. William Willis, raft and cockleshell voyager, nearly lost his life from a hernia attack. At any rate, special health problems should be discussed with your doctor, who should also be consulted for medical stores for the cruise. Recommended books, written by sailor-doctors, which discuss first aid supplies and medical treatment when there is no professional medical assistance available are *Advanced First Aid Afloat* by Peter F. Eastman, M.D.; *First Aid Afloat* by Paul B. Sheldon, M.D.; *Dr. Cohen's Healthy Sailor Book* by M.M. Cohen, M.D.; *Handy Medical Guide for Seafarers* by R.W. Scott, M.D.; *The Ship's Medicine Chest and Medical Aid at Sea*, published by U.S. Department of Health and Human Services; and *Your Offshore Doctor* by M.H. Beilan, M.D.

In addition to the usual bandages, gauze, adhesive tape, burn ointments, disinfectants, and other items found in first aid kits, there should be such supplies as splints, hypodermic syringes, butterfly bandages, thermometer, catheter tube, enema gear, sanitary napkins (for serious cuts), dental kit (such as the one made by Dent-Aide), sutures, ace bandages, forceps, eye patch (Robin Knox-Johnson missed not having one), local anesthetic (Xylocaine, or Novocaine, and perhaps an ethyl chloride spray), seasickness remedy (perhaps Bonine, Marezine or Bucladin), ordinary pain killers (aspirin, codeine, or Talwin), severe pain killers (Demerol is often recommended); diarrhea medicine (Lomotil and Paregoric are recommended), laxative (Milk of Magnesia or Metamucil perhaps), and antibiotics (broad spectrum, such as penicillin, ampicillin, or Tetracycline, and special antibiotics for specific infections). Dr. Eastman's book deals with antibiotics in some detail. He also recommends two sulpha drugs for certain infections, Sulfadiazene and Azo-Gantrisin.

As Dr. David Lewis has warned, the singlehander must be careful in taking heavy doses of strong, pain-killing drugs that cause unwanted sleep or might adversely affect his judgment. At times, he might have to endure more pain than he wants in order to be alert during situations that demand careful navigation and seamanship. For a sailor who must stay awake, Dr. Sheldon suggests Benzedrine, but he warns that the drug should only be used for a temporary crisis, as continued use could result in cumulative fatigue and serious errors in judgment. It could also lead to hallucinating in certain cases.

Seasickness remedies such as Dramamine can cause extreme drowsiness in some individuals. The remedies in the previous list of supplies will rarely put a person to sleep, I have heard, but they may have different effects on different people and so should be tried when it is not vital to stay awake. In any event, it is important that serious seasickness is kept under control as much as possible, because dehydration can render a singlehander completely helpless. When repeated vomiting prevents the retention of liquids and oral seasickness remedies, an antiemetic such as Compazine can be taken by injection or suppository, or scopolamine can be administered with a Transderm® disc stuck behind the ear. Bucladin, in the form of a small yellowish pill, is effectively retained because it is placed under the tongue and soon absorbed into the body.

The old proverb, "An ounce of prevention is worth a pound of cure," is most appropriate for one who sails alone far from medical help. Proper diet and rest, of course, will help avoid many ailments. Wearing the proper clothing can avoid chills and overexposure that could lead to colds, various infections, or even hypothermia. Especially valuable are really waterproof foul-weather gear, (PVC or polyurethane-covered nylon is recommended and several BOC racers raved about Dorlon brand), thermal underwear, clothing made of layered materials, gloves, towel scarves, and watch caps. Natural fabrics and/or polypropylene is recommended for clothing worn next to the skin. Some singlehanders carry wet suits, dry suits, and even survival suits in cold waters. Bill Homewood is sold on the Bayley Suit; the Mustang suit produced by The Survival Technologies Group is shown in Figure 9-10. In hot weather light clothing, wide-brimmed hats, awnings, and sunscreen lotions can prevent not only sunburn, but also certain other skin problems and heat exhaustion (provided ample water and salt are taken). Other skin ailments such as common saltwater rash can be minimized with careful attention to cleanliness, frequent washing in fresh water (provided the supply is ample), and the use of talcum powder or Desitin. Burns can be avoided with proper gimbals, pot holders, safe fuels, safety belts, and cooking while wearing foulweather gear in rough weather (John Letcher uses a long vinyl apron). Injuries from falls are best avoided with sound safety practices and equipment (see Chapter 8, Safety Considerations).

Exercise is vital to good health, of course, and the singlehander is usually active, but certain muscles and parts of the body are quite often neglected in small boats. Prolonged sitting may lead to drowsiness, stiffness of joints, and poor blood circulation, aside from the sore bottom known in modern parlance as "fiberglarse." It is well for the sailor to work out an exercise routine that puts to use the neglected muscles and keeps the blood flowing.

It is certainly advisable that the singlehander about to make a voyage give some thought to survival just in case he has to abandon his boat at sea. Basic life raft requirements have been suggested in Chapter 8, but here some thoughts are presented on the gear that goes into the raft. Important items for a very complete survival kit are: signal mirror; flares (hand-held and parachute with Very pistol);

Figure 9-10. An exposure suit such as this Mustang Cruiser™, is worth serious consideration for high-latitude singlehanders. It is not as cumbersome as it appears to be. (Courtesy of Survival Technologies Group, Inc.)

orange smoke flares (for daylight use); small strobe light (the kind that is attached to a horseshoe buoy); freon horn; waterproof flashlight and spare batteries; dye marker; air pump and perhaps extra bottles of CO_2 for raft inflation; sea anchor; repair kit with screw-type wooden plugs for punctures, bailer; knife in sheath; fishing kit with hooks, line, lures, and a gaff or spear head; first aid kit with antibiotics, pain killers, and seasickness remedy; EPIRB radio locator beacon; portable VHF radio; paddles; a short mast in two sections; radar reflector; a cloth (for sail, rain catching, or spare canopy); emergency navigation kit with small plastic sextant, almanac, compass, pencils and pad, watch, pilot chart, etc.; marline; a coil of line; small tool kit with pliers, forceps, scout knife, wire, hacksaw blade, screwdriver, etc.; sunscreen lotion; Halazone tablets to purify water; matches in a waterproof container; solar stills; plastic bottles of fresh water; two sponges (one for bailing and the other for mopping up condensation); and emergency rations (including vitamin and mineral tablets, hard candy, yeast, canned milk, beer, pemmican, milk tablets, bouillon, garlic, peanut butter, raisins, etc.).

This sounds like a lot of gear, but most of it can be packed in a couple of heavy, plastic, waterproof ice bags. These can be put in empty sailbags containing a life jacket or two for flotation and stowed in a handy cockpit locker or in the lazarette.

A sturdy lanyard should be attached to each bag. If any of the survival items listed are not kept in the bags, it is a good idea to write with indelible ink on each bag what is missing so that it can be obtained at once during an emergency.

For a more thorough discussion of life raft survival, see Chapter 11, Handling Emergencies at Sea.

The slack bilges and moderately narrow beam of *Gipsy Moth IV* give a strong hint as to why Chichester found her to be excessively tender. (Courtesy of *Yachting* magazine)

10

Alone Against the Elements

SOONER OR LATER, EVERY PASSAGE-MAKING singlehander encounters heavy weather. His boat-handling procedures will not be exactly the same as those on a fully crewed vessel because of the need for more prompt action and one-step-at-a-time operation. The helm can be manned for a limited time only. Sails must be shortened or removed early, and the boat must be made capable of fending for herself if the storm lasts for any length of time.

In a blow, the solo sailor simply shortens sail and lets the self-steering gear take charge, or in heavier weather he may strike the steering vane and heave to, quite often under a deeply reefed mainsail or storm trysail alone, or with a storm jib aback (sheeted to windward) and the helm lashed down.

Other tactics include lying ahull, lying to a sea anchor, and running off at slow or fast speeds.

Continuing on course under greatly reduced sail is often the easiest thing to do when conditions permit. However, the feasibility of this action depends to a large extent on how the boat is behaving and the weather trend. It can be risky to leave the self-steering gear in charge when the boat is running or reaching in steep seas. Angus Primrose's Moody 33 rolled upside down in less than horrendously heavy weather during the 1976 OSTAR. The accident happened in mid-Atlantic while Primrose was down below and his boat *Demon Demo* was sailing herself on a reach. She righted herself but lost her rig. It should be pointed out that this boat, which Primrose himself designed, may not have the best range of stability for the worst weather offshore. She has a lot of freeboard, suggesting a high center of gravity, and a great deal of beam. Under the beam/displacement Capsize Screening Formula given in Chapter 4, this boat is borderline. Several years later Primrose was drowned when *Demon Demo* again capsized, this time in a Gulf Stream gale off the U.S. East Coast.

Lying Ahull

A particularly attractive tactic for the singlehander who can only man the helm for a limited period of time is lying ahull. One merely takes down all sail, battens down, and lets the boat drift as she will, finding her natural position and retreating from the seas. The vast majority of monohull cruisers sailing today will lie ahull about beam-on or perhaps with the stern slightly up to the wind and seas. Having the bow closer to the seas with no headway could strain the rudder when the boat is pushed backwards by a breaking sea. Most vessels that assume a more stern-up attitude will forereach slowly while they drift off to leeward. The helm should be restrained with shock cord or other elastic material to relieve strain on the rudder, and often the helm is lashed alee somewhat to inhibit excessive forward speed. The offshore singlehander can then retreat to the shelter of the cabin, but the rolling motion may be considerable. He should have numerous hand holds to grip and safety belts to hold him securely in the galley, at the chart table, and in his bunk. It is equally important that all gear be well secured so that it cannot fall or be flung around the cabin in the event of a severe roll-over or capsize.

Some of the numerous practitioners of the hulling tactic (lying ahull) are Marin-Marie, Jean Gau, John Guzzwell, Francis Chichester, Chris Loehr, Alex Rose, Chay Blyth, and Clare Francis. It is interesting to compare this group of singlehanders, because their voyages range in time from 1933 to almost the present, and their vessels represent a variety of moderately deep, ballast-keel monohulls, the general type best suited to hulling. For the most part, this suitability has to do with the relatively high range of stability afforded by a ballasted keel of ample weight and depth. An excessively deep keel with great lateral plane, however, could be less successful, for it might overly inhibit leeway and cause the vessel to trip when she moves sideways.

Be this as it may, Marin-Marie successfully lay ahull in a deep-draft vessel with great lateral plane during a violent Atlantic storm in early August 1933. His 36-foot craft, the gaff-rigged cutter *Winnibelle*, was somewhat similar to the famous Colin Archer-designed Norwegian double-enders except that she had slightly less beam, greater draft, and a heavily ballasted keel. With her rather high metacenter and short rig, *Winnibelle* was naturally a vigorous roller, but despite this, her motion was tolerable when hulling under bare poles in a real blow. Marin-Marie wrote, "The *Winnibelle*, lying at right angles to the sea, was a great deal easier in her motion than she had been running before the Trades, when she had given me such hell, the bitch!" Wisely, he spread his mattress on the cabin sole to avoid being rolled out of his bunk and rested when he could, while the cutter lay beam on with the helm lashed down, drifting at 1½ or 2 knots to leeward. Marin-Marie did not try to estimate the wind's velocity, but it was so strong that when he went on deck he could not stand up and could only move about on his hands and knees.

Jean Gau's *Atom* was also a double-ender, one of the famous Tahiti ketches designed by John Hanna (Chapter 4). She had considerable beam and displacement, but by modern standards, had a rather modest amount of ballast on her long, moderately-shallow keel. In September 1957 *Atom* rode out hurricane Carrie, the same storm that sank the large bark *Pamir* with a loss of 80 lives. The little double-ender lay ahull with her helm lashed alee in 120-knot winds while her

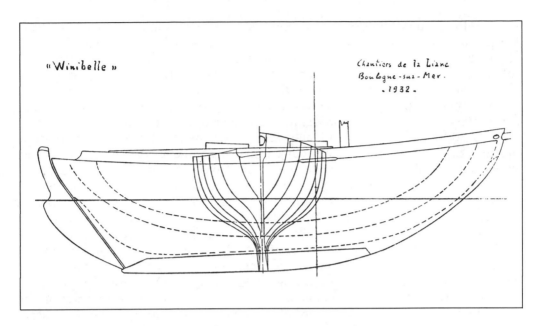

Figure 10-1. Plans of the *Winnibelle* show the size of her lateral plane and wine glass sections. (From *Wind Aloft, Wind Alow* by Marin-Marie)

Marin-Marie's *Winnibelle* lay ahull successfully despite her sizable lateral plane and tendency to roll when running. (From *Wind Aloft, Wind Alow* by Marin-Marie)

master closed himself in in the cabin and "slept, ate, read, and drew pictures." This is the storm tactic usually employed by Gau in extremely heavy weather, but it should be mentioned that on one occasion the method utterly failed and *Atom* was rolled completely over. This accident, which will be described in detail later in the chapter, does not necessarily disprove the merits of hulling, even for a Tahiti ketch. It simply demonstrates that the tactic can fail in particular weather and sea conditions. When *Atom* capsized, she was in one of the world's most dangerous stretches of water, off the Cape of Good Hope, where a southwest storm of over 70 knots opposed the fast-moving Agulhas current causing unbelievably high, steep seas. Perhaps no tactic could have prevented *Atom* from turning over in those conditions, but the beam-on position merely resulted in a capsize, whereas a position with bow or stern into the wind might have resulted in a far worse pitch-poling (somersaulting end-over-end). In 1971 this same boat survived five days of battering from hurricane Ginger when she was about 300 miles from Bermuda. Again she was left to her own devices, drifting off under bare poles, while Gau, then 69 years old, stayed below eating, napping, and pumping the bilge. The latter activity reminds us of the importance of having a bilge pump operable from below.

In contrast to the heavy double-enders, the 21-foot *Trekka*, sailed around the world by John Guzzwell, was a light-displacement yawl with a fin keel and separated rudder attached to a skeg. In June 1958, off the coast of Australia, she encountered a tropical cyclone that lasted for six days. She lay beam to the wind and seas with her helm lashed down and all sails furled while drifting to leeward at the rate of one knot, according to Guzzwell's estimate. In this manner, she rode the waves well but gradually ran out of sea room. To reduce drift towards the lee shore, Guzzwell improvised a drag from two heavy warps and an eight-foot length of lumber. One warp was made fast to the bow and the other to the stern. They lessened the boat's drift, but her motion was not as comfortable as before, when she had no drag. After the wind had shifted and moderated, Guzzwell tried running off dead before the high seas under a storm jib while towing the drag astern, but *Trekka* did not behave well and was nearly pooped by seas breaking over her stern. John lowered the jib, took in his drag, turned broadside to the seas, and lashed his tiller down; once again the little yawl rode the seas like a duck.

Francis Chichester had many heavy-weather experiences, but the one that sticks in my mind is the gale he encountered during the 1960 OSTAR, with winds gusting up to 100 m.p.h. His boat was the 40-foot sloop *Gipsy Moth III*, a racing-cruising type of moderate proportions designed by Robert Clark. She had a rather deep conventional keel, a cutaway forefoot, and a raking rudder attached to the keel. In the storm's early stages, Chichester described an appalling din, "a high-pitch screech or scream dominating. Plenty of spray peppering everything and seas hitting periodically with a bonk! Crash!" The sloop lay ahull, stripped of all sail and with her main boom lowered and lashed to the deck. Evidently her motion was not too violent, for with the wind at an estimated 90 m.p.h. Chichester went below and had a meal of fried potatoes, onions, and three eggs, and then "went to sleep reading *The Tempest.*" Later, however, when the wind increased even more, *Gipsy Moth* began to forereach excessively and take quite a pounding from the seas. In an effort to slow her down, the singlehander streamed astern a large auto tire at the end of 10 fathoms of anchor chain and 20 fathoms of warp, but still the boat reached ahead at about three knots. I am not too surprised that the drag failed to slow her more, because it might have tended to hold the stern up slightly and thus encourage forereaching. Nevertheless, *Gipsy Moth III* weathered the blow satisfactorily.

It seems rather odd that in 1971 Chichester ran off before a 60-knot blow in his larger and faster *Gipsy Moth V* instead of trying to lie ahull. He told us in his book, *The Romantic Challenge*, that the boat behaved dangerously, knocking down repeatedly while running before the wind at 10 knots (once the speedometer showed 12½ knots) under a small storm jib sheeted flat, and then later under bare poles. He tried slowing her by heading up into the wind, but she would not turn past the beam-on position. Chichester expressed great concern about how anyone could manage a very fast monohull sailboat in such weather conditions. Apparently he lay with the wind and seas abeam only temporarily and never really gave the hulling tactic a chance. Perhaps he was hesitant to do so because of the extreme knockdown he had experienced when lying ahull in *Gipsy Moth IV*. That boat, however, was said to be unusually tender. At any rate, we can only speculate on how *Gipsy Moth V* would have behaved when left to herself under bare poles with the helm lashed down. It seems likely that she would have lain approximately broadside to the seas but would have forereached at a moderate to fairly fast speed. A tiny, flat riding sail aft and possibly a heavy anchor hung at long scope from the bow might have been helpful in keeping her head up to or slightly above the beam-on position, thus inhibiting forereaching.

A clue to the hulling behavior of *Gipsy Moth V* might be obtained from the experience of Chay Blyth's *British Steel*, when this boat lay ahull between Australia and the Cape of Good Hope near the end of April 1971. Both *British Steel* and *Gipsy Moth V* were designed by Robert Clark, and although their rigs differed somewhat, their hulls were very similar in their lines and dimensions. It has been said that Blyth's boat was designed for going to windward, while Chichester's was for sailing downwind, but this distinction has probably been overrated, for both craft look very much alike in form and underwater profile, each having similar, abbreviated, fin keels and separate, skeg-mounted rudders. As a matter of fact, *Gipsy Moth V* has slightly more draft, a feature conducive to good windward performance, even though she was intended to excel when sheets were well eased. Be that as it may, there are few significant differences between the shape of the two hulls. When Blyth drifted under bare poles beam to a wind exceeding 60 knots with steep seas, he did not express any great anxiety over excessive speed. His chief concern regarding the boat's behavior seemed to be her rolling and/or knockdowns, but he never mentioned her heeling past about 50 degrees.

Two strong advocates of hulling are Alec Rose, who sailed the 36-foot yawl *Lively Lady* around the world in 1967–68, and Chris Loehr, a master mariner and sailmaker who made several heavy-weather passages alone in the 28-foot sloop *Lento*. Rose's boat was heavy and fairly narrow, with a spoon bow having little overhang, a deep forefoot, long, deep keel, counter stern, and slack bilges. Loehr's craft was a Great Dane, designed by Aage Utzon based on traditional concepts. She was fairly heavy with slack bilges and a moderately long keel, but with a cutaway forefoot and a raked outboard rudder. Concerning the hulling tactic, Loehr said, "I believe any ship will find its natural position in the sea. . . . There is something about nature you cannot fight. Just as your body quickly finds the most comfortable position when you sit down, so does a boat on the ocean." Alec Rose put it only a bit differently: ". . . it is safer to lay ahull. That is to strip off all sails and let the yacht go with the sea and take up her own position." He went on to explain that *Lively Lady* would lie with the wind just forward of the beam, with a list to leeward, and forereaching "slightly." He said the boat was often "thrown about unmercifully" but no more so than if other tactics had been employed. Furthermore, he wrote that he would lie ahull "in the very fiercest storms."

Clare Francis successfully lay ahull in a Force 10 gale with 35-foot seas during the 1976 OSTAR. Her Ohlson 38, *Robertson's Golly*, had a stability range of about 135 degrees, higher than the norm for a modern racing cruiser. Here's what Clare wrote about her experience: "The *Golly* lay ahull in her usual fashion, beam on to the waves but sometimes a little stern-to, sometimes a little bow-to. When a breaking crest roared up she would heel over, let it crash into her side and then shake off the water, ready for the next. I always braced myself for the wave that would roll her a little too far or drop her into a trough but it never came, for the *Golly* was a real old seadog and never let herself be caught out. Several times waves filled the cockpit or shot over the boat, but apart from a sharp lurch or a small roll the *Golly* remained unperturbed." We had a similar experience in our sistership *Kelpie* when she lay ahull for 15 hours during a mid-Atlantic Force 10 gale. We had tried heaving to and then running off, but found her much better behaved and comfortable stripped of all sail, lying about beam to the seas with the helm lashed alee. She made about two knots of leeway and left a square drift to windward which seemed to smooth the seas, causing them to break just before they struck the hull.

By no means do all singlehanders advocate the hulling tactic or "lying doggo," as Naomi James put it. In fact, Hal Roth once wrote me, "I have lain ahull many dozens of times in gales in which the wind has blown from one direction for many hours and has created even, regular waves. But in fast-moving depressions in which the wind direction and wave train sequence have changed, the easy and regular waves become irregular and most-troublesome monsters that threaten a small vessel like an elephant's foot poised above a peanut."

Although there are many experienced sailers who reject hulling in the heaviest weather, it is interesting that the tactic was generally preferred even on fully-crewed boats in the aforementioned *Ocean Cruising Survey* by Jimmy Cornell. The following is quoted from the book's section on heavy weather seamanship.

> The surveys include a wide range of boats of both heavy and light displacement, large and small, with long and fin keels, so it was very difficult to find a common denominator which would have enabled me to draw some general conclusions on the subject of dealing with heavy weather. However, discussing heavy weather techniques with the most experienced skippers, among whom over a dozen had sailed in excess of 50,000 miles, I detected in each of them a profound confidence in the seaworthiness of their boats. Every one of the skippers I spoke to, who had weathered extreme conditions by dropping all sail, lying ahull, battening down, and leaving the boat to look after itself, stressed the wisdom of such an action and found this tactic more satisfactory than trying to battle with the elements.

Even the strongest advocates of hulling would seldom recommend the tactic on all occasions. I, for one, would not lie beam to the seas when they were predominately steep "plungers" rather than spilling breakers. Also, I would be sure my boat had a high stability range, at least 130 degrees (the stability range of most stock racer/cruisers can be obtained from the United States Yacht Racing Union or International Yacht Racing Union, or else the range can be determined by a naval architect). In addition, the boat should have a sturdy, well-crowned cabin trunk with ample supporting posts, beams, or bulkheads to prevent a collapse. While delivering a Hinckley-built boat, a friend of mine suffered a knockdown in a gale, and the boat's windows popped out—a result, he claims, of the moderately crowned (i.e., relatively flat) cabintop oil-canning inward. Any boat lying ahull in the worst possible weather should be prepared for a possible 180-degree rollover. This means having a strong boat that is absolutely watertight and gear that is stowed securely enough to withstand an inversion.

Heaving To

When a boat is hove to, her headway is mostly stopped by heading up and bringing the wind well forward of the beam while sailing under greatly reduced sail. Sometimes this can be done with one tiny, centrally-located sail, but more often headway is better slowed by using two small counteracting sails, one being backed to offset the thrust of the other. Heaving to under counteracting sails in a sloop, cutter, or yawl with a large foretriangle, is normally best done with a deeply reefed main or storm trysail working against a spitfire or storm jib hanked on an inner forestay rather than the headstay. This plan provides superior balance as well as

Figure 10-2. Heaving to under sail.

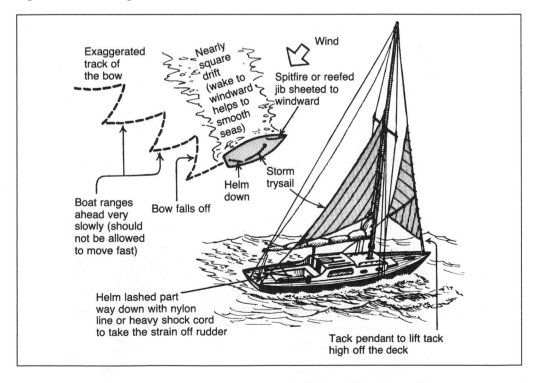

more deck space around the sail for greater security. The trysail is sheeted free of the boom to the side deck, while the spitfire is sheeted to windward in order to counter the trysail's forward thrust. The helm is lashed down (rudder to windward) so that when the boat gains headway she will head up and lose way. Then the backed spitfire together with the force of the seas will cause the bow to fall off until the trysail fills again, driving the boat forward to repeat the process. The advantage of this tactic over lying ahull is that the bow is usually held closer to the wind, and therefore the boat is less subject to being rolled over by a steep breaking sea taken on her beam. Disadvantages are that the boat will not yield quite as much as when drifting off to leeward, and part of the time she will drive very slowly into the seas, increasing their impact. Furthermore, heaving to may require more sail handling effort, and in the worst conditions sails may blow out or overpower the boat.

Using Sea Anchors

Most modern sailors in storms offshore seem reluctant to use sea anchors unless the boat is small, shallow-draft, and with a very low range of stability, or unless it is imperative to slow the boat's drift towards a lee shore. The principal reason for this reluctance is that most of today's deep-keel yachts, especially those with a cutaway forefoot and considerable windage ahead of the vertical turning axis, will not lie bow-to an anchor streamed from the bow. They simply fall off the wind and forereach while imposing severe strains on their anchoring gear. Some argue that a huge parachute anchor must be used to really hold the boat steady, but observe how most modern boats range back and forth even on their fixed moorings in relatively still waters. The unyielding types of sea anchors also create strains that can damage the boat as well as her gear and prevent her from giving to the seas or in effecting rolling with the punches. Another argument against the large parachute is the difficulty of streaming and retrieving it without entanglements.

For a boat that will not keep her head up, it is often a better tactic to stream the anchor astern, provided there is ample freeboard aft, a small, fast-draining

Figure 10-3. Fenger-type drogue (*left*). Galerider drogue (*right*). (Courtesy of Hathaway, Reiser, and Raymond)

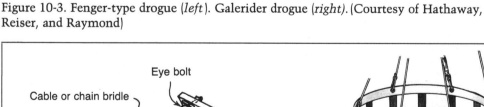

cockpit, and sturdy, lock-in storm slides for the companionway. The best anchoring system for this purpose is one that is fairly elastic, allowing some give to lessen impact with the waves and to avoid excessive strains from shock loading. Two such anchors (normally referred to as drogues) are illustrated. One is an early design by the previously mentioned innovator Frederic A. Fenger. The other is a modern, easily stowable type known as the Galerider® made by the sailmakers Hathaway, Reiser, and Raymond. Its parabolic shape and open web construction not only reduce shock loading, but allow enough drift for steering control.

A proper sea anchor that holds the boat more firmly, however, can be valuable on any small, shallow craft such as a lifeboat, dinghy, or open boat that can be made to lie with its bow up, for such a craft should seldom be allowed to get broadside to breaking seas due to the risk of rolling over. In the early days of offshore singlehanding, many small-boat sailors such as Gilboy, Andrews, Lawlor, and Blackburn used standard sea anchors (See Figure 7-1). To relieve violent jerking strains, Blackburn used a spiral steel spring at the inboard end of his rode. This could be used today utilizing a modern shock absorber of nylon, shock cord, or a rubber snubber. Care must be taken with the latter, however, to see that its metal thimbles do not chafe the rode.

A more modern example of a small boat using a sea anchor successfully is the case of Robert Manry in the 13½-foot modified centerboard dinghy *Tinkerbelle*. During her Atlantic crossing in 1965, she rode out several blows with a drogue streamed from her bow. She kept her head to the wind and seas, but this position could be held only when her outboard rudder was unshipped. At certain times Manry found it helpful to hoist a scrap of sail aft on the permanent backstay to act as a riding sail.

Many times sea anchors have been improvised with some success. Fred Rebell, the amazing do-it-yourselfer who crossed the Pacific in the 18-foot open boat *Elaine*, made an effective drogue out of his centerboard. During a gale near the end of the passage between Hawaii and California in December 1932, *Elaine* lay hove to under a triple-reefed mainsail sheeted in flat. She was keeping her bow somewhat toward the seas but was shipping a great deal of water, and on one occasion she took a bad knockdown that half filled her. Rebell decided that he should lower sail and stream a drag from the bow, but he had no sea anchor. After racking his brain, he thought of the centerboard, which was a large, heavy metal plate. It must have been a job to remove the board during the storm's height, but Rebell extracted it from the well, rigged some sort of bridle, and launched the affair over the bow. It veered around crazily at the end of its rode but apparently succeeded in holding the *Elaine*'s bow to the seas. I wonder, however, if there was not

The open boat *Elaine*, whose centerboard Fred Rebell utilized to make an effective drogue during his solo crossing of the Pacific in 1932.

another, more subtle advantage to such a tactic. By removing the board, Rebell also raised it completely and, although he sacrificed some stability, he also removed a sizeable underwater appendage on which the boat could trip. Thus he could have increased his boat's resistance to being rolled down. At any rate, *Elaine* came through the blow relatively unscathed.

As mentioned earlier, auto tires are sometimes used for drags. Bob Griffith (not a singlehander, but a remarkable seaman, who circumnavigated Antarctica in the 52-foot ferrocement cutter *Awahnee*) told me that at times he carried as many as 12 tires. Solo sailor Bill Murnan carried an aircraft tire aboard his steel Seabird yawl, *Seven Seas II*. He sometimes towed it astern edgewise but found that it caused greater drag when towed from a bridle in an upright position.

Running Off (Scudding)

Running off before the wind under bare poles is a classic means of weathering a storm, but it may not always be suitable for a singlehander because the tactic normally requires someone at the helm, and there is obviously a limit to the time one person can steer in very severe conditions. It has been suggested that a singlehander can scud before a storm with the self-steering vane controlling the vessel, but in the worst weather such a practice could be extremely dangerous. Of course, there are a number of requisites for scudding, even when the helm is manned. First of all, there must be ample sea room, because the vessel may move with considerable speed; second, she must be readily controllable while running. She must not yaw, squat, or root her bow excessively. Her performance will depend primarily on two factors: the nature of the seas and the boat's design characteristics, such as the fullness of her bow, length of keel, location of the rudder, kind of stern and so forth.

Spray proved well suited to the scudding tactic under the right sea conditions. Slocum ran her off before a gale near Cape Horn in 1896 while carrying a reefed forestaysail sheeted flat and towing two long hawsers. The helm was lashed amidships, and evidently the *Spray* was able to steer herself. There are not many modern yachts, however, that can safely steer themselves for any length of time before the heaviest weather offshore.

Bernard Moitessier devised a method of scudding at high speed before the exceptionally high seas of the southern Pacific, but the technique required his hand on the helm. His procedure in the very worst conditions, which he claimed was suggested from the writings of Vito Dumas, was to head off directly before the wind, stripped of all sail and towing no drags, until his boat was approached by a steep following sea. At this time he would head up slightly so that the stern was about 15 to 20 degrees from being square to the seas. This attitude was held until the crest rolled under the quarter and the boat settled into the trough of the next following wave. The boat's slight angle to the seas, he claimed, would inhibit surfing and cause the boat to heel somewhat, which would also discourage rooting (having the bow dig in). He found it necessary to keep his boat moving sufficiently fast at all times for good steering control, normally close to but not exceeding (if possible) the hull speed. Moitessier stated that towing drags failed to slow his *Joshua* and merely hampered steering in those great seas of the high latitudes in the South Pacific.

Another solo skipper of a double-ender, Robin Knox-Johnston, used the scudding tactics in the huge seas of the South Pacific, but he usually towed a drag in the form of a 100-fathom, 2-inch, polypropylene warp. With her long keel and a tiny storm jib sheeted flat and set far forward at the end of her long bowsprit, Robin's 32-foot ketch *Suhaili* was able to keep her stern up to the seas with the helm unattended. The long warp was streamed in a somewhat unusual manner, for, although it was towed astern, it was streamed in a bight with both ends secured forward and leading down either side of the boat. The singlehander claimed that this method allowed more stretch in the line to provide "give" against the force of the seas, and, of course, the bight helped smooth the crests. A further benefit might be that if the helm should need attending, the drags would not hamper steering excessively due to their being secured far ahead of the rudder.

Other drags that can slow the boat without overly tethering her are towed sails, drogues such as the previously mentioned Galerider, and even metal anchors. Singlehander Bill Doherty successfully weathered a Force 10 gale off the coast of Ireland in his 18-foot Herreshoff Goldeneye by towing a 15-pound mushroom anchor attached to a 12-foot length of chain shackled to 200 feet of nylon rode. He called it the "ultimate storm tactic," at least for his boat.

During his remarkable solo voyage from Australia to Antarctica in later 1972 and early 1973, Dr. David Lewis used a method similar to Moitessier's of scudding at high speed before gales. Under a tiny storm jib, he ran off in his 32-foot sloop at an angle of about 20 degrees to the following seas. The tactic demanded that the helm be controlled, but Lewis was able to accomplish this by rigging steering lines that led into the cabin. Unfortunately, in the worst conditions the technique did

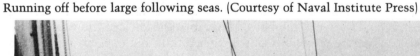

Running off before large following seas. (Courtesy of Naval Institute Press)

not succeed and in a late November gale, while running before waves about 40 feet high, *Ice Bird* was overwhelmed (see Chapter 11). She was smashed down by a breaking sea and rolled completely over. She righted immediately but suffered the loss of her mast and other damages.

It is impossible to say, on that particular occasion, how *Ice Bird* would have fared had she been hulling. She probably would have rolled over, but, with very little forward speed, perhaps the capsizing would have been less damaging. In at least one respect *Ice Bird* may not have been entirely suitable for high-speed scudding, for her keel was of moderate length only, with the attached rudder not as far aft as it could have been (according to the drawings I have seen) for optimum steering control. Scudding in the kind of sea conditions to which Lewis was exposed undoubtedly requires continued careful attention to steering, and during a lengthy storm, a singlehander could surely become exhausted whether steering from the cockpit or below. After reaching Cape Town following his third capsizing (Chapter 11), Lewis said, "I was greatly influenced by Moitessier. I thought it right to run her off before the wind but I don't know ... "

Since the disastrous Fastnet Race of 1979 when a number of boats capsized, many ocean racing sailors now believe in running off at fast speeds on fully crewed boats, because some of the IOR boats having low stability ranges fared well in the race by using this tactic. There are even a number of singlehanders who believe in moderate-to fast-speed scudding when there is plenty of sea room. Rachel Hayward told me that some of her more experienced competitors advised her to use this tactic in the 1984 OSTAR.

The advantage of fast scudding is that it gives the rudder best control and allows steering a weaving course that can avoid the most dangerous seas. But again, this requires that the helm be skillfully manned. It could be dangerous to leave a vane gear in charge, since vanes usually do not work well when running in steep following seas. Even an effective autopilot cannot steer a breaker-avoiding course, and in steep seas it could drive a fine-bowed boat into the back of the wave ahead, risking a broach or possible pitchpoling. A further risk in high-speed scudding for heavy displacement craft is that the boat's own wave system can reinforce a following sea, possibly causing it to break over the stern. There is less risk of this for light displacement boats that create a shallow wave system.

The Dreaded Capsize

There are various interpretations of the term capsize, but to me it means a knockdown or roll-down at least to the point where the vessel's righting moment becomes zero or where her stability changes from positive to negative. At this point, she has lost her ability to self-right. She may hang momentarily between positive and negative stability and then slowly right, or she may "turn turtle" (roll completely upside down with her keel in the air) where she could possibly remain for some time (perhaps indefinitely, if she is a multihull), or she might make a 360-degree roll-over.

More than a few singlehanders have undergone the frightening experience of a capsize. In fact, such accidents were quite common in the early days when ocean crossings were made or attempted in cockleshell boats with little or no external ballast. Johnson, Gilboy, Andrews, Lawlor, and Blackburn all capsized at sea.

Lawlor probably had the easiest time of it with his *Sea Serpent*, because she was fitted with about 600 pounds of lead on her keel, not enough to prevent a capsize, but very helpful when it came to righting the boat. Andrews, on the other hand, had no external ballast at all on his *Mermaid*, and, he capsized seven times during his attempted Atlantic crossing in 1891. On one occasion it took him 30 minutes of struggling to right the boat.

The log of Bernard Gilboy's solo Pacific crossing, which was rediscovered and published not many years ago, gives the understated details of his turning turtle approximately 240 miles from the Fiji Islands on December 13, 1882. His 18-foot, double-ended schooner, *Pacific*, broached to while running when a sea broke under her quarter, and she promptly rolled over bottomside up. Gilboy, who had been aboard the boat continuously for nearly four months, suddenly found himself underneath the overturned hull. Extricating himself, he surfaced on the windward side and managed to crawl onto her slippery, weed-and-barnacle-covered bottom. He struggled out of his heavy shirt and oilskin coat, which were weighing him down, and then set about figuring how to right the boat. This would be no easy job, because the masts and sails thrusting downward caused great resistance to being lifted, while the boat's broad beam made her very stable in the inverted position, and her shallow, unballasted keel contributed little as a counterbalance to assist in righting.

Gilboy had decided to dive under the boat and attempt to retrieve a line that could be used to help with the righting, when he noticed his sea anchor, with its line attached, floating to windward. The drogue was a sail-pattern type (similar in appearance to a squaresail), and evidently a bubble of air trapped under the canvas kept it on the water's surface. The singlehander caught hold of the drogue's line, the end of which was made fast on the forward deck, and hauled it up over the boat's bottom. This gave him something to pull on when trying to roll the hull upright. Gilboy positioned himself to leeward on the side of the hull opposite the line's attachment, and with his legs braced against the topsides, he pulled on the line with all his might. He tried repeatedly, but with no success. As his log stated, "It seemed to be a hopeless task." He persisted, however, and finally, "after an hour's hard work she began to right."

But Gilboy's difficulties were far from over. Although the half-swamped boat was now on her feet, the captain had great difficulty in keeping her upright. To lessen windage and top-hamper, he began to cut away the rigging and unship the masts, but before the job was completed, *Pacific* capsized again. This time Gilboy had less trouble righting her, and he succeeded in unshipping the masts, which he lashed together and made fast, along with some other loose gear, to the drogue line. The spars and gear floated to windward and acted as a drag to hold the boat's bow into the wind and seas to help prevent another capsizing. Gilboy scrambled aboard and began bailing for all he was worth with a large sugar-cube box. Water seemed to wash into his cockpit hatch faster than he could bail it out. There was a large watertight compartment forward of the cockpit, but Gilboy had failed to plug its limber holes, and so the compartment was partially flooded. After a long period of exhausting work and great anxiety, the boat began to gain freeboard, and about dawn the next day she was finally clear of water.

The crisis was over, but much food was lost or spoiled and the compass, rudder, and mainmast were gone. Gilboy devised a reasonably well balanced jury rig by substituting for the mainsail a triangular sail, which was hoisted to the head of the foremast, tacked down amidships, and boomed out with an oar. The single-hander gamely struggled on for about a month and a half longer, but, at the end of that time, his food and water were almost gone and he was weak and exhausted. Only 160 miles short of his destination in Australia, he allowed himself to be picked up by the schooner *Alfred Vittery.*

Modern monohulls, of course, nearly always carry external ballast on (or encased in) the keel, which not only increases the range of stability, but also helps with self-righting in the event of turning turtle. Most externally-ballasted mono-hulls that have had the misfortune to roll upside down have remained in the inverted position no longer than a few minutes, but occasionally a boat will become stabilized with her keel up.

Such was the case when the 19-foot *Cockle* capsized during her transatlantic race against two sisterboats, modified Hunter 19s, in November 1971. Her single-handed skipper, Alan Gick, was only about four days out from Falmouth, England, in the Bay of Biscay, a notoriously rough area, especially at that time of year, when his little *Cockle* turned turtle. She had been lying ahull during a blow that produced relatively short, confused seas about 20 feet high, when she was hit by an unusually high sea with a breaking top caused by the coincidence of two waves. Gick was below at the time, and he was thrown to the cabintop as his boat rolled completely upside down. Fortunately, the companionway hatch was closed so that the cabin was not completely flooded during the knockdown, but about half of the supplies and stores were flung or fell to the cabin top.

After recovering from his initial shock, Gick suddenly came to the frightening realization that his boat was not righting herself. Not even the steep seas washing over her bottom could roll her upright. The water level inside the cabin began rising, and the singlehander described his situation as similar to being inside a washing machine. He managed to don a life jacket and then inflated a rubber dinghy, which he hoped would keep the *Cockle* afloat. He had the strong feeling she was about to sink, although she had a certain amount of built-in flotation. Moments later, however, he reconsidered and deflated the dinghy in order to try to escape from the cabin and use the dinghy as a life boat. After about 12 minutes of being upside down, which must have seemed an eternity, the little vessel began to right. Her mast had broken, and the partial removal of its stabilizing effect, along with the free surface effect from water that had risen inside the hull, allowed her to roll back on her feet. The water level inside the cabin was then less than half a foot below the bridge deck, but Gick bailed frantically and evidently very efficiently, for he reported clearing the boat within about half an hour. The broken mast and tangled rigging were afloat to windward, and they acted as a kind of sea anchor. Gick managed to float them far enough away from the boat to prevent their damaging the hull, which lay almost broadside to the waves.

The blow continued, and, before dawn the next day, *Cockle* turned turtle again, but this time she did a rapid 360-degree roll-over. A mastless boat with small moment of inertia is more vulnerable to rolling over than one with mast intact, as the spar increases the inertia and slows the roll. Again stores and gear were flung about the cabin, so Gick took hammer in hand and nailed almost everything movable to the cabin sole. When daylight came, he shifted his drag, consisting of the broken rig and a 150-foot warp, to the stern. *Cockle* seemed to behave better tethered from her stern, but the blow showed no signs of abating, and Gick decided to call for help with an emergency radio beacon. Fourteen hours later an airplane spotted him and sent a ship to his rescue. Gick was eventually taken off, but *Cockle* could not be hoisted aboard the ship due to bad weather. The singlehander wrote, "It was heartbreaking to see her drifting away into the darkness."

Gick was at a loss to explain how his boat could have remained so stable in the upside-down position, since she had a ballast-displacement ratio of 50 percent. One partial explanation could be that the shifting stores falling to the cabin top contributed to the inverted stability, especially before the water in the hull had risen and, of course, the boat's moderately broad beam contributed to the problem.

Another possible contributing factor to the *Cockle*'s predicament was that the keel's center of gravity may have been relatively high due to its shape and distribution of ballast, and the flotation might have been concentrated at higher locations for better advantage when capsized. At any rate, Alan Gick's experience teaches us some valuable lessons:

1. There is high risk in a very small boat crossing such a notoriously rough body of water as the Bay of Biscay at other than the most favorable time of the year.
2. Broad beam, light displacement, and small size all increase the risk of capsizing.
3. All gear, stores, and ballast must be absolutely secured to prevent shifting during the worse possible knockdown in heavy weather at sea.
4. Lying ahull can be dangerous in such a boat in short and steep confused seas that have breaking tops of the plunging variety.
5. Consideration might be given to *sturdy* masthead flotation and suitable rigging to support it on all capsizable boats having questionable self-righting characteristics (even monohulls) that might venture offshore.
6. There is not necessarily a cause for urgent concern if a well-ballasted boat with moderate beam does not right immediately after turning turtle, because, as water slowly rises inside her hull, the free surface effect and the lessening of the load waterline beam will be helpful to righting.

When monohulls having well-ballasted keels capsize, the cause is usually extraordinary wave action. Often these waves are encountered during stormy seasons in areas where there is tremendous fetch, and/or where there are shoals (not always charted) or strong currents that cause steep, plunging seas; then there are the freak, or rogue, waves that will soon be described. Probably the most notorious regions for producing dangerous seas are those in the high southern latitudes, especially in the general vicinities of Cape Horn and the Cape of Good Hope.

Marcel Bardiaux experienced two rapid 360-degree roll-overs while sailing around Cape Horn from east to west in 1952. He is generally credited with being the first singlehander to round the Horn against the prevailing winds and safely clear the shores of South America. This feat, accomplished near the beginning of the Antarctic winter in a mere 31-foot, homemade racing-cruiser, has been described as the equivalent to climbing Mt. Everest. Bardiaux's boat, *Les 4 Vents*, was uniquely fitted for the passage. In anticipation of a possible capsizing, Bardiaux had secured flotation in the form of 24 five-gallon GI tins to the underside of the deck. He felt that these tins in conjunction with the lead ballast on the keel would immediately right the boat from an inverted position.

When Bardiaux rounded Cape San Diego, the southeast tip of Tierra del Fuego, to pass through Le Maire Strait on his way to the Horn, weather conditions were simply appalling. He was being set to windward by a 9-knot current flowing against a 50-knot gale! Experienced sailors need little imagination to realize what short, steep, tumbling seas were created by such an opposition of wind and water flow. *Les 4 Vents* had made several boards to windward under a deeply roller-reefed mainsail, which Bardiaux could only set after dipping the sail in sea water to unfreeze it, when the wind freshened and backed to the southwest putting Cape Horn dead to windward. Bardiaux could make no progress to weather despite the powerful current, and so he hove to; *Les 4 Vents* was then thrown backwards by the breaking seas. In an effort to counteract this sternway, Bardiaux scrambled below to get his sea anchor. Moments later, a comber taken on the beam tumbled the cutter, throwing Bardiaux to the cabintop amid a shower of loose gear. A flood of water burst through the companionway, but the boat quickly righted herself. The singlehander struggled out of the cabin and slammed shut the companionway doors, but then *Les 4 Vents* turned turtle again. This time she did not right as promptly due to the shifting of equipment and stores, and Bardiaux was submerged in the icy water. When she did turn upright, the mast was still intact, but the storm trysail, headsails, and dodger were gone. The powerfully built Bardiaux remained on board by clutching the twisted dodger frame, which was bolted to the deck.

Les 4 Vents was half filled and listing badly, but Bardiaux streamed a long warp and 5 fathoms of anchor chain, which seemed to steady the boat, while he manned the pump. When the bilges were mostly cleared, he hoisted a scrap of sail and made for what shelter he could find. Soaked to the skin and in subzero temperatures, the singlehander slowly worked his boat into countercurrents and smoother water along the coast. It was totally dark when he reached Aquirre Bay and dropped the hook in 60 fathoms.

Bardiaux was shaken but not deterred by his ordeal, and he set off again 30 hours later to beat past the Horn. On May 12, 1952, in a storm of hail and snow, the determined Frenchman left Cape Horn to starboard. He then stood about 25 miles to the SSW, came about, weathered Hermite Island (northwest of Cape Horn), and eventually fought his way through floating ice and strong winds into Beagle Channel. From there he proceeded to Cook Bay and out into the Pacific. Bardiaux's singlehanded near-wintertime doubling of the Horn in a small, homemade boat has to be ranked with the most astonishing of all sailing feats.

In many ways, *Les 4 Vents* was well-prepared for her venture, having buoyancy tanks, a small cockpit, a well-rounded cabin trunk, small portholes, bolted dodger frame, and so forth. But on the other hand, she had no deck-enclosing life lines, minuscule coamings, and a less-than-satisfactory means of blocking off the companionway.

When the weather deteriorates to survival conditions, it seems that the safest location for the crew members is below, perhaps strapped in their bunks, but if it is necessary that someone be on deck for steering or some other purpose, he should be attached with a stout safety line. Not everyone has the strength of Bardiaux to hang on with bare hands alone during a capsize or severe pooping. The safety line should probably be of considerable length, because otherwise the sailor might be held too long under water during a roll-over or extreme knockdown. Singlehander Ambrogio Fogar, sailing the 38-foot sloop *Surprise,* was rolled over in the Tasman Sea during a cyclone in 1974. Only moments before she turned turtle, Fogar was washed overboard, but he remained tethered by a long safety line. He actually watched his vessel roll through 360 degrees from the end of the line. With sufficient ballast in her keel and moderate beam, *Surprise* righted promptly, and Fogar was able to haul himself back on board.

Multihull Seamanship

Unlike monohull boats, unballasted multihulls often capsize from wind force rather than wave action. An exception, however, was Tom Corkill's 25-foot trimaran *Clipper One*, which turned turtle about 200 miles northwest of the Cape of Good Hope. She had been lying ahull in a blow and was stripped of all sail when a steep sea broke against her beam. It stove in the cabin side and threw the boat upside down. Corkill was below at the time, and after his initial recovery from the tumbling, he forced open the companionway hatch, took a deep breath, and swam down and out from under the upturned boat. With lungs nearly bursting, he bobbed up into a roaring gale. Clad only in shorts and a jersey, with the seas washing over him, he had to cling to the bottom of the craft for 18 hours. An important factor that led to Corkill's rescue was that *Clipper One*'s bottom was painted with a bright "air-sea-rescue" orange paint that enabled the overturned vessel to be spotted by a ship.

Without special systems of self-rescue such as those described in Chapter 3, there is little chance of a singlehander righting a multihull; thus all precautions should be taken to avoid capsizing. Most of these were discussed in Chapter 7. In Corkill's case, perhaps the most effective measures would have been sturdy masthead flotation with extra strong rigging (although this is a controversial preventative); small, strong cabin sides and windows; the ability to lie end-to those particular seas; and the ability to avoid tripping. In respect to the latter, *Clipper One* was heavily loaded and had taken on a considerable amount of water, which evidently shifted, and, together with the extra weight, caused her leeward ama to dig in. A proper bilge pump operable from the helm and also from below might have been helpful. Trimaran designer Robert Harris wrote, "It is also possible that had Corkill pumped out his *Clipper* before retiring she would have been buoyant enough to remain upright."

With further regard to tripping, it is important to keep the centerboards up. In the 1968 OSTAR, Bill Howell lay ahull in the catamaran *Golden Cockerel* (later called *Tahiti Bill*) with her daggerboards up during a lengthy gale and managed to stay upright. Without a grip on the water his boat was simply thrown to leeward by the waves. Although Robin Knox-Johnston advised keeping the windward board of catamaran partway down in extremely heavy weather, he had in mind running off with the seas taken on the quarter, not on the beam.

Because of the multihull's low range of stability, many authorities feel that these craft should be kept largely end-to the seas by either running off or lying to a sea anchor. Dick Newick is opposed to lying ahull in his trimarans and advocates using a sea anchor or two. In one gale on board a 31-foot Val tri of his design, he had success streaming a large sea anchor from the bow of the main hull and a smaller one, on a shorter, weighted rode from the windward ama. He wrote me that this method "takes care of the odd wave from a different direction that has been known to capsize boats." Newick says that many of his newer offshore multihulls are designed with consideration for taking heavy seas on the stern, and in these craft he would favor lying to a sea anchor off the stern.

During the 1980 OSTAR, Bill Homewood weathered a severe storm by using sea anchors on his Val trimaran, but he nearly capsized and now favors keeping the boat moving at moderate speed under a triple reefed main. For sea anchors, he recommends a fairly elastic rode with weight on it (diver's lead weights) eight to 10 feet from the anchor to hold it down in deep water.

Freak Waves

In the literature of the sea, one often finds references to "freak" waves. These are gigantic crests towering high above their neighbors. Occasionally, also, there may be abnormally deep troughs, sometimes referred to as "holes in the sea." Monstrous freak waves are fortunately rare; when they do exist, they are often formed by the mixing of several different wave trains (systems of related waves moving at about half the speed of the individual waves) during prolonged storms at sea, sometimes after a wind shift, or perhaps by the shelving of underwater shoals or the opposition of strong, offshore currents. Slocum and Gerbault met freak seas of considerable size, and each singlehander avoided being washed overboard by climbing aloft. One might think a safer place would be in the enclosed cabin. After

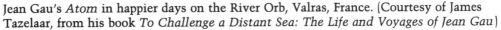

Jean Gau's *Atom* in happier days on the River Orb, Valras, France. (Courtesy of James Tazelaar, from his book *To Challenge a Distant Sea: The Life and Voyages of Jean Gau*)

spotting the approaching wave, Slocum had time to douse his sails and haul himself up the peak halyards, and Gerbault climbed his mast halfway to the truck. Each vessel was completely buried by tons of water and neither capsized.

Jean Gau, however, was not so lucky. He met with a huge tumbling sea near the Cape of Good Hope that rolled his double-ender *Atom* completely upside down. The capsizing took place during the singlehander's second circumnavigation, in 1966. The *Atom* had been lying ahull under bare poles during a blow that gusted up to 72 knots in a region noted for dangerous seas, when she was overwhelmed. Published writings by Jean are presently all too rare, but the following excerpt appeared in the Autumn 1966 issue of the Slocum Society's journal, *The Spray* (translated from the French in "Le Midi Libre," May 1966):

> In the night of February 27th, at about 3 A.M., I heard a strange distant sound. It increased in intensity. It appeared to be the roar of a distant waterfall. Second by second it increased. I could not believe it was real. I wondered what would happen. As the roar increased, I instinctively grabbed the edge of my bunk. In a tremendous explosion the huge wave hit the starboard side and tons of water fell on deck. I was thrown against the deck beams and buried under all objects which were on the starboard bunk opposite mine; navigation instruments, charts, etc. The cabin lamp went out.
>
> To my amazement and for the first time, *Atom* had capsized completely (keel uppermost). I had kept all the openings closed except for a small porthole at the end of the cabin. Through this opening a powerful jet of water entered the cabin, flooding everything. For an undefined period of time I felt paralyzed, awaiting the end. I knew that one day or the other, I would meet one of those monstrous waves which would bury me and my boat. I really thought that moment had arrived, but suddenly thanks to its heavy keel, the boat righted itself. In a desperate effort, I took the decision, which appeared senseless at the time, to reach safety. I was nearly buried under wet blankets and other assorted objects, and it was only after I freed myself that I was able, although heavily bruised, to reach the deck. The sea around the boat was a raging mass of water, but what gave me a feeling of horror was to see that *Atom* had been dismasted. It was a frightful sight, the stumps of the masts sticking out of the deck. The mast, boom and the bowsprit with the sails still lashed on had carried downwind, but were held back by the shrouds and the stays. The dinghy which had been solidly lashed on the cabin top had torn its fastenings and disappeared.
>
> All this happened within a second, maybe less. The sight was so discouraging that I felt nothing more could be done. I made an effort to look at things calmly and thought it was not the time to sit there and do nothing. The boat was still afloat, and maybe there was still some way of reaching safety. *Atom* and I had been together for a great part of our lives and were destined to sail or sink together. She had saved my life several times, and it was now my turn to do all that was humanly possible to save her.

And save her life he did. After cutting away the smashed rig and setting it adrift, Gau set to work pumping the bilge and repairing his drowned engine. The following day he succeeded in getting the auxiliary started, and on March 2 he arrived at Mossel Bay on the southern coast of South Africa. When an astounded witness to his arrival asked Gau why he sailed alone in such a little boat, the circumnavigator replied that he could not help it. "More than anything else," he said, "I love my boat, the sea and adventure."

John Letcher on his *Island Girl*, which he sailed solo from Hawaii to Alaska using mostly sheet-to-helm self-steering. Later she was run down by a ship. (Photo by Warren Roll, Honolulu Star Bulletin)

11

Handling Emergencies

O N A FULLY-CREWED VESSEL, emergencies can be difficult enough, but they will be infinitely more serious for the singlehander. Many of the experiences recounted here are worth telling for their adventure value and for the courage or endurance they display. But moreover, they serve as examples of correct or occasionally incorrect action and teach valuable lessons in seamanship to all who make, or aspire to make, shorthanded passages.

Collision and Damage Control

Perhaps the greatest hazard faced by a solo voyager is vulnerability to collisions. Obviously, one cannot stand watch all of the time, and considerable sleep and rest are essential for the preservation of strength, good health, proper spirits, and sound judgment. Thus the vessel must be left in charge of herself for a large part of the time during a passage, and then she is subject to the possibility of colliding with ships, other boats, flotsam, or even formidable marine life such as whales. Actually the danger is not so great as it might seem when the singlehander takes the proper precautions, as discussed in Chapters 7 and 8, but there is always a certain degree of risk.

The most serious collision threat is probably from ships, and especially fishing vessels. Despite the fact that merchant ships stick closely to established traffic patterns and channels near large ports and to steamer lanes when offshore, modern ships move at high speeds, lack maneuverability, are sometimes under-crewed and lacking in adequate lookouts, and depend for much of the time on radar observation, which is less reliable than the human eye unless visibility is very poor.

253

Fishing vessels do not necessarily stick to established routes, even though fishing grounds and ports are generally well known. Some singlehanders are extremely concerned about the possibility of being run down by ships, while others seem casual to the point of being fatalistic. Robert Manry, for instance, spent much time sleeping during the day and standing watch at night. On the other hand, John Guzzwell wrote me concerning his voyage in *Trekka*, "Don't know about being run down by steamers. I'm a heavy sleeper."

Singlehander John Letcher has given considerable thought to the risks involved in sleeping at night on a shorthanded passage. His interest in this subject is more than academic, since he was run down on two occasions, once by a steamer when alone and once by a fishing vessel when his wife was his shipmate. The following account, taken from his book *Self-Steering for Sailing Craft*, describes the time when he was alone:

> From Hawaii I sailed *Island Girl* north to Alaska in 1964, arriving in Sitka early in September. I laid her up there for the winter, and early the next summer I returned for two unforgettable months of cruising and climbing in the fiords and islands of Southeast Alaska; then in mid-August, alone again, I sailed from Sitka to return to Los Angeles.
>
> The passage was fast, and in pleasure it suffered only from being in the wrong direction—from a remote, wild, exciting region toward a much less thrilling destination, not the way a voyage should be. Fair, fresh winds prevailed, the little black twins drove us over 100 miles almost every day, and the only uncomfortable experience was the northerly gale off northern California. At dusk of the 20th day we made a good landfall, picking up the lights of the coast near Point Conception. This cape is the dividing line between the chill, foggy Pacific Coast weather and the relatively warm, gentle climate of Southern California, so I felt we were almost in home waters.
>
> That night I saw the lights of many ships—one or two per hour—passing a little way inshore. We were running under twins, but by midnight the wind had almost died and progress—and maneuverability—had become very poor. One northbound ship appeared for a long while as if it were going to pass a little outside us, but rather close. I assumed they were seeing my lights, and was a little annoyed that they would pass so close. As their lights grew closer, and the muffled whine of turbines and the rush of the bow wave came across the water to me, I turned on my searchlight and aimed it at the ship. This was to let them know I was annoyed. Imagine my horror when the ship turned and came directly toward me! White over white, red beside green, the group of lights approached with an awful noise, growing by the second, and there was not the slightest chance of getting out of its path. As the pale bow loomed out of the darkness, I dived through the companionway and instantly there was a terrible jolt and a rending crash. In a few seconds of shuddering vibration the ship's side rushed past, then we were wallowing in the foamy, hissing wake as their stern light drew rapidly away. They never knew we were there.
>
> It turned out that there was no contact between our hulls. I believe that they were a little off their aim, so that their bow wave washed *Island Girl's* hull aside, but her rig rolled into the side of the ship. The mast was broken in three places, the forestay, headstay, and bowsprit were all broken, and the upward pull on the forestay lifted the deck and clamps so the sheer strakes were split on both sides almost back to the chain plates. I got away with my life and felt very lucky. *Island Girl* was towed to Santa Barbara and I refitted her there.

That was a truly frightening experience, but it may be of some comfort to others, who fear being run down by ships, to know that a boat can be fended off by the ship's bow wave (during a nearly head-to-head meeting) so that, unless the collision is dead on center, there is a good chance that there will be only slight, if any, contact between the two hulls. This increases the odds for survival tremendously, although the rig is very apt to be damaged. John told me that he dove below at the last minute before impact, because he considered that the cabin was the safest place to be during a head-on collision. Also, he said that the mast fell on the companionway and blocked it, and this emphasizes the advisability in having another hatch for an alternate exit. I agree with John that the cabin is the safest place to be when there is damage to the rig only, but with serious hull damage that would result in a rapid sinking, a safer location would probably be on deck near the life raft.

Just before starting the second edition of this book I received an interesting letter from Captain Ed Purdy, who pointed out that John Letcher was run down in the western terminus of the Santa Barbara Channel, Traffic Separation Zone. Captain Purdy quite rightfully suggested that my readers should be informed that such zones, boldly marked with magenta strips on charts, are exceedingly dangerous areas for a small boat after dark. In fact, Rule 10 of the U.S. Coast Guard's *Navigation Rules* warns of navigating near terminations of traffic separation schemes. Section (H) of Rule 10 states: "A vessel not using a traffic separation scheme shall avoid it by as wide a margin as is practicable," while Section (J) says: "A vessel of less than 20 meters in length or a sailing vessel shall not impede the safe passage of a power-driven vessel following a traffic lane." In simple terms, keep well clear of those areas at night, particularly if you are sailing an engineless boat in light airs.

Being a very scientific-minded fellow, John calculated the probability of being run down by a ship on his 2,500-mile solo passage from Hawaii to Alaska. He reasoned that he could sail blindly back and forth continuously over those waters for over 80 years and expect to be run down only once in a thousand voyages. If daylight hours were assumed safe and nine-tenths of the ships stuck to charted lanes, the probability of collision for a single passage would be about one in 20,000.

Francis Stokes is even more optimistic. He wrote me that he guessed (very roughly) that his chances of being run down by a ship were possibly one in a million or one in ten million. Still he was not without worries, for he wrote, "Rightly or wrongly, one has a fairly persistent fear of collisions with ships."

Quite often, of course, when the weather permits, ships can be heard or smelled from downwind. The odor of smoke, the sound of whining turbines, the throbbing of diesel engines, the thrashing of screws when ships are light, and even the roar of bow waves can be detected by the singlehander in poor visibility or from his cabin when he is not sound asleep. These sounds often carry well at sea, especially in calm, foggy weather. In some cases, underwater sounds, the turning of a propeller, for instance, can noticeably reverberate through the hull shell. Many passage-making sailors develop a keen sensitivity for unusual sounds. They can sleep through a din of normal noises such as rattling blocks, creaking lines, and the gurgling of water flowing past the hull, but a strange, unexplained sound can wake them. This kind of sensitivity may at times seem almost clairvoyant, as in the case of Hans de Meiss-Teuffen, who crossed the Atlantic alone in 1946 aboard the 34-foot yawl *Speranza*. He entered in his log (on July 18): "Slept two hours, 1 a.m.

to 3 a.m. Woke at three with the urge to have a quick look on deck. And there, only 300 yards off, a fishing motor vessel!" Needless to say, a singlehander should never count on any mental alarm systems to warn him, but there is some degree of comfort in knowing that they often work and that acute sensitivities are often developed by offshore sailors. Michael Richey, who bought the famous *Jester* from H. G. Hasler in the mid-1970s, wrote, "The experience of waking mysteriously at the right time seems to be a common one. It would be foolish to rely heavily on it, but it can certainly be taken into account."

Frank Casper told me that before he began sailing alone, an irresponsible crewmember was nearly the cause of his being run down. On a passage between the Panama Canal and the Galapagos Islands, Casper and his single crew stood watch and watch, one sleeping while the other kept a lookout on deck. One dark night, while the skipper was asleep below, the crewmember decided to take a nap on deck. He closed the companionway doors and stretched out just behind them on the bridge deck. Casper, having the aforementioned seamanlike sensitivities, awoke to the sounds of an approaching steamer. He tried to rush on deck, but his sleeping crewman lying against the companionway doors completely blocked that exit. Frank then ran forward and sprang through the forward hatch just in time to see the great bow of the ship bearing down on him. Rushing aft, he quickly started the engine, threw the helm hard over, and barely escaped a collision. Frank cited this experience as one of the reasons why he prefers to sail alone.

For all of us who sail when there is risk of collision with boats or ships, there is a valuable lesson to be learned from Casper's close shave, and that is to have the engine ready for instant use. This would usually mean having the main switch turned on, and the fuel and exhaust valves open; seeing that the bilges are clear of

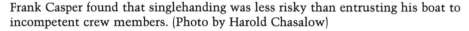

Frank Casper found that singlehanding was less risky than entrusting his boat to incompetent crew members. (Photo by Harold Chasalow)

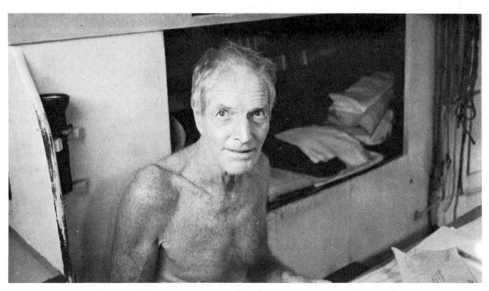

fumes (they should be anyway, at all times); seeing that the bilge water is below the level of the blower's exhaust hose when the fuel is gasoline; and running the engine for a short time at regular intervals to keep it in good working order.

Other lessons can be learned from Tania Aebi's experience when she was run down by a ship in the traffic separation zone near the Suez Canal. Tania made the mistake of going below after dark to make a cup of coffee while in the middle of a traffic lane, which allowed her sloop *Varuna* to stray into the path of a fast-moving tanker. Alerted by the vessel's horn, she hurried on deck to turn the helm but could not immediately cast off the tiller from its connection with the self-steering gear, because it was tied with a knot that took at least five seconds to release. Fortunately, the ship's bow missed her by 10 feet, and *Varuna* was struck a glancing blow by the stern section, which only caused some damage to the rig. The obvious lessons are to stand a continual watch in traffic separation zones, use running lights, have the engine ready, and be sure the helm can be quickly released.

Radar reflectors on small boats are definitely helpful but obviously only when the ship is radar-equipped and when the equipment is being properly used. An unusual way of getting a ship's attention was tried successfully by Chay Blyth. During his circumnavigation in *British Steel*, Blyth carried explosives, which were fuse ignited and sounded like fairly heavy guns. Early one morning before dawn, near the Cape of Good Hope, he spotted a ship headed towards him. Blyth flashed his emergency lights and sounded his foghorn, but the ship did not alter course. When she was only about 50 yards away, the singlehander fired an explosive. With that, the ship suddenly sheered off, heeling sharply, and barely missed *British Steel*. After the incident Blyth entered in his log, "I'm shaking like a bloody leaf. I just can't control it. We've been close to being run down before but never as close as this."

Except for heaving to at night, there is little a singlehander can do about preventing collisions with flotsam. The best plan is to be sure one's boat is strongly constructed to withstand violent impact, see that there is some means of keeping the vessel afloat if she should happen to be holed, and of course see that there is a proper means of abandoning and calling for help. A vessel can be kept afloat with permanent or even inflatable flotation, with watertight bulkheads, or by providing an effective method of plugging the hole, such as with a collision mat (see Chapter 8 and Figure 11-1).

Wooden boats seem a little more vulnerable to being holed than those properly built of heavy fiberglass, ferrocement, or steel. Peter Tangvald, for one, lost his old, but strongly-built, wooden cutter *Dorothea* during a West Indies passage in March 1967 when she struck what was thought to be a large piece of flotsam, perhaps a floating tree trunk. *Dorothea*, which had previously carried Tangvald safely around the world, promptly filled with water and forced her solo skipper to abandon ship in a seven-foot plywood dinghy, which is far from the safest kind of lifeboat. Peter had little time to get off his sinking craft, but he remained remarkably cool-headed, and plotted his position on the chart table with the inrushing water swirling around his legs. Then he quickly gathered together the gear, water, food, flashlight, clothes, compass, and so forth that he would need for his escape. His position was about 40 miles southwest of Barbados, and Peter figured his best chance for survival was to head for the Grenadines, approximately 55 miles to leeward, making all the speed he safely could. He rigged a jury squaresail from an

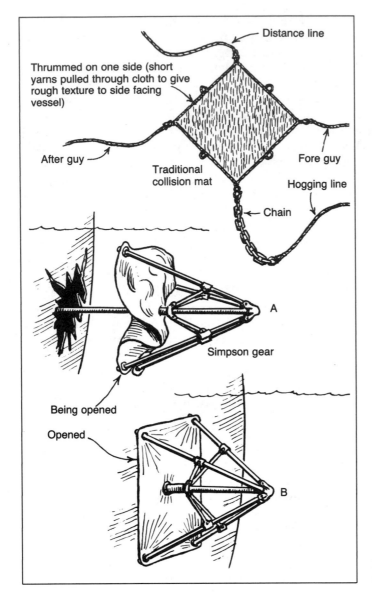

Figure 11-1. Damage control.

old awning, using an oar for the mast and a boat hook for the yard. A steamer passed close aboard in the middle of the night and Peter repeatedly flashed SOS signals with his powerful light, but to no avail. After 20 hours of somewhat frightening sailing, which required the utmost concentration to keep the boat from swamping in the rough seas kicked up by the fresh trade winds, Tangvald reached Cannouan Island, where he landed in a nearly exhausted condition.

There are a few lessons to be learned from Peter Tangvald's experience. One, not often thought about, is that when a boat has a tight ceiling or inside liner, a damaged area may be inaccessible. Peter could not locate his leak or attempt to stop it, because of the permanent ceiling construction. Many modern boats are just as bad or worse with their fiberglass liners, which often make it difficult to reach the hull shell, fastenings, wiring, hoses, valves, and so forth. Also, there were at least two important items of equipment that Peter found he needed, namely a pocket knife and flares. An EPIRB, portable VHF, or radio transmitting on 2182 kHz would have improved his chances of being picked up by the steamer; and a life raft or inflatable boat would have served him well, but it is reassuring to learn that a well-designed dinghy, even one as small as Tangvald's, can survive in fairly rough seas when it is well handled.

Incidentally, a fin keel whose leading edge is not swept back is exceedingly vulnerable to damage in the event of collision with submerged objects. John Letcher once hit a submerged floating log in his fin-keeler *Island Girl*, and even though she was moving slowly, the impact was severe enough to loosen the strakes next to the garboards. The collision could have sunk the boat except that her bottom was covered with copper sheathing for worm protection, and this inhibited extreme leaking.

Multihulls or very fast monohull racers may be more vulnerable to collisions with flotsam or relatively stationary objects than monohull cruisers. *Jet Services* had to be abandoned after striking a tree trunk in the 1984 OSTAR, and in 1986 BOC racer *Airforce* sank after she struck what was thought to be a submerged container (the deliberate dumping of cargo containers at sea is a deplorable practice that should be stopped immediately with the toughest laws). Although multihulls and racing monohulls have less displacement and thus carry less momentum, they normally travel at higher speeds and are often more lightly constructed. High speeds not only contribute to the extent of damage, but also, for a given period when there is no look-out, increase the chances that a collision will occur due to the rapidity of convergence with the stationary object. When Eric Tabarly crashed into an anchored freighter at night not long after the start of the 1968 OSTAR, his trimaran *Pen Duick IV* was making 15 knots. (Tabarly had been standing watch but had temporarily ducked below to heat some coffee.) Only about 15 minutes elapsed between the time he carefully checked the horizon for ships and the time of the collision. *Pen Duick*'s unusually high strength-to-weight aluminum construction allowed her to survive the impact, but she sustained a four-foot gash in one float, and her rig was damaged. Tabarly was forced to abandon the race and limp back to port.

In the 1972 OSTAR, Bill Howell's catamaran *Tahiti Bill* rammed a slow-moving Russian trawler only about 100 miles from the finish line. The accident took place during daylight hours but in dense fog. *Tahiti Bill* suffered a stove-in bow, but fortunately she had a watertight bulkhead that kept the hull from filling entirely. The Russians said they had not seen the catamaran when they looked at their radar 20 minutes before the accident. This points up not only the risks involved in sailing fast (though Howell was only making seven knots) without a lookout or in poor visibility, but also the fallibility of depending solely on radar to avoid collisions, especially when the screen is only checked occasionally.

Racers in the 1986–87 BOC Challenge were required to have watertight bulkheads forward and aft, but that didn't prevent *Airforce* from sinking. Fortunately, her skipper, Dick Cross, was rescued by a Navy helicopter. One BOC boat, *Ecureuil d'Aquitaine*, even had a false crash bow of foam, while an earlier racer, *Koden Okera V*, had a bow bumper to fend off icebergs.

Whales and Dangerous Sea Life

Many sailors venture offshore in small boats with little concern of being attacked by or colliding with sea creatures. This hazard seems to be the kind one would read about in a high-adventure or science-fiction story, but true reports of hull damage and even sinkings caused by marine life are not uncommon. The culprits are whales, killer whales, sharks, and, occasionally, swordfish. Whales in particular seem to cause the most damage. During the 1984 OSTAR, for example, four boats made violent contact with whales during the race, while another hit occurred before the start. The 29-foot *Go Kart* was forced to retire after being holed, and the 30-foot *Tjisje* was hit so hard that she sank. Her skipper, Henk Van De Weg, was rescued by a Coast Guard helicopter after he activated his Argos transmitter.

Going back to an early singlehanded voyage, Bernard Gilboy was attacked by a swordfish during his Pacific crossing in 1882. The fish rammed Gilboy's double-ended schooner *Pacific* at high speed and put its sword clean through the bottom of the hull. After giving the boat a shaking, the fish withdrew its blade, leaving a spurting hole in the planking. The singlehander stuffed the hole with a wick and some rags, which stopped the leak surprisingly well. Another early singlehander who was attacked by several swordfish was Howard Blackburn during his Atlantic crossing in *Great Republic* in 1901. By throwing coils of line on top of the fish, he eventually drove them off before his boat was impaled. Blackburn's biographer, Joseph Garland, suggests, however, that such a tactic could be dangerous in that it might cause further provocation.

William Andrews, who feared almost nothing, was all but terrified of whales. During the latter part of his 1892 voyage in *Sapolio*, he encountered a pod of large finbacks not far from the coast of Spain, and he made the following remarks in his log:

> At 5:30 a herd of fin-back whales came feeding straight for the boat, the wind being so light I could do nothing but keep on and take my chances with their flukes. I seized my shark tickler, rattled it on the boat, made a noise and yelled at them. All to no avail. On they came, with their mouths wide open and with blow holes big enough to crawl into. I commenced to tremble and feel shakey in the knees. When within fifty feet, O, how they made the water boil! I thought they would sound, and felt relieved; but no, I saw them coming under the boat, and as they rose to the surface and blowed all around me they were going in different directions, and so slowly. This they kept up for fifteen minutes, while I seized hold of a rope for safety, and seizing my paddle, used it very dexterously for a few minutes, thinking, from previous experience, that I might frighten them off. But no, still they glided under the boat, nicely and easily avoiding collision with each other and us. Finally, one slipped off, and I felt better; then another and another. One more curious than the others remained around for some time, when he slunk away after his beastly companions. I tell you, my friends, that I stood there holding the tiller trying to avoid those tons of bone and muscle, and without much headway on the boat, with the water boiling and foaming with the commotion they made, turning the boat every which way, completely beyond my control, and I wondering which way my course was, as the compass was whirling, too, they blowing their misty breaths in my face—I tell you again, friends, it wants nerve food a little better than I have with me.

At one time during his circumnavigation in *Lehg II*, Vito Dumas sailed between two whales that were sleeping side-by-side. The 31-foot ketch actually tried to climb their backs. Dumas wrote that the bow lifted up and then slid off the shiny, slippery mound of flesh. Fortunately, the monsters did not wake up despite their being so rudely jostled, and *Lehg II* slowly "elbowed" her way between them while the singlehander watched in awe.

Another singlehander, D.M.R. Guthrie, collided with a sleeping blue whale, the world's largest animal, while sailing his 30-foot sloop *Widgee* from Antigua to Bermuda in 1969. The impact was sufficient to roll the sloop over on her beam ends and awaken the whale. It thrashed the water in anger and narrowly missed striking the hull with its fluke. After the whale departed, Guthrie found a lump of torn skin and blubber caught in the rigging, and the rudder shaft was bent and jammed. Two days were spent working on the rudder, and repairs were finally effected by cutting away the jammed part with a chisel.

A school of small pilot whales deliberately attacked Alan Eddy's 30-foot Seawind ketch *Apogee* in mid-ocean during his circumnavigation. Possibly provoked by a collision with the ketch, the creatures repeatedly charged and butted her until the cabin sole was loosened, but the sturdy fiberglass hull built by the Allied Boat Company withstood the battering.

In contrast, Bill King's *Galway Blazer II* was severely damaged by a sea creature despite the boat's strong construction of molded plywood. The accident occurred in the waters just south of Australia in December 1971 when a collision stove in the hull on one side just below the waterline. At first the singlehander thought that he had been rammed by a killer whale. The assumption was not unreasonable because the aggressive mammal has a record of occasional attacks on small craft. A highly publicized example was the sinking by killer whales of Dougal Robertson's schooner *Lucette* near the Galapagos Islands in 1972. Subsequent research into the holing of *Galway Blazer*, however, led King to the belief that his vessel actually had been struck by a great white shark, a ferocious creature commonly found in those waters where the accident took place.

King's struggle to keep his boat afloat is an epic of seamanship and a remarkable example of endurance, for the singlehander was over 60 years old and not in perfect health. When the collision occurred, King was below, and he saw a circular portion of the hull spring inward and burst into jagged splits. He rushed on deck attempting to see what he had struck and then promptly threw the boat about onto the opposite tack in order to lift the damaged area out of the water. The sheets were trimmed in flat, and the boat was held off the wind to induce heeling. Occasional waves still washed through the hole, however, and it took considerable time and effort to clear most of the water from the bilge with a hand pump. Incidentally, I would like to stress an important point, that the heeling of a damaged hull should be accomplished with a method that minimizes headway, because forward speed will cause greater leaking and perhaps further damage.

After a tremendous struggle, the singlehander managed to stuff the hole with sponge rubber and nail a piece of Dacron cloth over the outside of the entire damaged area. This required that he hang upside down from the rail with his head immersed and later that he lower himself over the side in a bosun's chair. Periodically King had to break off from his work to pump the bilge. Once the outside repair

Bill King's *Galway Blazer II* under tow before the start of the Golden Globe race.
(Nautical Publishing Company; from *Capsize* by Bill King)

was accomplished, the damaged area, which still leaked, was attended to from inside the hull. King packed the hole with rubber strips, and he cut shores from a spare boom. These were placed against the sprung portion of the hull and held firmly by wedging their opposite ends against a strength member on the boat's other side. *Blazer* was still making some water, and her skipper was forced to pump off-and-on throughout the entire night after the accident.

The next day further repairs were made. King made up and rigged collision mats which were held in place by 13 ropes passed under the hull. In addition, he nailed on strips of sheet copper, applied seam compound and sticky tape, and wedged in some more shores. It took about three days of work to all but stop the leaking. After this, King sailed 400 miles to Fremantle, Australia, with the boat moving sluggishly with the cat's cradle of lines under her bottom. He encountered some heavy weather, but the repairs held, and he reached port safely.

As a result of his experience, Bill King advises offshore sailors to carry such emergency repair equipment as a collision mat (see Figure 11-1), broad-headed nails, a heavy-duty stapling gun with stainless steel staples, and a wet suit for overboard repairs in cold waters. King recommends a triangular collision mat and one backed with foam rubber or thrummed as shown. Of course, it is doubtful that the nails and staples could be used effectively on most boats built of materials other than wood, but self-tapping screws could possibly be used on fiberglass hulls and softwood wedges or bungs on metal hulls. It seems advisable that all offshore boats carry a few small sheets of lightweight plywood, sheets of copper and lead, and poles or extra spars that can be cut into shores. King successfully used a sticky yellow tape (which he thought was mercury chromate) that could be made to adhere to a split under water. Of course, caulking compounds intended for use under water, such as those used on swimming pools or the kind of epoxy putty that hardens when submerged, could be very handy. Another leak-stopper that I have seen used effectively is a mixture of cup grease and soft putty. Globs of this waterproof mix should be smeared into a split or wide seam and covered with canvas, plywood, or sheet metal.

A unique damage control device has been invented by Barry Simpson in England (see Figure 11-1). It works on the principle of an umbrella, in that it can be thrust through a hole from inside the boat (while the device is folded) and then opened up, so that the unfolded fabric will cover the hole on the outside of the hull. The device has been produced, and details on it were featured in *Yachting Monthly* magazine (June 1974). Needless to say there must be immediate access to the hole, and a hatchet, ax, or wrecking bar may be needed to get through the ceiling or liner. The Simpson device might be easier to rig than a conventional collision mat, but the latter would probably allow easier jury repairs to the hole.

There have been many suggestions concerning defensive measures against sea creatures. Some sailors advocate trying to scare them off with sounds, such as explosives, engine and propeller noises, or the high-pitched sound from fathometers. The suggestion has even been made that sound recordings of whales or killer whales be played through a transducer mounted on the hull, which might repel certain kinds of dangerous sea life. The main trouble with this defense is that sounds from a particular creature might attract members of the same species. For instance, the sound emitted by killer whales might scare off certain whales or sharks, but perhaps it could attract killer whales. Other sounds, such as explosions or even the noise of a propeller, might conceivably be irritants that could provoke an attack. In fact, M. J. Gilkes, who served with a whaling fleet, wrote that sperm whales in particular have a penchant for charging straight at the propeller of a whale-catching boat. Where whales are concerned, he recommends practicing Br'er Rabbit's strategy to "lay low and don't say nuffin."

Jerry Cartwright had a most unusual and frightening experience during the 1972 OSTAR when he was listening to a BBC broadcast on the radio concerning whale extinction. The program played loud sounds of whales communicating, when suddenly a huge sperm whale surfaced alongside his boat. Fortunately it did not attack, but it gave the singlehander a good scare. Jerry felt there was a good possibility that the sounds had attracted the whale, for, as he wrote, "the timing seemed too perfect for coincidence."

Another controversial point is the effect that colored bottom paints have on sea creatures. William Andrews often painted the bottoms of his boats black as a defense against whales. Bill King and others suspect that red and even white bottom paint can attract sea predators. Their reasoning is based on assumption that red is associated with blood and white with the foam whipped up by a wounded creature. On the other hand, an experienced charter boat captain claims that, based on his own observations, some whales are repelled by red but attracted by blue bottom paint.

At present, it appears that the only sure defense against all kinds of sea creatures is the construction of one's boat. Strongly made hulls of heavy fiberglass, ferrocement, or steel probably offer the best protection, especially when they are well-rounded and well-stiffened with frames, bulkheads, stringers, and other structural supports. It seems important that any vulnerable skeg be strengthened and glassed over at its top in the bilge area in order to prevent an inflow of water in event that the skeg should be broken off. Several boats have been sunk as a result of whales damaging their skegs. No matter how well his boat is built, however, the careful offshore sailor must be prepared for emergency repairs. Adequate shores could be vital. Frank Casper told me about his friend John Goetzke, an occasional singlehander whose wooden boat was attacked by killer whales. Six frames on the port and starboard sides were cracked, but Goetzke saved his boat by staying below and wedging numerous shores against the inside of the hull.

In a lighter vein, it has been said that nothing will make a whale disappear faster than producing a camera. One offshore sailor even suggested playing a tape recorder that reproduces the sound of camera shutter clicks!

Grounding and Lee Shores

Every bluewater sailor has a healthy respect for a lee shore, but it can be a special source of anxiety for the singlehander. When closely approaching or following a coast, he must stand watch almost continuously because a sound sleep or even a period of rest below without heaving to could result in a grounding. Bernard Moitessier lost his *Marie-Thérèse II* on the rocky shores of St. Vincent Island, West Indies, in 1958 when he took a nap after turning control of his boat over to his self-steering gear. The singlehander relied on an alarm clock to awake him before he was too close to the island, but the alarm failed to ring or he never heard it, and Moitessier did not wake up until his boat was in the breakers. He escaped relatively unharmed, but the boat was pounded into a total wreck.

Jean Gau's beloved ketch *Atom*, which twice carried him around the world and had been his home for 26 years, was nearly lost on the beach at Assateague Island, Maryland, in 1971, right after she had weathered hurricane Ginger. The singlehander did not even fall asleep, though he was dead tired after the storm. He had simply gone below for a rest and to listen to the radio when he was about 14 miles off the coast, which lay to windward. That seemed a safe enough action, but while he was in the cabin, there was a drastic wind shift that put the shore to leeward. With his senses dulled by fatigue and being somewhat distracted by the radio, Jean was unaware of his impending predicament. At one o'clock in the morning, he heard the hissing of breakers, and he rushed on deck, but it was too late. *Atom* was already in shoal water and she immediately grounded with sickening thumps. As a result of an unusually high tide, the ketch carried far up on the beach where she was left high and dry after the water receded. At dawn, Gau stepped ashore unhurt and set off on foot to look for help. Fortunately, he soon found it, more than he ever dreamed he would. The Coast Guard, National Park Service, U. S. Navy, native watermen, and other volunteers all contributed their efforts to free the stranded *Atom*. Her minor damages were repaired. She was pumped clear of sand and made watertight with caulking, plywood patches, and a fast-setting cement. A three-foot-deep trench was dug around her and then to the

Jean Gau's Tahiti ketch *Atom* receives an assist from volunteers after being blown ashore on Assateague Island, Maryland, in 1971. The vessel was eventually refloated and towed in for repairs. (Photo by O. V. Wootton)

sea. She was pivoted so that her bow faced the water, and finally she was pulled free by a Coast Guard utility boat.

Slocum, Pidgeon, and Dumas all had similar experiences. Slocum hugged the shore too closely while sailing down the coast of Uruguay in December 1895 and grounded on a sand bottom. Although *Spray* was left high and dry at low tide, Slocum gives his readers no real details of how he managed to refloat his heavy craft. He said only that he dislodged her with the help of a "German and one soldier and one Italian he called 'Angel of Milan.'" It can only be assumed that he kedged off at high water, since a heavy anchor had already been laid out with considerable difficulty.

Pidgeon ran his yawl *Islander* aground because he fell asleep while too close to shore near Cape Town, South Africa, in June 1924. Fortunately, he grounded on a sand beach (narrowly missing rocks) in moderate surf. It wasn't long, however, before the wind freshened to gale force and the yawl began to be tumbled over from one side to the other. Pidgeon cleverly prevented his boat from being seriously damaged by bending a line to his topping lift, carrying it ashore, and securing it there. The line held the masthead steady and thus put a stop to the destructive tumbling motion. She survived the pounding but was driven far up on the beach.

A signed photo of Harry Pidgeon at the helm of *Islander*. His grounding off Cape Town, South Africa, is a reminder that even expert sailors occasionally make serious errors in judgment.

When the weather moderated, *Islander* was jacked up so that planks and rollers could be placed under her. Then she was pulled afloat with a powerful winch on a small steamer anchored a short distance offshore.

Some particularly important lessons might be learned from Dumas' experience. Beating in his ketch *Lehg II* along the coast of Argentina in 1943, the singlehander made boards of two hours each with the helm lashed. Perhaps an unpredicted current carried him too close to shore, but at one point when Dumas came on deck after a brief rest below, he saw breakers about 100 yards ahead. He had no knife with him to cut the lashing and wasted precious moments untying the tiller. By the time the helm was freed it was too late, and the ketch grounded on a sandy beach. This points up not only the value of carrying a knife, but also the advisability of tying the helm with a slip knot or a loop that can be slipped easily off the end of the tiller or wheel spoke.

Wisely, Dumas stayed at the helm and left his sails drawing so that his boat would be driven far up on the beach. In calm water, this could well have been the wrong tactic, but there was a heavy swell and surf, which made it imperative for the boat to be securely beached so that she would not be continually lifted and dropped on the bottom. Dumas even unloaded the boat to lighten her so that she would be left as nearly as possible high and dry. Several days later, *Lehg II* was pulled free by a trawler with a long coir cable.

One of the most remarkable incidents involving salvage following a grounding was the case of Alain Gerbault's cutter *Firecrest* when she struck a reef after snapping her anchor chain in the Wallis Islands, just north of Fiji, in 1926. She pounded on the reef for about an hour and then suddenly fell over on her beam ends. Gerbault abandoned ship and began swimming for shore when, to his amazement, he noticed that the cutter was following him. The pounding had broken all her keel bolts, which caused the ballast keel to drop off. With almost all stability gone, the extremely narrow boat simply flopped on her side and drifted across the reef. She then lodged on a sandy beach.

To refloat *Firecrest* it was necessary to find the four-ton piece of lead ballast and float it across the lagoon, shore up the cutter, forge 10 new bolts (some of which were over three feet long), move the ballast underwater and align it with the cutter's wood keel so that the bolt holes matched exactly, and then careen the boat after the ballast was bolted on so that she could be moved back across the reef into deep water. All of this had to be done on a remote island that had no facilities for such an operation. It took the help of 50 natives, two Chinese carpenters, the chief engineer from a passing tramp steamer (who had a forge and machine shop), and part of the crew of a French naval vessel. The heavy ballast had to be fitted to the keel twice, because the first time the bolts were too small in diameter, and they allowed water to spurt in through their holes. The whole operation took nearly two months, but *Firecrest* was made almost as good as new.

The aforementioned singlehanders who saved their grounded vessels did so mainly because they had considerable help, but some others had little or no assistance. Two such examples were the circumnavigators Marcel Bardiaux and C. H. (Rusty) Webb. The latter fetched up on a coral reef off Barbuda in the West Indies in 1968. His 58-year-old wooden ketch *Flyd* was severely damaged with 21 holes in her hull. All by himself Webb patched his boat with sheets of copper and canvas. This necessitated underwater work without diving gear over a period of 14 days. Each copper patch required about 60 nails, which had to be hammered in while Webb held his breath beneath the boat. He said at first that he could only drive one nail at a time, but that later he was able to manage two or three nails without surfacing. When repairs were finally completed, the singlehander sailed his patched-up boat more than 4,000 miles to England with the repairs leaking so much that he had to pump the bilge every two hours.

Marcel Bardiaux also grounded on a coral reef, and he did so with such force that the impact threw him overboard and gave him a severe cut on the forehead. The grounding took place in 1954 on an incorrectly charted shoal that was out of sight of land and 65 miles from the nearest port, Noumea, in New Caledonia. Bardiaux's sloop *Les 4 Vents* was being badly damaged by seas that repeatedly slammed her against the coral, and it was obvious that she would have to be dislodged promptly while she was still watertight. The powerful singlehander immediately set to work kedging off. This required taking out on foot a heavy anchor and chain, which were carried and dragged over jagged coral washed by breakers. He used a portable windlass of his own design to drag the boat ahead until she was at short scope, and then the anchor had to be carried out again. This operation had to be repeated many times before *Les 4 Vents* could be pulled free. By then, she was so badly damaged that she was leaking seriously and seemed in imminent danger of sinking in deep water. However, the sloop had a number of buoyancy cans secured under her deck for the primary purpose of improving her ability to self-right, and these, together with a large rubber life raft that Bardiaux spread out and inflated below, supplied enough flotation to keep her from foundering. The Frenchman then sailed her, passing no less than 27 vessels wrecked on the same reef, all the way to Noumea with the hull half-filled, and it was reported that he reached his destination with the decks awash.

A big factor in avoiding grounding and other mistakes in seamanship is the avoidance of extreme fatigue. Ben Dixon, who sails alone occasionally, told me that he nearly lost his sloop *Sundowner* when she dragged onto a lee shore, because he was so tired that he failed to set his anchor properly.

Then there is the case of Gary Mundell, who became a castaway after grounding his Cape Dory 27 *Petrel* on a deserted South Pacific atoll in 1985. He lost his boat and was forced to spend 50 days on Caroline Island before being rescued by a French oceanographic vessel. Prior to the grounding, Gary had figured he was well clear of the island and went below for a nap after having been awake for almost 36 hours. Two and a half hours later, while her skipper slept, *Petrel* struck and careened over the island's outlying reef, where she became hopelessly trapped. It certainly seems possible that Mundell would have been more cautious and perhaps his navigation would have been more accurate had he been well rested. Once again we see how deep fatigue leads not only to carelessness, but also to errors in judgment. The singlehander should get all the rest possible whenever the opportunity arises.

Rigging Problems

Rigging failure is a problem frequently encountered on any passage-making vessel. Lines chafe through, halyards can jam in their blocks, tangles occur aloft, spreaders occasionally come loose, fittings fatigue from the constant motion, booms may break, and even dismastings are not uncommon. Of course, these difficulties are extremely trying for the singlehander, who must pull himself aloft to make repairs or must haul broken spars aboard and set up heavy gear and jury rigs alone. Effecting permanent or even makeshift repairs alone at sea calls for tremendous forethought, effort, patience, and often ingenuity, as illustrated by the experience of David Guthrie.

Guthrie was alone in mid-Atlantic aboard his small sloop when the end of the main halyard ran aloft. This necessitated a trip to the masthead in waters that were far from smooth. Guthrie had a large, conic sea anchor aboard, and it occurred to him that he might be able to utilize its drag to assist him in going aloft. His plan was to keep sailing under a headsail and to attach a bosun's chair to one end of a spare halyard and secure the sea anchor to the halyard's other end. Then he would throw overboard the sea anchor, which would remain relatively stationary, and the boat's headway would pull the chair with Guthrie in it to the masthead. The plan also required that the singlehander carry aloft the end of a trip line leading to the apex of the sea anchor so that it could be tripped to allow descending after the runaway halyard had been retrieved.

The idea was a good one, but its execution brought about some unanticipated problems. One was that the boat's speed of between four and five knots hoisted Guthrie entirely too fast, and a more serious difficulty occurred when the trip line was found to be too short as a result of its having been led inadvertently under the stern pulpit. This mistake caused the trip line to act before Guthrie was at the masthead, and down he came, fortunately with no serious injuries resulting. Once he was back on deck and the trip-line slackened, he was yanked aloft again by the strain of the sea anchor. After returning to the deck again, Guthrie was somewhat shaken, and having been "hoist by his own petard," he decided to postpone the experiment until the following day.

I never heard whether the halyard was eventually retrieved by this unusual method, but the plan definitely had merit and would have worked well had the boat been moving a bit more slowly and had the trip line been longer. In fact, my cousin Charles Henderson used a similar method in going aloft after weathering a typhoon in the China Sea. He was not alone but was shorthanded, and he used a bucket secured to the end of a halyard that was dropped overboard as an assist in going up the mast.

Most singlehanders, of course, use more conventional methods of going aloft. Many have ratlines and/or mast steps, and these are not only useful for climbing the masts to make inspections and rigging repairs, but also for conning the vessel in clear waters where there are submerged reefs or other shoals. Marcel Bardiaux not only had steps, but also even had a way of rigging steering lines from the tiller leading up the mast so that the boat could be steered from aloft. Many singlehanders haul themselves up the mast with a tackle, and a few of the more athletic types climb up hand over hand for simple jobs aloft when the boat's motion permits. On a boat without mast steps or ratlines, however, it would seem to be an unnecessary risk for a singlehander to go aloft even a short distance without rigging either a bosun's chair or a ladder.

The difficulties involved in going aloft when alone and in a rough sea were vividly described by Robin Knox-Johnston. In late January 1969 during his non-stop circumnavigation aboard the ketch *Suhaili*, the large reaching jib's halyard parted and Knox-Johnston made several attempts to reach the masthead in order to reeve a new halyard. The first effort ended with an egg-sized bump on his eyebrow when the ketch rolled and swung him against the end of a spreader. The next day, when the sea seemed a bit more calm, he tried again. He hauled himself up with a tackle and had reached the upper spreaders when the boat started pitching severely. He waited 10 minutes or so for the motion to stop, but to no avail. Meanwhile the jib on the deck began to wash overboard. He decided to make a quick dash for the masthead. He wrote, "Both hands were on the tackle which I did not dare let go of or I would have fallen 32 feet. My legs couldn't hold on round the mast as the mainsail was in the way and I swung forward. I managed to cushion the return swing and fend myself off the mast with my feet, and I swung straight out towards the mizzen. Somehow I got caught the wrong side of the mainsail, which stopped me being swung forward again and I was able to grab one of the backstays with a leg and then get a hand free for the same purpose—and there I hung, lurching wildly, until she eased up."

What a helpless feeling Robin must have had while swinging back and forth from the masthead, unable to use his hands and with no one on deck to steady him with a downhaul line. He managed to make it back to the deck uninjured, if somewhat shaken, but the new halyard was not reeved, and for some time thereafter the topping lift was used as a substitute for the halyard.

Robin's experience not only points out the added advantage of a strong topping lift that is controllable at the deck, but also shows how handy proper mast steps can be for the singlehander. Robin might have had an easier time with the mainsail lowered so that he could have wrapped his legs or a life line around the mast, but, on the other hand, the hoisted sail might have been a considerable help in dampening the boat's rolling motion. Unquestionably, it is a good idea for anyone hauling himself aloft to have a quick and easy means of securing the fall of the tackle so that he can use his hands at a moment's notice. A commonly used method is to pass the fall under the bosun's chair bridle and then secure it with a bosun's hitch (Figure 11-2) over a hook on the bottom of the tackle's lower block. For maximum security, I would prefer an extra half-hitch.

Several OSTAR racers, including Mike McMullen, Phil Weld, and Brian Cooke, have used mast-climbing assists called jumars. These are metal clamps often used by mountain climbers, which attach to a rope and operate in somewhat the manner of a cam cleat, allowing the rope to move through the clamp in one direction but preventing movement in the opposite direction. A jumar can be attached to a bosun's chair in such a way that it will accept and jam the fall of the hoisting tackle and thus hold the chair, at least temporarily, when the singlehander releases his grip on the tackle's fall. A rolling hitch or related knot such as the magnus hitch serves the same purpose.

A number of singlehanders have made remarkable repairs aloft while underway. During the first BOC Challenge Francis Stokes was forced to put bolts through the trailing edge of his streamlined aluminum spreader because the welded seam was being squeezed open as a result of shroud compression. Modest almost to a fault, Francis made light of the repair and gave few details when I talked to him, but I can well imagine the difficulty he had drilling holes from a shifty bosun's chair with every motion of the boat being magnified aloft. It was indeed fortunate that he was able to spot the problem and correct it, for a collapsed windward spreader often results in a dismasting.

In calm weather it is advisable for the solo voyager to climb the mast occasionally to check for chafe, wear, fatigue cracks, or anything amiss. Even periodically looking aloft through binoculars can warn of a problem. As for Stokes' particular mishap, it is safer not to have such spreaders on a seaboat, but if they are used, the welds should be carefully inspected. On racing boats it is common practice to file down the trailing edges of streamlined spreaders to a fairly sharp point, which can weaken the welds. Incidentally, there is little benefit to having a streamlined spreader unless it is mounted in such a way that it is rotated on its axis and angled downward 10 to 15 degrees. This is done to lessen windage when the boat is heeled.

Brian Cooke also made a remarkable repair aloft on *British Steel* during the 1972 OSTAR when a tang for a lower shroud broke. The tang was a stainless steel plate that was too thin and perhaps had its hole for the shroud's pin bored too close to the tang's edge. At any rate, the fitting broke between the hole and the edge, and Cooke felt compelled to repair it at night while in a confused sea following a blow. This involved five trips up and down the mast and working with one hand only (the other was needed to hold on). Evidently, Cooke made a figure-eight loop of wire around the mast at the spreader, though I am not sure how he avoided blocking the mainsail's track. The upper end of the shroud was then fastened to the wire loop.

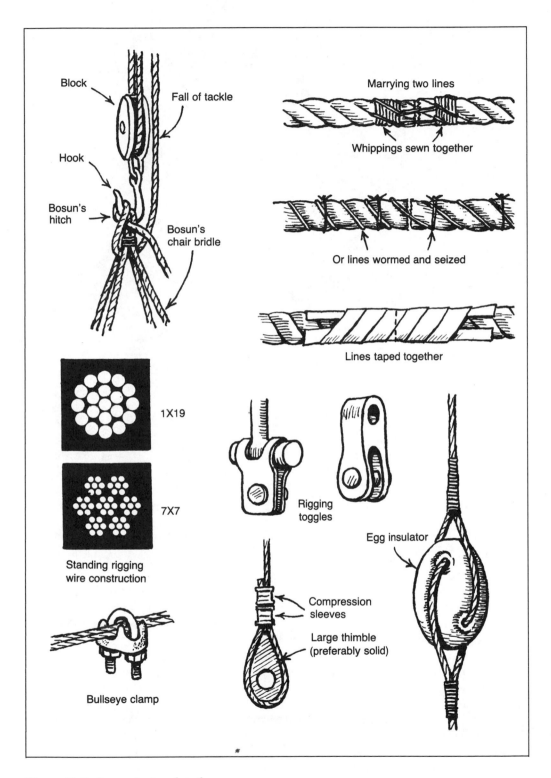

Figure 11-2. Some rigging details.

Brian Cooke aboard the 49-foot trimaran on which he hoped to achieve the goal sought by Chichester, to sail 4,000 miles in 20 days. (Courtesy of John Rock)

One of his greatest trials during the repair job was replacing a cotter pin with one hand in the dark while being swung around violently by the boat's motion. In many cases, a common shower-curtain ring can make a very handy temporary substitute for a cotter pin, since it can be inserted and snapped with one hand. It only takes one moment of impatience or carelessness when working aloft for dire consequences to result. A few years later, Brian Cooke fell from the mast of his trimaran *Triple Arrow* during his attempt to set a solo speed record, the one sought by Francis Chichester, to sail 4,000 miles on a nearly straight course in 20 days. He fell more than 40 feet to the deck and crushed some vertebrae but miraculously made it home. To help avoid falls while making difficult repairs aloft, a climber should always wear a safety harness and clip on to a solid part of the rig.

Chay Blyth is another singlehander who had more than a few rigging problems necessitating working aloft during his circumnavigation on *British Steel* in

1970–71. On one occasion he wrote that he spent the "entire day" clearing up a tangle of halyards. After weathering a lengthy gale about midway between Australia and South Africa, he found that all of his headsail halyards had parted, necessitating going 65 feet up to the masthead (one of the disadvantages of single-handing such a large boat) and threading tail lines (messengers) through the halyard sheaves. Blyth also said the operation involved cutting away a broken wire halyard, no mean job at such a height while trying to hang on for dear life. After this experience, he decided to replace the mizzen halyard *before* it parted.

Although Blyth climbed aloft to do this job, a worn halyard can often be replaced without climbing the mast by marrying (joining end-to-end by sewing, worming, and/or taping) (Figure 11-2) the end of the old halyard with the end of its replacement so that the new halyard can be reeved through its block simply by pulling it through from the deck. Synthetic lines can usually be married by heating and melting their ends so that the ends stick together, but seizing and tape should also be used to insure adhesion. Incidentally, a very crude temporary halyard might be rigged for a storm trysail by throwing a line over a spreader. Chichester used such a method to clear his mizzen staysail halyard on *Gipsy Moth IV* during his 1967 circumnavigation. After trying in vain to shinny up the mast, Sir Francis tied a shackle to the end of a heaving line and threw it over a spreader. This line was then used to pull over the halyard.

British Steel had some galvanized wire halyards which seriously wore or broke, and this brings up the question of whether stainless steel is not the superior material for rigging. Captain John Illingworth, noted authority on rigging, whose firm designed the rig for Alec Rose's *Lively Lady*, specified that her standing rigging be galvanized wire of 7 x 7 construction (seven strands of seven wires each). The argument for such rigging, instead of the usual stainless steel wire of 1 x 19 construction (one strand of 19 wires), is that the 7 x 7 is flexible and can be bent into eyes and spliced (see Figure 11-2). The stainless 1 x 19 wire, however, must use swaged terminal fittings, which are subject to failure as a result of cracks or other defects that are sometimes difficult to detect. On the other hand, properly done swaged fittings are considerably stronger than splices, there is less stretch in the 1 x 19 rigging, and highly reliable methods of inspecting stainless fittings have recently been developed. These inspections include checks with gauges (to detect flat areas and unevenness), magnets, dye or fluorescent penetrants, and even X-rays.

For greatest reliability, especially in tropical waters, many voyagers prefer to use mechanical terminals such as Norseman and Sta-Lok fittings. These can be disassembled and easily reassembled for occasional internal inspections.

Many modern high-tech boats have rod rigging, which has become quite reliable in recent years, but for the greatest dependability and ease of replacement in remote regions, I still prefer wire cable, which usually gives some warning of failure and continues to have some strength even when a few strands have broken. Philippe Jeantot won the rugged 1986–87 BOC Challenge with some broken strands in his rigging. In fact, he's pictured on the cover of a leading magazine standing next to a stranded shroud that I would hesitate to take on an inland cruise, but it held under the toughest conditions.

For running rigging, flexible stainless steel wire of 7 x 19 construction can be bent into eyes and fastened quite reliably with compression sleeves, which can be clamped without difficulty by using a portable hand press. Of course, U-type bullseye clamps (Figure 11-2) can also be used in emergencies. As a matter of fact, Alec Rose had wire splices fail during his circumnavigation, and on two occasions he made very seamanlike temporary repairs with bullseye clamps after bending the wire in eyes around thimbles. Later, in Melbourne, Australia, permanent repairs were made with swaged eyes, and they were said to be entirely satisfactory.

Lively Lady also broke a masthead tang, and designer-author Douglas Phillips-Birt tells us that this was probably due to crystallization and fatigue. Such failures are not uncommon on offshore craft that are subject to prolonged periods of motion, and every effort must be made to prevent or alleviate alternating movements and bending moments on the fittings. This is usually best accomplished with extensive use of rigging toggles, which may come in a variety of designs (see Figure 11-2), but which always function as universal joints to prevent metal fatigue. The safest policy is to use toggles at the top and bottom of any shroud or stay that is subject to alternate motions and stress from various directions. In the case of *Lively Lady*, Phillips-Birt suggests that Rose may have contributed to the tang's failure by putting "an unfair bending load" on it when he cast off one of his twin headstays (topmast forestays in British terminology) and led it aft around the spreader as an emergency substitute for a parted lower shroud. This was a necessary jury arrangement to safeguard against loss of the mast when the shroud broke at its upper splice. Of course, the mast was also endangered when the tang failed, but Rose made a temporary repair by using a masthead halyard as a substitute for the broken headstay until he could reach the nearest port where a new tang could be fitted.

As mentioned in Chapter 5, twin headstays are often considered a boon to the singlehander, for in addition to providing backup mast support, they enable him to change jibs with a minimum of effort. There are drawbacks with the rig, however, due to possible jamming of hanks, chafe on the jib's luff, and difficulties in keeping an equal tension on each stay. One method of overcoming the latter problem, tried by Mike McMullen on his *Binkie II*, was with the use of a U-bolt to which each twin stay was attached at the stemhead (Chapter 5). The rig was not entirely successful, however, since the U-bolt broke during the 1972 transatlantic race. McMullen replaced the broken fitting with a spare, but it caused him considerable anxiety for the rest of the passage. He wrote, "I sailed with the constant threat of it [the U-bolt] breaking again, and had it happened I would have been hard pressed to finish." The use of a triangular plate at the bottom of the twin stays connecting them to a single turnbuckle has proven quite satisfactory in many cases (see Figure 5-7).

Women have also made amazing repairs aloft. During the 1986 Route du Rhum race, Florence Arthaud reportedly climbed her 90-foot mast hand-over-hand to repair a broken halyard.

New Zealand circumnavigator Naomi James made a difficult repair that involved bolting on a jury shroud tang from a bosun's chair. Although Naomi was not entirely satisfied with her jury rig, it was strong enough to keep the mast intact when her *Express Crusader* capsized in the Southern Ocean.

Even more remarkable was the repair made by 43-year-old Teresa Remiszewska during an OSTAR. In mid-ocean, Teresa noticed a crack in her wooden mast near the upper spreaders. Hoisting a rope ladder with wooden steps, she removed the spreaders, resecured them at a lower position on the mast, and then shortened and readjusted the rigging to tighten the shrouds. The operation took an entire week.

The singlehander who suffered the most rigging failures without losing the mast would have to be Alain Gerbault in *Firecrest*. His sails constantly ripped or blew out, running and standing rigging parted, and gear often broke or partially failed. These problems were primarily due to inadequate preparations, for his equipment was old and tired, even rotten, at the time he cast off. Of course, he had more than his share of heavy weather, and it could truthfully be said that the cotton sails used in Gerbault's time were not as strong as those made of modern synthetics. Nevertheless, a suit of cotton sails carried John Guzzwell around the world without any major failures over a period of about four years. Gerbault showed poor judgment in fitting out his boat, but we must give him credit for outstanding endurance and seamanship in overcoming many of his problems.

On one occasion, in the South Seas, he had to claw off a lee shore in heavy weather. When he had made almost enough offing, the mainsail split at a seam. Gerbault was forced to lower the sail and hurriedly sew up the seam before his boat drifted onto a coral reef to leeward. He finished the job just in time to avoid a serious grounding.

Another time, the end of his bowsprit broke and Gerbault was forced to make a difficult jury repair, which involved cutting a slot in the end of the broken sprit, inserting an iron pin, and rigging a new bobstay. The latter was the hardest job of all, as it involved cutting a piece from the anchor chain and shackling it to *Firecrest*'s stem at a point just below the waterline. To accomplish this, Gerbault had to hang head down from the bowsprit while repeatedly being deeply submerged by the boat's pitching. He described himself as being alternately dipped and brought up "dripping and sputtering to repeat the dose again and again."

Gerbault's trials obviously show us the importance of having sound gear, plenty of extra fittings, and spare rigging, including extra chain suitable for emergency repairs. Furthermore, the experience with the broken bowsprit points up the value of having halyard downhauls, because when the break occurred it was necessary to hand sail promptly to avoid losing the mast. Wind pressure held the mainsail so firmly against the rigging that Gerbault had to rig a purchase to the downhaul to lower it. He could not luff up to relieve the wind pressure on account of the slack headstay (due to the broken bowsprit), which gave no forward support to the top of the mast.

Another singlehander who experienced bowsprit problems was Bernard Moitessier. During his circumnavigation (Chapter 2), a ship approached to receive his written message, came too close, and damaged the rig of his ketch *Joshua*. The heavy steel bowsprit was severely bent and it seemed impossible for one man alone at sea to make the repair. Moitessier tried, nevertheless, and after careful planning used a four-part tackle, large winch, and a gin pole to pull the bowsprit straight. The repair was a complete success and the Frenchman wrote of his exuberance: "Incredible, the power of a tackle on a winch—I feel I am going to cry, it's so beautiful—the bowsprit begins to straighten out, very, very slowly. I am wild with joy!"

A totally different and less serious problem but one that can cause a singlehander no end of trouble, is the jamming of a halyard aloft. This is usually caused by the halyard jumping over the lip of its sheave and becoming jammed between the sheave and the shell of its block or wall of its sheave box. When such a jam occurs, sail can neither be lowered nor further hoisted, and forcibly hauling on the halyard only increases the jam. Robin Knox-Johnston experienced this difficulty in heavy weather during his circumnavigation. It was essential that the mainsail be lowered because the *Suhaili* was threatening to broach, but the boat's motion made it impossible to climb aloft to unshackle the halyard. Robin solved the problem temporarily by slacking the luff of the roller-reefed sail by unrolling three turns off the boom and then hauling the outboard end of the boom up against the mast and frapping the mainsail to its spars. In his book, *A World of My Own*, Robin does not give details of the frapping operation, but I assume that he used the fall of a halyard to wind around the mast, boom, and sail, in effect, brailing the whole affair from the deck.

The jamming problem is best avoided by having a sufficiently deep groove in a sheave intended for wire with the narrowest possible space between the sheave and its housing, by using wire of a proper size, and by using fairleads to keep the halyards where they belong. In addition, there should be a separator between the side-by-side sheaves, and stops on halyards to prevent their eyes or end fittings from being pulled into their sheaves. Robin's experience also points out once again the value of a proper topping lift that is controllable from the deck.

Naturally, it makes sense for a singlehander to be as sure as possible that his rigging is sound and free of chafe before he gets underway. The rubbing of lines and sails cannot be stopped entirely, but it should be minimized with reinforcing patches on sails, baggywrinkle, fairleads, straps of shock cord, and constant vigilance. Before he embarked on his 'round-the-world voyage, Chay Blyth was so concerned about chafe prevention that in the boatyard in which his *British Steel* was being fitted out, he was given the nickname of "Chafe Bligh." It was this kind of attention to detail that helped him complete one of the most difficult voyages of all time.

Dismasting

The rigging failures described so far did not result in the loss of a mast, but sometimes when a vital fitting, shroud, or stay breaks, the whole rig will go by the board. This situation can be a desperate one for the singlehander and may demand the highest level of seamanship. The victim of such an accident must first of all clear up the wreckage and prevent the broken mast from battering a hole in the hull, and then he must either call for help, use his auxiliary power, or construct a jury rig that will allow him to limp to the nearest port. If he is rescued by a ship, he may have to abandon his boat unless she is small enough to be taken aboard the ship. In some cases, the boat might be taken in tow, but this usually necessitates her being towed faster than her hull speed (about 1.35 times the square root of her waterline length for a displacement hull), and serious damage is apt to result. In fact, bandleader-singlehander Bob Miller lost his sloop *Mersea Pearl* in just this way while she was being towed by a merchant ship at 15 knots following his dismasting in the 1972 OSTAR. Gerbault's famous *Firecrest* was lost in a similar manner.

Unless a dismasted boat is quite near other vessels so that flares can be seen, she must depend on her radio to call for help. A boat equipped with a radiotelephone often uses her backstay for the antenna, and, of course, after the mast breaks, the radio is put out of commission. This happened to Bob Miller and also to Murray Sayle aboard the ketch-rigged *Lady of Fleet* in the same race. Miller was able to rig a jury antenna by erecting a nine-foot plank which he screwed to the topsides, while Sayle managed to salvage his antenna from the broken mainmast and rig it to the mizzen mast. Sayle was also taken in tow, but his boat survived being pulled at high speeds, primarily because she was a catamaran and could plane easily.

Another possible risk in using the backstay for an antenna is that the stay may be weakened by insulators. Sandy Munro on the catamaran *Ocean Highlander* lost his mast for this reason during the 1968 OSTAR. Unbeknownst to Munro, the insulators used were about half as strong as those specified. It is a wise plan to use egg-type insulators (Figure 11-2) that prevent sharp bends in the wire and allow the part of the stay above and below the insulator to remain connected in the event that the insulator should break. Also, incidentally, it is not the safest practice to bend a non-flexible 1 x 19 stay around in a loop to fasten it to an insulator. The better construction for looping is 7 x 7 wire (see Figure 11-2). To enable radio transmission after a dismasting, many offshore sailors carry whip antennas that are independent of the rigging, although they are less efficient. All boats, particularly those not equipped with single sideband or ham radios, should carry EPIRBs (Chapter 8), which continuously send out distress signals on emergency frequencies when the beacons are activated. One of these devices brought help to Alan Gick in 1971 when his 19-foot *Cockle* was dismasted at sea after she had capsized during an informal transatlantic race against two sister boats (Chapter 10). Many others, particularly capsized multihull sailors, have been rescued through the use of EPIRBs in more recent times.

Bob Salmon and his 24-foot sloop *Justa Listang* were taken aboard a ship after a dismasting following the failure of a shroud tang during the 1972 OSTAR. The rescue did not take place, however, until about four days after the accident, and Salmon had the opportunity to set up and use an effective jury rig. Having two spinnaker poles, he was able to make an A-frame by securing the end of each pole near the chainplates and clipping their opposite ends to a metal ring. Then he rigged a forestay and twin backstays that were secured to the same ring, and the A-frame was pulled to the vertical position with the backstays. His sail consisted of an inverted jib hanked to the forestay. It had no halyard but was set or handed by raising or lowering the A-frame. Salmon said the sail worked well downwind, and it helped steady the boat's motion, which was exceedingly quick with the sail down. Incidentally, the shroud tang that caused the dismasting failed in a mere Force 3 or 4 breeze after having survived much stronger blows, including a Force 9 gale. Thus it seems that metal fatigue was responsible. Again we are reminded of the importance of preventing fittings from bending with the use of adequate toggles or by other means.

Perhaps the most remarkable experience involving an improvised A-frame was that of Canadian master mariner John Hughes during the second BOC Challenge. John's 41-foot sloop *Joseph Young* was dismasted 4,000 miles from South America. The mast broke at a usually vulnerable spot just above the gooseneck, where a lot of holes are customarily drilled or cut into a mast. Hughes devised an

Galway Blazer II under jury rig after her capsize and loss of foremast. Notice the A-frame supporting the headsail. (Nautical Publishing Company; from *Capsize* by Bill King)

A-frame similar to Salmon's by lashing together two spinnaker poles and was able to round Cape Horn under tiny sails hoisted from the joined poles. He sailed for 45 days, covering 4,400 miles under jury rig before reaching the Falkland Islands, where he put in for repairs. There he had to wait a lengthy period for a new mast, but he made it back to the race's finish at Newport, Rhode Island in time for the awards ceremony. It is amazing that the flimsy rig, supported only by a cat's cradle of lines and with the pole ends planted in two rag-filled coffee cans, could survive a couple of knockdowns off Cape Horn. Hughes was rightfully given a hero's welcome when he returned home.

Bill King also used an A-frame jury rig after being dismasted following a capsize in his Chinese-lug-rigged schooner *Galway Blazer II* during the Golden Globe Race for singlehanders in 1968. Actually, King's emergency rig was a permanently-installed bipod of aluminum poles, hinged to the deck, which lay flat when not in use but could be hauled upright after a dismasting. During the capsize, *Blazer* lost her foremast, but the stayless mainmast, made (like the foremast) of spruce sheathed in fiberglass, was left standing. It was bent, but was partially usable. King's first job was to cut away the broken foremast before it pounded a hole in the hull. Then, after waiting for wind and seas to subside, he erected the bipod, which carried a small jib, and hoisted a few panels of the fully battened mainsail. The latter sail was hoisted on the bent mainmast, but had that mast gone by the board, there were provisions for hoisting on the bipod a lug sail that could

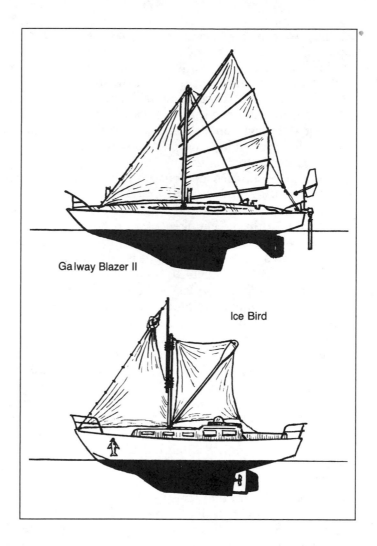

Figure 11-3. Jury rigs.

be used in conjunction with the jib (see Figure 11-3). The lower ends of the bipod were fastened to slides on tracks running for a limited distance fore and aft on each side of the boat in order that the jury rig's position could be shifted longitudinally for the best possible balance.

King had been capsized and dismasted by huge, confused seas following a gale in an area 1,100 miles southwest of Cape Town, South Africa. Fortunately he did not have to sail the entire distance to port under jury rig. He radioed for help and was towed the last 200 miles to Cape Town by the 52-foot ketch *Corsair II*, which came out from Cape Town especially for the purpose.

Another of several boats dismasted by capsizing was Jean Gau's double-ended ketch *Atom*, which was tumbled by a "freak" wave not far from the Cape of Good Hope in 1966 (Chapter 10). The capsizing left *Atom*'s rig a complete shambles with both masts and her bowsprit broken and overboard but tethered by their rigging. After he had recovered from the initial shock of the accident, Gau set to work cutting away the rig, because the spars were pounding the boat and threatening to sink her. He worked in total darkness with the boat rolling violently and heavy seas washing over the deck, while hurricane force winds nearly tore off his clothes and took away his breath. For three hours he worked on the rigging with a hacksaw and pliers. At one point a wave tore the hacksaw from his hands and it was lost overboard. A South African sailor who spoke to Gau soon after the misadventure told me that the singlehander continued cutting the wire with pliers and a hacksaw blade held between his fingers. At any rate, *Atom* was saved and she reached port under her auxiliary engine.

Gau's experience demonstrates another advantage of an auxiliary engine which is kept in good working order, and also shows the wisdom of carrying suitable tools for cutting away the rigging. There are times when a singlehander will not be able to bring a broken spar on board, and, if it is damaging the hull, it will have to be cut loose. Heavy-duty rigging cutters are recommended, but a good hacksaw can also do the job and it is not a bad idea to carry a spare.

During the 1964 OSTAR, Mike Ellison suffered a dismasting similar to King's when his lug-rigged *Ilala* lost her unstayed foremast in confused seas following a gale. The whipping mast broke off about five feet above the deck. Although the mainmast was left standing, a previously broken halyard block limited the use of that mast. The block had fallen because its bronze eye had worn through. Ellison had difficulty climbing the mast because of the motion, and, according to one account, his rope ladder was too short to reach the truck. Using a spare halyard that was insufficient to carry the full load of the mainsail, he devised a way of hauling aloft a new main halyard block with a strap around the mast. When the block was aloft, Ellison could pull on the new main halyard and tighten the strap so that it would not slide down the tapered mast. With this rig he could hoist four-fifths of the mainsail. Then with a long oar he erected a jury foremast that could carry three panels of the foresail. With this flimsy rig he limped 1,500 miles to Newport, Rhode Island, arriving there almost a month after his dismasting.

It would seem that large, unstayed masts are rather prone to breakage. Mike Ellison commented, "A lot of homework will have to be done before large unstayed masts become reliable and generally acceptable." Yet *Jester*'s smaller, unstayed mast survived 12 Atlantic voyages before breaking when *Jester* was rolled in a North Atlantic gale. *Lady Pepperell*'s freestanding carbon fiber masts survived a pitchpoling in the first BOC Challenge. In one respect unstayed masts are more reliable because they do not depend on fittings that can break. In steep, confused seas following a gale, which can cause violent rolling and possibly a capsizing (as in Bill King's case), it may be advisable to set substantial sail at once to dampen roll, steady the masts and control steering. Ellison's experience also demonstrates the vulnerability of bronze fittings to abrasion, the value of mast-climbing equipment, and the wisdom of carrying spare halyards.

Many singlehanders have been dismasted, but few have suffered more from this problem than has Dr. David Lewis. He lost his mast (not for the first time) shortly after the start of the 1960 OSTAR. A windward spreader failed on his 25-foot *Cardinal Vertue* and caused the wooden mast to break just above the spreader sockets. Lewis got the broken mast aboard before it damaged the hull, and despite the boat's violent rolling, he shinnied up the mast stump and secured to its top a couple of blocks for halyards. The doctor had religiously practiced climbing the mast before the race, and now his preparedness was paying off, because he had to climb the gyrating stump twice and lash the blocks in place while hanging on with one hand. With the mainsail scandalized and with a double-head rig, consisting of a trysail and a number three staysail, the *Cardinal Vertue* had a fairly efficient jury rig that allowed her to sail back to Plymouth, where the race had begun. A new mast was made in record time, and Lewis set off again two days later to cross the Atlantic successfully and take a third place in the race.

Three years later, on a voyage to Iceland and back in the catamaran *Rehu Moana* with crew aboard, Lewis was twice dismasted. These accidents were due mostly to the fact that he was using experimental rigs. Undoubtedly the intrepid doctor's worst dismasting, however, occurred when he capsized three times on his attempted solo circumnavigation of Antarctica. Twice he was rolled over in late 1972 on the passage from New Zealand to Palmer Station, and the accident was repeated in early 1974 on a passage from Antarctica to Cape Town where the adventure was finally terminated. After each dismasting Lewis was able to make jury rigs and carry on alone despite incredible adversities.

On the first occasion, he was in the latitude of the Screaming Sixties, to the south of that point on earth which is most distant from land. A depression had actually dropped the barometer's pointer off its scale (about 28 inches), and winds were estimated at 100 miles an hour, while seas reached heights of 40 feet. It was so cold that the temperature was below freezing inside the boat, which was appropriately named the *Ice Bird*, and the drinking water was frozen in its keel tank. In these appalling conditions, the 32-foot steel sloop was smashed and rolled completely over, through 360 degrees, by a breaking sea. She righted but was half-filled with water, the mast was down, broken off about seven feet above the deck, the cabin house of ⅛-inch steel had a large split, and the forward hatch (not being flush) was wrenched loose by a shroud that fouled it.

Lewis literally had to fight for his life. He pulled the sprung hatch nearly closed with a tackle and then emptied the bilge while water continued to spurt through the hatch and cabin split when the boat rolled. It has been said that there is no bilge pump as efficient as one scared man with a bucket, but Lewis spent more than six hours bailing with a bucket to drain *Ice Bird*. Later, with frost-bitten hands, he unscrewed the turnbuckles and cast off the broken rig. When the blow abated, he set up a very inadequate jury rig consisting of a spinnaker pole supporting a knotted storm jib. The makeshift mast kept breaking away until it was all but worthless.

Two weeks after her first capsizing, *Ice Bird* was rolled over again in a Force 11 storm. This time, however, damage was not so extensive and there was less water in the bilge, partly because the ventilators were stuffed with rags. About one week later, the doctor devised a satisfactory jury rig. He made a new mast from the heavy main boom, which was just under 12 feet long. Raising it was no easy task for one man with injured hands working on a violently rolling deck. Incidentally, a mastless boat's rolling motion can sometimes be slowed by moving heavy weights such as anchors, ballast, and water containers to the top of the cabin trunk. He raised the mast by fitting one end of the boom into the mast step on deck while the other end rested in the erected boom crutch, and then rigging a line from the top

Dr. David Lewis' *Ice Bird* with her jury mast after her third capsizing during the attempt to circumnavigate Australia. (Photo by Margo Mackay)

of the boom to the bow and back aft to a halyard winch. Guys were rigged to hold the jury mast steady, and then it was winched up to the vertical position. The new spar was able to carry a trysail and jib. Under this rig, Lewis sailed 2,500 miles to Palmer Station, where he arrived at night after threading his way through floating ice and rocks, to make fast alongside Jacques Cousteau's oceanographic vessel, the *Calypso*.

The third capsizing took place about 800 miles southwest of Cape Town. A new mast fitted in Antarctica went by the board and again Lewis erected the boom. He even extended its length by lashing a spar to it as a sort of topmast. A long oar served as a sprit to hold out the peak of the jury mainsail. A fair-sized jib was also carried on a stay running from the stem to the topmast. With this rig and without the benefits of a self-steering gear or an engine, because they were inoperable, Lewis took three weeks to reach Cape Town. Surely *Ice Bird*'s passage from New Zealand to South Africa via Antarctica was one of the most remarkable solo voyages of all times, and Lewis must be considered not only an extraordinary seaman but also one of the foremost experts on dismastings and jury rigs.

Sickness and Injury

Life at sea in a small boat is a healthy one, but even the heartiest sailor is subject to sickness or accidents. A disabling illness or injury could be disastrous for a singlehander far offshore. Precautions against debilitation would obviously include exercising special care when working the boat; carrying and using proper safety equipment (Chapter 8); keeping up one's health with good diet, rest, and proper clothing; carrying adequate medical supplies and instruction books (Chapter 9); prior thought on avoidance and treatment of common physical ailments; and prior basic instructions from a doctor (or medical book) on self-treatment. Common afflictions are injuries from falls, burns from cooking, injuries resulting from spar or fitting failures, cuts from using a knife or tools, rope burns, infections, salt-water sores, seasickness, sunburn, heat exhaustion, food poisoning, fever, sprains, toothache, etc.

It is highly advisable that a solo voyager have a thorough physical examination before setting forth, but it is amazing how casual about this sort of thing some singlehanders can be. For instance, Robin Knox-Johnston told an interviewer from *Rudder* magazine that he never conferred with his doctor or dentist before he left on his non-stop solo circumnavigation, which lasted 10½ months. Even when the sailor enjoys uncommonly good health, a thorough physical can detect a latent malady that might occur at sea. A case in point is Peter Tangvald, an occasional singlehander who suffered a heart attack offshore but fortunately when there was a companion on board. For five days Tangvald lay in his bunk, crippled with pain and unable to work the boat. Also, I have heard of a few elderly shorthanded sailors suffering from prostate gland enlargement resulting in inability to urinate. Sailors with prostate problems or with past histories of urinary infections should be sure to check with their doctors and carry a catheter with instructions for use before embarking on a voyage.

A source of worry for some is the threat of appendicitis. More than one offshore sailor has had his appendix removed before going on a cruise, even when it had caused no previous trouble. This is an extreme precaution, however, that many people are not willing to take. There is the well-known case of William A. Robinson, who nearly lost his life from an acute attack of appendicitis after cruising shorthanded to the Galapagos Islands in 1934. Nowadays, we have antibiotics that may cure, or at least inhibit, serious infections. It is of some comfort to read in Dr. Paul Sheldon's book, *First Aid Afloat:* "On antibiotic treatment alone in 41 consecutive cases of later proven appendicitis at sea on ships without doctors not one life was lost." Dr. Sheldon goes on to say, however, that in some cases surgery might have to be done later. During his circumnavigation, Robin Knox-Johnston had a severe abdominal pain that he feared was appendicitis. It lasted for four days but turned out to be only indigestion, according to Robin. Had it been appendicitis, he would have been out of luck, since he was a thousand miles from the nearest "decent" port, and, surprisingly, he carried no antibiotics.

Vito Dumas could have used some modern antibiotics (though he did have a disinfectant which was administered by injections) when his arm became horribly infected in 1942 during his solo circumnavigation. The arm became grotesquely swollen and almost unbearably painful. Dumas developed a high fever and became so desperate that he seriously considered amputation. In his book *Alone Through the Roaring Forties,* he vividly described the predicament: "A decision had to be made. That night must be the last with my arm in this condition. Land? I could not reach land in time. If by tomorrow things had not improved, I would have to amputate this useless arm, slung around my neck and already smelling of decay. It was dying and dragging me along with it. It was septicaemia. I could not give in without playing my last card.

"There were several suppurating open wounds in the hands, but I could not localize the septic focus in this formless mass. With an axe, or my seaman's knife, at the elbow, at the shoulder, I knew not where or how, somehow I would have to amputate."

This hair-raising incident ended happily, though, for Dumas fell asleep (or passed out), and while he was unconscious the infected arm burst open and drained itself. Amputation was no longer considered necessary and several days later the courageous singlehander had almost fully recovered.

Pain killers as well as antibiotics can be extremely valuable, if not essential. As Sir Alec Rose, who suffered from a bad back, has said, "nothing exhausts one so quickly as pain." Proper pain killers might have spared Leonid Teliga some excruciating suffering during his circumnavigation. During the voyage on his yawl *Opty,* Teliga was struck in the abdomen with a boom, which reportedly helped develop or accelerate cancer. The brave sailor, who died not very long after he rounded the world, said almost nothing about his affliction, but his log reveals that the cancer developed rapidly and caused such terrible pain that he tried to seek relief by chewing on his blanket, and during one series of paroxysms he seemed to lose his mind for several days.

Although some pain killers are extremely effective, the singlehander must be careful that what he takes will not dull his sensibilities, cause unwanted sleep, or adversely affect his judgment. Dr. David Lewis gave this warning when he compiled a list of medical supplies for the participants in the 1960 singlehanded transatlantic race; "Morphia may so impair judgment that for a lone sailor who has to rely on himself, it is rather a means towards suicide than a treatment." Lewis suggested aminode hydrochloride for severe pain, but it would be wise for the singlehander to consult with his own doctor.

Minor pain killers should be taken for the relief of such ailments as headaches and bad teeth. More than a few singlehanders have been afflicted with persistent toothaches. William Andrews, for instance, was bothered to such an extent on his voyage in *Sapolio* that he pulled out his own tooth with a pair of pliers. In modern times, Bill Homewood suffered from a dental condition that gave him persistent headaches during the 1984 OSTAR. Obviously, the ocean voyager would do well to visit a dentist before casting off and carry a dental kit with instructions.

The determination and courage of some singlehanders to carry on when they have serious physical ailments is sometimes incredible. Aside from the cases of cancer victims Leonid Teliga, Walter Koenig and Francis Chichester, mentioned in Chapter 2, there is the unpublicized example of Commander George Farley, who, after being discharged from the Royal Navy because he had diabetes, crossed the North Atlantic alone in the stormy month of September 1966 aboard his 23-foot sloop *Dawn Star.* He had the most difficult task of giving himself daily injections of insulin, which included boiling the needle while the boat was tossed about by continuous heavy weather consisting of a procession of lows, four full gales, and a

Leonid Teliga aboard *Opty.* Although he suffered excruciating pain from a rapidly developing cancer, Teliga managed to complete his singlehanded circumnavigation. (Photo by Donald R. Holm)

hurricane. On an earlier cruise, he almost lost his life when his supply of insulin went bad from excessively hot weather.

Injuries from accidents are not uncommon, but fortunately they are seldom completely disabling. This was hardly true for Jerry Cartwright, however, when he was thrown out of his bunk during the 1969 transpacific race for singlehanders. Jerry turned in one night without securing his bunk board, and when his 29-foot sloop *Scuffler II* was hit by a gust that caused her to round up and drop off a wave, he became airborne. Landing on his head against the bunk on the boat's opposite side, he sustained a serious blow that resulted in a concussion (subsequent X-rays revealed a long crack around the right side of his skull). The next three weeks were a nightmare for Jerry. He suffered from deafness in one ear, vertigo, lapses in memory, and almost continuous nausea with prolonged periods of vomiting and consequently dehydration. It is a great credit to his courage, tenacity, and seamanship that he was able to carry on alone and reach Hawaii, where he was promptly hospitalized.

Jerry admits to making a mistake in not securing himself in his bunk. He wrote, "I forgot a prime rule of the sea—constant vigilance." Very often rules are obvious, and it is easy to give lip service to them, but how difficult it is to live by them with never a moment of laxity or carelessness. Experiences like Jerry's remind us in a general way of the need for extra caution when alone and specifically of the need for proper, easy-operable bunk boards or lee cloths (perhaps even automobile-type seat belts), adequate hand rails above and below deck, safety belts, and lanyards with adequate places to snap on, skid-proof surfaces, and a minimum of clutter and fittings on deck that can cause tripping (see Chapter 8).

Of special value to a disabled singlehander is a reliable self-steering device. Cartwright said, "I remember feeling a profound sense of gratitude for that steering vane." (It was a Gunning pendulum type, by the way.) Of course, there is one situation when the self-steerer could be a decided disadvantage, and that would be if the singlehander should happen to fall overboard. There is the story of one solo sailor who deliberately dove off the bow of his boat and surfaced in time to grab her stern, but taking such chances seems tantamount to playing Russian roulette. Even in calm weather a self-steering boat could easily catch a puff of wind and leave her swimming master floundering in her wake.

Dr. Alain Bombard had a close call of this kind during his bold Atlantic crossing in the rubber dinghy *L'Hérétique* when he lost a cushion overboard and dove in to recover it, even though he took the precaution of lowering sail and putting out a sea anchor. After reaching the cushion, he turned around and saw his boat drifting away faster than he could swim. The sea anchor, which was a parachute type, had fouled its lines in such a way that it had collapsed and was causing little drag. Despite the fact that Bombard had been a champion swimmer, he could not reach the boat until, luckily, the lines became untangled and allowed the parachute to open. The safest policy for a singlehander who insists on swimming is not only to lower sail, but also to attach himself to the boat with a line and also to rig a boarding ladder, because there have been cases of swimmers who were too exhausted to pull themselves aboard. Of course, there is also the added danger of sharks, which can appear very suddenly.

No one knows how many singlehanders have accidentally fallen overboard while their boats were self-steered. There are probably not many of these accidents, but derelict boats of solo sailors are occasionally found, as in the case of the boat of John Pflieger, Commodore of the Slocum Society Sailing Club, who most probably fell overboard while sailing his *Stella Maris* from Bermuda to St. Martin in 1966. In more recent times Mike Flanagan, Jacques de Roux, and Loic Caradec were lost overboard. Many others have been washed overboard and pulled themselves back aboard by their safety harness lanyard.

One extremely lucky solo sailor was Fred Wood, who was knocked overboard when his boat *Windsong* accidentally jibed during a passage from Tahiti to Hawaii. Fortunately, Wood was a strong swimmer, and he happened to be only five miles from Christmas Island when the accident occurred. It took him seven hours to reach the island, and then he had to pick his way through a jagged coral reef before landing. He managed to keep away from the dangerous surf by listening to the differences in sound produced by the breaking waves.

As mentioned in Chapter 8, a means of reducing the hazard of being left astern by a self-steering boat after a fall overboard is to tow a long tripping line that will disengage the self-steering gear when it is pulled. Very often it is possible to grab a long line towed astern when it is floating and has a rescue quoit or buoy attached.

Life Raft Survival

Occasionally, lone sailors have finished their voyages in a life raft or lifeboat after the mother ship has sunk. One of the longest trials of endurance was experienced by Steve Callahan after his 21-foot sloop *Napoleon Solo* collided with a submerged object after withdrawing from the 1982 Mini Transat race and sank 450 miles west of the Canary Islands. Steve climbed into his six-man Avon life raft and for the next 76 days drifted 1,800 miles southwest to the island of Marie Galante in the West Indies.

Inflatable dinghies or rafts of heavy-duty nylon coated with hypalon or neo-prene (synthetic rubber) are extremely durable, but they must be protected from chafe, as, for example, where the sea-anchor line leads over the bow. Dr. Bombard tells us that his dinghy needed slight deflation during hot days to allow for expansion of the air inside. He also thinks a wood flooring inside an inflatable dinghy is very important. Some of the better life rafts have an air chamber in the bottom for comfort and insulation. An important feature is stability pockets or a large water ballast bag to keep the raft from capsizing, but in warm waters far from land or shipping lanes you want a stability system that allows mobility under sail.

Thirst, starvation, and exposure pose grave threats to the survival of castaways. A controversy has existed about drinking sea water ever since Dr. Alain Bombard made his celebrated solo Atlantic crossing in the inflatable rubber dinghy *L'Hérétique* in 1952 without food or water to prove that man can live off the sea itself. Certain French authorities on survival endorsed Bombard's theories, but many British and American authorities disagree and are adamant that a castaway should never drink sea water under any circumstances.

Actually, I think that at least some of the controversy stems from a misunderstanding of the French doctor. He never claimed that sea water could entirely replace fresh water as a drink, but rather argued that very small amounts could be drunk to augment fresh water or to replace it temporarily over a short period of time before dehydration has begun. He also reasoned that the amount of salt consumed by drinking sea water should not exceed the normal amount taken in when eating ordinary meals and using it for seasoning. He wrote, "I would consume the permissible daily intake of salt by swallowing it in sea water." Although Bombard admitted, "Everyone knows that sea water is dangerous," he claimed "the essential thing, therefore, is to maintain the body's water content at its proper level during the first few days before fish can be caught. The only solution is to drink sea water." But he warned, "It is essential not to wait for dehydration before drinking sea water." Bombard's fresh water came from catching rain, from condensation, and especially from squeezing the juice out of fish, which he did with a fruit press.

Dr. Hannes Lindemann, who seemed to make his Atlantic crossing in the Foldboat partially for the purpose of disproving the Bombard theory, concluded that salt water should not be drunk unless there is sufficient fresh water on board. He wrote, "A small amount of salt water may be drunk as a salt replacement, but that is all."

Regardless of the controversy and the fact that some doctors feel Bombard has done more harm than good, the courageous Frenchman undoubtedly made some contributions. He demonstrated that it is possible to survive for long periods at sea without supplies of food and water (whether he did it because of, or in spite of, his theories), and that should give encouragement to all castaways. He showed that a sufficient catch of fish can supply a surprising amount of water (when a press is carried) as well as proteins and fats. Eating plankton, which he caught in a fine-mesh net, can supply enough Vitamin C to stave off scurvy. Incidentally, Francis Brenton, who ran out of food while crossing the Atlantic in an outrigger canoe in 1967, also ate plankton as well as barnacles, eelgrass, and mushrooms that grew inside his boat. He suffered no serious ill effects from this diet, but it should be pointed out that many survival experts warn against eating plankton because certain types have spines that may cause irritation, and there is a possibility that poisonous dinoflagellates could be consumed. Bombard caught fish with a home-made harpoon and also had some success using hooks baited with flying fish that fell on board. He found that a light at night would sometimes bring "an absolute shower of fish."

Some lessons can be learned from Poon Lim, who survived a record-setting 133 days alone on a life raft in the South Atlantic (1942–43). Lim caught small minnows by baiting a hook made from a flashlight spring with a barnacle. Then he caught large fish, up to 20 pounds, on a large hook made from a nail, which he baited with a minnow. He put the large hook through the minnow's tail so that the bait fish remained alive and wriggling. For water, Lim caught rain in an awning suspended from four uprights at each corner of his square raft. Birds were occasionally snared when they lit on top of the awning.

In summation, a few general conclusions might be drawn from the studies of survival experts and the experiences of castaways:

Sea water should not be drunk except for perhaps a very limited amount (some say a pint a day) to augment an ample fresh supply. Salt intake should not exceed the amount normally consumed. Sea water should never be taken when a person is dehydrated. Even advocates of drinking sea water say that it should not be consumed for longer than five days at a time. When there is a lot of salt lost from the body through sweating, the occasional drinking of a limited amount of sea water will do no harm, and it may be helpful in replacing lost salt, provided fresh water is also drunk to clear the kidneys. John Voss drank a glass of sea water a day for his health, and Chichester occasionally did the same after a great deal of sweating in order to alleviate cramps in his leg muscles.

Sea water may be desalted with a chemical kit containing briquettes of silver aluminum silicate, with a solar still, or with a Gore watermaker, a filtration system which makes use of ambient temperature differences between the air and the sea water. The solar still consists of an inflatable plastic sphere, which contains a black cloth that absorbs the sun's heat and causes condensation through evaporation of sea water in a storage compartment. The device is capable of producing a maximum of two pints of fresh water per sunny day. Steve Callahan had three solar stills in his life raft, and they saved his life. Each one produced an average of $1\frac{1}{4}$ pints of water per day and lasted for about 25 days before wearing out.

If water is scarce, little if any food should be eaten, as digestion uses up body fluids. Some experts say that the consuming of protein requires the drinking of two pints of fresh water on the same day.

Exposure and despair are the greatest enemies of shipwreck victims. Those who perish usually do so not because they starve to death or die of thirst, but because they lack proper protection from the wind, water, and sun, or because their morale breaks down, and they lose the will to fight for their lives. A canopy or cover and warm clothes provide the best protection from exposure, while the spirit can be bolstered with survival knowledge, having a definite plan of action, and keeping reasonably busy. Many standard life rafts contain (or should contain) survival manuals along with emergency supplies and a pilot chart showing currents, prevailing winds, and steamer lanes.

After the castaway is rescued, he may drink a moderate amount of fluids but he must take solid food very gradually. Gorging on rich food immediately after the ordeal could cause serious illness, or even death.

A demonstration by Joshua Slocum of his emergency still for producing a limited amount of fresh water. A fire under the bucket of sea water produced steam, which was then cooled by evaporation. (Courtesy of *Yachting* magazine)

A final word on abandoning ship is not to do it unless it is certain the vessel is about to founder. Many times boats have been needlessly abandoned because their crews felt that sinking was imminent, but days later the derelicts have been found afloat even though their bilge pumps were unmanned. Complete preparations should be made for abandonment during a serious emergency, but the actual drastic step should not be taken until, perhaps, the decks are all but awash. There is a saying that you should step *up* into a life raft from your sinking boat.

Every offshore skipper of a fully crewed vessel should take heed of Murphy's law, which states: "If anything can go wrong, it will." For the lone sailor preparing to set forth on an extended voyage in rough waters, it will be most prudent if he thinks in terms of what my wife calls Henderson's law: If anything *can't* go wrong, it will.

PART IV

Singlehanding for Everyone

Tania Aebi, who set off as an inexperienced 18-year old, emerged from her circumnavigation as a mature, confident sailor. (Photo by Susan Thorpe)

12

Gaining
Singlehanded Experience

WE CAN'T ALL BE SLOCUMS OR Chichesters, and I'm sure that many sailors have no particular desire to emulate the masters. There seems little doubt, however, that many an avid sailor would enjoy an occasional sail or weekend cruise alone just for the satisfaction of doing it or because the right crew is hard to find. Maybe crew is available, but they are inexperienced, so in effect, it is necessary to handle the boat alone.

Let us suppose that you have a small stock cruiser (about 30 to 35 feet long) not specifically modified for singlehanded sailing, and you want to take her out alone. You are new at singlehanded sailing and are a bit nervous about the possibility of getting into trouble and making a spectacle of yourself. The answer to this worry is thorough preparation and careful planning ahead.

Preparing For Your First Solo Sail

To begin with, see that your boat is properly equipped. A few items of special importance for singlehanding are sheets that are within easy reach of the helm; steering lines and/or means of locking the helm; a proper adjustable topping lift leading to the masthead (not a short strop securing the boom to the backstay); adequate clearance between the boom and backstay (not always the case); stowage compartments or lockers near the helm; decks clear of unnecessary gear or fittings that could cause tripping or fouling of lines; all engine controls near the helm; sheet winches (preferably the self-tailing kind) near the helm; suitable headsails that allow good visibility; a steering compass that may also be used for taking bearings; a long, lightweight boathook; and a handy place to stow the anchor (perhaps on the bow pulpit or a stemhead roller chock) where it will be out of the way but available for instant use.

There are a number of ways to simplify setting, reefing, and furling sails. First of all, if you plan on doing a lot of solo sailing, I would order sails made of fairly soft Dacron with a minimal resin filler because today's standard sail cloth is extremely stiff and slippery, making it difficult for one person to handle.

A number of labor-saving systems, now available for sail handling, were discussed in Chapter 5.

Before getting underway, locate and put in an accessible place every piece of gear that will or might be needed. For example, see that binoculars, chart, horn, sail stops, winch handles, and personal items such as sunburn cream and dark glasses are near the helm. Shelves just inside the companionway and winch-base stowage compartments are handy for these items. Speaking of personal gear, let me stress the importance of wearing proper skidproof deck shoes and carrying in your pocket a knife with screwdriver and folding spike. Pliers and a small adjustable wrench can be carried in a leather case hung from the belt, and by all means carry a spare sail stop attached to your belt or in a pocket.

Don't leave your mooring or marina berth until all lead blocks are in place, headsail sheets have been properly rove, the anchor and rode are ready for use, sails and lines that might be needed are conveniently stowed, food and drinks are in a handy location, all loose items are made secure so that they cannot fall during a knockdown, hat and foulweather gear are available, and so forth. Bend on the proper size jib one person can handle in the velocity of wind you expect, and by all means see that it is high enough off the deck to allow good visibility. The sail may require a tack pendant. Be sure that everything is rigged so that lines cannot foul. The anchor, for instance, should not be stowed where the headsail sheets can foul it when coming about. In some cases, it might be advisable to rig a line that will act as a fouling preventer similar to the one shown in Figure 12-1. It is a good idea to tie the headsail sheets to the clew grommet with bowlines, but tie the knots in such a way that they cannot foul on the shrouds. The end of the line where it finally emerges from the knot should be facing away from the shrouds and not toward them. This is also explained in Figure 12-1. A bowline facing the wrong way can foul even when shroud rollers are used, and the singlehander does not want to have to make a trip forward to clear it.

If your boat lacks a self-steering vane, rig simple steering lines as suggested in Chapter 7, which run from the tiller through blocks on each side of the cockpit and then forward. The ends of the steering lines can be secured to jam cleats mounted in the vicinity of the mast, or, if there are no jam cleats, the lines can be made fast to the grabrails or lifeline stanchions forward with simple slip-knots that can be released quickly. Jam cleats can also be mounted on the tiller, but I prefer two half hitches that can be slipped over the tiller end in order to free it immediately in an emergency. The important point to remember when the helm is lashed is that you must be able to release it *quickly* from either forward or aft because of boat traffic or for some other reason. If the boat has a wheel, the best plan is usually to fit the emergency tiller when the system works freely. Almost every boat with a wheel has this provision, or at least should have. As mentioned earlier, sometimes the emergency tiller will have to be rigged backwards (see Figure 12-2) in order to clear the wheel when there is a steering pedestal just forward of the rudder post head.

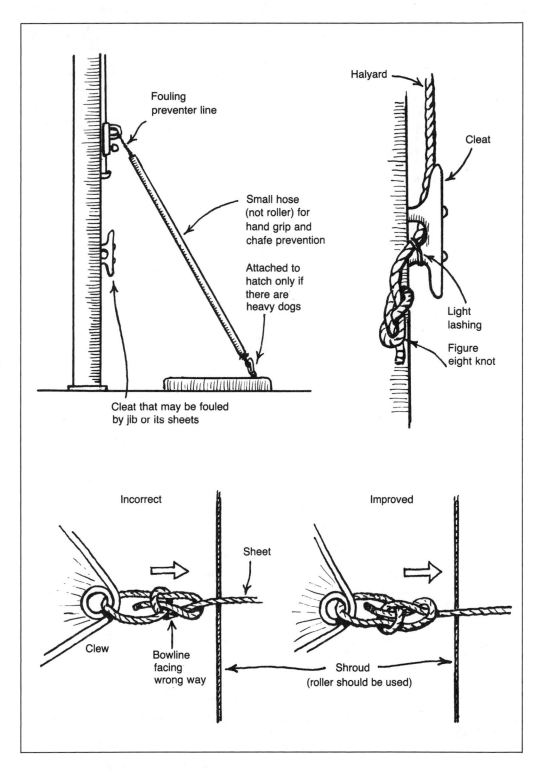

Figure 12-1. Fouling and jamming protection.

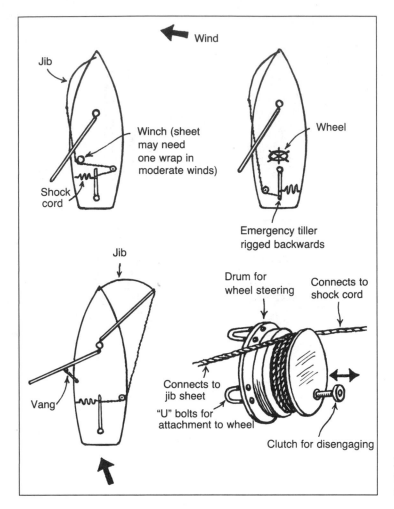

Figure 12-2. Simple
temporary
self-steering.

Obviously, this arrangement necessitates reverse steering, with the tiller pushed down to make the boat turn downwind, and pulled up to turn the boat into the wind. Boats with excellent directional stability may not need steering lines led forward, but keep in mind that when you make a sail change or any time you lower or hoist a sail, any boat's balance will change and she will need a helm correction.

Getting Underway

Before casting off, check the weather, wind, and tide conditions. Analyze carefully just how your boat will be affected when she leaves her dock or mooring. Will her bow be blown off? Is the current setting her against the dock? Should she be warped around the other way or moved closer to the end of the dock? Which direction should be taken in leaving the mooring?

A reliable engine will simplify getting underway. After starting the engine, be sure it is warmed up and running smoothly before casting off. It is a good idea to doublecheck that the water intake and fuel valves are open, because sometimes the effect of these valves being closed will not make itself known until the boat is underway. In most cases, docking lines should be looped around their piling or dockside cleat and then led back to the cockpit for easier control when there are no people to help on the dock (see Figure 7-3). If a dinghy is being towed, its painter should be fitted with cork floats so there is no possibility of its fouling the propeller. Also, all loose lines on the deck, such as jib sheets, ought to be belayed with their coiled ends in the cockpit so they cannot fall overboard and be sucked into the prop.

After you are well away from the dock or mooring and are running under power in open waters, try lashing your helm so that the boat will hold a reasonably straight course. In most cases the boat will have a slight tendency to turn to port due to having a right-hand propeller, assuming the shaft is on the centerline and is not angled to counteract the torque. It is a simple matter to secure the tiller by belaying the appropriate steering line, usually the port line when the boat has the normal tiller and customary torque. Of course, some boats have other means of locking the helm, such as a friction screw on a wheel, or a tiller "comb," which consists of a toothed, metal strip fastened to the deck running athwartships under the tiller that will accept a metal fin on the tiller's underside. I prefer steering lines, however, that can be released quickly from aft or forward. The boat cannot be expected to hold a steady course for very long, but long enough to allow you to move about getting the sails ready to hoist. While you are preparing the main halyard, untying stops, and so forth, it is important to look around. *The importance of keeping a continual lookout while singlehanding in crowded waters cannot be overstressed.*

When the sails are readied for hoisting, go aft, slow the engine, head into the wind, and relash the helm to hold the bow into the wind's eye. If the halyards lead back to the cockpit, the helm may not need lashing, but otherwise, of course, you must go forward to make sail. Customarily, the mainsail is raised first and then the jib. Keep tension on the main halyard until just before hoisting, because in a choppy sea, a slack halyard can jump around to the wrong side of the spreaders, which could cause an awkward situation for a singlehander. Be sure halyard ends are secured so that they cannot possibly go aloft. Some cleats are designed with a hole through their bases so that the halyard ends can be run through and knotted. This is a good plan, but keep the knot pulled a short distance away from the cleat and perhaps lash it there with light marline (see Figure 12-1) so that it won't interfere with belaying the line and perhaps cause a jam. If the halyards are internal, a figure-eight knot in the end will usually prevent the line from disappearing into the mast; there is no need to run the line through the base of its cleat. But check on this to be sure the halyard cannot escape into the mast exit. Be sure that the halyards are properly coiled and hung after sail is hoisted.

Sail Handling Techniques

Once you are under sail, cut the engine. After figuring your course, trim the sails for proper balance. The average, well-balanced boat normally will have her sails trimmed to carry a very slight weather helm when close-hauled in a moderate breeze, but when she is being singlehanded her sails should be trimmed for almost perfect balance, i.e. with neither weather nor lee helm. This probably will mean that the headsail will be trimmed slightly flatter than usual, and the mainsail cracked just a bit. Many boats require that the mainsail be eased about four inches farther than normal in a 10-to-12-knot wind. If the boat is well balanced and her sheets properly trimmed, she should be capable of steering herself to windward for short periods, perhaps for 15 minutes or longer under ideal conditions. Of course, a sudden gust, wind shift, irregular seas, or powerboat waves may knock her out of the groove, but the helm can be readjusted quite easily. This self-steering capability, even if only for brief periods, is of great value to a singlehander, because it frees him to move about attending to chores and various needs.

It is more difficult to make a modern boat without a vane gear or autopilot sail herself on a beam, broad, or quartering reach, but simple methods have been devised with sheet-to-helm connections such as those described in Chapter 6. An effective plan is to rig a small staysail inside the jib, as shown in Figure 6-9. The staysail is backed slightly, and its sheet is led through blocks to the windward side of the tiller, while a shock cord is rigged to pull the tiller to leeward. When the boat luffs, the staysail exerts more force on the tiller to correct the course, but when she bears off the staysail exerts less force allowing the shock cord to make the correction.

A simpler but less effective method is to forego the staysail and merely rig the jib sheet to the windward side of the tiller. Take the leeward sheet and lead it from its winch to a lead block on the windward side of the cockpit and then back to the tiller. The sheet's pull is counteracted by the tension of shock cord from the tiller to the leeward side of the cockpit (see Figure 12-2). To hook up the lines, first straddle the tiller and hold it between your legs while facing forward with the boat on her desired course. Then, using your hands to pull on the shock cord and sheet, balance the tension between the two lines and tie them to the tiller, the sheet first and then the shock cord. I find it convenient to throw a couple of hitches over the tiller end for the sheet but to tie the shock cord on its own standing part with a rolling hitch for easy adjustment. The boat should then take over steering herself for temporary periods at least. If she starts to head up, the jib will pull harder and pull the helm up, which will cause her to bear off to the original course; but if she falls off, the jib will become partially blanketed by the mainsail and pull less hard, which will allow the shock cord to pull the helm down, thereby causing the boat to head up to her original course. The jib may have to be trimmed a bit flatter than normal so that it will be partially stalled when on course; if the boat begins to luff, the flow will become attached (rather than turbulent), causing greater efficiency and thus the jib will pull harder.

Some experimentation will be necessary in selecting the right size shock cord and setting the proper tension, trimming the sails for best advantage, and determining the proper number of wraps of the sheet around the winch. In moderate conditions, one wrap around the winch may be about right, but in lighter airs it might be best not to use any wraps, especially when an emergency tiller is used, because unless the wheel steering can be disconnected, the emergency tiller will have to turn the wheel and this will obviously take more effort. One method of avoiding this extra effort is to attach to the wheel a steering drum such as the one made by Marine Vane Gears and illustrated in Figure 12-2. If the drum is used or the emergency tiller is rigged backwards (as mentioned earlier) or your standard tiller can be folded over to aim aft, then the leeward sheet will be led directly to the tiller and the shock cord rigged to windward. These matters obviously will vary with individual boats. When coming about, the jib sheet and the shock cord can easily be slipped over (or otherwise disengaged from) the tiller end, and then, of course, the self-steering system will have to be rigged for the new tack.

If the helm is manned, a boomed headsail with a traveller will allow you to come about very easily without touching a line, but it is not really difficult to singlehandedly tack the usual jib having double sheets when its overlap is not excessive. A 150 percent jib, one having an LP (a perpendicular from luff to clew) 1½ times as long as the base of the foretriangle, should slide around the mast by itself, and it will provide a lot more power than a self-tending working jib. Rollers around the shrouds will allow the jib to slide around the shrouds with minimal chance of fouling and chafing.

The normal procedure for tacking a double-sheet jib would be to wrap about two turns of the windward sheet around its winch and see that the winch handle is available, cast off the leeward sheet and take all but about three or four wraps off its winch, and turn the helm with one hand while holding the leeward sheet in your other hand. When the boat is almost head-to-wind, slack the leeward sheet, throw off the remaining turns from the winch, and, after the bow passes through the wind's eye, haul in on the opposite sheet hand-over-hand as far as possible. Then wrap about two or three more turns around the winch in use while alternately correcting the helm. Hold the helm steady with your leg or body, insert the winch handle and crank in the jib until it is correctly trimmed. A few hints: See that the sheet being slacked is coiled or flaked down and clear to run; put only a couple of turns around the windward winch to begin with in order to avoid an override; let the sail blow clear of the spreaders before hauling it in; and look around for other boats before and during the operation.

As mentioned earlier, self-tailing winches are best for singlehanding, but if you don't have them, there is a simple, inexpensive substitute. The Paul Elvstrom-designed Watski Wincher® is a rubber cap that fits over a small to medium-size standard winch. The Wincher does its job after the sheet, wrapped around the winch drum, climbs up and jams under the cap. There is also a cleating groove on top. The device is no substitute for a proper self-tailer, because there is no stripper to remove the tail of the line from the winch, but I find it momentarily helpful to position my knee near the tail so that it acts as a stripper, pushing the line away from the drum.

Should you find it necessary to change headsails during your solo sail, the advantage of having the steering lines led forward becomes apparent when the unwanted headsail is dropped and the balance of the boat changes. With steering lines led forward, you can correct the helm from the foredeck, eliminating the need to go aft.

Rigging some form of net or lacing between the forward life lines will help keep the lowered sail aboard. The question of whether or not to lead the jib halyard back to the cockpit was discussed in Chapter 5. In my opinion, it is better to keep the halyard at the mast so that it can be more easily controlled when the jib is being lowered, unless perhaps, you use the Gerr downhaul described in Chapter 5.

One handy method of lowering the jib is to back it, that is, pull in somewhat

The Watski Wincher® is an inexpensive substitute for a self-tailing winch.

on the windward sheet, or tack and let the sail go aback, and then lower it. Another method is to run off and let the mainsail blanket the sail. In this case, the sheet will have to be slacked with an overlapping jib in order to bring the clew inboard. That spare sail stop comes in handy for securing the sail when it is down. It is often helpful to have stops or spare lashing lines rove through the cabin-top grabrail forward. When lowering the sail, cast off the halyard and take all but one turn off its winch, then lead the halyard forward under its winch. While standing on the bow, slack away the halyard with one hand while pulling down and gathering in the jib with the other hand. When the sail is about halfway down, you may find that you can let go the halyard and use both hands for gathering in the jib, but be sure the halyard is not fouled and that its bitter end cannot possibly go aloft.

If you have a single jibstay it may be easier to remove the lowered sail completely before hanking on its replacement. However, it is faster to hank on the replacement jib beneath the original jib before that sail is lowered. Then, drop the original sail and unhank it, leaving the tack attached. Lash the doused sail to the rail or lifeline, transfer the halyard and sheets to the new sail and hoist. Of course, new sheets and proper leads should have been provided for the replacement jib before it was hoisted.

Flying A Spinnaker

The self-confident singlehander who wants to get the most boat speed may even set a spinnaker in light airs. As most sailors know, however, the modern parachute spinnaker can be a contrary devil to handle, and even fully-crewed racing boats have had numerous problems with this temperamental sail. It seems most prudent to set the 'chute only when the wind is light and in waters that are fairly free of boat traffic.

Prior to getting underway, prepare the spinnaker for hoisting, either by turtling (folding and stuffing into a special container or bag) or stopping (rolling or bunching up and tying with easily breakable stops). The stopping method assures more control in a breeze, but since most singlehanders set spinnakers only when the breeze is light, the turtling method should suffice. If prior turtling has been overlooked, the operation can be done in the cockpit while underway without too much difficulty.

One method is to secure the head to something solid with a lashing (merely to hold it steady) and then, with the sail in the bottom of the cockpit to keep it from being blown by the wind, sort out the two leeches and bring them together to prevent the sail from becoming twisted when it is hoisted. Working down from the head to the foot, the two leeches are accordion-folded, and they can be held in place by stepping on them. When the entire length of the leeches has been folded, the loose bulk of the sail is stuffed into the turtle or bag, and then the folded leeches are neatly laid on top of the bulk with the head and two clews hanging out of the bag's top. I find it convenient to have a piece of shock cord in the bag's neck to hold it closed yet still allow the sail to be hoisted out of its bag. The bag can then be taken forward and secured to the pulpit. Of course, the halyard is attached to the head, and the guy and sheet attached to each clew.

An alternative to turtling the spinnaker is the use of a "Spinnaker Sally," produced by Jack Fretwell of Millwood, Virginia, 22646 or the somewhat similar spinnaker sock originally called "Spee Squeezer," produced by Parbury Henty in London, England. The Sally consists of a number of interconnected plastic rings carried stacked together above the head of the sail when it's flying and pulled down to enclose and furl the sail. Socks are cloth sleeves that are pulled down to contain the 'chute when it is handed, and the sleeve is pulled up to fly the sail. U.S. sailmakers produce spinnaker socks under various trade names such as the Snuffer (North Sails) and the Stasher (Ulmer-Kolius). Although entanglements are possible, the sock system worked well enough for 100-pound Clare Francis in the 1976 OSTAR and helped her set a transatlantic speed record for women.

Let's suppose you're setting your 'chute from a turtle. After the turtled spinnaker is secured forward and lines are attached to its corners, the pole is hooked onto the mast and the lift and downhaul (foreguy) are attached. In light airs, I prefer to rig these lines to the pole's middle to permit end-for-end jibing (to be described soon) without the need of changing the downhaul's position, which would be required if the line were attached to the pole's end. The hook-up is illustrated in Figure 12-3. The outboard, spinnaker-pole end fitting is generally hooked onto the guy, and, incidentally, there should be a lanyard adjustable at the pole's middle to control the end fittings' spring-loaded pins. After all lines have been attached, hoist the pole with its lift until it is almost horizontal, and then haul in on the guy until the tack (windward clew) of the sail is perhaps about three feet from the pole end and the pole is positioned slightly forward of being square to the wind. The secret in performing such a complicated operation singlehanded is to see that all elements are pre-set. This doesn't mean that they are set to positions of final trim but only to positions where the sail is most easily managed immediately after it is hoisted. Pull the sheet as taut as you can without pulling the spinnaker leech very far out of its bag. The sail is now ready for hoisting.

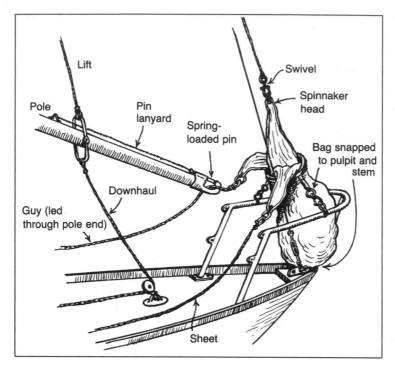

Figure 12-3.
Spinnaker hook-up.

The spinnaker halyard is best led aft to the cockpit where the singlehander can steer by straddling the tiller or conveniently make helm corrections with his leg while hoisting the sail. The hoisting operation should be done rapidly to help prevent hourglassing. The sheet and guy should be belayed nearby to port and starboard. In any breeze at all, it may be best to keep the boat almost dead before the wind, so that the 'chute will be blanketed until it is completely hoisted. Then, with the sail up and the sheet and guy partially adjusted, head up into the wind until the 'chute fills. Once on the desired course, final adjustments for proper trim can be made quite easily one at a time. In my opinion, it is best to lead the pole lift and downhaul as well as the halyard back to the cockpit

Jibing can be a bit tricky, but pre-setting the various lines involved can simplify the operation. Run off almost dead before the wind and square the pole, bringing it aft until it touches the forward shroud. Secure the helm, and go forward to the mast. After grabbing the sheet and holding it in the crook of your arm, unhook the pole from the mast and hook it onto the sheet which will become the new guy. The pole is now secured to both lines, but you now unhook the old guy, which will become the new sheet, and hook the free end of the pole to the mast. The lift and downhaul will have been pre-set, so you won't have to touch them. Be sure there is enough slack in the new guy to allow the pole-end hook to reach its eye on the mast. Unless the guy has been led forward, it means another trip back to the cockpit. Once the 'chute is jibed, return to the cockpit to turn the helm slightly and jibe the mainsail. This method, commonly called end-for-ending, is the one I prefer, but no doubt the dip-pole method can be used. This involves raising the pole to a high point on its mast track so that its outboard end can be dipped down and swung over inside the forestay. It is the easiest method in a strong wind, but in such conditions, setting a spinnaker alone can hardly be recommended.

Handing the 'chute is most easily accomplished when the boat is run dead before the wind so that the sail is blanketed. When the various lines are led aft, the whole operation can be done from the cockpit. Steering with your legs, ease the guy forward until the pole touches the forestay, and then cast off the guy entirely and let it run through the end of the spinnaker pole (be sure the guy shackle is tied closed if there is a fresh breeze). Next, cast off the halyard, and, with one or more turns around its winch (depending on the strength of wind), clamp the freed halyard between your elbow and side to hold it temporarily. Haul in on the clew with its sheet, and alternately lower the spinnaker while pulling it (with the sheet) under the main boom that should be trimmed in somewhat. As the 'chute is gathered in, it can be pulled into the bottom of the cockpit or stuffed down the companionway. Alternately lower and gather in a bit at a time by using one hand for each operation, or by letting the halyard run under your arm to free both hands for gathering in.

Nowadays, many singlehanders carry cruising spinnakers because they are easier to handle than conventional ones. Sold by sailmakers under various trade names such as Flashers®, Gennakers®, or Multi-Purpose Sails®, cruising spinnakers are asymmetrical in shape and do not require a pole. The tack is attached to the jibstay and held down by a pendant to the stem head. The trade-off for less gear and greater ease of handling is less speed than a poled-out spinnaker, especially when running. Although there is less chance of wrapping a cruising spinnaker around the jibstay, hourglassing the sail as a result of a twist and stay wrapping are still possible. The aforementioned spinnaker sock is one solution to these problems, but its use should not be necessary in light weather when proper care is taken. An undersized standard symmetrical 'chute can also be used without a pole.

Running Wing-And-Wing

If the wind is fresh, or you simply don't want to expend the effort of setting a 'chute, a wung-out jib works quite well. It can be boomed out or can be carried without a pole on the side of the boat opposite the mainsail. With the latter method, the boat is simply sailed by the lee, and the jib is allowed to jibe while the mainsail is not. The secret in keeping the jib drawing is to keep sailing very slightly by the lee. This requires a constant hand on the helm in order to keep the jib full without jibing the mainsail. I would strongly recommend rigging a vang or preventer line from the boom to some point forward in order to prevent accidentally jibing the mainsail. A preventer is advisable anytime you leave the helm while running, whether you are sailing by the lee or not. It is not a bad idea to use the Walder boom brake described earlier because several singlehanders have been injured by accidental jibes.

To boom the jib out to windward, rig the spinnaker pole as though you were going to set the 'chute, with one end of the pole hooked onto the mast and the other end raised with the pole lift. Lead the windward jib sheet through the outboard end of the pole, slack the leeward sheet, and haul the jib out to the pole end. This is a fairly stable rig, and the boat may even be made to steer herself in smooth water. The windward jib sheet is secured to the tiller and its pull is counteracted by a length of shock cord on the opposite side of the tiller (see Figure 12-2). Should the boat bear away and sail quite far by the lee, her jib will become partially blanketed, and the shock cord will correct the helm; but if she should head up above her course, the jib will exert a greater pull than the shock cord, and the sheet will make the helm correction. Don't neglect to carry the vang or preventer on the main boom.

Piloting Close to Shore

When sailing alone in shoal water, don't become so absorbed in the technique of sailing that you neglect your piloting. It is important to know where you are at all times. Keep track of all buoys and channel markers you pass and keep a local chart at hand near the helm. As said in Chapter 7, a folded chart or chart book and a grid of parallel lines printed on a sheet of plastic (to obviate the need of parallel rules) are very handy, especially when the grid and chart can be fitted together and enclosed in a transparent case of stiff plastic. It may be helpful to carry a pad of tracing paper so that a simple sketch chart of an unfamiliar anchorage can be traced from the proper chart, with only the most important features noted. This simplified chart can be read at a glance while entering the harbor.

The compass should be in plain view from any position around the helm and preferably pedestal-mounted so that bearings can easily be taken. Binoculars should be kept near at hand for finding channel markers or buoys, observing their numbers and watching the flow of the current. Note the state of the tide and anticipate the current because an adverse flow could delay the time of arrival until after dark. Plan on entering an unfamiliar harbor in broad daylight, preferably when the sun is fairly high. Particular care should be taken to get in early if bad weather is making up. Upon reaching a strange anchorage, it is always wise to slow down

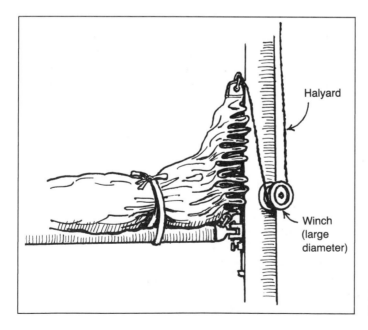

Figure 12-4. Securing the main halyard.

and to be certain that the channel, landmarks, navigation aids, and so forth are well understood before entering.

Returning home from a solo cruise, be careful not to become careless through overconfidence at being in familiar waters. It is generally the safest plan to start the engine and lower sails, or at least the headsail, before entering the harbor. Head into the wind with the engine running slowly and the helm lashed. Allow plenty of room for rounding up and making headway to windward, because handing sails takes more time when one is alone. Be sure the topping lift is attached before lowering the mainsail. Furl the sails and tie them temporarily with a minimum number of stops. Leave the halyards attached for the time being in case the engine should quit, but pull them taut to prevent them from whipping around and fouling aloft. Lead the main halyard under the low mast winch (see Figure 12-4) so that it can be tightened without pulling the sail aloft.

A reliable auxiliary is most useful when maneuvering in close quarters, and especially when anchoring, shooting a mooring or docking. But the solo sailor should not become so dependent on it the he or she cannot manage the boat under sail alone. Docking under sail was discussed in Chapter 7 and is not easy for beginning singlehanders to master. Anchoring under sail, on the other hand, is a skill easily mastered by the beginner with a little practice.

Anchoring

Whether coming to anchor under sail or power, it is a good idea to lower the headsail or roll it up if you have a roller-furling jib. Then the bagged sail (still hanked on) can be swung forward and stuffed between the bow pulpit and the headstay high up, where it is out of the way, will not interfere with the anchor rode and bow chocks, and will not become covered with mud from the ground tackle when the anchor is weighed again. When anchoring under sail, the boat is normally rounded up to the wind. Walk forward to the anchor, and, after headway is completely lost, lower the hook, paying out the rode only after the boat drifts backwards and/or her bow blows off. Be sure the mainsheet is well slacked and free to run so that the sail will not fill. If the boat is extremely cut away under water forward, her bow may blow off so rapidly that she will not make any sternway. In this case, it might be advisable to lower the anchor while headed downwind, usually with the mainsail sheeted in fairly flat to reduce speed and steering control lines led forward in case the boat tries to round up. I would not advise doing this if the rode is chain, as it could scar the topsides or underbody when the boat overrides it. After sufficient scope has been paid out to make a fairly flat angle between the rode and bottom, the rode is snubbed so the anchor will dig in. If there is any doubt whether the flukes have a good bite on the bottom, it is a good idea to wait until the boat comes head-to-wind, then pay out more scope, and push the main boom far to windward, so that the boat is blown astern, causing the anchor to dig in.

There are several means of releasing the anchor from the cockpit, a simple method being to hang the anchor at the stem from a wood toggle that can be tripped with a line leading aft, as shown in Figure 12-5. One must be careful, however, that the boat is making sternway (or headway if sailing downwind) when the hook is dropped, because the rode can become fouled if it is dumped on top of the anchor.

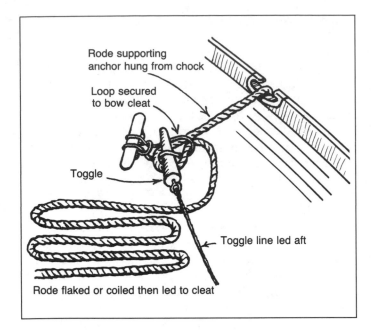

Rode supporting
anchor hung from chock

Loop secured
to bow cleat

Toggle

Toggle line led aft

Rode flaked or coiled then led to cleat

Figure 12-5. A simple anchor release.

Many sailors prefer to go forward where they can give the rode more careful attention, pay it out gradually, and better snub it.

It is easier to dig the hook in under power. After the anchor has been lowered and the boat has drifted back against her payed-out rode so that she lies head-to-wind, momentarily reverse the engine to be sure the flukes have a good bite on the ground. Then put the gear in neutral and go forward to let out more rode, enough for a scope-to-depth ratio of 5:1 or 6:1 if there is sufficient swinging room. It is especially important to be securely anchored in a protected harbor with good holding bottom and where there is ample swinging room, preferably away from other craft, to avoid having to weigh anchor or take other corrective actions in the middle of the night should your boat or a neighbor's start to drag. If you want to anchor by the stern in fair weather and light airs, it is a simple matter to drop the anchor astern from the cockpit and snub it while the boat is making headway. Should it be necessary to transfer the rode to the bow in the event it breezes up, the end of the rode should be run to the bow cleat before the line is cast off astern. Anchoring by the stern could be risky because the weather could deteriorate while the singlehander is asleep.

Building Confidence With Experience

After some experience in daysailing alone and a few successful overnight solo cruises you will develop a more intimate familiarity with your boat and a stronger confidence in your seamanship. This experience will serve you well, not only in solo and shorthanded work, but also aboard fully crewed vessels and especially during emergencies. It could lead to more ambitious projects, such as an extended inshore cruise or perhaps a coastal passage.

If making a singlehanded passage, you might catch an hour or more of sleep by taking an offshore tack or heaving to when there is sufficient sea room and no boat or ship traffic. Normally, snatches of sleep should only be taken during the day, but brief napping might be done at night under ideal conditions if the boat is well lighted. Prior to the passage, experiment with various methods of heaving to, lying ahull, backing the jib, lying to a sea anchor, and so forth. Estimate the boat's drift and headway for each method under a variety of conditions.

The occasional singlehander who sails only short distances may never aspire to an extended passage alone, but with enough experience in solo daysailing and overnight cruising, there is no reason why you cannot become a blue-water voyager if you so desire. Many years ago, Jim Crawford, who later became an offshore singlehander, asked Harry Pidgeon a question about how he managed to sail around the world alone. The circumnavigator replied, "You can sail one day, can't you, Jim? That's all it is—one day after another."

Biscuits Lu...British Steel...Credit Agricole: today's racing scene sports a growing number of boats honoring not the gods of the sea, but the gods of commerce.

13

Future Directions and Developments

IT SEEMS VERY PROBABLE THAT in the future an increasing number of sailors will be cruising or at least day-sailing alone or shorthanded. To some extent, the increase will be due to factors that are causing a growth in the popularity of boating in general, such as the population explosion, more leisure time for the average person, more boats available through modern production, and a back-to-nature resurgence stimulated to a large degree by contemporary awareness of pollution problems and preservation of the ecology. Specifically, singlehanding may be expected to gain in popularity for certain psychological and practical reasons. The latter will have to do with the lack of availability of crew as more people obtain their own boats, and also the fact that boats with the newest gear should become increasingly easy to handle shorthanded or alone. Psychologically, solo sailing relates to an increasing desire for independence and individuality. This is not only a desire to escape or experience a change from crowding and the emotional pressures of contemporary life, but it is a reaction against our modern society in which people are often mere cogs in a large machine and identities are numbers fed to a computer. Another factor is that the tremendous number of solo voyages successfully made in recent years by all kinds of people, including women, teenagers, and old men, will inspire others to follow, and will add a snowball effect to the growth of singlehanding.

Still another stimulus to shorthanded sailing is the tremendous advancement in technology that allows easier, more comfortable, and safer sailing today. Satellites spinning overhead can provide an almost instant means of determining one's position; the Argos rescue system gives the lone sailor in remote regions a feeling of security; electronic and computer advancements allow vastly improved systems of self-steering, weather predicting, and communicating. With such devices as self-tailing winches and more reliable roller furling/reefing gear, sail handling has been simplified, allowing one or two people to manage larger and thus safer, more comfortable boats.

Despite the promise of growth and a generally positive outlook for the future of singlehanding, there are some negative aspects and undesirable trends. Some of these are the production of stock boats that are unsuitable for singlehanding and the use of unwholesome boats for solo racing; regulations that could prohibit or at least discourage seamanly solo passages in small craft; unfairness in solo competitions, a preoccupation with setting records and publicity; and a fast-spreading growth of commercial sponsorship, which places unnatural demands on solo sailors.

Many stock boats have undesirable features because craftsmanship and careful detail are lacking as a result of mass production; design emphasis is often placed on round-the-buoys racing (despite the fact that a small percentage will be used for that purpose); short-cuts and oversights are common in modern construction; and flimsy gear is more the rule than the exception. Having a sound vessel, an important requirement for any sailor, becomes essential when one sails alone, and especially so when cruises are made offshore. When the average stock boat is taken to sea, she should be given a thorough going over by a qualified surveyor. The hull can be strengthened by reinforcing bulkheads, beefing up or stiffening flexible areas, bolting or bonding hull-to-deck connections, strengthening the area around the mast step, glassing over the bilge in way of a vulnerable skeg to prevent flooding in case it should break off, and so forth. Rigging and fittings can be made a size larger than normal, and standard equipment should often be replaced by high-quality gear for best security. Of course, some stock boats are built to high standards and need little modification, but many are deficient, and a few are positively deplorable.

To summarize some of the requirements mentioned earlier in this book a seagoing boat should not be extremely heavy, light, or beamy. She should be strongly built and have a low center of gravity to provide a long range of stability (perhaps to 130 degrees of heel or more). Freeboard should be high and the hull reasonably balanced for good directional stability at various angles of heel. The cockpit should be deep but small in volume and with ample scuppers for quick drainage. Be sure there is a high companionway sill or bridge deck to prevent downflooding. All hatches, ports, and locker lids must be designed to allow quick, sure closing and watertight integrity. Centerline hatches are the safest. The cabin trunk needs to be well braced and rounded. Windows should be small and preferably glazed with Lexan. The hull-deck connection should be watertight and preferably bolted rather than riveted. All fittings need through-bolts with adequate backing plates. In the case of most cheap stock boats, the rigging should be a size larger than standard. Cast aluminum fittings should be treated as suspect and perhaps replaced. Keel-stepped masts are stronger than those stepped on the cabin-top. The rudder (and tiller), skeg, propeller, and fin keel are vulnerable to damage and should be inspected.

The Impact of Racing and Record Breaking

Unhealthy boats are also resulting from the great emphasis on solo racing. This has encouraged the building of monstrous, impractical, and expensive monohulls or multihulls. Multihulls have their good points, of course, but they are more subject to capsizing, and despite the accomplishments of Eric Tabarly, Alain Colas, and others, multihulls hardly seem the most suitable craft for extended offshore solo cruising. In fact, catamaran enthusiast Bill Howell once admitted, "I don't think an ocean racing cat such as I've got here is a singlehanded boat." Trimarans are better accepted for offshore work, but usually when there is a crew of more than one. Even the British tri enthusiast and author, D. H. Clarke, has written, "If you want to sail alone across an ocean in a trimaran, and you believe it is necessary to take as many precautions as possible to prevent a capsize plus gadgets to save you after you have capsized, then the only advice I can really give you is don't go by tri, go by monohull!"

A principal objective for transatlantic solo racing, put forth by H. G. Hasler in 1957, was "to encourage the development of suitable boats, gear, and techniques for singlehanded ocean-crossing under sail." Few sailors could find fault with that philosophy, but many recent solo racing boats indicate that the development trend has strayed quite far from Hasler's original concept. The late Hasler himself would seem to agree with this, for he once said ". . . not very much has been done to make boats easier and more comfortable to sail," and, "I thought that everyone would think as I did—that one would like to sail with the minimum of exertion and the minimum of fatigue, but this has not proved true." In regard to the huge *Vendredi 13*, Hasler described her as "a fascinating experiment in the wrong direction." I can only imagine what he said about the monstrous *Club Méditerranée*.

Even a magnificent creation such as Dodge Morgan's *American Promise* is a high-tech, high-budget boat that few singlehanders could afford if they wanted her. Furthermore, her systems may be overly complex for the average sailor who might not be able to repair the gear if it should happen to break down in heavy weather. There is a danger in becoming overly dependent on computer/electronic or any electrical equipment that can let you down when the going gets rough.

It is probable that the vast majority of singlehanders (or would-be singlehanders) or shorthanded sailors are neither "blood-and-thunder" adventurers in the extreme nor super-dedicated racers. The majority are quite ordinary sailors who are interested in safe, leisurely cruising, involving a minimum of risk and anxiety. They want a smart sailing boat with good speed, seakindliness, and easy handling characteristics at a reasonable cost. In my opinion, this is the kind of boat that should be developed—not impractical, oversized, expensive, and overly sensitive craft that demand feats of endurance to make them perform.

Sponsorship is a controversial subject. There are good and bad points in being financed by an industry or newspaper to race or make a voyage singlehanded. The big advantage of this arrangement is that it enables qualified sailors without financial means to undertake such ventures. Arguments against sponsorship include distasteful commercialism that detracts from the purity of the sport; the disadvantage in a competition of those who cannot acquire sponsorship; the encouragement in developing expensive, sophisticated gear that is beyond the means and desires of the ordinary sailor; and the added sense of responsibility and obligation to a sponsor felt by the singlehander.

The latter can be a very serious burden for many sailors. Hasler, for one, wrote, "I have a considerable aversion to being sponsored. . . . For me it would be horrible to start a transatlantic race and feel that you had to do well in order to give your sponsors a return for their money. The greatest freedom I value is the freedom to give up off the Eddystone Light if you don't like it."

Donald Crowhurst suffered over the sense of obligation he felt toward his sponsors, and some say that this was a major factor that led to his demise. He felt forced to make his voyage (in the 1968 Golden Globe race) and to leave before he was mentally or physically prepared. Frank Page, an English yachting correspondent, wrote that "Crowhurst spent his last night on shore weeping in his wife's arms, but still unable to take the awful decision to call off the enterprise which involved so many other people relying on him." It might be argued the Crowhurst was mentally unstable, but any completely normal sailor can feel heavy pressures from responsibility to his sponsor that could adversely affect his best judgment. One can only wonder about the influence of media hype on the decisions of Tania Aebi to sail home during the hurricane season and of Bill Dunlop to attempt a circumnavigation in a 9-foot boat, a stunt which cost him his life.

As for the boats and gear made possible by sponsorship, they are usually very expensive and far beyond the means of the average unsponsored sailor. Of course, this makes possible the development of certain sophisticated gear and boats, but such gear and specialized, custom-made boats can give an unfair advantage to racing singlehanders with sponsors. In the 1968 transatlantic race, there were complaints and criticisms that the winner, Geoffrey Williams, had decided advantages with his specialized, low-freeboard ketch and her equipment, which included loran and radio access to a shore-based computer that provided optimum course recommendations. Nowadays most serious racers are loaded with gadgets such as onboard computers, weather facsimile equipment, GPS satellite navigation, and Argos transponders. Without sponsorship it is difficult for the average singlehander to acquire such gear. Sponsorship also produced *Vendredi 13* and *Club Med*, which are not only highly specialized boats designed to win a particular race, but are very impractical and hard-to-handle giants for ordinary singlehanding. Fortunately, a size limitation was put on OSTAR racers before the 1980 race, but this was later extended, and it seems that the size of solo racers is again creeping upward. It is also true that the quest for speed has produced boats of questionable seaworthiness (or at least seakindliness) that are very tricky to handle. We may soon reach the point, if we haven't already, where the most competitive solo boats can only be managed by superpeople using the most high-tech, expensive, and vulnerable gadgetry.

It seems the only sensible course is to put some emphasis on characteristics other than a boat's top speed, which, for the racers at least, has been blown far out of proportion. The accentuation of elapsed time for a racer might be de-emphasized in a number of ways: by further limiting size and displacement; staggering starts; emphasizing separate prizes for monohulls and multihulls in different size categories; restricting sponsorship to discourage super-boats; developing a more fair handicap system with awards for corrected time; and, possibly, emphasizing seamanly performance awards. The main arguments against these measures is that development would be inhibited, and it is probably true the "far-out" ideas would be restricted. On the other hand, such measures might encourage the development of practical vessels and gear, the kind that would be of use to the everyday sailor who occasionally sails alone and often cruises shorthanded.

A form of handicapping has been used in the most recent transatlantic races, but the simple rating system used has been called unfair and totally unrealistic, and furthermore not much attention is paid to the winner of the handicap award. How many people knew that *Voortrekker* won the award in 1968 or that the *Blue Smoke* won the monohull handicap trophy in 1972? Public interest seems to be in the order of arrival of the finishers. Staggered starts with the small boats starting first might take some of the attention away from the large craft, but what many knowledgeable people feel is needed is a realistic handicap rule. This rule should attempt to assess more fairly the speed of the boats and encourage wholesome, practical types. No handicapping system is perfect, of course, but perhaps some consideration should be given to a non-IOR type of rule, and one that measures or approximates all forms of resistance. The relatively new IMS (International Measurement System) is a step in the right direction, for it considers such previously neglected factors as wetted surface, ultimate stability, and velocity prediction in various wind conditions, points of sailing, angles of heel, and degrees of loading. The present IMS is not perfect, though, because it is overly complicated, boat measurements are difficult, it restricts some possibly desirable means of producing speed (water ballast, for instance), requirements for accommodations are too demanding for solo racers, and several speed-affecting factors (pitching characteristics, for instance) may not be adequately considered. Solo ocean racers need an improved rule of their own. Almost any sailor will agree that multihulls and monohulls cannot be rated equitably to compete against each other, and so they should be raced in separate classes. Everything possible should be done to minimize comparisons in the elapsed time of these entirely different types of craft, because it is as pointless as comparing the speeds of a porpoise and a race horse. They are just different animals.

Room for Innovation

Whether racing or not, a singlehander wants (or should want) maximum safety, convenience, and comfort. A great deal of progress has been made in these directions with the research and development of Waller, Hammond, Marin-Marie, Hasler, King, McLeod, Greene, Terlain, Morgan, and many others, but the singlehander still has important unfilled needs.

It has often been said that the possibility of collision with ships is the offshore or coastal singlehander's greatest risk. This may be especially true today with ships becoming increasingly automated and visual watches apparently becoming more lax. An improved, fully automatic, omnidirectional radar alarm of considerable range and volume that is reliable close to shore would be of great value. Perhaps it could be similar to the type pioneered by Noel Bevan (see Chapter 8). Also, it might be well to legalize the use of masthead strobe lights for singlehanders, when they are offshore away from an area where these lights could possibly be confused with aids to navigation. Of course, strobe lights are permitted as flare-ups under the Rules of the Road, but they are not legal for continual use (see Chapter 8). Another need is a really effective emergency noise-maker, perhaps a loud siren, or explosives, such as those used by Chay Blyth, to warn ships of a small boat's presence.

Singlehanders' flag, as designed by Mimi Rehor.

In my opinion, it would be a good idea to devise a special signal for singlehanders, perhaps a large flag flown from a conspicuous spot such as the backstay to notify other boats in the area that the solo vessel may be somewhat limited in its maneuvering ability for lack of a full crew. Of course, two black balls (or two red lights at night) can be displayed to indicate the vessel is not under command under Rule 27 (a) of the Inland and International Rules of the Road, but these signals are often impractical, not clear to many boatmen, and not strictly correct when the singlehander is on deck. One suggestion would be a white flag with one large red or black hand on it. If this flag were publicized (in chart books, cruising guides, and elsewhere), it should be easily recognizable as the singlehander's signal. Since the first edition of this book was published, Mimi Rehor, who extensively single-handed a Magellan 35, thought well enough of the solo flag idea to design and produce one (shown in the accompanying photograph). Incidentally, Phil Weld also thought this flag was a good idea and suggested it be endorsed by the Cruising Club of America.

Research is needed in the control of damage resulting from collisions not only with vessels, but also with flotsam and marine life. Improvement could be made in plugging and sealing compounds, in materials that will harden instantly under water, collision mats, methods for repair from within the hull, ways of securing other materials to fiberglass, flotation, and watertight compartments.

A great deal of work has been done on self-steering systems, but there is still room for improvement. Vane gears might be made stronger, simpler, and easier to reduce in area and remove completely when not needed. Their performance could be improved in light airs, when running in following seas, and on fast multihulls. High-torque autopilots could be made less electrically demanding, more water-proof, and less expensive. Electrical systems could be made more reliable, and there is definitely a need for more efficient battery chargers that can use natural power such as wind, sun, water moving past the boat, or wave action.

Sail-changing and reefing systems could also be improved. One of the greatest chores the singlehander faces is shortening down and changing headsails. Many roller systems need to be made stronger, more dependable, more efficient, and more versatile for the combination of jib changing, variable reduction, and balancing for self-steering. Mainsail roller furling needs further development to increase sailing efficiency and reliability under all conditions. All gear for singlehanders needs to be extremely reliable because a person alone cannot afford to cope with constant breakages.

Singlehanded cruisers need a better means of "anchoring" at sea so that they can sleep and seek shelter with peace of mind in heavy weather or when there is a danger of grounding in fair weather. Good sea anchors, such as the Shewmon product, have been developed that anchor a boat, and there are good drogues such as the aforementioned Galerider that merely slow the boat. But what is needed is a very elastic system that will keep a boat end-to the seas to reduce vulnerability to capsizing. Sailor/engineer Donald J. Jordan has been working on such a system and has obtained some promising results with his so-called series drogue, which consists of a series of small cones on a tow line. The system has not yet been perfected, but hopefully it will soon be developed to the point where it will be a real improvement over existing systems and afford some variability in drag requirements.

Hasler and a few others have put much thought into comfort below deck. Their ideas should be made available to all shorthanded offshore sailors. The concept of a gimballed chair, for instance, was pioneered by Chichester and King. In its perfected form, such a chair would be completely padded and would support all parts of the body. It would be completely adjustable, gimballed in all directions, and usable for navigating, eating, cooking, reading, writing, and even sleeping. Further research might be done on controlling deck operations from below and improving visibility from the cabin without resorting to large windows (a periscope?). There also seems to be room for improvement in the galley. For instance, there could be more gimballing, greater security, better compartmentation for stowage, better stove fuel that is both safe and convenient, and so forth.

There is much room for the development of sophisticated gear, especially in reliability, low power drainage, and economy. Cheaper facsimile weather equipment, low-power drainage auto-steering controlled by a gyro compass, and inexpensive satellite navigation are the kinds of systems that would be useful. However, basic time-tested systems such as celestial navigation, sail trimming for self-steering, and the "cocked weather eye" should never be forgotten or neglected. Where singlehanding is concerned, the simplest way of performing an operation is usually the best way.

Regulations Affecting Singlehanding

One of the most troublesome problems relating to the future of singlehanded sailing is the effect of federal and international regulations that threaten to restrict or even terminate solo voyaging. The most dogmatic rule, which can only be interpreted one way, is put forth in the International Regulations for Preventing Collisions at Sea, commonly called COLREGS. Rule 5 of both the International and Inland Rules of the road states, "Every vessel shall at all times maintain a proper look-out by sight and hearing as well as by all available means appropriate in the prevailing circumstances and conditions so as to make a full appraisal of the situation and of the risk of collision." This rule makes long distance singlehanding illegal, because the lone sailor obviously can't stand watch continuously. Nevertheless, the proliferation of solo voyaging and organized offshore racing for single-handers continues despite the violation of Rule 5. The regulation is not being enforced, and so long as this is the case, singlehanded voyaging will probably continue to flourish. It seems unlikely that the rule will be enforced on loners unless they sail large, heavy, fast-moving boats that can seriously damage other vessels in the event of a collision.

In regard to federal regulations that could possibly have a retarding effect on offshore singlehanding, I have in mind the U.S. Coast Guard's authority to designate a boat "manifestly unsafe" for a specific voyage. Such power could be good or bad, depending on how it will be used. Certainly it should be used to stop crackpot stunts and to prevent costly searches and rescues, but the line between a stunt and feat of seamanship is sometimes very thin, and one might wonder about the qualifications of a particular Coast Guard officer who is authorized to forbid or terminate a voyage. Had such a regulation always been in existence, would the voyages of Johnson, Andrews, Lawlor, Blackburn, Slocum, Pidgeon, Manry, Casper, and others have been terminated, and *should* they have been stopped? These are questions that cannot be answered easily, nor should they be considered lightly. Undoubtedly some of those voyages were manifestly unsafe, but it can be dangerous to give government officials the power to regulate and suppress the sense of adventure and the exploring instincts of people.

There is no question in my mind that the 1987 voyage of blind sailor Jim Dickson (Chapter 2) should have been delayed until Dickson was better prepared, his boat was better equipped with well-tested backup gear, and the season offered more favorable weather. Yet I deplore his castigation over national television and in print by William F. Buckley, Jr., who made the dogmatic assertion that blind people lack the vital sense for a full appreciation of sailing. Being a sailor himself, Buckley should know that sailing involves *all* the senses, and with a blind person's ability to make full use of senses other than sight, he can derive immense pleasure from sailing. But the important point is that courageous sailors like Dickson, who are setting inspiring examples for all handicapped people, should be encouraged to do their thing, *provided* they are thoroughly prepared in every way.

When passing judgment on a voyage, perhaps the ultimate consideration should be danger to people other than the voyager. In my opinion, any real seaman who knows what he is doing has the right to risk his own neck, but he has no right to risk the lives of others. If he uses good judgment about standing watch in crowded waters, sleeps during the day, uses alarms, is self-sufficient, acts in a seamanly manner, and does not expect to be rescued, he exposes others to very little danger. One of the reasons I admire so many of the early singlehanders—the real loners who had no ham radios, Argos transponders, or even short distance radios—is that they were utterly on their own. Seamen like Slocum, Blackburn, and Dumas would have accepted help, no doubt, but they never counted on being rescued in the event of trouble. Just because the modern sailor has the ability to communicate, he should not feel that the world owes him help. He must realize that search and rescue operations can be very costly, risk lives, and cause damage to the sport through bad publicity.

The responsible and independent solo seaman should have the right to seek adventure, fulfill his desires for freedom, and exercise his instinct to explore. A strong case for this is made by J.R.L. Anderson in his book *The Ulysses Factor.*

Anderson feels that such adventurous escapades as singlehanded voyaging not only fulfill deep internal needs, but also have an important influence on the public, largely by giving inspiration to low-level adventure. In fact, Anderson considers the exploring instinct, which he calls the Ulysses Factor, to be a major hope for the future of humanity. Although not everyone will agree with him, perhaps, it is plain to see that the quashing of a carefully planned voyage is a responsibility that should not be taken lightly. Boat inspections by federal authorities or race committees should be made only by the most qualified inspectors who are intimately familiar with the problems involved. Not only should the boat be judged, but also the voyage plan and especially the voyager, for a lubber can be lost in a well-found vessel, while a proficient seaman can survive in a cockleshell.

In my opinion, stunt-type voyages need not be completely discouraged. We have to allow adventurers to live out their dreams. But, of course, the stunter must be well prepared in every way with the best possible plan, boat, and gear. He should be a level-headed seaman, not merely a publicity seeker going off half-cocked, and his proposed stunt should be carefully researched. It is amazing how often sailors set out to accomplish something that has already been done. There is a real need for some organization to keep track of worldwide sailing records and feats continuing the fine work done by Britisher D.H. Clarke. Perhaps the Slocum Society could perform such a service or maybe the International Yacht Racing Union.

Despite the problems discussed, I think the future of solo and shorthanded voyaging seems bright. Interest and participation are on the increase, and even though this means more crowded anchorages, there is still plenty of open, unpolluted water offshore. Furthermore, the increasing number of voyagers creates a demand for better boats and gear, which cannot but help every sailor. Even those who have no desire to sail alone can benefit from development in solo equipment and a study of singlehanding techniques, for, sooner or later every sailor, willingly or not, will find himself or herself sailing shorthanded.

The rewards of singlehanding are many: the feeling of independence, sense of accomplishment, self-confidence gained from success, and gratification of the sense of adventure. Francis B. Cooke once wrote that the singlehander "is not only captain of his little ship but also captain of his soul, enjoying a freedom of action unobtainable in any other way."

Appendix A. Singlehanded Circumnavigations

A collection of solo (or mostly solo) non-racing world cruises or circumnavigations

Completion Date	Master	Vessel	Route
1898	Joshua Slocum, USA	Spray (36 ft.)	E to W via Strait of Magellan (first solo circumnavigation)
1925	Harry Pidgeon, USA	Islander (34 ft.)	E to W via Panama Canal (circumnavigated again in 1937)
1929	Alain Gerbault, France	Firecrest (39 ft.)	E to W via Panama Canal
1932	Edward Miles, USA	Sturdy & Sturdy II (37 ft.)	W to E via Red Sea
1938	Louis Bernicot, France	Anahita (41 ft.)	E to W via Strait of Magellan
1939	Wladyslaw Wagner, Poland	Zjawa & II, III (29 ft.)	E to W via Panama Canal
1943	Vito Dumas, Argentina	Lehg (31 ft.)	W to E via Cape Horn
1952	Alfred Peterson, USA	Stornoway (33 ft.)	E to W via Red Sea
1952	Bill Murnan, USA	Seven Seas II (30 ft.)	E to W via Panama Canal
1952	Yves Le Toumelin, France	Kurun (33 ft.)	E to W via Panama Canal
1957	Jean Gau, France/USA	Atom (30 ft.)	E to W via Panama Canal (circumnavigated again in 1967)
1958	Marcel Bardiaux, France	Les 4 Vents (31 ft.)	E to W via Cape Horn
1959	John Guzzwell, Britain	Trekka (21 ft.)	E to W via Panama Canal (set record for smallest boat to circumnavigate)
1961	Joseph Havkins, Israel	Lammerhak II (23 ft.)	E to W via overland Mexico
1963	Adrian Hayter, New Zealand	Sheila II (32 ft.)	England-New Zealand eastward
		Valkyr (26 ft.)	England-New Zealand westward
1965	William Nance, Australia	Cardinal Vertue (25 ft.)	W to E via Cape Horn
1966	Michael Mermod, Switzerland	Genève (24 ft.)	E to W, Peru to France
1966	Frank Caspar, USA	Elsie (30 ft.)	E to W via Panama Canal
1966	Pierre Auboiroux, France	Neo-Vent (27 ft.)	E to W via Panama Canal
1967	Francis Chichester, Britain	Gipsy Moth IV (53 ft.)	W to E via Cape Horn (first one-stop)
1968	Johann Trauner, Austria	Lei Lei Lassen (26 ft.)	E to W via Panama Canal
1968	Alan Eddy, USA	Apogee (30 ft.)	E to W via Panama Canal
1968	Wilfried Erdnan, Germany	Kathena (25 ft.)	E to W via Panama Canal
1968	C. H. (Rusty) Webb, Britain	Flyd (29 ft.)	E to W via Panama Canal
1968	Alec Rose, Britain	Lively Lady (36 ft.)	W to E via Cape Horn
1969	Walter Koenig, Germany	Zarathustra (25 ft.)	E to W via Panama Canal
1969	Alfred Kalies, Germany	Pru (25 ft.)	E to W via Panama Canal
1969	Roger Plisson, France	François Virginie (24 ft.)	E to W via Panama Canal
1970	Robin Lee Graham, USA	Dove (24 ft.), Return of Dove (33 ft.)	E to W via Panama Canal (youngest male circumnavigator)
1971	Chay Blyth, Britain	British Steel (59 ft.)	E to W via Cape Horn (first non-stop circumnavigation 292 days)
1972	Jorgen Meyer, Germany	Paloma (34 ft.)	W to E via Cape Horn
1973	Wolf Hausner, Austrian	Taboo (32 ft. catamaran)	E to W via Panama Canal

Completion Date	Master	Vessel	Route
1973	Bill King, Britain	*Galway Blazer II* (42 ft.)	W to E via Cape Horn
1973	Dima Grinups, Sweden	*Sandra II* (27 ft.)	E to W via Panama Canal
1973	Goran Cederstrom, Sweden	*Tua Tua* (27 ft.)	E to W via Panama Canal
1973	Chris Baronowski, Poland	*Polonez* (45 ft.)	W to E via Cape Horn
1974	Yoh Aoki, Japan	*Ahodori II* (20 ft.)	W to E via Cape Horn *(took record from Trekka for smallest boat to circumnavigate)*
1974	Edward Allcard, Britain	*Sea Wanderer* (36 ft.)	E to W via Cape Horn
1974	Ambrogio Fogar, Italy	*Surprise* (38 ft.)	E to W via Cape Horn
1974	Ryusuke Ushijima, Japan	*Gin Gitsune* (31 ft.)	W to E via Cape Horn
1974	Kenichi Horie, Japan	*Mermaid III* (29 ft.)	W to E via Cape Horn *(set monohull record 276 days)*
1974	Alain Colas, France	*Manureva* (76 ft. catamaran)	W to E via Cape Horn *(record 168 days)*
1975	Heinrich J. Henze, Germany	*Leda* (25 ft.)	E to W via Panama Canal
1975	Richard Konkolski, Czechoslovakia/USA	*Nike* (24 ft.)	E to W via Panama Canal *(first of 3 circumnavigations)*
1975	John Struchinsky, Britain	*Bonaventure De Lys* (25 ft.)	E to W via Panama Canal
1975	Jules Garnet, France	*Memory* (46 ft.)	E to W via Panama Canal
1976	Webb Chiles, USA	*Egregious* (37 ft.)	W to E via Cape Horn *(202 days; broke monohull record)*
1976	Klaus Alverman, Germany	*Plumbelly* (26 ft.)	E to W via Panama Canal
1976	Julio Vilar, Spain	*Mistral* (23 ft.)	E to W via Panama Canal
1976	Utz Muller-Tren, Germany	*Frauken* (39 ft.)	E to W via Panama Canal
1977	Ann Gash, Australia	*Ilimo* (26 ft.)	E to W via Panama Canal *(yacht shipped from Ghana to England)*
1977	Gidaliahu Shtirmer, Israel	*New Penny* (25 ft.)	W to E via Cape Horn
1977	Georgi Georgiev, Bulgaria	*Cor Caroli* (30 ft.)	E to W via Panama Canal *(monohull record 201 days)*
1977	Ed Boden, USA	*Kittywake* (25 ft.)	E to W via Panama Canal
1977	Barry Loeckler, USA	*Freedom* (36 ft.)	E to W via Panama Canal
1977	Donald Ridler, Britain	*Eric the Red* (26 ft.)	E to W via Panama Canal
1978	Krystena Chojnowska-Liskiewicz, Poland	*Mazurek* (31 ft.)	E to W via Panama Canal *(first woman to circumnavigate)*
1978	Naomi James, New Zealand	*Express Crusader* (53 ft.)	E to W via Cape Horn *(first woman to circumnavigate via Cape Horn)*
1978	Elico Kasemier, Holland	*Bylgia* (40 ft.)	E to W via Cape Horn
1978	Brigette Oudry, France	*Gea* (34 ft.)	W to E via Cape Horn
1978	G. Lagarrique, France	*Mikenos* (31 ft.)	E to W via Panama Canal
1979	Kees Den Hartoog, Holland	*Sentign* (39 ft.)	W to E via Cape Horn
1979	Stant Blunt, USA	*Rupipaki* (26 ft.)	E to W via Panama Canal
1980	Tom Blackwell, Britain	*Islander* (58 ft.)	E to W *(2 1/2 circumnavigations in same boat)*
1980	Dean Vincent, USA	*Eos* (39 ft.)	E to W via Panama Canal
1980	Richard B. Sweat, USA	*My Honey* (30 ft.)	E to W via Panama Canal

Completion Date	Master	Vessel	Route
1980	Zbigniew Pulchalski, Poland	Miranda	E to W via Panama Canal
1980	David Scott Cowper, Britain	Ocean Bound (41 ft.)	W to E via Cape Horn (previously completed E to W circumnavigation. First to circumnavigate Cape Horn in both directions)
1980	Henry Jaskula, Poland	Dar Przemysla (47 ft.)	W to E via Cape Horn (non-stop & without assistance)
1980	Horst Timmreck, Germany	Brigitte (31 ft.)	W to E via Cape Horn (163 days)
1981	Leslie Powles, Britain	Solitaire of Hamble (34 ft.)	W to E non-stop (without replenishment; previously made westabout circumnavigation)
1981	Paul Rogers, New Zealand	Spirit of Pentax (55 ft.)	W to E (1¼ times around non-stop)
1981	Jonathan Sanders, Australia	Perie Banon (34 ft.)	W to E (first to complete 2 non-stop circumnavigations; revictualled at sea)
1981	Jan Swertz, Belgium	Tahani & Peti (30 ft. & 41 ft.)	E to W via Cape Horn
1981	Harald Kolzer, Germany	Rosi II (22 ft.)	E to W via Panama Canal
1982	Patrick Childress, USA	Juggernaut (27 ft.)	E to W via Panama Canal
1982	Pleum Van Der Lugt, Holland	Zee Uwse Stromen (35 ft.)	W to E (set time record for non-stop antipodal circumnavigation 286 days)
1983	Mark Schrader, USA	Resourceful (40 ft.)	W to E (first American to circumnavigate via 5 Southern capes)
1983	Webb Chiles, USA	Chidiock Tichborne I & II (18 ft.)	E to W ¾ circumnavigation (record distance for open boat)
1984	Andrew Urbanczyk, USA	Nord IV (30 ft.)	E to W via Panama Canal
1986	John Sowden, USA	Tarmin (24 ½ ft.)	E to W via Panama Canal (3 circumnavigations in same boat)
1986	James Baldwin, USA	Atom (28 ft.)	E to W via Panama Canal
1986	Henry Pigott, Britain	Glory (19 ½ ft. junk-rigged)	E to W via Panama Canal
1986	Dodge Morgan, USA	American Promise (60 ft.)	W to E via Cape Horn (fastest non-stop antipodal circumnavigation 150 days)
1987	James Hatfield, Britain	British Heart II & III (29 ft.)	E to W via Strait of Magellan
1987	Alan Butler, Canada	Amon-Re (26 ft.)	E to W via Panama Canal (smallest multihull solo circumnavigation)
1987	Philippe Monnet, France	Kriter Brut de Brut (70 ft. tri.)	W to E via Cape Horn (fastest solo circumnavigation 129 da. 19 hrs. 17 min.)
1987	Julia Hazel, Australia	Jeshan (28 ft.)	E to W via Panama Canal
1987	Tania Aebi, USA	Varuna (26 ft.)	E to W via Panama Canal
1987	Sergio Testa, Australia	Acrohc Australis (12 ft.)	E to W via Panama Canal (smallest boat to circumnavigate)
1988	Kay Cottee, Australia	Blackmore's First Lady (36 ft.)	First non-stop circumnavigation by a woman

Appendix B
Honor Roll of
Blue-Water Singlehanders

Gary Adams
Sharon Sites Adams
Tania Aebi
Edward Allcard
Klans Alverman
William Andrews
Yoh Aoki
Florence Arthaud
Pierre Auxboiroux
James Baldwin
Chris Baranowski
Marcel Bardiaux
Jim Bates
Edith Baumann
Ed Beddow
Guy Bernardin
Olivier Berner
Louis Bernicot
Mike Best
Noel Bevan
Mike Birch
Howard Blackburn
Tom Blackwell
David Blagden
Stant Blunt
Chay Blyth
Ed Boden
Michael Bohmann
David Bonner
Max Bourgeois
Jack Boye
Amy Boyer
M. Boyle
Monique Brand
Andrew Bray

Jock Brazier
Richard Broadhead
Tony Bullimore
Bob Bunker
Nigel Burgess
R. Lancy Burn
Alan Butler
Chris Butler
Michael Butterfield
Dan Byrne
Steve Callahan
Reggie Calvert
Loic Caradec
Francois Carpente
Patrice Carpentier
Jerry Cartwright
Frank Caspar
Ida Castigliani
Goran Cederstrom
Geoffrey Chaffey
Albert Chaltin
Joel Charpentier
Pierre Chassin
Francis Chichester
Patrick Childress
Webb Chiles
Pat Chilton
Krystyna Chojnowska-
   Liskiewicz
Frank Clark
Richard Clifford
Jack Coffey
Alain Colas
Brian Cooke
Alex Corozzo

Kay Cottee
David Scott Cowper
James Crawford
Donald Crowhurst
Peter Crowther
Bruce Dalling
Olivier Dardel
Colin Darrock
Ann Davison
Bertrand de Castelbajac
Willy de Roos
Jacques de Roux
John de Trafford
Clyde Deal
Hank Dekker
Kees Den Hartoog
Claude Desjardine
Wayne Dickinson
Jim Dickson
Gerard Dijkstra
Graeme Dillon
Ben Dixon
William Doherty
Steve Dolby
Tom Donnelly
Colin Drummond
Patrick Dumas
Vito Dumas
Bill Dunlop
Alan Eddy
Ludwig Eisenbraun
Christopher Elliot
Ginger Elliott
Mike Ellison
Bertil Enbom

Dave Englehart
Wilfried Erdman
Franco Faggione
George Farley
Monk Farnham
Yvon Fauconnier
Marie-Claude Fauroux
Bruno Fehranbach
Jim Ferris
Mike Flanagan
Andre Foezon
Ambrogio Fogar
Tom Follett
Colin Forbes
Michel Formosa
Loik Fougeron
Albert Fournier
Phillipe Fournier
Mario Franchetti
Clare Francis
Jerry Freeman
Robert Gainer
Jim Gannon
Jules Garnet
Ann Gash
Jean Gau
Daniel Gauthier
Georgi Georgiev
Alain Gerbault
Heinrich Gerbers
Daniel Gilard
Bernard Gilboy
Alain Glicksman
Robin Lee Graham
Kai Granholm
Paul Graute
Max Gravelean
Walter Greene
E. Grenapin
Dima Grinups
Tom Grossman
D. M. R. Guthrie
John Guzzwell
Geoffrey Hales
Eric Hall
Desmond Hampton
Harry Harkima
H. G. Hasler
James Hatfield
Wolf Hausner
Rene Hauwaert
Joseph Havkins
Adrian Hayter
Rachel Hayward
Julia Hazel
Claus Hehner
Heinrich J. Henze

Margaret Hicks
John Holtom
Bill Homewood
Michel Horeau
Kenishi Horie
Guy Hornett
Jeff Houlgrave
Bill Howell
Valentine Howells
John Hughs
John Hunt
Colin Irwin
Naomi James
Rob James
Herman Jansen
Henry Jaskula
Kazimierz Jaworski
Philippe Jeantot
Alfred Johnson
Robbie Jones
Tristan Jones
Hank Jukkema
A. V. Kaariatta
Alfred Kalies
Mike Kane
Eilco Kasemier
Ikjo Kashina
Nick Keig
Derek Kelsall
William L. King
Jack Kingsley
Wolf Kirchner
Olav Kivikoski
E. F. Knight
Robin Knox-Johnston
Noriko Kobayashi
Walter Koenig
Harald Kolzer
Richard Konkolski
Heiko Krieger
Vassil Kurtev
Jean Lacombe
G. Lagarrique
Colin Laird
Titouan Lamazon
David Landgraf
Spence Langford
Bob Langyel
Si Lawlor
Judy Lawson
Yves Le Cornec
Olivier le Diouris
Pierre Le Normand
Yves Le Toumelin
Bob Lengyel
Rene Lescombe
Vincent Levy

David Lewis
Hannes Lindemann
Mark Linksi
Barry Loeckler
Eric Loizeau
Alonso Lopez
Ed Lormand
Warren Luhrs
Sven Lundin
Bob Lush
Tony Lush
H. A. McAulay
Richard McBride
Fred McCallum
James McClintock
Hugh McCoy
John MacGregor
Jock McLeod
Mike McMullen
R. T. McMullen
Halvard Maibire
Michael Malinovsky
William Maney
Robert Manry
John Mansell
Alain Marcal
Claude Marsault
Remy Marsault
John Martin
Christian Marty
Ake Mattson
Jean Maurel
Michael Mermod
Jorgen Meyer
Anne Michailof
E. E. Middleton
Edward Miles
Bob Miller
Nicolette Milnes-Walker
Martin Minter-Kemp
Mike Mitchel
H. G. Mitchell
Bernard Moitessier
John Moon
James Moore
Dodge Morgan
Patrick Morvan
Philippe Mounet
Oliver Moussey
Paul Muller
Utz Muller-Tren
Frank Mulville
Gary Mundell
Didier Munduteguy
Sandy Munro
Tony Murdock
Bill Murnan

Phillipe Museaux
Shoji Nagayama
William Nance
Barry Nelson
Ian Nicolson
Roy Nugent
Yves Olivaux
Gen Oshika
Brigitte Oudry
Marc Pajot
Stephen Pakenham
Bernard Pallard
David Palmer
Beppe Panada
Jean Claude Parisis
Solomon Parker
E. Vidal Paz
Lionel Pean
Douglas T. Peck
Axel Pederson
Jaques Peignon
Gerard Pestey
Eric Peters
Alfred Peterson
Karl Peterzen
Jack Petith
Bruno Peycon
Lois Peyron
Stephon Peyron
Peter Phillips
Guy Piazzini
Harry Pidgeon
Henry Pigott
Mike Plant
Roger Plisson
Henry Pottle
Philippe Poupon
Leslie Powles
Angus Primrose
Jean-Claude Protta
Zbigniew Puchalski
Ian Radford
Raymond Rawls
Fred Rebell
Bertie Reed
W. B. Reese
Mimi Rehor
Teresa Remiszewska
Michael Richey

John Ridgeway
John Riding
Donald Ridler
David Robertson
Bernie Rodriguez
Kees Roemers
Paul Rogers
Franz Romer
Alec Rose
Hal Roth
David Ryan
Masato Sako
Pentti Salmi
David Sandeman
Jonathan Sanders
Murray Sayle
David Schaal
Ludwig Schlimboch
Mark Schrader
Robert Scott
Keith Sedwick
Josiah Shackford
John Shaw
Max Shean
Gidaliahu Shtirmer
Pierre Sicouri
Tony Skidmore
Joshua Slocum
E. Everett Smith
Howard Smith
Mac Smith
Norton Smith
John Sowden
Andrew Spedding
Gerry Spiess
Phil Steggall
Richard L. Stevenson
Francis Stokes
John Struchinsky
Eric Sumner
David Sutcliffe
Rosie Swale
Richard B. Sweat
Jan Swertz
Eric Tabarly
Yuko Tada
Shun Takeich
Peter Tangvald

Josh Taylor
Ty Techera
Goos Terschagget
Sergio Testa
Nigel Tetley
Alan W. Thomas
Peter Thurley
Horst Timmreck
Luis Tonizzo
Hiroshi Totsuka
Johann Trauner
Andrew Urbanczyk
Ryusuke Ushijima
Henk Van de Weg
Jean-Luc Van Den Heeds
Pleum Van Der Lugt
Wytze van der Zee
J. Van Donselaar
Simon Van Hagan
Hans Van Hest
Giampaola Venturin
Alain Veyron
Jean-Marie Vidal
Hugo Vihlen
Julio Vilar
Dean Vincent
Ingeborg Von Heister
Jean-Jacques Vuylsteker
Wladyslaw Wagner
William Wallace
Borje Wase
Jill Watkins
Bill Watson
Bruce Webb
C. H. (Rusty) Webb
Linda Weber-Rettie
Phil Weld
Frank Wells
Alexander Welsh
David White
Annette Wilde
Geoffrey Williams
Leslie Williams
William Willis
Martin Wills
Stuart Woods
James Young
Jean Yves-Terlain

Note: My apologies to those who might have been overlooked.

Completion Date	Master	Vessel	Route
1980	Zbrigniew Pulchalski, Poland	Miranda	E to W via Panama Canal
1980	David Scott Cowper, Britain	Ocean Bound (41 ft.)	W to E via Cape Horn (previously completed E to W circumnavigation. First to circumnavigate Cape Horn in both directions)
1980	Henry Jaskula, Poland	Dar Przemysla (47 ft.)	W to E via Cape Horn (non-stop & without assistance)
1980	Horst Timmreck, Germany	Brigitte (31 ft.)	W to E via Cape Horn (163 days)
1981	Leslie Powles, Britain	Solitaire of Hamble (34 ft.)	W to E non-stop (without replenishment; previously made westabout circumnavigation)
1981	Paul Rogers, New Zealand	Spirit of Pentax (55 ft.)	W to E (1 1/4 times around non-stop)
1981	Jonathan Sanders, Australia	Perie Banon (34 ft.)	W to E (first to complete 2 non-stop circumnavigations; revictualled at sea)
1981	Jan Swertz, Belgium	Tahani & Peti (30 ft. & 41 ft.)	E to W via Cape Horn
1981	Harald Kolzer, Germany	Rosi II (22 ft.)	E to W via Panama Canal
1982	Patrick Childress, USA	Juggernaut (27 ft.)	E to W via Panama Canal
1982	Pleum Van Der Lugt, Holland	Zee Uwse Stromen (35 ft.)	W to E (set time record for non-stop antipodal circumnavigation 286 days)
1983	Mark Schrader, USA	Resourceful (40 ft.)	W to E (first American to circumnavigate via 5 Southern capes)
1983	Webb Chiles, USA	Chidiock Tichbone I & II (18 ft.)	E to W 3/4 circumnavigation (record distance for open boat)
1984	Andrew Urbanczyk, USA	Nord IV (30 ft.)	E to W via Panama Canal
1986	John Sowden, USA	Tarmin (24 1/2 ft.)	(3 circumnavigations in same boat)
1986	James Baldwin, USA	Atom (28 ft.)	E to W via Panama Canal
1986	Henry Pigott, Britain	Glory (19 1/2 ft. junk-rigged)	E to W via Panama Canal
1986	Dodge Morgan, USA	American Promise (60 ft.)	W to E via Cape Horn (fastest non-stop antipodal circumnavigation 150 days)
1987	James Hatfield, Britain	British Heart II & III (29 ft.)	E to W via Strait of Magellan
1987	Alan Butler, Canada	Amon-Re (26 ft.)	E to W via Panama Canal (smallest multihull solo circumnavigation)
1987	Philippe Monnet, France	Kriter Brut de Brut (70 ft. tri.)	W to E via Cape Horn (fastest solo circumnavigation 129 da. 19 hrs. 17 min.)
1987	Julia Hazel, Australia	Jeshan (28 ft.)	E to W via Panama Canal
1987	Tania Aebi, USA	Varuna (26 ft.)	E to W via Panama Canal
1987	Sergio Testa, Australia	Acrohc Australis (12 ft.)	E to W via Panama Canal (smallest boat to circumnavigate)
1988	Kay Cottee, Australia	Blackmore's First Lady (36 ft.)	First non-stop circumnavigation by a woman

Appendix B
Honor Roll of
Blue-Water Singlehanders

Gary Adams
Sharon Sites Adams
Tania Aebi
Edward Allcard
Klans Alverman
William Andrews
Yoh Aoki
Florence Arthaud
Pierre Auxboiroux
James Baldwin
Chris Baranowski
Marcel Bardiaux
Jim Bates
Edith Baumann
Ed Beddow
Guy Bernardin
Olivier Berner
Louis Bernicot
Mike Best
Noel Bevan
Mike Birch
Howard Blackburn
Tom Blackwell
David Blagden
Stant Blunt
Chay Blyth
Ed Boden
Michael Bohmann
David Bonner
Max Bourgeois
Jack Boye
Amy Boyer
M. Boyle
Monique Brand
Andrew Bray

Jock Brazier
Richard Broadhead
Tony Bullimore
Bob Bunker
Nigel Burgess
R. Lancy Burn
Alan Butler
Chris Butler
Michael Butterfield
Dan Byrne
Steve Callahan
Reggie Calvert
Loic Caradec
Francois Carpente
Patrice Carpentier
Jerry Cartwright
Frank Caspar
Ida Castigliani
Goran Cederstrom
Geoffrey Chaffey
Albert Chaltin
Joel Charpentier
Pierre Chassin
Francis Chichester
Patrick Childress
Webb Chiles
Pat Chilton
Krystyna Chojnowska-
    Liskiewicz
Frank Clark
Richard Clifford
Jack Coffey
Alain Colas
Brian Cooke
Alex Corozzo

Kay Cottee
David Scott Cowper
James Crawford
Donald Crowhurst
Peter Crowther
Bruce Dalling
Olivier Dardel
Colin Darrock
Ann Davison
Bertrand de Castelbajac
Willy de Roos
Jacques de Roux
John de Trafford
Clyde Deal
Hank Dekker
Kees Den Hartoog
Claude Desjardine
Wayne Dickinson
Jim Dickson
Gerard Dijkstra
Graeme Dillon
Ben Dixon
William Doherty
Steve Dolby
Tom Donnelly
Colin Drummond
Patrick Dumas
Vito Dumas
Bill Dunlop
Alan Eddy
Ludwig Eisenbraun
Christopher Elliot
Ginger Elliott
Mike Ellison
Bertil Enbom

Books About Singlehanded Sailing

Aebi, Tania. **Taking the World by Storm.** Newport, Rhode Island: *Cruising World*. 1988. A collection in book form of articles that originally appeared in *Cruising World* about a young American girl who sailed alone around the world in a 26-foot boat.

Allcard, Edward C. **Single-Handed Passage.** London: Putnam. 1950. **Temptress Returns.** New York: Norton. 1953. **Voyage Alone.** New York: Dodd-Mead. 1964. Solo voyages by a famous circumnavigator. Allcard is a strong individualist with definite opinions, but his advice should be heeded, for he has the background of a naval architect and surveyor and has had a lifetime of oceanic singlehanded experience. His cruising grounds have included such formidable waters as those near Cape Horn.

Anderson, J. R. L. **The Ulysses Factor.** New York: Harcourt-Brace-Jovanovich. 1970. A profound and provocative book about the exploring instinct in man. It deals in detail with the motives of singlehanders (also of flyers and mountain climbers).

Andrews, William A. **A Daring Voyage** and **Columbus Outdone,** logs of two early transatlantic passages in the small boats *Nautilus* and *Sapolio* under the title **Dangerous Voyages of Capt. William Andrews.** New York: Abercrombie & Fitch. 1966. Compilation, editing, and brief biography by Richard Henderson.

Anthony, Irvin. **Voyagers Unafraid.** Philadelphia: Macrae Smith. 1930. Stories about early transatlantic voyagers written in what has been described as a "shiver-my-timbers" style, but highly entertaining.

Bardiaux, Marcel. **4 Winds of Adventure.** New York: John de Graff. 1961. First half of an eight-year solo circumnavigation in a home-built racing cruiser, including a "wrong-way" rounding of Cape Horn near the beginning of winter.

Barton, Humphrey. **Atlantic Adventurers.** Southhampton: Adlard Coles. 1953. Records of small-craft passages across the North Atlantic by a designer-surveyor and highly experienced offshore sailor. Interesting critical comments and asides.

Belcher, Bill. **Wind-Vane Self-Steering.** Camden, Maine: International Marine Publishing. 1981. A how-to book on planning and building your own vane-controlled self-steering system.

Bernicot, Louis. **The Voyage of the Anahita.** London: Hart-Davis. 1953. Understated account of the sixth solo circumnavigation by a masterful seaman.

Bladgen, David. **Very Willing Griffin.** New York: W. W. Norton. 1974. Preparations and Atlantic crossing in 1972 of the smallest OSTAR entry.

Blyth, Chay. **The Impossible Voyage.** New York: G. P. Putnam's Sons. 1972. Account of the "uphill" (against prevailing winds) circumnavigation in 1970–71 in *British Steel* by a former paratrooper and transatlantic oarsman.

Bombard, Alain. **The Bombard Story.** London: Readers Union. 1955. The **Voyage of the Heretique.** New York: Simon and Schuster. 1954. Transatlantic passage in an inflatable boat without supplies by a French doctor to prove that castaways can survive for lengthy periods without food and water.

Borden, Charles. **Sea Quest.** Philadelphia: Macrae Smith. 1967. One of the most complete collections of abbreviated cruising accounts by an experienced offshore sailor. Not exclusively about singlehanders, but most of the solo voyages up to about the mid-Sixties are included.

Brenton, Francis. **Voyage of the Sierra Sagrada.** Chicago: Regnery. 1968. Voyage from the Caribbean to Chicago and thence transatlantic with minimal equipment in a dugout canoe by a true contemporary adventurer. He was eventually lost at sea according to reliable reports.

Caldwell, John. **Desperate Voyage.** New York: Ballantine Books. 1949. The Pacific crossing of a double-ended cutter after World War II for the purpose of reuniting the skipper with his sweetheart in Australia. According to an acquaintance of Caldwell, the book was heavily ghost written, much to the chagrin of the author because it is so full of nautical blunders.

Callahan, Steven. **Adrift.** Boston: Houghton Mifflin. 1986. True solo survival story by a naval architect who spent 76 days in a life raft after his 21-foot boat was sunk not very far west of the Canary Islands.

Chichester, Francis. **Alone Across the Atlantic.** New York: Doubleday. 1961. **The Lonely Sea and the Sky.** New York: Coward-McCann. 1964. **Along the Clipper Way.** London: Hodder & Stoughton. 1966. **Gipsy Moth Circles the World.** New York: Coward-McCann. 1968. **The Romantic Challenge.** New York: Coward-McCann & Geoghegan. 1971. The first book listed describes Chichester's transatlantic passage in the 1960 OSTAR, when he won the race in *Gipsy Moth III*. The second book is his autobiography through his voyage in 1962. **Along the Clipper Way** is an anthology of literature relating to the Australian clipper ship routes, including commentary and some extracts from the writings of singlehanders. **Gipsy Moth Circles the World** deals with Chichester's one-stop circumnavigation in the *Gipsy Moth IV*; **The Romantic Challenge** tells of his attempt to set a solo speed record by sailing 4,000 miles in 20 days aboard the *Gipsy Moth V*. These books are well worth reading not only for the vicarious adventure they afford, but also for their technical information; the famous seaman pulls no punches in his criticism of boats and gear.

Chiles, Webb. **Storm Passage.** New York Times Books. 1977. **Open Boat: Across the Pacific.** New York: W. W. Norton. 1982. **The Ocean Waits.** New York: W. W. Norton. 1984. The first listed book tells the story of Chiles' record-setting circumnavigation in his Ericson 37. The latter two books recount his remarkable open boat voyage which covered about three-quarters of the distance around the world.

Clarke, D. H. **The Lure of the Sea.** London: Adlard Coles. 1970. The author, an English trimaran enthusiast and small-boat-voyage researcher, deals with aspects of voyage preparation.

Cornell, Jimmy. **Ocean Cruising Survey.** Granada Publishing. 1983. Information on ocean cruising resulting from interviews with dozens of voyagers, many sailing alone. **World Cruising Routes.** Camden, Maine: International Marine Publishing. 1987. A practical guide to choosing the best route for long-distance cruising in the most popular yachting areas of the world.

Cooke, Francis B. **Single-Handed Cruising.** London: Edward Arnold & Co. 1924. A how-to book by a late English "dean" of boating writers. Many of the techniques are old-fashioned but often not outdated, for there is merit in certain methods that have been time-tested and proven.

Davison, Ann. **My Ship Is So Small.** New York: Sloan. 1956. Well-written account of the first solo transatlantic passage by a woman.

deRoos, Willy. **North-West Passage.** Camden, Maine: International Marine Publishing. 1977. Remarkable voyage made mostly solo through the ice-choked Northwest Passage aboard a 34-foot, steel-hulled ketch.

Devine, Eric. **Midget Magellans.** New York: Harrison Smith & Hass. 1935. Early, well-known voyages in small boats, including some singlehanders.

Dumas, Vito. **Alone Through the Roaring Forties.** New York: John de Graff. 1960. The remarkable solo circumnavigation in the southern westerlies by *Legh II* which earned the first Slocum Award for her Argentinian skipper. Tantalizingly inexplicit on some points of seamanship.

Dykstra, Gerard. **Self-Steering for Sailboats.** Sail Books. 1980. A guide to stock autopilots and wind vane systems. Although somewhat outdated, the principles are sound.

Eddy, Alan. **So You Want to Sail Around the World.** New York: Allied Boat Co. (no date). Promotional publication for Allied describing Alan Eddy's circumnavigation, mostly solo, in the Seawind ketch *Apogee*.

Fenger, Frederic A. **Alone in the Caribbean.** Reprinted by Wellington Books. 1958. Fenger, a naval architect and experimenter with self-steering rigs, writes of a six-month cruise through the Lesser Antilles in the 17-foot sailing canoe *Yakaboo*.

Francis, Clare. **Come Hell or High Water.** London: Pelham Books, 1977. A personal account of this British sailor's participation in the 1976 OSTAR, during which she set a solo record for women.

Garland, Joseph E. **Lone Voyager.** Boston: Little, Brown & Co. 1963. A well-researched, fascinating biography of Howard Blackburn, the fingerless singlehander who made two transatlantic passages in small sloops and an attempted Atlantic crossing in a dory.

Gerbault, Alain. **The Fight of the Firecrest.** London: Hart-Davis. 1955. **In Quest of the Sun.** New York: Doubleday. 1955. The first book describes the French circumnavigator's slow and trouble-fraught transatlantic passage, for which he earned the first Cruising Club of America Blue Water Medal. The second book is an account of his adventures while completing the circumnavigation. Gerbault's later books became involved with sociology and philosophy at the expense of seamanship.

Gilboy, Bernard. **A Voyage of Pleasure.** Edited and annotated by John Barr Tompkins, Cambridge, Maryland: Cornell Maritime Press. 1956. The log of Gilboy's half-year, nonstop transpacific passage in the 19-foot boat, *Pacific*, in 1882–1883.

Gilles, Daniel. **Alone.** U.S. Edition by Sail Books, Inc. 1976. History of the OSTAR races through 1976; originally published in France.

Graham, Robert D. **Rough Passage.** Boston: Houghton Mifflin. 1937. A fast, solo cruise from England to Newfoundland in the 30-foot cutter *Emanuel* in 1933.

Graham, Robin Lee. **Dove.** New York: Harper & Row. 1972. Popular book describing the voyage of the youngest solo circumnavigator in the 24-foot *Dove* and 33-foot *Return of the Dove*. Ghost writing and commercializing the account so that it is directed to a general readership detracts from the value of the book for the experienced sailor.

Groser, John. **Atlantic Venture.** London: Ward Lock & Co. 1968. Good account of the singlehander's transatlantic race of 1968 by the sports editor of the London *Observer*.

Guzzwell, John. **Trekka Round the World.** London: Adlard Coles. 1963. A splendid book about a seamanly solo circumnavigation in a tiny, home-built yawl. Informative and entertaining.

Heaton, Peter. **The Sea Gets Bluer.** London: Black. 1965. A collection of extracts from the writings of well-known voyagers. Some singlehanders included.

Hiscock, Eric. **Voyaging Under Sail.** London: Oxford University Press. 1959. This is only one of many fine books by the late circumnavigator who has cruised all over the world with his wife, Susan, in a number of boats called *Wanderer*. Of all the Hiscock books, **Voyaging Under Sail** probably includes the most information relating to solo sailing, and it has a valuable chapter on voyage planning.

Horie, Kenichi. **Kodoku.** Rutland, Vermont: Charles E. Tuttle. 1964. A singlehanded, transpacific passage from Japan to California in 1962 in the 19-foot sloop *Mermaid*, by the famous Japanese solo circumnavigator.

Holm, Donald. **The Circumnavigators.** Englewood Cliffs, New Jersey: Prentice-Hall. 1974. This book and Charles Borden's **Sea Quest** probably are the most comprehensive collections of abbreviated accounts of small boat voyages. Many, but by no means all, were made singlehanded.

Howells, Valentine. **Sailing Into Solitude.** New York: Dodd-Mead. 1966. Account of the author's race across the Atlantic in the folkboat *Eira* in the 1960 OSTAR.

Jackson, Willis Carl. **The Log of the Carla Mia.** The Raintree Press. 1980. A solo passage across the Atlantic aboard a Seawind ketch in 1978; poignantly described by a 55-year-old librarian who was later lost at sea.

James, Naomi. **At One With the Sea.** Hutchinson/Stanley Paul. 1979. Good account of the first solo circumnavigation via Cape Horn by a woman.

Jones, Tristan. **The Incredible Voyage.** Avon. 1980. Entertaining solo exploits by the colorful Welsh shellback who, one suspects, does not allow the telling of his amazing experiences to be overly hampered by facts. More practical how to information is to be found in Jones' **One Hand For Yourself, One For the Ship.** New York: MacMillan. 1982.

King, William Leslie. **Capsize.** Lymington, England: Nautical Publishing. 1969. The story of King's participation in the Golden Globe round-the-world race for singlehanders in 1968 and the roll-over of his Chinese lug-rigged *Galway Blazer II*. The singlehander was forced to withdraw from the race but subsequently completed his circumnavigation.

Klein, David, and M. L. King. **Great Adventures in Small Boats** (originally called **They Took to the Sea**), New York: Collier Books. 1963. Excerpts and commentary about famous small boat voyages. Some of the early, better-known singlehanders are included. The book is somewhat unusual in that it is organized topically rather than chronologically.

Knox-Johnston, Robin. **A World of My Own.** London: Cassell. 1969. The winner of the Golden Globe race, who is credited with the first non-stop solo circumnavigation, tells how he did it in the double-ended ketch *Suhaili*.

Letcher, John. **Self-Steering for Sailing Craft.** Camden, Maine: International Marine Publishing. 1974. Mostly expository and technical writing about an important subject for singlehanders. A few accounts of Letcher's own singlehanding experiences are included.

Le Toumelin, J. Y. **Kurun Around the World.** New York: E. P. Dutton & Co. 1955. **Kurun in the Caribbean.** London: Rupert Hart-Davis. 1963. Singlehanded voyages including a solo circumnavigation in a Norwegian double-ender by a respected Breton seaman.

Lewis, Dr. David. **The Ship Would Not Sail Due West.** New York: St. Martin 1961. **Ice Bird.** New York: W. W. Norton. 1976. The adventurous doctor, who rounded the world with his family on a catamaran and attempted to circumnavigate Antarctica alone, has written books related to voyaging or navigation. The first book deals with singlehanding in the 1960 OSTAR, and it includes a valuable appendix on health and medical supplies. **Ice Bird** deals with the doctor's Antarctic cruise.

Lindemann, Dr. Hannes. **Alone at Sea.** New York: Random House. 1958. Descriptions of two amazing transatlantic passages, one in a narrow dugout canoe without outriggers and the other in a rubber-canvas foldboat. The skipper of these unseaworthy craft was a German doctor interested in survival techniques.

MacGregor, John. **The Voyage Alone in the Yawl Rob Roy.** London: Rupert Hart-Davis. 1954. (First published in 1867.) A mini-voyage across the English Channel in a tiny canoe yawl by an early promoter of singlehanded sailing and distance canoeing. MacGregor was very popular in the late nineteenth century and inspired much emulation.

Manry, Robert. **Tinkerbelle.** New York: Harper & Row. 1966. Although this book is about a feat that must be considered a stunt, crossing the Atlantic in a 13^1/$_2$-foot boat, it is well-written, informative, and thoughtful. Some useful details are given about gear and stores.

Marin-Marie. **Wind Aloft, Wind Alow.** New York: Charles Scribner's Sons. 1947. Two solo transatlantic passages, one under sail in the double-ender, *Winnibelle,* and the other under power in the motorboat, *Arielle,* by a French marine artist and masterful seaman. Marin-Marie was a pioneer in self-steering arrangements.

McMullen, R. T. **Down Channel.** London: Horace Cox. 1893. A classic book describing cruises based in England between 1850 and 1891 by a no-nonsense sailor of the old school. His singlehanding of the 20-ton yawl *Orion* is described in some detail.

Mermod, Michel. **The Voyage of the Geneve.** England: John Murray. 1973. An "almost" circumnavigation alone by a Swiss sociologist and long-distance canoeist in a 25-foot double-ended, converted lifeboat.

Merrien, Jean. **Lonely Voyagers.** New York: G. P. Putnam's Sons. 1954. A compendium of accounts of many transoceanic and round-the-world small boat voyages, most of them singlehanded. Includes a list of 120 long voyages by one or two people in small boats from 1849 to 1953.

Middleton, E. E. **The Cruise of the Kate.** London: Longmans, Green & Co. 1870. A singlehanded voyage around England in a 21-foot canoe yawl by an emulator of MacGregor.

Milnes-Walker, Nicolette. **When I Put Out To Sea.** England: Collins. Transatlantic crossing under sail by the third woman to do it alone. The author is a psychologist who was primarily interested in her own reactions to the voyage. Her book is an interesting, non-technical account, and it offers some good tips on the daily routine and provisions.

Moitessier, Bernard. **The First Voyage of the Joshua.** New York: William Morrow. 1973. **The Long Way.** Garden City, New York: Doubleday. 1975. Two voyages by the innovative French singlehander. The first, made with his wife, describes in detail the high-speed scudding technique he developed for heavy weather in the South Pacific. **The Long Way** is the account of his nonstop solo sail one and a half times around the world during and after his participation in the Golden Globe race. Entertaining and instructive.

Mulville, Frank. **Singlehanded Cruising and Sailing.** Camden, Maine: International Marine Publishing. 1981. Some good advice on cruising alone offshore by an experienced singlehander.

Neal, John. **Log of the Mahina.** Pacific International Publishing Co. 1976. Combination journal and guide resulting from a partly solo cruise to the South Pacific in a Vega 27.

Nicolson, Ian. **Sea Saint.** London: Peter Davies. 1957. A solo Atlantic crossing from Nova Scotia to England by a British naval architect and surveyor in the 32-foot sloop, *St. Elizabeth,* in 1954.

Page, Frank. **Sailing Solo to America.** New York: Quadrangle Books. 1972. Story of the OSTAR races with the main emphasis on the 1972 race by a yachting correspondent of the London *Observer.*

Pidgeon, Harry. **Around the World Single-Handed.** New York: Appleton. 1933. First circumnavigation of the second man to sail around the world alone, in the home-built, 34-foot Sea Bird yawl, *Islander.* The book is not as exciting as some because of Pidgeon's fine seamanship.

Rebell, Fred. **Escape to the Sea.** London: Murray. 1951. An amazing west-to-east solo crossing of the Pacific in the 18-foot open boat, *Elaine*, by a do-it-yourself greenhorn who made his own navigation instruments and used home-made charts traced from an ancient Atlas.

Ridler, Donald. **Erik the Red.** London: William Kimber. 1972. The story of the author's cruise from England across the Atlantic to the West Indies and back in a boat he built himself, a 26-foot transom-stern dory with a plank keel and a Chinese lug rig.

Rogers, Stanley. **Tales of the Fore-an-Aft.** London: George G. Harrap & Co. 1935. A collection of voyages including those of some singlehanders presented in a somewhat dramatic style.

Rose, Alec. **My Lively Lady.** New York: David McKay. 1968. A fast circumnavigation in the southern westerlies by a "grand old man" of solo voyaging. Some interesting technical information in the appendices.

Slack, Kenneth E. **In the Wake of the Spray.** New Brunswick, New Jersey: Rutgers University Press. 1966. The lovingly-done, painstaking research and analysis of Slocum's *Spray* and her replicas. A fascinating book, but one with the possible danger that it could lead a novice into acquiring a less-than-ideal boat for offshore work.

Slocum, Joshua. **Sailing Alone Around the World.** New York: Sheridan House. 1983. (Originally published by The Century Company 1899.) *The* classic on singlehanded cruising by the retired clipper-ship captain who became the first solo circumnavigator. The book is inspirational, charming, and probably will be read forever, but it has a glaring deficiency for sailor readers: lack of technical details.

Slocum, Victor. **Captain Joshua Slocum.** New York: Sheridan House. 1950. A very interesting biography of Joshua by his oldest son. Details of his various commands and many voyages, including the one in the *Liberdade*, a home-built, 35-foot dory-sampan.

Spiess, Gerry. **Alone Against the Atlantic** (with Marlin Bree). Control Data Publishing. 1980. The west-to-east transatlantic crossing in 1979 by Spiess aboard the 10-foot *Yankee Girl*.

Tabarly, Eric. **Lonely Victory.** London: Souvenir Press. 1964. **Ocean Racing.** New York: W. W. Norton. 1970. Refreshingly understated books by the famous French singlehander, who is one of the most dedicated ocean racers. **Lonely Victory** gives details of his OSTAR victory in 1964, while **Ocean Racing** is a summary of his ocean racing experiences, mostly solo, with interesting details of his various craft named *Pen Duick*.

Tangvald, Peter. **Sea Gypsy.** New York: E. P. Dutton. 1966. A voyage around the world, singlehanded at times, in the 32-foot cutter *Dorothea* by a well-known ocean sailor. Tangvald is highly opinionated but a competent and resourceful seaman.

Tazelaar, James, and Jean Bussiere. **To Challenge a Distant Sea.** Chicago: Contemporary Books. 1977. The story of Jean Gau, who made two singlehanded circumnavigations and 11 singlehanded transatlantic crossings in his Tahiti ketch, *Atom*. Includes excerpts from his logs.

Teller, Walter M. **The Search for Captain Slocum.** New York: Charles Scribner's Sons. 1956. A well-researched biography of Slocum; most interesting but a bit depressing, as it brings out an unattractive side of our hero.

Tetley, Nigel. **Trimaran Solo.** Lymington, England: Nautical Publishing. 1970. The account of Tetley's record-breaking solo circumnavigation and subsequent loss of his trimaran, *Victress*, during the Golden Globe race.

Tomalin, Nicholas, and Ron Hall. **The Strange Last Voyage of Donald Crowhurst.** New York: Stein & Day. 1970. The fascinating story of the demise of Crowhurst, a competitor in the Golden Globe race, who faked a voyage around the world and died from an apparent suicidal leap into the sea. Source material for the book is taken from detailed logs, photographs, and tapes found on his derelict trimaran.

Voss, John C. **The Venturesome Voyages of Captain Voss.** New York: C.E. Lauriat. 1926. A classic book about Voss' voyages, including his near-circumnavigation in the dugout canoe, *Tilikum*. He rarely sailed alone, but once made a long passage singlehanded when his crew was lost over the side. Much good advice on how to handle a small boat in heavy weather, but one should not be misled into thinking a modern yacht will behave as did the *Tilikum* when lying to a sea anchor.

Vihlen, Hugo S. **April Fool.** Camp Hill, Pennsylvania: Dolphin Book Club. 1974. Account of crossing the Atlantic in a 6-foot boat; obviously a stunt but one that was carefully planned and a fascinating challenge.

Violet, Charles. **Solitary Journey.** London: Rupert Hart-Davis. 1954. An interesting solo cruise from England to Malta and return in the 20-foot yawl *Nova Espero*, a boat that had previously crossed the Atlantic.

Weld, Philip S. **Moxie.** Boston: Little, Brown & Co. 1981. Well-written narrative about the 1980 OSTAR by the 65-year-old winner who became America's best-known modern singlehander.

A Note on Sources

A number of readers of the first edition have asked about my sources of information. My interest in the history of small boat voyaging goes back to when I was a teenager. I began reading and taking notes on the subject so many years ago that it is about impossible to list all sources. Some information has come from correspondence or conversations with singlehanders and also from studying most of the books in the aforepresented bibliography; but much of the early history in this book resulted from page-by-page searches through early newspapers and magazines found in such repositories as the Library of Congress, Enoch Pratt Library, Boston Public Library, B. W. Blunt White Library, Mystic Seaport, Inc., U.S. Naval Academy Library, and The Maritime Historical Association.

Two well-known nautical historians were particularly helpful and supportive. Richard Gordon McCloskey, the scholarly founder of The Slocum Society, was a great person to have on my side (he could be scathing when agin' you), and he gave me not only information, but also a respect for accuracy and literary shipshapeliness. The popular yachting writer Alfred Loomis was very encouraging, and he left me his entire set of early *Sprays*, journals of The Slocum Society, which were loaded to the gun'ls with small boat history. Another important source of information has been Englishman D. H. (Nobby) Clarke, a longtime self-appointed keeper of bluewater sailing records. Nobby and I have been corresponding off-and-on since about 1973. We've had arguments about certain details, some of them petty perhaps, but I think we've helped each other sort out the facts. For greatest accuracy it certainly helps to have a variety of sources so that the "facts" can be confirmed. As a novice researcher I was quick to learn that you cannot believe everything in print, nor even first-hand recollections.

The following list includes some of the newspapers, magazines, and other materials I have consulted:

The World, New York: beginning 1888
Rudder, Sail, and Paddle: beginning 1891
Rudder: beginning 1891
Boston Daily Advertiser: beginning 1891
New Bedford Evening Journal: beginning 1892
Boston Post: beginning 1891
Boston Morning Journal: beginning 1891
Boston Daily Globe: beginning 1891
The Beverly Citizen: beginning 1891
Western Mail, Cardiff, Wales: 1891
The Strand Magazine, England: 1901
Haymers Guide (private depository of ships' records)
Yachting: beginning 1912
Yachting Monthly (England)
The Skipper: beginning 1953
The Argonaut
The Flying Fish (Journal of the Ocean Cruising Club)
The Singlehanded Sailor (Venice, California)

Yachting World (England)
Le Yacht (France)
Newswave (Survival Technologies Group)
The Daily Telegraph (England)
New York Times
The Capital (Annapolis)
Smithsonian (Washington, D.C.)
Sea History (National Maritime Historical Society)
The Sun (Baltimore, Maryland)
Los Angeles Times
National Geographic Magazine
The Washington Post
Hakluyt Minor (edited by Richard Gordon McCloskey)
National Fisherman (Rockland, Maine)
Blackwood's Magazine (England)
Sarasota Herald-Tribune
South African Yachting
Sea Breezes (England)
The Spray: beginning 1955
The Telltale Compass
Practical Sailor
Seven Seas Cruising Association Bulletins
Yacht and Boat Owner (England)
Cruising World
Sail
Sailing
Motorboating and Sailing
Sea
Yachts and Yachting (England)
The Yachtsman (England)

Index